PUBLIC FINANCE

PUBLIC FINANCE
SECOND EDITION

Ambar Ghosh

Chandana Ghosh

PHI Learning Private Limited

Delhi-110092

2014

₹425.00

PUBLIC FINANCE, Second Edition
Ambar Ghosh and Chandana Ghosh

ISBN-978-81-203-4998-8

The export rights of this book are vested solely with the publisher.

Second Printing (Second Edition) ... ... **June, 2014**

Published by Asoke K. Ghosh, PHI Learning Private Limited, Rimjhim House, 111, Patparganj Industrial Estate, Delhi-110092 and Printed by Mudrak, 30-A, Patparganj, Delhi-110091.

To

*our great and beloved teacher Professor Dipak Banerjee
who introduced us to and whetted our interest in the highly exciting,
controversial and challenging world of public finance*

CONTENTS

3   PRINCIPLES OF TAX EQUITY 58–101

4   EFFICIENCY OF TAXATION 102–153

▌PREFACE

The book formerly titled as **Economics of the Public Sector** in its first edition has now been retitled as **Public Finance (2/E)** to meet the needs of the students of Economics, both at undergraduate and postgraduate level. The book presents lucidly all the major theories of public finance relevant to our country. The reason why we allow our book to go into its second edition is that the undergraduate texts that exist today give a verbal exposition to the subject. This is unsuitable for serious students of economics for two reasons. First, verbal exposition of theories developed using mathematical models is usually vague and hard to comprehend. Second, such an exposition does not equip the students with the basic tools and techniques of economic analysis. Our book seeks to remove both these deficiencies. It uses elementary mathematics to present the theories, and develops simple mathematical models to derive major results in every area. The book illustrates graphically the working of the models and derivation of the results, and then explains the economic intuition of the results in detail. This brings all the assumptions and the underlying framework to the fore, and thereby, makes comprehension of the subject a lot easier. The second edition updates the data of the first edition.

In other words, this book explicitly states all the assumptions underlying a theory and shows how the results follow logically from the assumptions. Efforts have been made not to leave any gap or hazy area. The emphasis is on rigour. At the same time intuition of each result is explained in detail. Our long experience of teaching undergraduate students in different institutes has shown us that this is an effective way of reaching different categories of students in the best possible manner. They find this kind of presentation really exciting and easy to comprehend. They also develop the skill to handle the basic tools and techniques of economic analysis.

In addition, another distinguishing feature of the book is that it contains a large number of review questions as well as both analytical and numerical problems on every topic to help the students apply the tools and techniques learnt, and thereby, develop a sound understanding of the subject.

Wherever relevant, the book illustrates the theories with the help of simple examples from the Indian economy. Moreover, it assesses India's economic policies in the light of the theories discussed in the book. This drives home the relevance of the subject and makes the theories meaningful to the Indian students.

We owe our greatest debt to our great teachers who trained us in logical thinking, precision and rigour. In this context, we also fondly remember our students whose illuminating questions and responses prompted us to rethink, and thereby, improve our understanding of the subject.

Ambar Ghosh
Chandana Ghosh

1

INTRODUCTION

Chapter Objectives

The objectives of this chapter are to

(i) explain the objective of the theory of public finance.
(ii) illustrate with the help of a hypothetical government budget what the theory of public finance seeks to do.
(iii) elucidate the contending views regarding the role of the government in a society.

1.1 THE CONSTITUENTS OF THE PUBLIC SECTOR

The public sector refers to the one that is owned, controlled and operated by the government. Government in Indian context means not only the central government but also the state governments and their subsidiaries, viz., the local self governments such as the panchayats and the municipal bodies. Public sector provides different kinds of productive services, which are of considerable use to the people. It consists of two types of production units: those that are organized on commercial principles and those that are not. All the production units that are of the latter type are together referred to as public administration and defence. Obviously, the whole administrative apparatus consisting of the legislature, executive and judiciary, which are respectively responsible for enacting laws, enforcing and maintaining laws and settling legal disputes, is included in this group. So is the whole set-up of national defence, which protects the country from foreign invasion. These productive units do not sell their services but supply them free of cost to the citizens. Similarly, all the three tiers of government run many educational institutions, hospitals, health centres etc., which supply their services either free of cost or at very low prices that cover only a negligible portion of their average cost of production. These are also included in public administration and defence. The government-owned firms

1

which are commercially organized are referred to as public sector enterprises. They set the prices of their products at remunerative levels on the basis of the demand and supply conditions of their products. In addition to the production units that belong to government administration and defence, Government of India and also the state governments are actively engaged in the production of many goods and services, which are sold at remunerative prices in the market. Steel Authority of India Limited (SAIL), which produces and sells steel, Bharat Sanchar Nigam Limited (BSNL), which sells telecom services in the market are some of the examples of public sector enterprises.

1.2 GOVERNMENT'S BUDGET, ECONOMIC ACTIVITIES OF THE GOVERNMENT AND ECONOMICS OF THE PUBLIC SECTOR

The purpose of this introduction is to whet students' interest in the economics of the public sector or the theory of public finance. Every year at the end of March we wait with bated breath for the presentation of the budget of the Government of India in the parliament by the finance minister of the country. Why do we do that? It is because it affects us in myriad ways. However, before discussing how it affects us, it is advisable to briefly describe the budget of a hypothetical government and its different components. *The budget that the government presents on the last day of every financial year is a record of the government's estimated or projected incomes and expenditures for the coming financial year.* Budget of a hypothetical government is shown in Table 1.1. It is divided into two accounts, revenue account and capital account. Expenditures and receipts that have no direct bearing on government's future income and expenditure are recorded in the revenue account, while those *that have* are shown in the capital account. Let us illustrate with examples. Consider loans taken by the government. It is recorded on the receipt side of the capital account because, unlike taxes, loans mean an increase in future expenditure of the government due to interest payment on the loan. Again, investment expenditure of the government means, for example, building of a power plant by NTPC, a public sector enterprise that generates power. It will yield profit in future and thereby add to future surpluses or profits of the public sector enterprises. Hence it is recorded as an item of expenditure on the capital account. Government's expenditure on defence or administration in contrast does not yield directly any profit in future, since these services, as we have mentioned in the earlier section, are supplied to the individuals free of cost. Hence these expenditures are regarded as public consumption and recorded in the revenue account.

From the hypothetical budget presented in Table 1.1 it is clear why government's budget is so important to us. Changes in taxes and subsidies alter prices of commodities we buy, affect incomes we earn from various sources and thereby change our incentives to undertake different kinds of activities such as saving, investment, labour supply etc. Changes in government expenditures again have important implications for our expectations regarding the current and future availability and quality of different kinds of essential goods and services, which the government supplies. If, for example, there is an increase in expenditure on defence, roads, power, education, health, water supply etc., we expect an improvement in the current and future supplies of these commodities. This again has far-reaching implications for our incentive structure. Government's budget is, therefore, of enormous significance to all of us.

Table 1.1: Budget

(a) Revenue Account

Revenue receipt	Revenue expenditure
Direct taxes	Defence and administration
Indirect taxes	Education and health
Non-tax receipts, such as fees and surpluses	Subsidy
of public sector enterprises	Transfer payments
	Interest on public debt

Revenue deficit = Revenue expenditure – Revenue receipt

(b) Capital Account

Capital receipt	Capital expenditure
Recovery of loans	Investment of public sector enterprises
Proceeds from sales of assets	
Loans taken from the public	
Loans taken from the central bank	

Fiscal deficit = [Total revenue expenditure + Total capital expenditure] – [Total revenue receipt + Total non-debt creating capital receipt (which is the sum of recovery of loans and proceeds from sales of assets)]. Fiscal deficit shows how much the government has to borrow to finance its expenditures.

How does the government draw up its budget? In other words, how does the government decide on what kinds of expenditure it will undertake and how much should each kind of expenditure be? How does the government decide on the modes of financing its expenditures? Does the government take these decisions arbitrarily? Do they depend only on the whims of the finance minister? The answer is of course an emphatic no. All the decisions mentioned above are taken on the basis of certain well-laid out principles and the task or objective of the theory of public finance or economics of the public sector is to derive these principles. We shall now discuss in greater detail what the theory of public finance does using this hypothetical budget as an illustration.

1.2.1 Expenditures in the Revenue Account

Let us consider the revenue account. Focus on its expenditure side first. The first two items show that government spends on defence and administration as well as on health and education. Government in every country is solely responsible for maintaining internal law and order and protecting the country from foreign invasion. The government also in many countries including ours owns and runs schools, colleges, hospitals and health centres. The question that immediately springs to our mind is that why should the government undertake these activities and if it has to, then what should be the optimum scale of provision of these services? Public finance seeks to provide an answer to these questions. Chapter 2 addresses these issues.

Next item of expenditure is subsidies. They represent sums of money given to firms engaged in the production of certain goods and services. Subsidies may be given to consumers also on their consumption of certain specific types of goods and services. In India, for example, subsidies are given, among others, to producers of education and agricultural inputs. Subsidies are also given to consumers of food. Government gives subsidies because theory of public finance shows that subsidies on production and consumption of certain goods are necessary for efficient allocation of resources. This means that in the absence of subsidies production of these goods will be less than what *the people desire*. Chapter 2 addresses the issues of efficient allocation of resources and subsidies.

Next comes transfers. Theory of public finance also recommends transfer payments to certain sections of population to achieve desirable distribution of income. Actually, public finance theorists have developed many approaches to optimum income distribution, namely, utilitarian approach, egalitarian approach, 'maximin' approach of Rawls (1972) and categorical equity. Utilitarian approach defines optimum income distribution as the one that maximizes aggregate social welfare, which is the sum of welfare levels of all the individuals in the society. Under certain conditions, which we shall explain in Chapter 3, this approach calls for equalization of incomes of all the individuals. If, however, taxes imposed by the government to change the income distribution affect the decisions of the taxpayers regarding labour supply, maximization of social welfare may allow for considerable inequality in income distribution. Egalitarian approach on the other hand does not attach any significance to the concept of the sum of individuals' welfares. It regards every individual to be of equal importance to the society. Hence it recommends equal income for everyone. This approach can accept inequality only on grounds of health or larger number of dependents. Thus it is acceptable to give larger income to an individual with poor health or larger number of dependents. Rawls, a well-known philosopher, has developed 'maximin' approach to income distribution. It defines optimum income distribution as the one, which maximizes the welfare level of the poorest individuals. This approach may also imply considerable inequality in income distribution. To illustrate, suppose that a rich lady is taxed to make a transfer payment to a poor person, who works as her driver. If this reduction in income induces the rich lady to sack her driver and drive her car herself, it can make the poor person worse off despite the transfer. Thus, Rawls' criterion for optimum income distribution may also allow for considerable income inequality. Most countries including India, however, follow the concept of categorical equity in their approach to income distribution. This approach considers an income distribution just as long as everyone in the society is assured of a minimum level of income, which is sufficient to meet her requirements of certain basic necessities, such as food, clothing, shelter etc. Government of India has defined a poverty line income, which is the minimum income that is required to meet the basic nutritional requirements of an individual. Various poverty alleviation programmes have been launched in India to make transfer payments to the people below the poverty line income.

1.2.2   Receipts in the Revenue Account: Financing of Revenue Expenditure

Government has to make all the different types of revenue expenditures noted above. It has to provide defence and administration since, as we shall explain in Chapter 2, market fails to provide these services, even though they are absolutely essential to the society. Government also, for reasons elucidated in Chapter 2, subsidises production and consumption of various goods and services as market on its own will produce these services in too little quantities relative to their social requirements. Transfer payments are necessary to achieve categorical equity. However, how will the government finance these revenue expenditures? This takes us to the receipt side of the revenue account of the budget. The largest item on this side on the revenue account is taxation. Government has coercive power. It can force people to pay taxes. One of the major objectives of public finance is, therefore, to develop principles of taxation to prevent abuse or arbitrary use of power of taxation by the government. Government finances bulk of its revenue expenditure by means of taxation. There are two types of taxes: direct and indirect. Direct taxes are those taxes that are imposed directly on individuals. Direct taxes apply to individuals' income, wealth, gifts, inheritance and consumption expenditure. Even though people's consumption expenditures can be taxed in principle, such taxes do not exist anywhere. Joint stock companies or corporations in every country are regarded as independent entities separate from their owners or shareholders. Hence in every country in addition to personal income tax, i.e., taxes on individuals' income, there are taxes on incomes of corporations as well. These taxes are referred to as corporate tax or corporation income tax. They are also regarded as direct taxes. In fact, personal income tax and corporation income tax are the two major direct taxes in India. Chapters 6 and 7 deal with these taxes in detail.

Indirect taxes on the other hand are in-rem taxes, i.e., they are taxes on goods and services. Indirect taxes apply to sales or purchases or production or imports of different types of goods and services. Taxes that apply to sales and production of goods are referred to as sales and excise taxes respectively, while those on imports are called customs duties. Chapter 7 contains a detailed discussion on sales and excise taxes. *Indirect taxes*, as we shall explain in detail in Chapter 2, are the opposite of subsidies. They *are usually imposed on goods whose costs of production and ill effects of consumption do not remain confined to their direct producers and consumers.* Consider the case of cigarettes. Ill effects of smoking affect not only the smokers but also everyone in their vicinity. Similarly, if effluents of a firm producing pesticides are dumped in rivers and seas, fish population and, therefore, output of fishermen is adversely affected. Left to itself, as has been explained in Chapter 2, market will produce these goods in quantities that are much larger than what is optimum from the society's point of view. Indirect taxes, if imposed on these goods at appropriate rates, as you will see in Chapter 2, will reduce their outputs to the socially optimum level. Of course indirect taxes are not imposed only on the kind of goods mentioned above. They are imposed also on other goods, as revenues yielded by direct taxes are often grossly inadequate. This is particularly true of LDCs like India where quite a large part of GDP originates in the unorganized sector comprising of small production units. It is extremely costly to keep tabs on such incomes and tax them. In fact, major part of India's tax revenue comes from indirect taxes. However, in recent years direct taxes' share in total tax revenue has been growing.

Even though indirect taxes generate the bulk of the tax revenue in India, theory of public finance, which is concerned with equitable distribution of the tax burden among individuals, recommend direct taxes for the sake of equity. In fact, to ensure equity theory of public finance emphasizes direct taxes and recommends either individual's income or individual's consumption as the tax base. Chapter 3 discusses in detail this issue of equitable distribution of the tax revenue to be collected to finance government expenditure.

Taxes impact an economy in myriad ways. Most taxes affect individuals' behaviour. A tax on individuals' income, for example, reduces individuals' incentive to earn wage income by supplying labour, interest income by lending out their saving, rental income through residential investment etc. Indirect taxes on purchase or sales, or on production or imports of goods usually affect producers' supply and buyers' purchase decisions. As a result of individuals' and firms' responses to taxes, allocation of productive resources across different sectors of production may change. This may lead to deviations of outputs of different goods and services from those that best satisfy individuals' requirements for these goods and services. In other words, taxes by altering individuals' and firms' economic decisions and thereby changing allocation of productive resources may lead to a decline in 'individuals' welfare over and above what is entailed by the transfer of the tax revenue from the individuals to the government. This issue is referred to as that of efficiency of taxation. Theory of public finance examines in detail the efficiency aspect of every kind of tax and seeks to suggest ways of minimizing inefficiency of the tax structure. Chapter 4 contains a detailed discussion on this issue.

There are other problems with taxes. Taxes, as we have discussed above, affect individuals' behaviour and choices. This has another important implication. *Burden of a tax may not be borne entirely by the people who are liable to pay the tax to the government by the statute of the tax. They may succeed in shifting the tax burden partly or even fully to others.* Let us illustrate this point with an extreme example. Suppose that a tax at the rate of Re. 1 per kg is imposed on the sale of rice and in response to it sellers of rice raise the price from its pre-tax level by Re. 1. Rice is a necessity. Hence, it may be reasonable to assume that its demand is completely price inelastic. Therefore, market for rice will be in equilibrium at this higher price in the post-tax scenario. Suppose that the total demand for rice and, therefore, the equilibrium quantity of rice bought and sold is 100 kg in both the pre-tax and post-tax equilibria. Sellers of rice, therefore, pay the government Rs. 100 as tax. However, they are not actually bearing the burden of the tax. They are actually receiving the same price (after paying the tax) as that in the pre-tax situation and selling the same quantity of rice as before. Hence their income remains unaffected. On the other hand buyers pay an additional amount of Re.1 for every unit of rice purchased. Clearly, therefore, the entire tax of Rs. 100 is actually paid by the buyers. Thus, the actual distribution of the burden of a tax may vastly differ from the distribution specified by the statute of the tax. The former is referred to as the economic incidence and the latter as the statutory incidence of a tax. The tax authority must have a clear idea about the economic incidence of a tax to design a just tax structure. Incidence of different kinds of taxes constitutes the subject matter of Chapter 5.

The last item on the receipt side of the revenue account is the surpluses of the public sector enterprises. We have already explained above what public sector enterprises are. Their profits or surpluses are a source of financing government's revenue expenditure.

1.2.3 Receipts and Expenditures in the Capital Account

Let us now focus on the capital account. On the expenditure side there is only one item, viz., investment or capital expenditure of the government. It refers to investment expenditures of the public sector enterprises. Public investment plays a vital role in the development of Indian economy. To gauge the significance of public investment in India, it may be better to delve into history and focus on the efforts of the government at developing our economy since independence. The period between 1950 and 1990 is referred to as the Mahalanobis era, since the government during this period played a very active role in developing the economy following the strategy formulated by P.C. Mahalanobis. The strategy is known as Mahalanobis or alternatively Nehru–Mahalanobis strategy of economic development. Setting up of heavy and basic industries was at the core of the Mahalanobis strategy. However, private entrepreneurs at that time did not consider it profitable to invest in such industries. Hence government had to build those industries. That is how public sector enterprises came into existence in India. Banks and insurance companies were nationalized too. The objective was to develop a sound financial infrastructure that would command the faith of the public. In the pre-independence period the financial sector was small and rudimentary. Failures of financial institutions were quite common. People did not have much faith in these financial institutions either. Following nationalization of financial institutions, government invested heavily in them to bring the majority of the people of the country within the reach of the organized financial institutions. The objective was to mobilize as much saving as possible to finance investments that were essential for industrialization. Mahalanobis programme of economic development, which was an inward looking or import substituting strategy, aimed at achieving self-reliance by acquiring the capability of producing all the goods India needed. Despite its many failings, it succeeded in achieving its goal of self-reliance by setting up a highly diversified industrial sector and a nation-wide organized financial sector. From the eighties, however, policies started deviating from the Mahalanobis programme. Restrictions on investment, import and external commercial borrowing were relaxed and these policies led to a sharp increase in India's external debt, which eventually culminated in a BOP crisis in 1990. India had to seek financial assistance from the IMF. Conditionalities attached to the loan in turn forced India to supplant the Mahalanobis strategy with the structural adjustment programme (SAP) in the middle of 1991. The major feature of SAP consists in relaxation of all controls over the economic activities of private economic agents and opening up of the economy to foreign trade and international capital flows. One important part of SAP is the programme of stabilization, which identifies the size of fiscal deficit, i.e., the amount of government borrowing, as the only factor responsible for macroeconomic instability. (See the definition of fiscal deficit below Table 1.1.) It, therefore, puts stringent restrictions on the size of fiscal deficit. Following the adoption of SAP, government sought to reduce its fiscal deficit mainly by cutting down its investment expenditure, which in turn led to acute shortage of crucial infrastructural inputs such as power, roads, ports etc. As a result, following a brief spurt in the growth rate buoyed by the opportunities thrown up by the liberalization of controls over import, investment, external borrowing etc., the economy entered into a recession on account of the paucity of crucial infrastructural inputs.

Let us now focus on the receipt side of the capital account. There are two major items, viz., proceeds from the sale of government assets and government borrowing. The former mainly consists of proceeds from the sale of shares of public sector enterprises. Restricting fiscal deficit means putting a ceiling on government borrowing. One of the major objectives of public finance is to examine the implications of government borrowing and to suggest how much the government can borrow and which activities the government can or should finance by borrowing. Fiscal deficit can also be reduced by raising the sales of shares of public sector enterprises. However, is it prudent to do so? Economics of the public sector seeks to provide an answer to that as well. In sum, the theory of the public sector derives principles on the basis of which we can assess the merit of the IMF recommended stabilization programme. Chapter 9 deals with these issues in detail.

1.3 FISCAL FEDERALISM

India is a large federation consisting of a large number of states and union territories. While the latter are under the direct control of the central government, each state has its own state government. Every state government owes its allegiance to the central government. The Constitution of India specifies the fiscal or economic responsibilities of both the state and the central governments. It also lays down tax powers of the centre and the state governments. The question that obviously emerges in this context is, what is the rationale of distributing the economic or fiscal responsibilities and tax powers among different tiers of government instead of having them concentrated in the central government? Theory of public finance deals with this issue also. The part of public finance that addresses this issue is referred to as the theory of fiscal federalism. Chapter 10 discusses this theory in detail.

1.4 CONCLUSION

The objective of the theory of public finance is to identify areas where market fails to provide goods and services in quantities in which people want to have them and distribute income generated among individuals equitably. These are the areas of market failure and accordingly are in need of corrective government intervention ranging from direct provision of certain kinds of goods and services to transfer payments to weaker sections of people and taxation and subsidization of purchases and sales of certain commodities. It also seeks to determine optimum scales of government intervention or expenditures in different sectors and the optimum modes of financing the expenditures. The problems that it handles are extremely complex and the solutions that it has suggested so far are far from perfect. Many of them are controversial and quite a few of them are extremely difficult to implement. However, efforts are on to suggest better, more acceptable and easier-to-implement solutions.

Markets not only fail to, as we have discussed above and as should be clear from Chapter 2, allocate resources efficiently across different lines of production, they also quite often do not succeed in ensuring full employment of the productive resources such as labour and capital. In market economies output and employment fluctuate cyclically leading to alternating phases of recession and boom. In times of recession aggregate demand in the economy falls far below the full employment level of output leading to large-scale unemployment of both capital and labour. In periods of boom aggregate demand outstrips full employment output and thereby generates high rates of inflation. Since both unemployment and inflation are costly, governments everywhere seek to remove unemployment and inflation through fiscal and monetary policies. These activities of the government are referred to as stabilization. One major objective of the theory of public finance is to suggest ways of stabilizing the economy and point to the pitfalls in such programmes. Following the publication of Keynes' *The General Theory of Employment, Interest and Money* in 1936 in the aftermath of the Great Depression, government's role in the stabilization of the economy received tremendous importance. Until the end of the sixties Keynesian ideas held sway. However, since the beginning of the seventies Keynesian policies started losing ground. Though majority of the economists today subscribe to the Keynesian explanation of short run cyclical fluctuations in aggregate output and employment, most of the economists are skeptical about the efficacy of government's stabilization policies. For a discussion on some of these issues you can go through Mankiw (1990).

There is a heated controversy over the optimum size of the government. Some economists believe that political parties consist of self-seeking people who work only in their own interest and are, therefore, necessarily corrupt. They accordingly suggest minimization of the role of the government in a society. Others, however, think that in a well-functioning democracy there are enough checks and balances to keep the government on the right track. They, therefore, envisage a far greater role of the government in the economy. Mistrust in the efficiency of government's policies has deepened further since the collapse of the Soviet block, whose rapid economic progress in the post-revolution era was regarded as the epitome of success of government-controlled economic development. During the Keynesian era, bolstered by the Keynesian theory of the importance of the government in the stabilization of the economy and the successful development experience of the socialist economies, governments in developing countries including India played a major role in the development of the economy. They imposed all kinds of price and quantitative controls over the behaviour of economic agents to allocate resources in favour of those sectors, which they considered essential for the speedy development of the economy in the desired direction. Today, however, opinions on government's intervention in promoting development are sharply divided. There is the 'development view', which regards government control over financial and real resources in LDCs like India as necessary for the development of the economy (see, for example, Gerschenkron (1962)). In sharp contrast there is also the 'political view', which regards such controls as politically motivated and inimical to the growth and development of the economy. Some of the studies propagating the 'political view' are, Kornai (1979), Shleifer and Vishny (1994), and Porta, Lopez-De-Silanes and Shleifer (2002). The issue is clearly controversial. There are quite a few influential studies which attribute the Asian Tigers' success to government's regulation of financial flows and other policies (see, for example, Amsden (1989), Wade (1990) and Rodrik (1995), (1997)). In contrast, studies carried out by Young (1995) and Barth, Caprio and Levine (1999) in the context of South East Asia and Italy respectively churn out evidences in support of the political view. However, evidences suggest that the success of India's industrialization programme and the Green Revolution during the Mahalanobis era was due in large measure to the government initiatives and control (see, for example, Rakshit (1994) in this context). More generally, as pointed out by Stiglitz (1996), "developments over the past fifteen years have shown that well-designed government actions can improve living standards whenever there are imperfections of information or competition or incomplete markets—problems that arise in all economies, but especially in developing ones". One should sound a note of caution at this point. In a country where functioning of democracy is not up to the mark, political parties tend to collude, large sections of people are illiterate and economically weak and, therefore, vulnerable to political bullying, giving much leeway to the government may lead to considerable abuse of power and thereby cause more harm than good. See in this context Buchanan (1987). Majority of the economists today are of the view that both markets and the government are essential for smooth functioning and rapid progress of the economies. The role of the public sector economics today is, therefore, to identify the areas of both market failure and government failure and to suggest how the two sectors can optimally interact with one another to eliminate or at least minimize these failures.

================= **SUMMARY** =================

1. The public sector refers to the sector that is owned, controlled and operated by the government. It consists of public administration and defence, which comprise all the government enterprises that are not commercially organized and public sector enterprises, which are those government-owned firms that are run on profit motive.

2. Government's budget placed in the parliament on the last day of a given financial year is a record of the government's expected or projected incomes and expenditures in the coming financial year. Government does not prepare its budget arbitrarily. Its income and expenditure decisions are based on principles yielded by the theory of public finance.

3. Government's budget has two segments: revenue account and capital account. Government's incomes and expenditures that have direct bearing on future incomes and expenditures of the government are recorded in the capital account, while other incomes and expenditures are recorded in the revenue account.

4. Government seeks to achieve a desired distribution of income through tax-transfer policies. There are four major approaches to optimum income distribution, viz. utilitarian approach, egalitarian approach, maximin approach and categorical equity. None of these, except the second one, calls for complete equality of income.

5. Theory of public finance seeks to tell us what kinds of expenditure should the government incur and what their levels should be. It also seeks to prescribe the optimum methods of financing these expenditures. The major source of finance to the government is taxation. Equitable distribution of the tax burden among individuals is a major issue that the theory of public finance deals with.

6. Taxes alter individuals' behaviour and choices. This affects allocation of productive resources across different lines of production. As a result individuals' welfare may decline by an amount, which is larger than what is strictly entailed by the transfer of the tax revenue from the individual to the government. This aspect of taxation is referred to as the efficiency of taxation. It constitutes an important subject that the theory of public finance studies in detail.

7. The individuals on whom the burden of the tax falls by the statute of the tax may succeed in shifting the burden partly or fully to the others. Distribution of the burden of a tax as specified by the statute of the tax and the actual distribution of the burden of the tax are referred to respectively as statutory and economic incidence of the tax. Theory of public finance studies tax incidence in detail.

8. Theory of public finance also deals with government borrowing. It examines in detail the implications of such borrowing and suggests which expenditures the government can or should finance by borrowing. It also examines whether there should be any upper limit to government borrowing or fiscal deficit.

9. India is a federation of many states and union territories. While the latter are under the direct control of the central government, all the state governments owe their allegiance to the central government. The Constitution of India distributes fiscal responsibilities and tax powers among the central and the state governments. This kind of decentralization of government's fiscal responsibilities and tax powers is referred to as fiscal federalism. The theory of public finance provides the rationale of fiscal federalism and also derives principles on the basis of which fiscal responsibilities and tax powers should be distributed.

KEY CONCEPTS

✓ Government's budget
✓ Capital account
✓ Efficiency of taxation
✓ Egalitarian approach
✓ Categorical equity
✓ Fiscal deficit
✓ Stabilization

✓ Revenue account
✓ Tax equity
✓ Utilitarian approach
✓ Maximin approach
✓ Revenue deficit
✓ Fiscal federalism

REVIEW QUESTIONS

1. How will you define public sector?
2. What is a government's budget?
3. Why is the government's budget important to us?
4. What are the two divisions of the government's budget?
5. What kinds of revenue and expenditure are recorded in the revenue account of the government's budget? Explain.
6. What kinds of revenue and expenditure are recorded in the capital account of the government's budget? Explain.
7. What are the different approaches to optimum income distribution developed by public finance theorists? Explain each of them. Do those approaches call for equalization of everyone's income? Explain.
8. Distinguish between direct and indirect taxes. What are their chief uses?
9. What is meant by efficiency of taxation?
10. Explain the concept of statutory and economic incidence of a tax.
11. What are public sector enterprises? In which part of the government's budget their surpluses are recorded? Explain your answer.
12. What is meant by fiscal federalism?
13. What is stabilization?

PROBLEMS AND APPLICATIONS

1. Why are subsidies and interest payments recorded in the revenue account?

2. Why are sales of public sector enterprises' shares recorded in the capital account?

3. If the government decides to sell a plot of land it owns, in which account of the budget will the sales proceeds be recorded? Explain your answer.

4. Consider the classical model of income determination. Suppose that the government imposes taxes on the rich persons, who as a result decide to reduce their labour supply. Will the effect of their decision remain confined to them only? Explain your answer.

   (*Hint:* This will reduce the full employment level of output and employment. It means lower levels of interest, rental and profit income as well. Some of these incomes may accrue to the poor. If the services of rich and poor workers are complements, which is likely to be the case, fall in employment will reduce the employment of the poor labour as well. Poor workers' wage rate in this case is likely to fall too, as the demand for their services falls, while their labour supply decision is not affected. Poor workers are unskilled, while rich workers are skilled. Hence, they are unlikely to be substitutes and more likely to be complements.)

5. Suppose that the government wants people to reduce consumption of liquor. How can the government do that?

6. Suppose that a commodity is a necessity, with a vertical demand curve. Its supply curve has its usual upward sloping shape. Suppose that the equilibrium price and quantity of the commodity are Rs. 10 and 5000 units respectively. Illustrate the situation in a graph. Suppose that a tax at the rate of Rs. 2 is imposed per unit of sale of this commodity. Who are the persons on whom the burden of the tax falls by the statute of the tax and who actually bear the burden of the tax? Explain.

REFERENCES

Amsden, A. (1989): *Asia's New Giant: South Korea` and Late Industrialization*, Oxford University Press, New York.

Barth, J. Caprio, G. Jr. and Levine, R. (1999): Banking systems around the globe. Do regulation and ownership affect performance and stability? *Mimeo,* World Bank.

Buchanan, J.M. (1987): Tax reform as political choice, *Journal of Economic Perspectives* (Summer).

Gerschenkron, A. (1962): *Economic Backwardness in Historical Perspective*, Harvard University Press, Cambridge, MA.

Kornai, J. (1979): Resource constrained versus demand constrained systems, *Econometrica*, 47, 801–819.

La Porta, R. Lopez-De-Silanes, F. and Shleifer, A. (2002): Government ownership of banks, *The Journal of Finance*, 1.VII (1), 265–301.

Rakshit, M. (1994): Issues in financial liberalization, *Economic and Political Weekly*, September, 24, 2547–2552.

Rodrik, D. (1995): Getting interventions right: How South Korea and Japan grew rich, *Economic Policy*, 20, 55–107.

——(1997): Trade strategy, investment and exports: Another look at East Asia, *Pacific Economic Review* (1), 1–24.

Shleifer, A. and Vishny, R. (1994): Politicians and firms, *Quarterly Journal of Economics*, 109, 995–1025.

Stiglitz, J.E. (1996): Keynote Address at the Annual World Bank Conference on Development Economics, reprinted *in*: Bagchi, A. (Ed.), *Readings in Public Finance*, Oxford University Press, New Delhi.

Wade, R. (1990): *Governing the Market: Economic Theory and the Role of the Government in East Asian Industrialization*, Princeton University Press, Princeton.

Young, A. (1995): The tyranny of numbers: Confronting the statistical realities of East Asian growth experience, *Quarterly Journal of Economics*, 110, 641–680.

2 | PUBLIC GOODS, MIXED GOODS AND EXTERNALITY

Chapter Objectives

The objective of this chapter is to show how market failure occurs in the allocation of resources in the presence of social or public and mixed goods. The chapter accomplishes this in the following manner. It

(i) explains the meanings of social or public goods, private goods and mixed goods. Derives and explains the necessary conditions for optimum allocation of resources in the presence of only private goods. Also derives and explains the necessary conditions for optimum allocation of resources in the presence of both public and private goods.

(ii) identifies the differences in the two sets of conditions and explains them.

(iii) specifies the reasons for the failure of the market in providing social goods.

(iv) identifies and explains the problems the government faces in providing social goods.

(v) defines externality. Explains the linkage between externality and mixed goods and dwells on the reasons for market failure in the case of mixed goods.

(vi) discusses the measures the government can adopt to correct market failures in the case of mixed goods.

(vii) defines and explains the concept of merit goods.

2.1 INTRODUCTION

Theory of public finance deals with, among others, the issue of market failure. One of its major objectives is to identify the reasons why market fails to establish a Pareto optimum or efficient allocation of resources. *There are three major sources of market failure in this regard: public goods, mixed goods and imperfect competition.* Here we shall focus only on public or social goods and mixed goods, and the problems they give rise to. Goods are divided into three broad categories: public or social goods, private goods and mixed goods. To identify the type of a good, we have to first ascertain whether the good is excludable or non-excludable and rival or non-rival. In Sections 2.2 and 2.3 we shall explain what is meant by a good being excludable or non-excludable and rival or non-rival. In Section 2.4 we use these concepts to define public goods and private goods. Markets cannot provide public goods. They have to be provided by the government. Is it possible for the government to provide public goods efficiently? This is the question which is discussed in Sections 2.5, 2.6, 2.7 and 2.10. Section 2.5 derives the necessary conditions for optimum allocation of resources when only private goods are produced. Section 2.6 derives the necessary conditions for optimum allocation of resources when both private and public goods are produced in the economy. Section 2.7 compares these conditions with those in the earlier case. Section 2.8 focuses on mixed goods and the externalities they generate leading to market failure. It also discusses the measures that the government can adopt to resolve the problem. Section 2.9 focuses on a different category of goods, called merit goods. Finally, Section 2.10 examines whether government can provide public goods fulfilling the efficiency conditions.

2.2 EXCLUDABLE AND NON-EXCLUDABLE GOODS

If the owner of a good can prevent others from using the good, the good is excludable. Otherwise, it is non-excludable. The owner of an excludable good is, therefore, in a position to allow only those who are willing to pay for using the good to use it and prevent others from using it. The owners of non-excludable goods cannot prevent anyone from using the non-excludable goods they own. National defence is an example of a non-excludable good. If a system of national defence is put in place to protect a country from foreign invasion, then everyone living in the country will enjoy the security provided by it. If the producer of national defence asks some citizens to pay for the service and if they refuse to pay, it will not be possible for the producer to prevent them from enjoying the benefit of the service. Similarly, if a flood control facility is set up to prevent an area from being flooded, everyone living in the area will enjoy its benefits irrespective of whether she pays for the services of the facility or not. The producer of the service is not in a position to prevent all those who are living in the area but refusing to pay for the service from enjoying the benefit of the service. Besides national defence and flood control facility, administration that maintains internal law and order of the country, boundary wall of a housing estate etc. are all examples of non-excludable goods. In contrast, items of food, clothing etc. are all excludable. The owner of a readymade garment store, for example, allows only those to take away the garments who pay the price asked for, and is capable of preventing others from using his garments.

The important point that is made above is the following. Since owners of non-excludable goods cannot prevent anyone from using the goods, they cannot force anybody to pay for using them. Obviously, in a market economy profit maximizing produces will supply only excludable goods. They will never produce non-excludable goods.

2.3 RIVAL AND NON-RIVAL GOODS

If use of a particular unit of a good by one person does not prevent others from using the same unit of the good at the same time, the good is non-rival. Otherwise, the good is rival. Take the case of a non-crowded road. If a person uses the road, that does not prevent others from using the same road at the same time. Therefore, a non-crowded road or a non-crowded bridge is non-rival. In contrast, consider a piece of cake. If a person eats it up, others cannot eat it. So it is rival. Similarly, if a person wears a shirt, then others cannot wear it at the same time. Therefore, shirts are rival. In fact, almost all the items of food and clothing are rival, while national defence, administration, facilities to control flood and water logging etc. are all examples of non-rival goods. Just like non-excludable goods a market economy cannot handle efficiently the non-rival goods either. Let us explain. If a non-rival good is produced or built, (take, e.g., a non-crowded road), then, from the point of view of the society, the marginal or additional cost of allowing one extra person to use the non-rival good is zero. This means that the society need not use any extra resources to allow one extra person to use the non-rival good. Therefore, from the point of view of the society an existing non-rival good is efficiently utilized, if every individual who derives some benefit from using the non-rival good is allowed to use it. If a positive price is charged for using a non-rival good, then the individuals who derive positive utility from its use, but whose utility from its use is too low to warrant the payment of the price, i.e., whose demand price for the use of the non-rival good is less than the price charged, will not use it. So, the society will lose some amount of utility that it could derive from the use of the non-rival good. Therefore, the utilization of the non-rival good from the point of view of the society will be suboptimum or inefficient. In a market economy if a profit-maximizing producer produces a non-rival good, he will obviously impose a user charge and thereby bring about inefficient utilization of the non-rival good. From the above it follows that *a market economy cannot provide non-excludable goods. Nor can it bring about efficient utilization of non-rival goods. In these areas, therefore, government intervention or government provision are needed.*

2.4 CLASSIFICATION OF GOODS

On the basis of the characteristics of the goods discussed above goods are classified into social or public and private goods. *Goods that are both non-excludable and non-rival are pure public or social goods, while those that are excludable as well as rival are pure private goods.* Here we use the terms pure public goods and public goods, and pure private goods and private goods interchangeably. Pure social goods, as we have already pointed out, have to be provided by the government.

Box 2.1: Distribution of Public Goods in India

Distribution of public goods varies widely across different regions of India. In an interesting study, Banerjee (2004) identifies certain key factors which he thinks might be responsible for the kind of uneven distribution of public goods that exists in India. These factors are geographical, historical and ethnic in nature. Of the geographical factors 'being coastal' is found to be the most important in influencing spatial distribution of public goods. The reason is that people living in coastal areas have greater exposure to international trade. Hence they are more aware of the kind of amenities that are available

---

(Contd.)...

(Contd.)...

in foreign countries. Accordingly, they demand public goods more fervently. Besides being coastal, other geographical factors are also found to be important. The cost of providing public goods in mountainous regions is much higher than that in the plains. Hence, the latter have larger share of public goods than the former. Per capita cost of providing public goods is much less in densely-populated regions than in thinly-populated ones. Accordingly, the former have a larger concentration of public goods in India.

Historical factors have also been found to be significant. Three different kinds of land tenure systems existed in India, namely, zamindari (landlord-based system), raiyatwari (peasant-based system) and mahalwari (village-based system). Zamindars (landlords) were politically quite strong and the British had relatively much less control over rent in the zamindari areas. In fact, rent in these areas was fixed forever in nominal terms. In other regions the British could and did raise rent whenever there was an increase in productivity. Accordingly, the British were much more interested in investing in productivity-enhancing infrastructure in non-zamindari areas. Landlords on the other hand were mostly absentee landlords who derived bulk of their income from non-agricultural sources. Hence, they had little incentive to invest in land. For these reasons areas under the zamindari system attracted much less public goods.

Ethnic factors are also found to be important. Minority communities have always been discriminated against. They constitute the bulk of the poor population with little access to education or health care facilities. They are much less aware of their rights and legitimate dues and, therefore, less articulate in their demand for public goods. Accordingly, as has been found by Banerjee, there is less availability of public goods in areas where the minority communities are predominant in population.

2.5 EFFICIENT ALLOCATION OF RESOURCES IN THE ABSENCE OF PUBLIC GOODS

To have a clear idea about the issue of market failure in the presence of public goods, we have to derive first the necessary conditions for optimum allocation of resources for the case where both private and public goods are produced in the economy. But before going into that, we shall have to consider the necessary conditions for efficient allocation of resources in an economy where only private goods are produced. We shall gain valuable insight into the problems posed by public goods by comparing the two sets of conditions for the two cases.

For simplicity we consider a simple economy where only two private goods, X and Y, are produced with only two factors of production, capital (K) and labour (L). Endowments of K and L are fixed and given by $\bar{K}$ and $\bar{L}$ respectively. There are only two individuals A and B. The analysis, though carried out for this simple case, can easily be extended to the more general case. Resource allocation in the economy is efficient or Pareto optimum, when allocation of $\bar{K}$ and $\bar{L}$ between X and Y and the distribution of produced X and Y between A and B are such that by changing them it is not possible to make any one of the two individuals better off without making the other worse off. In other words, resource allocation is efficient or Pareto optimum, when production of X and Y and their distribution between A and B are such that the utility of each individual is at its maximum possible level, given the utility level of the other individual. We can, therefore, derive the necessary conditions for efficient allocation of resources by carrying out the following optimization exercise:

$$\max U^A(X^a, Y^a)$$

subject to

$$U^B(X^b, Y^b) = \bar{U}^B \qquad (2.1)$$

$$X^a + X^b = F(K_x, L_x)$$

$$Y^a + Y^b = G(\bar{K} - K_x, \bar{L} - L_x)$$

$U^A(.)$ and $U^B(.)$ denote the utility functions of A and B respectively, (X^a, Y^a) and (X^b, Y^b) denote quantities of X and Y consumed by A and B respectively, $F(.)$ and $G(.)$ represent respectively the production functions of X and Y and K_x and L_x denote quantities of capital and labour employed in the production of X. When there is full employment of $\bar{K}$ and $\bar{L}$, quantities of capital and labour that are employed in the production of Y, which we shall henceforth denote by K_Y and L_Y respectively, are given by $(\bar{K} - K_x)$ and $(\bar{L} - L_x)$. Here the choice variables in the optimization exercise (2.1) are: X^a, Y^a, X^b, Y^b, K_x and L_x. Forming the Lagrangian expression, we have

$$Z = U^A(X^a, Y^a) + \lambda[U^B(X^b, Y^b) - \bar{U}^B] + \mu[F(K_x, L_x) - X^a - X^b]$$

$$+ \delta[G(\bar{K} - K_x, \bar{L} - L_x) - Y^a - Y^b]$$

The first-order conditions are given by

$$\frac{\partial Z}{\partial X^a} = \frac{\partial U^A}{\partial X^a} - \mu = 0 \qquad (2.1a)$$

$$\frac{\partial Z}{\partial X^b} = \lambda \frac{\partial U^B}{\partial X^b} - \mu = 0 \qquad (2.1b)$$

$$\frac{\partial Z}{\partial Y^a} = \frac{\partial U^A}{\partial Y^a} - \delta = 0 \qquad (2.1c)$$

$$\frac{\partial Z}{\partial Y^b} = \lambda \frac{\partial U^B}{\partial Y^b} - \delta = 0 \qquad (2.1d)$$

$$\frac{\partial Z}{\partial K_x} = \mu \frac{\partial F}{\partial K_x} - \delta \frac{\delta G}{\delta K_y} = 0 \qquad (2.1e)$$

$$\frac{\partial Z}{\partial L_x} = \mu \frac{\partial F}{\partial L_x} - \delta \frac{\delta G}{\delta L_y} = 0 \qquad (2.1f)$$

$$(K_y \equiv \bar{K} - K_x, \text{ and } L_y \equiv \bar{L} - L_y)$$

Solving these six FOCs along with the three constraints, we get the optimum values of the six choice variables and the three Lagrange multipliers. Eliminating the three Lagrange multipliers from the six FOCs, we get the three necessary conditions for optimal allocation of resources.

From (2.1a) to (2.1d), we get

$$\frac{\partial U^A/\partial X^a}{\partial U^A/\partial Y^a}\left(\equiv mrs^A_{x,y}\right) = \frac{\partial U^B/\partial X^b}{\partial U^B/\partial Y^b}\left(\equiv mrs^B_{x,y}\right) \tag{2.2}$$

where $mrs^A_{x,y}$ and $mrs^B_{x,y}$ denote respectively marginal rates of substitution of X for Y of A and B.

From (2.1e) and (2.1f), we get

$$\frac{\partial F/\partial K_x}{\partial F/\partial L_x}\left(\equiv mrts^x_{K,L}\right) = \frac{\partial G/\partial K_y}{\partial Y/\partial L_y}\left(\equiv mrts^y_{K,L}\right) \tag{2.3}$$

where $mrts^x_{K,L}$ and $mrts^y_{K,L}$ denote respectively marginal rates of technical substitution of K for L in the production of X and Y.

Finally, from (2.1a) to (2.1f), we get

$$\frac{\partial G/\partial K_y}{\partial F/\partial K_x}\left(\equiv mrtr_{x,y}\right) = \frac{\partial G/\partial L_y}{\partial F/\partial L_x}\left(\equiv mrtr_{x,y}\right)$$

$$= \frac{\partial U^A/\partial X^a}{\partial U^A/\partial Y^A}\left(\equiv mrs^A_{x,y}\right) = \frac{\partial U^B/\partial X^b}{\partial U^B/\partial Y^B}\left(\equiv mrs^B_{x,y}\right) \tag{2.4}$$

where $mrtr_{x,y}$ denotes marginal rate of transformation of X for Y.

Let us first explain why $[(\partial G/\partial K_y)/(\partial F/\partial K_x)]$ gives the marginal rate of transformation of X for Y. Marginal rate of transformation of X for Y gives the amount of Y that the society has to give up to produce one additional unit of X. One additional unit of capital, given labour, produces $(\partial F/\partial K_x)$ amount of X. Therefore, to produce one additional unit of X, given the amount of labour employed in its production, additional amount of capital required is $[1/(\partial F/\partial K_x)]$. If that much of capital is withdrawn from the production of Y, with the amount of labour employed in the Y sector remaining unchanged, output of Y will decline by $[1/(\partial F/\partial K_x)][\partial G/\partial K_y]$. Similarly, explain why the other term also gives the $mrtr_{x,y}$.

Conditions (2.2), (2.3) and (2.4) state respectively that, *when resource allocation is optimum, the marginal rate of substitution of X for Y is the same for every individual, the marginal rate of technical substitution of capital for labour is the same in the production of every good, and the marginal rate of transformation of X for Y is equal to the common marginal rate of substitution of X for Y.* These are, therefore, the necessary conditions for optimum allocation of resources when only private goods are produced in the economy. Let us now explain each of the three conditions.

Explanation of Condition (2.2)

When distribution of a given combination of X and Y, say, $\bar{X}$ and $\bar{Y}$, between A and B is optimum so that by changing the distribution it is not possible to make any one better off without making the other worse off, then condition (2.2) is satisfied. In fact, the FOCs of the following maximization exercise yields condition (2.2).

$$\max\ U^A(X^a,\ \dot{Y}^a)$$

$$\text{subject to}\quad U^B(X^b,\ Y^b) = \bar{U}^B$$

$$X^a + X^b = \bar{X}$$

and
$$Y^a + Y^b = \bar{Y}$$

Choice variables of the above maximization exercise are: X^a, X^b, Y^a and Y^b.

Let us now explain condition (2.2). Suppose that the distribution of a given (X, Y) between A and B is such that condition (2.2) is not satisfied. We shall show that in this case just by changing the distribution of the given (X, Y) between A and B it will be possible to make either of them better off without making the other worse off. This means that the initial distribution is not efficient. It, therefore, follows that if distribution of a given (X, Y) is efficient, it must satisfy condition (2.2).

Let us suppose that corresponding to the initial distribution of the given (X, Y), $mrs^A_{X,Y}$ $< mrs^B_{X,Y}$. In this case, if we transfer 1 unit of X from A to B, we can take away $mrs^B_{X,Y}$ amount of Y from B without making him worse off. A needs only $mrs^A_{X,Y}$ amount of Y to compensate for the loss of 1 unit of X and $mrs^A_{X,Y} < mrs^B_{X,Y}$. Thus, following this transfer of 1 unit of X from A to B, there will be an extra $(mrs^B_{X,Y} - mrs^A_{X,Y})$ amount of Y after keeping both of them on their initial indifference curves. This extra amount of Y can be given to either of them making him better off without making the other worse off. If it is distributed between both of them, both will be better off. Therefore, if the distribution of any given (X, Y) between A and B is efficient, it will satisfy (2.2).

Let us illustrate this condition graphically with the help of Figure 2.1 where we present an Edgeworth box whose length measures a given quantity of X, X_0, and the breadth measures a given quantity of Y, Y_0. We measure X^a and Y^a along the horizontal and vertical axes in the rightward and upward directions respectively with O as the origin, and X^b and Y^b along the horizontal and vertical axes in the leftward and downward directions respectively with O' as the origin. The point to note about the box is that every point in the box represents a unique distribution of the given combination of (X, Y), (X_0, Y_0), between A and B. Consider a point such as D, for example. At this point $O'C$ amount of X is owned by B, while the remaining part of X_0, $(X_0 - O'C)$, is owned by A. Again, $O'C'$ amount of Y is owned by B and the rest, $(Y_0 - O'C')$ amount of Y, is owned by A. We plot the indifference curves of A and B in this Figure. I_{1a}, I_{2a} etc. are indifference curves of A, while I_{0b}, I_{1b} etc. are indifference curves of B. Suppose that the government wants to distribute the given quantities of X and Y between A and B efficiently so that utility of each individual is maximized, given the utility level of the other individual.

What condition is satisfied when the government achieves its desired distribution? To know that suppose that the government wants to maximize B's utility keeping A on a given indifference curve, I_{2a}, say. The government achieves the desired outcome when the distribution corresponds to the point a on I_{2a}. At this point an indifference curve of B, I_{0b}, is tangent to I_{2a}. Hence, I_{0b} is the highest indifference curve of B that B can attain when A is on the given indifference curve, I_{2a}. All the indifference curves of B indicating higher utility levels are entirely below I_{2a} and, therefore, are unattainable, when A is kept on I_{2a}. All the other indifference curves of B, which pass through the other points of I_{2a} are above I_{0b} and, therefore, indicate lower levels of utility of B than I_{0b}. Thus, at the optimum point on I_{2a} the slopes of the two indifference curves are equal, i.e., $mrs_{X,Y}$ is the same for both the individuals. At every other point on I_{2a} an indifference curve of B cuts I_{2a}. Hence, at every such point values of $mrs_{X,Y}$ of the two individuals are different. Consider a point such as D to the left of A on I_{2a}. At such a point the absolute value of the slope of I_{2a}, $mrs^A_{X,Y} > mrs^B_{X,Y}$, the absolute value of the slope of I_{-1a}. Therefore, if from such a point one unit of X is transferred from B to A (indicated by the movement from D to E in Figure 2.1), the compensation that B requires in the form of additional Y, $mrs^B_{X,Y}$ (indicated by EF (approximately)), is smaller than the amount of Y that is to be taken away from A to keep him on the same indifference curve, I_{2a}. This amount is $mrs^A_{X,Y}$ (indicated by Ea (approximately)). Therefore, if Ea amount of Y is given to B, he will get aF amount more than the compensation he requires for the loss of one unit of X. Hence he will move over to a higher indifference curve. Thus, if we move leftward from D along I_{2a} redistributing X and Y commensurately between A and B, B will move to higher and higher indifference curves until the optimum point a is reached. Similarly, from any point to the right of a leftward movement along I_{2a} will take B to higher and higher indifference curves until the optimum point a is reached. We can carry out this exercise for every given level of utility of A or for every given

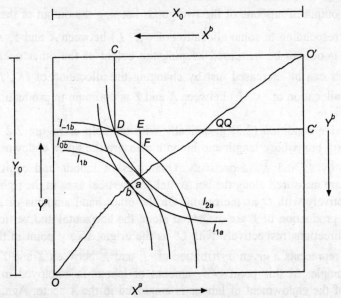

Figure 2.1:   Derivation of the optimum distribution of a given combination of X and Y between A and B.

level of utility of B. For every such given utility level of any of the two individuals there will be a unique optimum distribution given by the point of tangency of the indifference curve corresponding to the given level of utility of the individual whose utility is kept fixed and one indifference curve of the other individual. The locus of all such optimum points is called the contract curve. It is labelled QQ in Figure 2.1.

Explanation of Condition (2.3)

When production is optimally organized, i.e., when allocation of $(\overline{K}, \overline{L})$ between X and Y is such that output of neither can be increased without reducing the output of the other good (i.e., output of each good is at its maximum level, given the output of the other good), condition (2.3) is satisfied. In fact, FOCs of the following maximization exercise yield condition (2.3).

$$\max_{K_x, L_x} F(K_x, L_x)$$

$$\text{subject to} \quad G(\overline{K} - K_x, \overline{L} - L_x) = \overline{Y}$$

Let us now explain condition (2.3). Suppose that corresponding to some allocation of $(\overline{K}, \overline{L})$ between X and Y, i.e., corresponding to some (X, Y) produced, $mrts^X_{K,L} < mrts^Y_{K,L}$. If we transfer 1 unit of K from X to Y, we can take away $mrts^Y_{K,L}$ amount of labour from the Y sector keeping the output of Y unchanged. To compensate for the loss of one unit of capital, X sector needs only $mrts^X_{K,L}$ amount of labour and $mrts^X_{K,L} < mrts^Y_{K,L}$. Therefore, by transferring 1 unit of K from X to Y we can keep outputs of both X and Y unchanged and still have $(mrts^Y_{K,L} - mrts^X_{K,L})$ amount of labour unutilized. We can use this to increase either outputs of both X and Y or output of any one of the two goods keeping the output of the other unchanged. Therefore, if corresponding to some allocation of $(\overline{K}, \overline{L})$ between X and Y, $mrts^X_{K,L} \neq mrts^Y_{K,L}$, output of either good can be increased keeping the output of the other unchanged or outputs of both the goods can be increased just by changing the allocation of $(\overline{K}, \overline{L})$ between X and Y. Hence, when allocation of $(\overline{K}, \overline{L})$ between X and Y is optimum in production, condition (2.3) must hold.

We can derive condition (2.3) graphically with the help of Figure 2.2 where we present another Edgeworth box whose length and breadth measure the given endowments of labour and capital, denoted by $\overline{L}$ and $\overline{K}$ respectively. Quantities of labour and capital devoted to the production of X are measured along the horizontal and vertical axes in the rightward and upward directions respectively with O as the origin. On the other hand amounts of labour and capital employed in the production of Y are measured along the horizontal and vertical axes in the left and downward directions respectively with O' as the origin. Every point in this box, just as in the earlier case, represents a given distribution of $\overline{L}$ and $\overline{K}$ between X and Y sectors. Consider point A_2 for example. At this point $O'A_5$ amount of labour is employed in the Y sector, the remaining part of the endowment of labour is employed in the X sector Again, OA_6 amount of capital is employed in the X sector and the remaining part of the endowment of capital is employed in the Y sector. Let us now derive diagrammatically the condition that is satisfied, when the allocation of the given endowment of capital and labour is efficient. The allocation that maximizes the output of each good, with the output of the other good at a given level is efficient. Let us therefore identify the allocation that maximizes the output of Y, with the output of X at a given level, say X_0. The isoquants of X and Y are plotted in Figure 2.2. Focus on the isoquant corresponding to the given level of output of X, X_0. This isoquant is labelled X_0. Clearly, the maximum Y that can be produced, with the output of X equal to X_0, is given by the isoquant of Y that is tangent to the given isoquant of X. This isoquant of Y represents a given level of output of Y, which we denote by Y_1. This isoquant of Y is labelled Y_1. All the isoquants of Y that indicate higher levels of Y are unattainable as they lie entirely below this isoquant of Y. Those isoquants of Y have no common point with the isoquant X_0. This means that those higher levels of Y cannot be produced keeping the output of X at X_0. Every other point on the given isoquant of X, labelled X_0, lies above the isoquant of Y that is tangent to X_0. Hence, the isoquant of Y passing through every such point should intersect the isoquant, X_0, and lie entirely above the isoquant, Y_1. Obviously, all such isoquants represent lower levels of output than Y_1. At the point of efficient allocation, A_4, in Figure 2.2, therefore, marginal rates of technical substitution of labour for capital in the two industries are the same. At every other point on the given isoquant, X_0, $mrts_{L,K}$ of the Y sector is different from that in the X sector. Why are such points inefficient? Let us now explain the economic reason for that. Consider a point such as A_2 at which $mrts^X_{L,K} > mrts^Y_{L,K}$. If from such a point one unit of labour is transferred from the Y to the X sector (indicated by the movement from A_2 to A_3), the amount of capital that can be withdrawn from the X sector without affecting its output is the $mrts^X_{L,K}$ corresponding to A_2. This amount of capital is given by $A_3 A_4$ approximately. This amount of capital is much larger than the compensation in the form of additional K that the Y sector requires for the loss of one unit of labour. This compensation is the $mrts^Y_{L,K}$ corresponding to A_2. It is given by $A_3 A_7$ approximately. Therefore, if one unit of L is transferred from the Y to the X sector and $mrts^X_{L,K}$

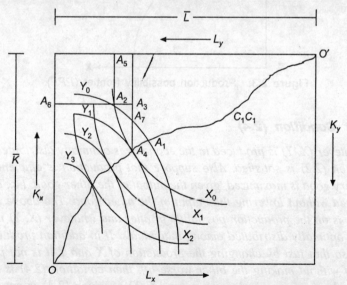

Figure 2.2:   Derivation of the necessary condition for optimum allocation of given endowments of factors of production.

amount of K is withdrawn from the latter and given to the former, the reallocation will raise Y without affecting X. At every point to the left of A_4 on the given isoquant of $Xm \neq rts^X_{L,K} > mrts^Y_{L,K}$. Therefore, by moving to the right from every such point along the given isoquant of X it will be possible to raise the output of Y keeping X unchanged until the optimum point is reached. Similarly, it can be shown that by moving to the left along the given isoquant of X from every point to the right of the optimum point on the given isoquant of X it will be possible to raise the output of Y keeping X unchanged until the optimum point is reached. (Do this yourself). This explains (2.3).

There is an optimum allocation of $\bar{K}$ and $\bar{L}$ for every given level of output of X or that of Y. The locus of all such allocations is the contract curve, C_1C_1. The set of all the combinations of X and Y corresponding to all the different points on the contract curve C_1C_1 is referred to as the production possibility frontier (PPF). It is shown in Figure 2.3. It indicates the maximum level of each good that the society can produce, given its endowment of factors of production and technology, corresponding to every different feasible level of output of the other good. Thus, when the economy is on the PPF, production is efficiently organized and condition (2.3) is satisfied. The absolute value of the slope of the PPF in the (X, Y) plane at any given point is the $mrtr_{X,Y}$ corresponding to the given point.

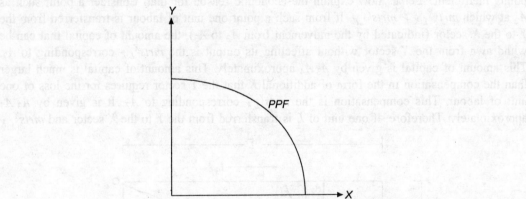

Figure 2.3:   Production possibility frontier (PPF).

Explanation of Condition (2.4)

Suppose that whatever (X, Y) is produced in the economy is optimally distributed between A and B so that condition (2.2) is satisfied. Also suppose that production is efficiently organized so that output of every good is maximized, given the output of the other good, i.e., output of neither good can be raised without lowering the output of the other good. The above conditions mean that the economy is on the production possibility frontier and whatever (X, Y) is produced from this frontier, it is optimally distributed among individuals. If in addition production of X and Y is also optimum so that just by changing the production of X and Y it is not possible to make anyone better off without making the other worse off, then condition (2.4) is satisfied. Let us explain. Suppose the economy produces a given (X, Y) at which (2.4) is not satisfied, but its production and distribution are efficiently organized so that both (2.2) and (2.3) are satisfied, i.e., the economy is on the *PPF* and the distribution of the given (X, Y) is such that the marginal rate of substitution of X for Y is the same for every individual. Suppose that at the given (X, Y), the slope of the *PPF*, $mrtr_{X,Y}$, is less than the common $mrs_{X,Y}$. If the economy now produces one additional unit of X and gives it to any one individual, the common $mrs_{X,Y}$ amount of Y can be taken away from him, keeping him on the same indifference curve. But to produce one additional unit of X the economy needs to sacrifice only $mrtr_{X,Y}$ amount of Y, which is less than the common $mrs_{X,Y}$. Therefore, by producing one extra unit of X, giving it to any one of the two individuals and reducing output of Y and also the consumption of Y of the individual who has got the extra unit of X by the required amount, $mrtr_{X,Y}$, it will be possible to make the individual who has got one additional unit of X better off. If the redistributing authority takes away from the individual who gets the extra unit of X the common $mrs_{X,Y}$ amount of Y instead of $mrtr_{X,Y}$, he will remain on the same indifference curve as before, but the authority will have (common $mrs_{X,Y} - mrtr_{X,Y}$) amount of Y undistributed. This amount of Y can be given to either individual making him better off without making the other worse off, or it may be distributed between both the individuals making both of them better off. Therefore, if (X, Y) is on *PPF* and distribution of (X, Y) between A and B is optimum and if along with this production of (X, Y) is efficient or Pareto optimum, then condition (2.4) must hold.

2.6 EFFICIENT ALLOCATION OF RESOURCES IN THE PRESENCE OF BOTH PRIVATE AND PUBLIC GOODS

We assume for simplicity that only one private good, X, and only one public good, G, are produced in the economy, with only two factors of production, capital, K, and labour, L. Endowments of K and L are fixed and are denoted as before by $\bar{K}$ and $\bar{L}$ respectively. Production functions of X and G are, $F(K_x, L_x)$ and $H(K_g, L_g)$ respectively. K_g and L_g denote quantities of capital and labour employed in the public good sector. There are only two individuals, A and B. Resource allocation in the economy is efficient or Pareto optimum, when allocation of $\bar{K}$ and $\bar{L}$ between X and G and the distribution of the produced X and G between A and B are such that by changing them it is not possible to make any one of the two individuals better off without making the other worse off. In other words, resource allocation is efficient or Pareto optimum, when production of X and G and their distribution between A and B are such that the utility of each individual is at its maximum possible level, given the utility of the other individual. Necessary conditions for optimum allocation of resources are, therefore, derived by carrying out the following optimization exercise:

$$\max \ U^a(X^a, G)$$

$$\text{subject to} \quad U^b(X^b, G) = \bar{U}^b$$

$$X^a + X^b = F(K_x, L_x)$$

$$G = H(\bar{K} - K_x, \bar{L} - L_x)$$

where $K_g = \bar{K} - K_x$ and $L_g = \bar{L} - L_x$. In the above optimization exercise the choice variables are given by X^a, X^b, G, K_x and L_x. The most important point to be noted here is that, unlike private goods, output of a public good cannot be distributed among individuals. A public good is non-excludable and non-rival. Hence, if a given quantity of a public good is produced in the economy, the whole of it will be available to every individual. Hence, in the utility functions of A and B, the whole output of the public good denoted by G enters as an argument.

Forming the Lagrangian expression, we have

$$Z = U^a(X^a, G) + \lambda[\bar{U}_b - U^b(X^b, G)] + \mu[X^a + X^b - F(K_x, L_x)]$$
$$+ \gamma[G - H(\bar{K} - K_x, \bar{L} - L_x)]$$

FOCs are, therefore, given by

$$\frac{\partial Z}{\partial X^a} = \frac{\partial U^a}{\partial X^a} + \mu = 0 \qquad (2.5)$$

$$\frac{\partial Z}{\partial X^b} = -\lambda \frac{\partial U^b}{\partial X^b} + \mu = 0 \qquad (2.6)$$

$$\frac{\partial Z}{\partial G} = \frac{\partial U^a}{\partial G} - \lambda \frac{\partial U^b}{\partial G} + \gamma = 0 \qquad (2.7)$$

$$\frac{\partial Z}{\partial K_x} = -\mu \frac{\partial F}{\partial K_x} + \gamma \frac{\partial H}{\partial K_G} = 0 \qquad (2.8)$$

$$\frac{\partial Z}{\partial L_x} = -\mu \frac{\partial F}{\partial L_x} + \gamma \frac{\partial H}{\partial L_G} = 0 \qquad (2.9)$$

We can solve these five equations along with the three constraints for the optimum values of the five choice variables and the three Lagrange multipliers. Optimum values of the five choice variables give us the optimum allocation of $\bar{K}$ and $\bar{L}$ between X and G, i.e., the optimum output levels of X and G and the optimum distribution of the optimum X between A and B. Distribution of the optimum output of G among individuals is not possible. The whole of it is available to every individual. From (2.5) to (2.9) we derive the following two necessary conditions for the optimum allocation of resources. From (2.8) and (2.9), we get

$$\frac{\partial F/\partial K_x}{\partial H/\partial K_G} (mrtr_{G,x}) = \frac{\partial F/\partial L_x}{\partial H/\partial L_G} (mrtr_{G,x}) = \frac{\gamma}{\mu} \qquad (2.10)$$

Dividing both the sides of (2.7) by μ and substituting for μ and (λ/μ) their values as given by (2.5) and (2.6) respectively, we get

$$\frac{\partial U^a/\partial G}{\partial U^a/\partial X^a} (mrs_{G,x}^a) + \frac{\partial U^b/\partial G}{\partial U^b/\partial X^b} (mrs_{G,x}^b) = \frac{\gamma}{\mu} \qquad (2.11)$$

From (2.10) and (2.11) we get the two necessary conditions

$$\frac{\partial F/\partial L_x}{\partial F/\partial K_x}(mrts_{L_x,K_x}) = \frac{\partial H/\partial L_G}{\partial H/\partial K_G}(mrts_{L_G,K_G}) \qquad (2.12)$$

and

$$\frac{\partial U^a/\partial G}{\partial U^a/\partial X^a} + \frac{\partial U^b/\partial G}{\partial U^b/\partial X^b} = \frac{\partial F/\partial K_x}{\partial H/\partial K_G} = \frac{\partial F/\partial L_x}{\partial H/\partial L_G}$$

$$\Rightarrow \qquad mrs_{G,x}^a + mrs_{G,x}^b = mrtr_{G,x} \qquad (2.13)$$

Condition (2.12) corresponds to condition (2.3) of the earlier case. Condition (2.12) is satisfied when allocation of $\overline{K}$ and $\overline{L}$ between X and G is such that output of each of the goods is maximized, given the output level of the other good. This means that condition (2.12) is satisfied when production of X and G is on the *PPF*. We can explain this condition the same way as (2.3). We shall discuss (2.12) in detail in the next section.

Condition (2.13) holds when production of G and X is on the *PPF* and the outputs of G and X and the distribution of the produced X between A and B are such that utility of every individual is maximized, given the utility of the other individual. We can derive (2.13) graphically also. To derive (2.13) graphically, as follows from our above discussion, we have to assume that production of G and X is on the *PPF* and distribution of the produced (G, X) between A and B is such that one of the two individuals is on a given indifference curve. Here we assume that individual B is on a given indifference curve. Under these conditions we shall graphically identify on the *PPF* the (G, X) that maximizes individual A's utility. That (G, X) represents the optimum allocation of resources between the two goods and then we shall derive the condition that is satisfied at the optimum allocation. We shall show graphically that the condition that is satisfied at the optimum allocation is (2.13). We shall carry out the whole graphical exercise described above with the help of Figure 2.4. The upper panel of Figure 2.4 shows the *PPF* and the given indifference curve of B labelled I_B^0 and the lower panel shows the consumption possibility locus of A (CPL^A). CPL^A shows corresponding to any given G the amount of X that can be made available to A, when the society produces that amount of X, which corresponds to the given G on *PPF* and B gets, along with the given amount of G, such an amount of X that he is on the given indifference curve, I_B^0.

CPL^A is drawn in the following manner. Consider a given (G, X), say (G_0, X_0), on *PPF*. The whole of G_0 is available to both A and B. Subtract from X_0 the amount of X that has to be given to B along with G_0 to keep him on the given indifference curve. This quantity of X is, say, X_0^b. Then the maximum amount of X that can be made available to A along with G_0 amount of G is $[X_0 - X_0^b]$. Therefore, $[G_0, X_0 - X_0^b]$ is a point on the CPL^A. X_0^b incidentally is shown to be equal to X_0 in Figure 2.4. Repeating this procedure for every feasible G, we get the CPL^A. If the *PPF* is concave and the given indifference curve of B is convex, then, as we shall show later, CPL^A is concave. We superimpose indifference curves of A in Figure 2.4 on CPL^A. The combination of G and X^a that maximizes A's utility on CPL^A will lie on the highest attainable indifference curve of A. The highest indifference curve of A attainable remaining on CPL^A is the one that is tangent to the CPL^A. The point of tangency is the optimum point. This point maximizes A's utility, when B is on the given indifference curve, I_B^0 and production is on PPF. This point gives us the optimum production of G. The point on PPF corresponding to this optimum G gives us the optimum production levels of G and X or the optimum allocation of $(\bar{K}, \bar{L})$ between G and X when B is on the given indifference curve. At the optimum point on CPL^A, as we have just mentioned, an indifference curve of A is tangent to the CPL^A. Thus, when production takes place on PPF and the allocation of $(\bar{K}, \bar{L})$ between G and X is optimum, the absolute value of the slope of CPL^A = the absolute value of the slope of the indifference curve of $A (\equiv mrs_{G,X}^a)$.

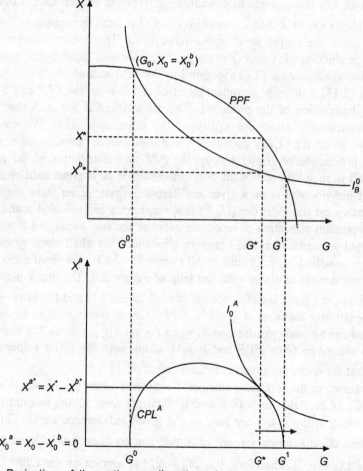

Figure 2.4:   Derivation of the optimum allocation of resources between private and public goods.

Note: For optimization the relevant region is the negatively-sloped portion of the CPL^A. As long as A is in the positively-sloped part of the CPL^A, an increase in G will raise his utility, since the amount of X available to him also rises. Hence, A's utility will be maximized only in the negatively-sloped portion of the CPL^A.

Let us now interpret the slope of CPL^A. It gives the amount of X that has to be taken away from A if the society produces 1 extra unit of G and reduces the output of X along the PPF and keeps B on the given indifference curve, I_0^B. If one extra unit of G is produced along PPF, society has to sacrifice $mrtr_{GX}$ amount of X. To keep B on the same given indifference curve with this one extra unit of G, $mrs_{G,X}^b$ amount of X has to be taken away from him. Hence, availability of X to A will go down not by the whole of $mrtr_{GX}$, but by $[mrtr_{GX} - mrs_{G,X}^B]$ and this gives the absolute value of the slope of CPL^A. (We have derived the slope of the CPL^A mathematically in the appendix to this chapter). Therefore, when resource allocation is optimum, the following condition is satisfied:

$$mrtr_{GX} - mrs_{G,X}^b \ (= \text{absolute value of the slope of } CPL^A)$$

$$= mrs_{G,X}^a$$

or
$$mrs_{G,X}^b + mrs_{G,X}^a = mrtr_{G,X}$$

Thus, we derive graphically condition (2.13). The point to note here is that for optimization the relevant region is the negatively-sloped portion of the CPL^A. As long as A is in the positively-sloped part of the CPL^A, an increase in G will raise his utility, since the amount of X available to him also rises. Hence, A's utility will be maximized only in the negatively-sloped portion of the CPL^A.

Let us now explain the necessary condition (2.13), derived above. Consider any point to the left of the optimum point on the CPL^A's negatively-sloped portion, which is the relevant portion for maximization of A's utility, given the constraints. The indifference curve of A passing through every such point will intersect the CPL^A from above, otherwise the indifference curve will intersect I_0^A. Hence, at every such point the absolute value of the slope of the indifference curve is greater than the absolute value of the slope of the CPL^A, i.e., at every such point $mrs_{G,X}^A > mrtr_{G,X} - mrs_{G,X}^B \Rightarrow mrs_{G,X}^A + mrs_{G,X}^B > mrtr_{G,X}$. If from such a point G is raised by one unit, the whole of it will be available to both A and B and from them $[mrs_{G,X}^A + mrs_{G,X}^B]$ amount of X can be taken away keeping them on the same indifference curves as before. Thus $[mrs_{G,X}^A + mrs_{G,X}^B]$ is the marginal social benefit of G in terms of X. However, to produce one additional unit of G, only $mrtr_{GX}$ amount of X is to be sacrificed, and it is less than $[mrs_{G,X}^A + mrs_{G,X}^B]$. Therefore, if one extra unit of G is produced, then even after keeping the two individuals on the same indifference curves as before $[mrs_{G,X}^A + mrs_{G,X}^B - mrtr_{G,X}]$ amount of X will be left over. If this is distributed to the individuals, then both of them will be better off. If the whole of it is given to A, then he will be better off, while B will remain on the same indifference curve as before. Therefore, at every point to the left of the optimum point on the CPL^A, marginal social benefit of G exceeds $mrtr_{GX}$, which is the marginal social cost of production of G in terms of X. Hence, from every such point by moving to the right along the CPL^A A can be made better off, without making B worse off. Similarly, at every point to the right of the optimum point on the CPL^A marginal social benefit of G is less than its marginal social cost of production. Hence, by moving to the left along the CPL^A, A can be made better off keeping B on the same indifference curve as before. (Show it yourself.)

We can also identify the optimum quantity of G using a different diagram. We have done this in Figure 2.5. It also brings out the meaning of condition (2.13) quite clearly. In Figure 2.5 $mrtr_{GX}$ or MC_{GX} schedule gives the values of $mrtr_{GX}$ corresponding to different values of G. Now $mrtr_{GX}$, which is the absolute value of the slope of PPF, gives the amount of X that the society has to sacrifice to produce one additional unit of G, i.e., it gives the marginal social cost of producing G in terms of X. Since PPF is concave, $mrtr_{GX}$ rises with an increase in G.

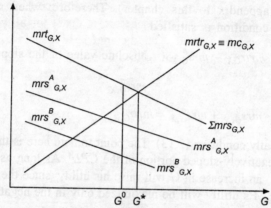

Figure 2.5: Derivation of the optimum allocation of resources between private and public goods.

The $mrs^B_{G,X}$ schedule gives the values of $mrs^B_{G,X}$ at different values of G when individual B is on the given indifference curve, I^B_0, as shown in Figure 2.4. It is obviously downward sloping. $mrs^A_{G,X}$ schedule gives the values of $mrs^A_{G,X}$ corresponding to different values of G when A is on CPL^A shown in Figure 2.4. As different points on CPL^A are located on different indifference curves of A, we cannot say a priori whether $mrs^A_{G,X}$ schedule is upward or downward sloping. However, in Figure 2.5, we have taken this schedule to be downward sloping for expository reasons. $\sum mrs_{G,X}$ schedule is derived by vertically summing up the $mrs^A_{G,X}$ and $mrs^B_{G,X}$ schedules. It gives corresponding to every value of G the sum of marginal rates of substitution of G for X of A and B taken together, i.e., it gives corresponding to every G the total amount of X that A and B together can sacrifice remaining on the same indifference curves as before if they get one additional unit of G. Now, if the society produces one additional unit of G, it becomes available to all the individuals at the same time. Hence, corresponding to every G the $\sum mrs_{G,X}$ schedule gives the marginal social benefit of G in terms of X, which is nothing but the total amount of X that all the individuals taken together can sacrifice remaining on the same indifference curves as before if they get one additional unit of G. The $\sum mrs_{G,X}$ schedule may be upward or downward sloping, since the sign of the slope of $mrs^a_{G,X}$ schedule is ambiguous. The only condition to be satisfied for maximization of A's utility, given the constraints, is that the $\sum mrs_{G,X}$ schedule should cut the $mrtr_{GX}$ or MC_{GX} schedule from the above. In fact we pointed out above in the context of Figure 2.4 that at every G less than its optimum value $\sum mrs_{G,X}$ exceeds $mrtr_{GX}$ and vice versa. In fact, one can deduce this from the second order condition for maximization as well. The optimum G, which we have denoted by G^*, corresponds to the point of intersection of the $\sum mrs_{G,X}$ and MC_{GX} schedules. This G corresponds to the point of tangency of the indifference curve of A, I_0^A, and CPL^A in Figure 2.4. At G^* the amount of X that all individuals together can sacrifice for one additional unit of G remaining on the same indifference curves as before is equal to the marginal social cost of producing G in terms of X, which is nothing but the amount of X that the society has to sacrifice to make one additional unit of G available to the individuals.

To see clearly why G^* is optimum, i.e., why G^* maximizes A's utility when B is on the given indifference curve and production is on PPF, consider a G, say G_0, which is less than G^*. At G_0, as shown in Figure 2.5, $mrs_{G,X}^a + mrs_{G,X}^b > MC_{G,X}$ or $mrs_{G,X}^a > MC_{G,X} - mrs_{G,X}^b$. Therefore, if one additional unit of G is produced along PPF, the amount of X that has to be taken away from A keeping B on the given indifference curve is given by the RHS of the latter inequality. However, the amount of X that can be taken away from A keeping him on the same indifference curve when one extra unit of G is produced is given by its LHS. At G_0 LHS > RHS. Therefore, by producing one extra unit of G, A's utility can be increased keeping B on the given indifference curve. This is true for every G less than G^*. Similarly, at every G greater than G^* LHS of the latter inequality is less than its RHS. Hence, from every such G A's utility can be increased keeping B on the given indifference curve by lowering the output of G and raising the output of X along PPF. (Prove this point yourself.)

We can explain Figure 2.5 in an alternative manner also. At any G, say G_0, less than G^*, $mrs_{G,X}^A + mrs_{G,X}^B > MC_{GX}$, i.e., marginal social benefit of G in terms of X is greater than the marginal social cost of producing G in terms of X. If one extra unit of G is produced, the amount of X the two individuals together can sacrifice remaining on the same indifference curves as before is larger than what they have to sacrifice. Thus, in this situation it is possible to make each individual sacrifice an amount of X less than his marginal rate of substitution of G for X to meet the cost of producing one extra unit of G and thereby make everyone of them better off. Thus, for every G less than the optimum G it is possible to make every individual better off by producing more G and less X along the PPF. For similar reasons it will be possible to make everyone better off by producing less G and more X, if G is larger than its optimum value. Work it out yourself.

2.7 COMPARISON BETWEEN NECESSARY CONDITIONS: CASES OF PURE PRIVATE GOODS AND PRIVATE AND PUBLIC GOODS

Let us now compare the necessary conditions of the two cases considered above. In the first case where only private goods are produced, the necessary conditions are given by (2.2), (2.3) and (2.4). In the second case where both private and public goods are produced, the necessary conditions are given by (2.12) and (2.13). We find that in the second case there is no condition corresponding to condition (2.2) of the earlier case. Conditions (2.12) and (2.3) are the same, while condition (2.4) of the first case corresponds to the condition (2.13) of the second case. However, (2.4) and (2.13) are different. Let us now explain these similarities and differences.

First, let us explain why in the second case there is no condition that corresponds to condition (2.2) of the earlier case. In other words, *in the second case there is no necessary condition for optimum distribution of any given (G, X) among individuals*. The reason is quite obvious. Distribution of a given (G, X) among individuals is optimum if by changing the distribution it is not possible to make someone better off without making at least one other individual worse off. Distribution of a given (G, X) among individuals can be changed only by changing the distribution of X since the whole of the given G is available to every individual. By changing the distribution of a given (G, X) among individuals an individual can, therefore, be made better off if and only if he is given more X. But that extra X can come only at the expense of at least one other individual. Therefore, in this case just by changing the distribution of a given (G, X) it is not possible to make any individual better off without making at least one other individual worse off. Hence, every distribution of every given (G, X) is optimum. This explains why there is no necessary condition for optimum distribution of a given (G, X).

Condition (2.12) of the second case is the same as condition (2.3) of the earlier case. This is the necessary condition for optimum allocation of the given endowment of factors of production among different goods in the sphere of production. When the allocation of the given $(\overline{K}, \overline{L})$ between X and G is optimum in production so that just by changing the allocation it is not possible to increase the output of any one of the two goods without reducing the output of the other goods, condition (2.12) is satisfied. The explanation of (2.12) is the same as that of (2.3). If, corresponding to any allocation of $(\overline{K}, \overline{L})$ between G and X, $mrts_{L,K}^{X} < mrts_{L,K}^{G}$, then by transferring one unit of L from X to G, taking away $mrts_{L,K}^{G}$ amount of capital from the production of G and giving to the X sector $mrts_{L,K}^{X}$ amount of capital, it will be possible to keep outputs of both X and G unchanged and still have a surplus of $\left(mrts_{L,K}^{G} - mrts_{L,K}^{X}\right)$ amount of capital. This much of capital can be used to increase the output of either or both the goods. Hence, if the allocation of $(\overline{K}, \overline{L})$ between G and X is optimum in the sphere of production, (2.12) is satisfied. The necessary condition for optimum allocation of resources in the sphere of production is the same in the two cases because private and social goods are different only on their uses side. The use or consumption of a social or public good is non-excludable and non-rival, while that of a private good is excludable and rival. However, there is no difference between private and public goods in the sphere of production.

Let us now compare condition (2.13) to (2.4). These two conditions correspond to one another. Both are necessary conditions for optimum allocation of resources, $(\overline{K}, \overline{L})$, when allocation of $(\overline{K}, \overline{L})$ is optimum in production and the distribution of the produced goods among individuals is also optimum. In the second case, however, distribution of the produced goods is always optimum. Both these conditions state that, when resource allocation is optimum, marginal social benefit of every good in terms of another is equal to its marginal social cost of production in terms of the other. The difference between (2.4) and (2.13) is due to the fact that, while *the marginal social benefit of a private good in terms of another is given by the common marginal rate of substitution of the private good for the other, marginal social benefit of a public good in terms of a private good is given by the sum of the marginal rates of substitution of the public good for the private good of all the individuals.* Let us now explain why. This difference is in fact due to the difference in the nature of private and social goods. Consider the first case, where only private goods are produced, first. Suppose one extra unit of a private good, say X, is produced. If it is given to any individual, it will not be available to any other individual. Therefore, marginal social benefit of X will be given by the extra benefit that the individual who gets it derives from it. When distribution of the produced goods among individuals in this case is optimum, the marginal rate of substitution, as we have explained earlier, is the same for everyone. Hence, in the simple two-good case we consider here, when distribution of the produced (X, Y) among individuals is optimum, $mrs_{X,Y}$ or marginal benefit of X in terms of Y is the same for every individual. In this case, therefore, marginal benefit of X in terms of Y to the society is equal to this common $mrs_{X,Y}$ or the common marginal benefit of X in terms of Y. Whoever gets the extra unit of X derives the same amount of benefit in terms of Y as given by the common $mrs_{X,Y}$.

In case of social goods, however, the situation is markedly different. If one extra unit of G is produced, it will be available to all the individuals. Hence, marginal benefit of G to the society is given not by the extra benefit that a single individual derives from the extra unit of G, but by the sum of the marginal benefits derived by all the individuals as everyone gets this extra unit of G. In our simple example the marginal benefit of G to the society in terms of X is $mrs_{G,X}^A + mrs_{G,X}^B$. If one extra unit of G is produced, it is available to both A and B and they together can sacrifice the above-mentioned amount of X and still remain on the same indifference curves as before. Hence, in the first case resource allocation between the two private goods, X and Y, is optimum, when marginal rate of transformation of X for Y, which is the marginal social cost of producing X in terms of Y, is equal to the common marginal rate of substitution of X for Y, while in the second case efficient resource allocation implies equality of the marginal rate of transformation of G for X and the sum of marginal rates of substitution of G for X of all the individuals. This explains the difference between (2.4) and (2.13).

2.8 MIXED GOODS AND EXTERNALITY

Externalities are a common phenomenon in a market economy. They lead to inefficient allocation of resources in such an economy. The government has to intervene to resolve the problems that externalities give rise to. Externalities are due to a specific type of goods, which are quite common in market economies. These goods are referred to as mixed goods. In what follows, we shall first define mixed goods and then externalities. After that we shall show the link between the two. Finally, we shall explain why market fails to establish an efficient allocation of resources in the presence of externalities generated by mixed goods and how the government can intervene to resolve these problems.

2.8.1 Mixed Goods

Goods that share the characteristics of both pure private goods and pure public goods are mixed goods. More precisely, goods that are excludable, but non-rival, e.g., a non-crowded highway or goods that are non-excludable, but rival, e.g., the crowded Howrah Bridge in the rush hours, are mixed goods. A road or a highway is excludable. It is possible for the owner of a road or highway to impose tolls on its use and prevent all those who are not willing to pay the toll from using it. However, a non-crowded road or highway is non-rival. Howrah Bridge in the rush hours is crowded and, therefore, rival. But it is not possible to impose tolls on its use. Imposition and collection of tolls will create so much traffic congestion that the whole road transport system of Kolkata and Howrah will collapse. Hence, Howrah Bridge in rush hours is rival but non-excludable.

Again, goods that are imperfectly excludable and/or only partly non-rival are also mixed goods. Important examples of this kind of mixed goods are education and health. Education and health are excludable and rival. The owners of a school, for example, can prevent whomever they want from taking admission in their school. This is true of a hospital also. Thus services rendered by schools and hospitals are excludable. Again, number of seats in a school or hospital is limited. A seat occupied by one cannot be occupied by any one else. Hence services rendered by schools and hospitals are rival. But they are excludable and rival only partially. This is because their benefits are reaped not only by their direct consumers, but also by others. In other words, benefits of education or health care services do not remain confined to the direct consumers of these services. They automatically spill over to others. Let us explain. As people get educated, social environment improves. Incidence of crime, drunkenness etc., falls. People are able to take informed decisions leading to an improvement in the functioning of democracy. Hence those who do not directly receive education benefit also. Similarly, if more people purchase health care services, rate of spread of contagious diseases falls benefiting others. In this sense education and health are partly non-rival. The recipients of education and health care services cannot prevent the benefits of consuming these services from being spilled over to others. Hence they are partly non-excludable as well. Goods such as cigarettes or liquor are also partly non-excludable and non-rival. Ill effects of their consumption spill over from their direct consumers to others adversely affecting their physical and mental health. Direct consumers of these goods cannot always stop this spillover. Thus, these goods are only imperfectly or partly excludable and rival and, therefore, belong to the category of mixed goods.

Non-rivalness and non-excludability of a good are by no means confined to its consumption or use, they may be a feature of its production as well. Production of chemicals and many other goods generates pollutants that make production of other goods costlier and affect people's health adversely. Drainage of industrial effluents into rivers and seas depletes fish population and thereby adversely affects output of the fisheries and poses health hazards for those who use the water of these rivers and seas for bathing or other purposes. Again, orchards raise output of honey of the neighbouring beekeepers. Costs and benefits of production of the goods cited above are, therefore, not completely internalized by their producers, they spill over to other producers and people as well. The producers of these goods in many cases cannot stop this spillover either. Hence, these goods are also only partially excludable and rival in their production, i.e., on their source's side. These goods also belong to the category of mixed goods.

Benefits and costs of consumption and production of mixed goods, as we have pointed out above, do not remain confined to their direct producers and consumers, they spill over to other producers and consumers as well. For this reason, as we shall explain in detail below, mixed goods cannot be provided efficiently by the market and government intervention may be needed to promote efficient provision of mixed goods.

2.8.2 Externalities

When activities of an economic agent directly affect the welfare of another and not indirectly via the market mechanism, externalities are generated. Consumption of cigarettes, for example, adversely affects the welfares of those who happen to be in the vicinity of the smokers. Smokers do not affect the welfare of these individuals through the market mechanism, but directly. The people who are adversely affected by the act of smoking by the smokers do not buy the smoke from the smokers. The smokers, therefore, generate externalities and these externalities are negative. The individuals who get themselves treated for contagious diseases generate positive externalities as their activities prevent the spread of the disease, reduce the risk of contagion and thereby increase the welfare of others directly and not through the market mechanism.

Externalities can arise not only in the sphere of consumption but also in that of production. A firm producing a good may emit pollutants in the environment adversely affecting other persons' health or reducing productivities in other sectors of production. Firms dumping effluents in rivers and oceans, for example, reduce output of fishermen and adversely affect the health of those who use that polluted water for bathing and other purposes. Firms and people whose output and health are affected by some firms' practice of dumping effluents in rivers and oceans do not pay the latter any thing for engaging in the practice. Hence, their suffering is an externality, a direct fall out of the practice of dumping effluents in rivers and oceans.

From the above it follows that the *goods whose benefits or costs cannot be fully internalized by the owners, i.e., the goods whose benefits and costs do not remain confined entirely to their consumers and producers, but spill over to others automatically, generate externalities. These goods, as we have explained above, are mixed goods.* In case of social or public goods, which are fully non-rival and non-excludable, the benefits spill over fully to others. Hence *the entire output of social goods may be regarded as a positive externality.* However, analysis of externalities is usually associated with the case of mixed goods only.

Externalities lead to suboptimum allocation of resources. The problem can be tackled in various ways. Some of these are Pigovian taxes and creation of markets. The problem may also be resolved through the initiative of the beneficiaries of the positive externalities or victims of negative externalities in the cases where it is possible for them to enter into a contract with the perpetrators of the externalities. When such contracts are infeasible, government can intervene to make such contracts feasible. We shall discuss these points below.

2.8.3 Pigovian Subsidy or Tax

Markets cannot produce mixed goods that generate externalities efficiently and there is room for the government, as pointed by Pigou, to intervene with tax-subsidy measures to make their output socially optimum. Let us explain the points made above with the help of Figure 2.6, which shows the demand and supply functions of a mixed good, X, whose consumption generates external benefits. It is imperfectly excludable and its use is also partly non-rival in the sense that its benefits are not completely internalized by those who consume it. They spill over automatically to other individuals as well. Hence X is a mixed good. We may regard X as education or health care services. It is possible to charge a price for the consumption of X, i.e., it can be bought and sold in the market. Note that schools can charge the students tuition fees for studying in schools. Similarly, hospitals can charge patients for the treatment they receive. Here we assume that X is bought and sold in a perfectly competitive market.

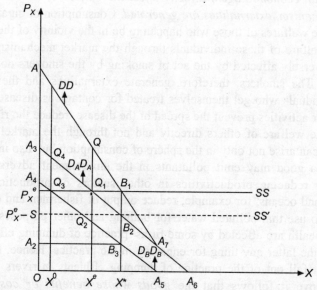

Figure 2.6: Mixed goods, externalities, optimum allocation of resources and Pigovian tax-subsidy scheme.

We further assume that there are two groups of individuals, A and B. Group A individuals directly enter into the market for X and purchase it. Individuals belonging to Group B do not directly purchase it, but benefit from others' consumption of X. D_AD_A and D_BD_B give demand schedules of the individuals belonging to groups A and B respectively. We shall refer to the individuals of Groups A and B by A and B respectively. For simplicity we assume that, besides X, only another good, a private good, Y, is produced. Price of X is denoted by P_x and it is given in terms of Y. D_AD_A, as usual, gives corresponding to every X the $mrs_{X,Y}$ or marginal benefit of X in terms of Y or the demand price of X in terms of Y of A. (To know why demand price equals $mrs_{X,Y}$ or marginal benefit of X in terms of Y see Appendix A.2.2)

D_BD_B on the other hand gives corresponding to every X the marginal benefit of X in terms of Y or demand price of X in terms of Y of B. Let us explain. B does not directly consume X, but he derives utility from A's consumption of X. If A gets one additional unit of X, then, other things remaining the same, B moves over to a higher indifference curve. To remain on the same indifference curve, therefore, B will have to sacrifice some given amount of Y. This is clearly the maximum amount of Y that B will be willing to sacrifice, if A is given one extra unit of X. This is thus B's marginal rate of substitution of X for Y ($mrs^b_{X,Y}$) or marginal benefit of X in terms of Y. This is also B's demand price of X in terms of Y. Let us explain. Suppose hypothetically B is charged a price in terms of Y for A's consumption of X. Let us denote it by P^b. If corresponding to any given level of A's consumption of X, the price charged to B is less than $mrs^b_{X,Y}$, B will gain if A's consumption of X rises. If A's consumption of X rises by 1 unit, B's gain in terms of Y will be ($mrs^b_{X,Y} - P^b$). Thus, as long as $mrs^b_{X,Y} > P^b$, B will gain if A's consumption of X rises. Similarly, if for any level of A's consumption of X, $mrs_{X,Y}^b < P^b$, B will gain if A's consumption of X falls. Therefore, B's gain will be maximum at that level of A's consumption of X at which $mrs_{X,Y}^b = P^b$. Suppose that this level of X is X_0. Clearly, if B is charged P^b for A's consumption of X, B will want A's consumption of X to be equal to X_0. Thus P^b or $mrs_{X,Y}^b$ corresponding to X_0 is B's demand price of X corresponding to X_0.

DD is the aggregate demand schedule. It is derived by vertically summing up $D_A D_A$ and $D_B D_B$. It gives corresponding to any given X the aggregate marginal benefit of A and B of the good X in terms of Y. DD, therefore, gives corresponding to every X marginal social benefit of X in terms of Y. In other words, it gives corresponding to every X the maximum amount of Y that the individuals of the two groups together can sacrifice without being worse off, if one additional unit of X is supplied to A.

SS gives corresponding to every X the supply price of X in terms of Y. This supply price is nothing but the marginal cost of production of X in terms of Y. We assume that production of X does not generate any externality. Therefore, marginal private cost of production of X equals its marginal social cost. Thus, the SS gives the marginal social cost of production of X in terms of Y corresponding to every X. As shown in Figure 2.6, aggregate social welfare is maximized at X^* corresponding to which marginal social benefit of X is equal to its marginal social cost of production. Let us explain. Consider any X, say X^e, less than X^* (see Figure 2.6). At X^e marginal social benefit of X in terms of Y is $Q X^e$. If one extra unit of X is produced and given to A, then B can sacrifice QQ_1 amount of Y remaining on the same indifference curve as before. As a result of this extra unit of X, A can sacrifice $Q_1 X^e$ amount of Y remaining on the same indifference curve as before. But the cost of producing this extra unit of X in terms of Y is only $Q_1 X^e < QX^e = QQ_1 + Q_1 X^e$. Thus, from this extra unit of X society's gain in terms of Y is QQ_1. By distributing this gain among individuals, for example, by taking away from A who gets this extra unit of X an amount of Y less than $Q_1 X^e$ and from B an amount of Y less than QQ_1 so that the total sacrifice of the two individuals equals the cost of producing the extra unit of X, it is possible to make both the individuals better off. Thus, society's welfare can be increased by producing more X as long as marginal social benefit of X exceeds its marginal social cost and conversely. Hence socially optimum output of X is X^*.

If, however, production of X is left to the market forces, only X^e amount of X will be produced, since X^e equates demand and supply in X's market where only Group A individuals bid for A.

Through a subsidy-tax programme it is possible for the government to raise the output of X to X^*. The supply schedule gives corresponding to every X the supply price or the minimum price at which the given amount of X is supplied. Suppose the government gives a subsidy, s, in terms of Y to the producers per unit of X supplied. This will clearly reduce the supply price by the amount s. This is because, if in the post-subsidy scenario producers charge a price, which is less than the original price by the amount s, they will effectively get the original supply price. The supply schedule will, therefore, shift downward by the amount s. If $s = B_1 B_2$, the SS schedule will shift downward and intersect $D_A D_A$, the demand schedule of the purchasers of X, at B_2 (see Figure 2.6) and the market will produce X^*. It should be noted that $B_1 B_2$ equals the demand price of X in terms of Y of B corresponding to X^*, $B_3 X^*$. This is the Pigovian subsidy scheme, which may be applied in case of mixed goods to bring about optimum allocation of resources.

Since the required unit subsidy equals the demand price of B corresponding to the optimum quantity of X, the subsidy is to be financed by imposing a tax equal to this demand price per unit of X supplied on Group B.

Let us now measure the total amount of gain to the society when the optimum quantity of X is produced under the tax-subsidy scheme specified above. Corresponding to any given quantity of X, say X_0, the total amount of Y that the individuals are willing to sacrifice for securing the given amount of X is given by the area under the DD schedule for the values of X from zero to X_0 (see Appendix A.2.2 for an explanation). The amount of Y that the society has to sacrifice to produce X_0 is given by the area under the SS schedule for the values of X from zero to X_0 (see Appendix A.2.2). Hence, gain to the society or to all the individuals taken together is given by the excess of the former area over the latter. This gain is maximized at X^* and it is given by the area of the triangle $AP^e_xB_1$ in Figure 2.6. One can easily check that the gain to the society will be less if any other quantity of X is produced. If for example X^e amount of X is produced, the gain to the society will be given by the area of the quadrilateral Q_1QA P^e_x. In this case the society's gain is less than its maximum level by the area of the triangle QQ_1B_1. The total gain to the society is distributed among Group A and Group B individuals. Let us now examine how this total gain is distributed among these two groups of individuals under the tax-subsidy scheme that makes the market produce the socially optimum quantity of X. In case of a buyer the gain from any unit purchased is given by the excess of the demand price corresponding to that unit and the actual price paid. Thus A's gain, as they face the price, $(P^e_x - s)$ in the optimum situation, is given by the area of the triangle, $A_3 (P^e_x - s)B_2$. B's gain on the other hand is given by $A_4A_2B_3$. The sum of these two areas equals $AP^e_xB_1$.

The problem with this scheme is that it is extremely difficult or costly to know the marginal benefit schedule of B with any degree of certainty. If the government does not have any information regarding the extent of marginal benefits generated by X, it cannot implement the Pigovian scheme. Efforts have, however, been made to design mechanisms that will induce individuals to reveal their preferences.

2.8.4 Creation of Markets

Besides Pigovian taxes, government can resolve the problem of suboptimum allocation of resources by creating markets for the external benefits of X. Suppose that the government issues coupons numbering X^* and gives them to A, who purchases X directly. The government also orders A to auction off all the coupons to B at the highest possible price. The sale of each coupon makes it compulsory for A to purchase 1 unit of X. Through this scheme the government actually creates a market for the external benefits of X. By buying a coupon B actually buys the benefit that he gets from A's consumption of one additional unit of X. Clearly, the highest price that B will offer for the X^* number of coupons, which enjoin on A to acquire X^* amount of X is, B_3X^*, as shown in Figure 2.6. The equilibrium in the coupons market is shown in Figure 2.7, where number of coupons is measured along the horizontal axis and price of coupons along the vertical axis. Here X gives the number of coupons as well as the number of units of the good X. This is because sale of one coupon means purchase of one unit of X. The vertical line SS

at X^* gives the given supply of coupons. Since purchase of one unit of coupon by B implies purchase of one unit of X by A as well, the demand schedule of B for coupons, which gives the demand price of B for coupons must be identical with his demand schedule for X. Thus the downward sloping line $D_B D_B$ in Figure 2.7 reproduces the $D_B D_B$ schedule of Figure 2.6. It gives corresponding to any given number of coupons the marginal benefit of B from A's purchase of the same number of units of X. Since, as follows from Figure 2.6, the marginal benefit of B from A's purchase of X^* number of X is $B_3 X^*$, he will purchase X^* number of coupons at the price $B_3 X^*$ only. Hence, the equilibrium price of coupons, as shown in Figure 2.7, is $B_3 X^*$.

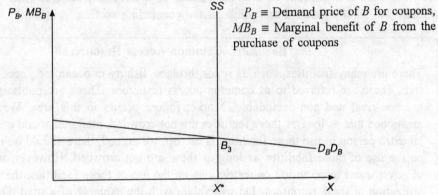

$P_B \equiv$ Demand price of B for coupons,
$MB_B \equiv$ Marginal benefit of B from the purchase of coupons

Figure 2.7: Mixed goods, externalities, optimum allocation of resources and creation of markets.

Clearly, if A gets from B the price $B_3 X^*$ for X^* number of coupons, the maximum price that he will be willing to pay for X^* amount of X, i.e., his demand price corresponding to X^* amount of X will rise by $B_3 X^*$. Hence, his demand schedule for X in Figure 2.6 will shift upward by $B_3 X^*$ corresponding to X^* amount of X and hence the market for X, as is clear from Figure 2.6, will be in equilibrium at X^*.

This scheme suffers from the same defect as the earlier one. Without the knowledge of the extent of external benefits generated by X, it is not possible to compute the optimum value of X or the optimum number of coupons. Hence this scheme is not feasible either.

2.8.5 Contract between Groups of Individuals

It has been pointed out by Coase(1960) that government intervention may not be necessary to achieve efficient output levels of mixed goods. The affected economic agents, beneficiaries or victims of the external effects and the perpetrators of the externalities may themselves enter into a contract with each other, when such contracts are feasible, to achieve the socially optimum outcome. This proposition is known as the Coase Theorem. Let us illustrate it with the help of Figure 2.6. Suppose that there is no government intervention and A faces the supply price P_x^e. If at this price they raise their purchase from X^e to X^*, they lose. Their loss in terms of Y is given by the area of the triangle $Q_1 B_1 B_2$, while B gains the area of the quadrilateral $Q_2 X^e X^* B_3$. The latter is larger than the former by the amount $Q Q_1 B_1$—(try to explain why). It should be noted that the gain to B is necessarily larger than the A's loss, since social welfare, i.e., the total welfare of the two groups of individuals together, is maximized at X^*. Hence, as X rises to X^*, gains to B will exceed A's losses. Therefore, B will find it profitable to enter into a contract with A asking him to purchase X^* and paying him in return an amount of Y larger than the area of the triangle $Q_1B_1B_2$, but less than the area of the quadrilateral $Q_2X^eX^*B_3$. Obviously, A will also find it profitable to accept the contract. Thus, according to Coase market itself will internalize the external effects and bring about an efficient allocation of resources.

However, the problem with the Coase theorem is that the contract that we specified above may not always be feasible. If B represents a large number of individuals, every individual may try to be a free rider, i.e., they might wait for others to make the contract and enjoy the gains for free. Even if B consists of a small number of individuals, the free rider problem may be present. We shall explain these points in the concluding section.

Box 2.2: Common Access Resources

There are many facilities, such as roads, bridges, fishing in ocean etc., access to which is free. These are referred to as common access resources. These are public goods as they are non-rival and non-excludable. Market failure occurs in this area. We have already mentioned that as long as these facilities are not crowded, marginal social cost of allowing an extra person to use these facilities is nil. So, we argued, there should be no restrictions on the use of these facilities as long as these are not crowded. However, in the absence of government intervention or restrictions on the use of these facilities, there occurs over utilization of these resources. Let us explain with the example of a road. Daily total cost of using the road to the motorists, denoted C, is usually an increasing function of the number of trips made on the road per day, which we denote by X. Let us illustrate with an example. If two hundred vehicles use the road daily, each passing the road only once, then the number of trips made on the road per day is two hundred. C consists of total cost of fuel, total time taken and total wear and tear of all the vehicles together in making the total number of daily trips. With the increase in X, the road gets more and more congested and as a result all the three components of cost rise and they are likely to rise at an increasing rate. Thus,

$$C = C(X); \ C' > 0 \text{ and } C'' > 0 \tag{B.2.1}$$

Average cost to a motorist of using the road or cost per daily trip to a motorist, denoted AC is, therefore, given by

$$AC = C(X)/X = AC(X); \ AC' > 0 \quad \text{(by assumption)} \tag{B.2.2}$$

Since the average cost rises with X, the marginal cost is higher than the average cost. The average cost schedule is shown in Figure B.2.1. It is labelled AC. The marginal cost schedule labelled MC lies above it. In the absence of any toll or user charge, the cost that an individual motorist has to incur to make a trip is this average cost. Let us explain. When there are a large number of individuals using the road, as is normally the case, an individual motorist has no control over X. Value of X is given to every individual *motorist*. If, for example, $X = 200$ per day, and an individual plans to make 10 trips daily, she has to incur on the average a cost of $[C(200)/200]$ per trip. In other words, to an individual

---

(Contd.)...

(Contd.)...

motorist AC corresponding to any given X may be regarded as the price she has to pay to make a trip. AC, therefore, gives the supply price of making trips to individual motorists. Equation (B.2.2) is, therefore, the inverse supply function of making trips to motorists. Demand for trips of the individual motorists should be a decreasing function of the price of making trips. Let the demand function of the ith motorist be $X_i = D_i(P)$, where X_i and P denote ith motorist's demand for making trips daily and the price of making daily trips respectively. Aggregating these individual demand functions over all individuals, we get the aggregate demand function. Inverting this aggregate demand function, we get the aggregate inverse demand function of daily trips of the motorists. It is given by

$$P = D(X); \ D' < 0 \qquad \text{(B.2.3)}$$

This inverse demand schedule, plotted in Figure B.2.1 and labelled DD, gives the demand price of every motorist for making daily trips corresponding to every X. The point to note here is that, since X is given to an individual motorist, $AC(X)$ is also given. Therefore, given X, the cost of making an additional daily trip to an individual motorist is $AC(X)$. On the other hand the demand price of daily trips of motorists corresponding to any given X is $D(X)$. Hence for every X for which $D(X) > AC(X)$, the price that any individual motorist has to pay to make an additional daily trip is less than the price he is willing to pay for making the trip. So every individual motorist will gain by raising the number of daily trips. Similarly, when $D(X) < AC(X)$, every individual motorist will gain by reducing the number of trips. Accordingly, the equilibrium value of X is given by

$$D(X) = AC(X) \qquad \text{(B.2.4)}$$

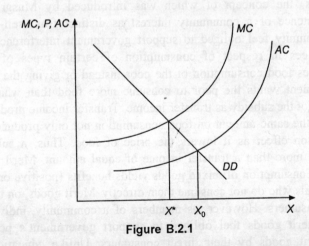

Figure B.2.1

The equilibrium value of X corresponds to the point of intersection of the DD and AC schedules. We denote this value of X by X_0. However, the socially efficient or optimum value of X is less than X_0. Let us explain. We know that the social marginal benefit of X

(Contd.)...

(Contd.)...

is the demand price $D(X)$, while the social marginal cost of X is $MC(X)$, which is given by $C'(X)$. $MC(X)$ is also plotted in Figure B.2.1. Socially optimum value of X is, therefore, given by

$$D(X) = MC(X) \qquad (B.2.5)$$

However, $MC(X)$ is, as we have pointed out above and as shown in Figure B.2.1, higher than $AC(X)$. Hence, the value of X that satisfies (B.2.5) is less than X_0. This socially optimum value of X is labelled X^* in Figure B.2.1. Thus the road in the absence of any restrictions will be over utilized. This phenomenon is referred to as *tragedy of the commons*.

The phenomenon may be explained as follows. Had there been just one individual making the trips, the additional cost of making one additional trip to him would be $MC(X)$ and the road would be optimally utilized. However, there are a large number of individuals using the road. Hence, to every single individual total number of trips made on the road per day, X, and therefore, $AC(X)$ are given. They are beyond his control. The number of trips made by a single individual over a day has no impact on X. Hence to a single individual $AC(X)$ is the extra cost of making an extra trip. This is the reason why there occurs over utilization or congestion of common access resources.

2.9 MERIT GOODS

Goods whose provision constitutes interference with individuals' wants are regarded as merit goods. Merit goods, the concept of which was introduced by Musgrave (1957, 1958), presuppose the existence of a community interest as distinct from self-interest. People as members of a community feel obliged to support government interference with individuals' tastes and preferences in respect of consumption of certain types of goods. When the government subsidises food consumption of the poor instead of giving the subsidy as transfer income, the government wants the poor to consume more food than what they would have consumed had they got the subsidy as transfer income. Transfer income produces just an income effect. A subsidy of the same amount on food consumption not only produces an income effect but also a substitution effect as it lowers the price of food. Thus, a subsidy raises poor's consumption of food more than a transfer income of equal amount. Merit goods are different from mixed goods. Consumption of mixed goods yields benefits (positive or negative) to all or some of the individuals who do not consume them directly. Merit goods, on the contrary, benefit only their direct consumers. However, as members of a community, individuals who do not directly consume merit goods feel obliged to support government's policy to encourage consumption of merit goods by their direct consumers. Unlike education or health, food consumption by the poor does not give any benefit to the non-poor. However, as members of the community the non-poor consider it their duty to support policies that raise the consumption of food of the poor beyond the level desired by the poor themselves. Government intervenes in case of mixed goods and social goods to ensure that individuals' tastes and preferences are satisfied in the best possible manner. In case of merit goods, however, government's intervention constitutes interference with individuals' tastes and preferences. All kinds of government aid given in kind are merit goods. If the aid had been given in cash, only a part of it would have been spent on the good in the form of which the aid in kind was given. By giving the aid in the form a specific good the government seeks to ensure that the aid recipients' consumption of the given good goes up by the whole value of the aid. Thus, the given good is a merit good. Obviously, aid in kind constitutes interference with individuals' choice. Like merit goods there may be demerit goods as well. Government interferes with individuals' choice to restrict the consumption of demerit goods below the level desired by the individuals.

2.10 CONCLUSION

Public goods and mixed goods constitute the foundation of an economy. Public administration and defence, roads and bridges, flood control facilities and drainage, sanitation, education and health constitute the crucial infrastructural services, which are essential for production. The greater the proportion of productive resources going into these sectors, as the modern growth theory tells us, the higher is the rate of growth of per capita income (see Barro (1990) and Lucas (1988) in this context). In case of both social and mixed goods government intervention is needed to promote efficient allocation of resources to these sectors. While government intervention through a tax-subsidy policy suffices in case of a mixed good, public goods have to be provided exclusively by the government. However, just as in the case of mixed goods, in the provision of public goods also the government faces insurmountable problems in identifying their optimum or efficient levels. *If the government, for example, produces less than the optimum quantity of a public good, the situation is unlikely to be revealed to the government. This happens on account of the problem of preference revelation or free rider problem.* Let us explain with an example. We shall take the help of Figure 2.5, where, as we have already explained, the optimum quantity of G is shown to be G^*. Suppose that the government produces a suboptimum quantity of G, $G_0 < G^*$. Corresponding to this quantity of G marginal social cost of production of G is less than the aggregate demand price of the individuals. Suppose, just for expository reasons, that the government charges to all the individuals together a price for G, which is equal to the supply price or the marginal cost of production of G. In other words, the government charges such prices to the individuals that the sum of these prices equals the supply price or the marginal cost of production of G. It is, therefore, possible for the government to charge to every individual a price less than his demand price. Suppose that the government does so. In this situation, if individuals get more G, they will be better off. In fact, if they get more G at any price less than their respective demand prices, they will be better off. They can reveal this to the government by offering to pay prices, which are less than their respective demand prices, but higher than the prices charged by the government. But chances are that they would not do that, i.e., they would not reveal their preferences to the government. The reason is the following. The individual will benefit, if he gets more of the social good at the higher price he offers. In case of a private good an individual can secure a larger amount of the good by offering a higher price. Since the good is excludable, the sellers will simply divert their sales to those who have offered higher prices from the others. As the good is also rival, those who did not offer a higher price will be deprived of the earlier supply of the good partly or fully. In case of a public good, however, this mechanism will not operate. Since the good is non-excludable and non-rival, the whole of its output is available to all and it is not possible for the seller to divert from others the existing supply of public goods to those buyers who have offered to pay higher prices. Thus, if an individual offers to pay a higher price, it will not reduce the supply of public goods to others. They will not be inconvenienced in any manner and, therefore, will not be under any kind of compulsion to make matching offers. If there are a large number of consumers of the public good, the price an individual pays will constitute only a negligible proportion of the marginal cost of producing the public good. Hence, if just one individual offers to pay a higher price, it will not enable the government to produce more of it. Let us illustrate the points made here with an example. If a Calcuttan wants Calcutta roads to be better and offers to pay more to the Calcutta Corporation, it will not inconvenience anyone else. Supply of roads or their quality to the other Calcuttans will not decline. Hence, they will not be under any compulsion to offer to pay more. Moreover, the additional amount that the individual offers to pay is such a negligible proportion of the cost of improving road conditions that the offer will not enable the Corporation to undertake any work to the desired effect. Every individual knows the points made above. Every individual knows that he is likely to fail to secure any additional public good by offering to pay more for the good. But he knows that he will get more public good if all or at least a large number of other individuals offer to pay more, it does not matter whether he also offers to pay more or not. Hence, instead of offering to pay more, he might choose to wait for others to make higher offers. In fact, he may decide not to make higher offers when others do so and thereby try to be a free rider. If all or most of the individuals think in this manner and try to be free riders, no one will offer to pay higher prices, i.e., no one will reveal his preferences to the government. Therefore, the government will not be able to know that it has produced a smaller than the optimum level of the public good.

Not all public goods, however, cater to a large number of individuals. There are many public goods, which serve only a small number of individuals. Take, for example, the case of a boundary wall of a housing complex. (Once the boundary wall of a housing complex is built, it caters to every inmate of the complex. It is not possible to prevent any inmate from enjoying the service provided by the boundary wall. Thus, the boundary wall is non-rival and non-excludable and, therefore, a social good). Though these social goods concern a small number of individuals only, still the free rider problem can arise. Everyone involved may think in the following manner. If he makes an offer for the good, others will choose not to make any offer at all and thereby try to be free riders. But, if he does not make any offer, then others will, as they prefer to pay and have the good instead of doing without it. Comparing these two situations, he may choose not to make any offer at all, i.e., he may choose to be a free rider, since in the case where he does not make any offer, but others do, he is better off. In this scenario, the public good will not be produced at all, even though its production benefits everyone.

The point may be explained with the help of Figure 2.6 where, suppose, $D_A D_A$ and $D_B D_B$ represent demand schedules of two individuals A and B respectively for a social good, X. DD is the aggregate demand schedule obtained by summing up vertically the two individual demand schedules. SS is the supply schedule of the public good, X. Accordingly, the value of X that corresponds to the point of intersection of the aggregate demand and supply schedules is the optimum level of output of X. However, this much of X is unlikely to get produced because of the way A and B might think about each other's behaviour. B may think that, if he chooses to purchase X, A may choose not to buy X at all and hence try to be a free rider, but if he does not bid for A, then A will. A may also think in a similar manner. In this case gains to B and A will be the following. When B alone bids for X, he will purchase X_0 amount of X. At this X his demand price is equal to the supply price. At every X less than X_0 his demand price is greater than the supply price and he gains by buying more X and vice versa. B will buy X_0 at the price P_X^e. His gain in this case is therefore given by the area of the triangle $A_4 P_X^e Q_3$ and A's gain will be $X_0 Q_4 A_3 O$. On the other hand, if A alone bids for X, he will purchase X^e amount of X at the price P_X^e. In this case A's and B's gains will be the area of the triangle $A_3 P_X^e Q_1$ and the area of the quadrilateral $X^e Q_2 A_4 O$ respectively.

Assuming $X_0 Q_4 A_3 O$ to be greater than $A_3 P_X^e Q_1$, both the individuals in this example gain more when they choose to be free riders. Accordingly, if both choose not to pay for X, no X will be produced. This is clearly an inefficient situation from the society's point of view. The example given here is quite plausible and because of the possibilities like this social goods may not be produced in optimum quantities even when they cater to only a few individuals.

The problem of preference revelation or the free rider problem noted above may stand in the way of realization of the Coase theorem also, it does not matter whether the number of beneficiaries or that of victims of the externalities is large or small. Argue this case yourself following the line suggested above.

Box 2.3: Case Study: India

India is a classic example where the problem of preference revelation or free rider problem has led to an acute shortage of social and mixed goods at the current juncture. Most of the public and mixed goods, except public administration, defence, health and education, are produced in the infrastructure sector in India. It covers the services of transportation (railways, road, ports and civil aviation), communications (telecommunications and postal services), electricity and other services such as water supply and sanitation, solid waste management and urban transport. According to the Economic Survey 2003–2004, "the lack of adequate infrastructure has been not only constraining the growth performance of the economy but has also induced significant costs in terms of welfare loss (for example, morbidity and water-borne diseases). It is widely recognized that a simple reliance on competitive markets is unlikely to produce efficient outcomes in infrastructure, a sector with pronounced public good characteristics of 'non-rivalness' and 'non-excludability'". Bulk of the infrastructure services are provided by the government. Because of their very nature, they cannot be priced at all, or, have to be supplied at low and, therefore, non-remunerative prices on efficiency grounds—recall that a positive price on the use of a non-rival good leads to inefficiency. Because of the free rider problem or the problem of preference revelation the individuals do not divulge how much they are really willing to pay for the social goods. The government, as we have already pointed out, has no means of knowing the exact extent of external benefits being derived by different economic agents from mixed goods. It is also enormously expensive and difficult to tax incomes originating in the unorganized or informal sectors, which contribute quite a significant part of GDP in countries like India. It is also politically costly to raise tax rates. For all these reasons the government cannot collect taxes on a scale that is required to provide social goods or subsidize the production of mixed goods in socially desired amounts.

(Contd.)...

(Contd.)...

The government resolved this problem of its failure to tax the individuals who derive the benefits of public and mixed goods far in excess of what they pay to the government in an innovative manner prior to the nineties through a system of SLR (statutory liquidity ratio). Under this system the banks had to invest a pre-specified proportion of their deposits in certain pre-specified unencumbered or newly issued government securities, which yielded very low rate of interest. Since investment in infrastructure yields very low return to the government owing to under-pricing and inadequate taxation, these low interest loans were the only means of sustaining adequate levels of investment in infrastructure and other areas producing mixed or social goods. This system was justified on following grounds. Had taxes and prices charged by the government reflected the marginal social benefits of public and mixed goods, returns on investments in these areas would have been equal to their true or socially desirable return, the return that is warranted by individuals' tastes and preferences. Because of under-pricing and inadequate taxation returns on these investments become much less than their socially desirable return. These social and mixed goods enter as inputs in the production of the other goods. Accordingly, the factors that reduce the rate of return on public investment below their socially desirable rate of return raise the rate of return on investment in non-infrastructure sectors above their socially desirable rate of return by a commensurate amount. If under these conditions both the private and the public sector compete for credit on an equal footing, too much credit will go into the private sector and too little to the public sector relative to what is socially optimum. Hence to bring about optimal allocation of resources, the government borrowed at a lower rate of return than the private investors. This justifies SLR.

SUMMARY

1. A good may be excludable or non-excludable. If the owner of a good can prevent others from using the good, it is excludable. Otherwise, it is non-excludable.

2. A good may be rival or non-rival. If consumption of a particular unit of a good does not prevent others from consuming the same unit of the good at the same time, the good is non-rival. Otherwise, it is rival.

3. Public goods are those goods which are both non-excludable and non-rival. A private good on the other hand is one which is both excludable and rival.

4. The necessary conditions for optimum allocation of resources when only pure private goods are produced are the following: (i) marginal rate of substitution of every good for every other good should be the same for every individual, (ii) marginal rate of technical substitution of every factor of production for every other factor should be the same in every sector of production, and finally (iii) marginal rate of transformation of every given good for every other good should be equal to the common marginal rate of substitution of the given good for every other good.

5. When public goods are produced along with the private goods, the necessary conditions that are satisfied when resource allocation between the private and the public good is efficient are the following: (i) marginal rate of technical substitution of every factor of production for every other factor of production should be the same in every sector of production, and (ii) the sum of the marginal rates of substitution of the public good for the private good of all the individuals should be equal to the marginal rate of transformation of the public good for the private good.

6. The difference between the necessary conditions in the two cases considered above is due to the differences in the characteristics of the private and the public good. Condition (i) of the first case has no correspond in the second case. This condition in the first case is satisfied, when distribution of the produced goods among individuals is optimum. When only one public good is produced along with one private good, which is the case considered here; every distribution of any given combination of the two goods produced, is optimum, since the whole output of the public good is available to everyone. Hence condition (i) of the first case has no correspond in the second case. Condition (ii) of the first case is the same as condition (i) of the second case. These are satisfied when allocation of the factors of production is optimum in the sphere of production so that output of each good is maximized, given the outputs of other goods. These conditions are the same because there is no difference between private and public goods on their sources side, i.e., they are similar as far as their production is concerned. They are different only on their uses side. This difference is responsible for the difference between condition (iii) of the first case and condition (ii) of the second case. Both conditions state that, when resource allocation is optimum, marginal social benefit of every good is equal to its marginal social cost. In both cases marginal social cost is given by the marginal rate of transformation. Marginal social benefit of a public good is, however, different from that of a private good. In case of the latter, it is given by the common marginal rate of substitution, since one extra unit of a private good, if given to any individual, cannot be made available to any other individual. In case of the former, however, it is given by the sum of the marginal rates of substitution of the public good for the private good. This is because, if one additional unit of public good is produced, it is available to every individual and hence marginal social benefit of public good should equal the sum of the marginal benefits from the public good of all individuals.

7. The government has to provide social goods. However, it is not possible for the government to provide social goods in optimum quantities because of the problem of preference revelation or the free rider problem.

8. There is a third category of goods called the mixed goods. Mixed goods share the characteristics of both private and public goods. They may be of various types. They may be excludable, but non-rival or rival but non-excludable. They may be imperfectly rival or excludable. This means that even though prices can be charged on their use, their benefits may not remain confined only to their direct consumers. They may automatically spill over to others. Mixed goods may be imperfectly excludable and rival in the sphere of production also, i.e., their costs instead of being confined to their producers alone may spill over to other producers and people. Mixed goods are the source of externalities in a market economy.

9. Market cannot produce mixed goods in socially optimum quantities either. Since exclusion principle and non-rivalness apply only imperfectly to these goods, costs and benefits of their production and/or consumption do not remain confined to the direct producers and consumers of these goods. They spill over to others generating externalities. To bring about efficiency in the allocation of resources between the mixed goods and other goods, the government has to intervene through a tax-subsidy programme or through creation of markets for externalities. However, the information the government needs to design the appropriate schemes is unlikely to be available to the government. Individuals generating these externalities and those affected by them may themselves enter into contracts with each other and internalize the externalities. However, such a possibility may not materialize because of the free rider problem.

10. Goods in case of which government intervention constitutes interference with individuals' choice are called merit goods. Even though consumption of merit good does not yield any utility or disutility to individuals who do not consume them directly, people as members of a community feel obliged to support government's policy to encourage (discourage) the consumption of merit (demerit) goods by their direct consumers. All government aids given in kind are merit goods.

KEY CONCEPTS

✓ Excludable and non-excludable goods
✓ Pure private good or private good
✓ Mixed goods
✓ Creation of markets for externalities
✓ Rival and non-rival goods
✓ Externalities in consumption
✓ Coase theorem

✓ Pure social/public good or public/social good
✓ Externalities in produnction
✓ Merit goods and demerit goods
✓ Free rider problem
✓ Pigovian tax/subsidy
✓ Interference with individuals' choice

REVIEW QUESTIONS

1. What is meant by (i) a non-excludable and (ii) a non-rival good. Illustrate with examples.
2. Define social or public, private and mixed goods. Illustrate with examples.
3. Derive the necessary conditions for optimum allocation of resources when only private goods are produced.
4. Derive the necessary conditions for optimum allocation of resources when private goods are produced along with the public goods.
5. Compare the necessary conditions for optimum allocation of resources of the case where only private goods are produced with those that obtain when public goods are produced along with the private goods.
6. Why does the government need to provide social goods? Why is it unlikely that the government will be able to provide public goods in socially efficient quantities? Explain your answer.

7. Why is government intervention necessary to promote efficient allocation of resources in the case of mixed goods? What kind of government policy is needed in this regard?

8. Is there any way that market itself can internalize the externalities?

9. What are merit goods? How do they differ from mixed goods?

====== **PROBLEMS AND APPLICATIONS** ======

1. (a) Suppose that the government provides protection against internal and external threats and disturbances. In other words the government provides public administration and defence. Let us denote the amount of service provided by public administration and defence by G. All private goods are clubbed together into a single private good. Let us denote the quantity of this private good by X. The production possibility frontier of this economy is given by $G + 0.5 X = 100$. Suppose that there are only two individuals, A and B, in this economy. Utility functions of A and B are given by $U^A = X^A G$ and $U^B = X^B G$ respectively. What are the optimum levels of G and X when B's utility level is kept fixed at 10 through an appropriate distribution programme?

   (b) Illustrate the solution graphically. Indicate the values of the vertical intercept and slope of PPF. What are the values of $mrtr_{GX}$, $mrs_{G,X}^A$ and $mrs_{G,X}^B$ at the optimum solution? Is there any relationship among these values? If your answer is yes, then explain it.

   (c) Derive marginal social cost and marginal social benefit of G as functions of G. Can you derive the optimum value of G from these functions? Explain and illustrate the solution graphically.

   (*Hint: PPF*: $X = \dfrac{1}{0.5} 100 - \dfrac{1}{0.5} G$, CPL^A: $X^A = \dfrac{1}{0.5} 100 - \dfrac{1}{0.5} G - \dfrac{10}{G}$; $G^* = 50$,

   $X^* = 100$. Marginal benefit of G of A when he is on CPL^A: $\dfrac{dX^A}{dG} = \dfrac{200}{G} - \dfrac{10}{G^2} - 2 -$

   we derive it by substituting the CPL^A into the value of $mrs_{G,X}^A$. Marginal benefit of G

   of B when he is on the given IC: $\dfrac{dX^B}{dG} = \dfrac{10}{G^2}$ —we get this by substituting the value

   of X^B as yielded by the equation of the given IC into the value of $mrs_{G,X}^B$.)

2. Consider an economy where only one private good, X, and one public good, G, are produced with just one input, labour (L). Labour requirements per unit of G and X are fixed and they are denoted by 1 and α respectively. Total endowment of labour in the economy is given at $\bar{L}$. There are N number individuals having the identical utility function, $X^i G$; $i = 1, 2, ..., N$. Suppose that the government has a distribution programme, which keeps every individual except one at a given level of utility, $\bar{U}$. How much G should the government produce, if it wants to maximize social welfare? Explain your answer. How does the optimum value of G change, if (i) labour endowment goes up, (ii) there

occurs a technological improvement that reduces α and (iii) value of $\bar{U}$ rises? Explain you answers.

(*Hint: PPF:* $\bar{L} = G + \alpha X \Rightarrow X = \dfrac{1}{\alpha} (\bar{L} - G)$. All individuals' utility, except the nth individual's, kept fixed at $\bar{U}$. So for each of the $N - 1$ individuals, value of X is given by $(\bar{U}/G)$. The amount of X to be given to all of them is, therefore, $(N - 1)(\bar{U}/G)$.

CPI^A: $X^N = \dfrac{1}{\alpha}(\bar{L} - G) - (N - 1)\dfrac{\bar{U}}{G}$. Work out the rest.)

3. Suppose that in an economy only two goods, one private good and one public good, are produced and the production possibility frontier is linear, i.e., the marginal rate of transformation of the public good for the private good or the marginal cost of production of the public good in terms of the private good is a constant. Suppose it has a redistributive tax-transfer policy, which keeps all individuals except one on given indifference curves. In this situation, if the government produces the efficient amount of the public good and collects from each individual a tax, which equals per unit of the public good supplied the $mrs_{G,X}$ of the individual, will the tax cover the total cost of producing social goods? Is the solution socially desirable? Explain your answer using a simple two-good-two-individual framework.

4. Most of the social goods are local and they are provided by local municipal bodies in urban areas and panchayats in rural areas. Kolkata Corporation is the municipal body in charge of providing the people of Kolkata with all the civic amenities. Kolkata Corporation divides its jurisdiction into different wards and people of each ward elect a representative to the Corporation. This representative is called the councillor. Suppose that the councillor of a ward identifies drainage as the area of improvement in her ward. She has to determine the optimum amount of expenditure on drainage. Even though she does not know the utility functions of the individuals, she finds a way of getting some idea about the marginal social benefit of drainage. Drainage makes it convenient for people to commute; it also reduces incidence of diseases. Drainage also reduces depreciation of houses. All this gets reflected in an increase in the rental values of houses, land etc., in the area served by the drainage facility. She, therefore, figures out that an improvement in drainage mainly gets reflected in an increase in the rental values of houses and land net of depreciation (net rental value). She also finds that there are many similar wards in Kolkata, which differ mainly in the levels of drainage. Observing the rental values net of depreciaton costs in all these localities, she derives the relationship between aggregate net rental value of all the land and houses of the given ward and the level of drainage. Suppose that this relationship is given by $R = 500D^{.5}$, where R and D denote the aggregate net rental value and the level of drainage respectively. What is the social marginal benefit of drainage? The cost of drainage, which is not difficult to estimate, on the other hand is given by $C = D$. Derive the optimum level of D.

(*Hint:* The increase in the aggregate net rental value following a unit increase in D is the social marginal benefit of D. From this chapter we have learnt that the efficient level of social good is the one at which marginal social benefit equals marginal social cost. $D^* = 625$, where D^* is the socially efficient level of D.)

5. Suppose that you are the pradhan of a gram panchyat, an elected body of the representatives of a village. He is in charge of providing the villagers with social goods. Suppose that the villagers are too poor to afford any drinking water facility. How will you decide whether setting up of tube wells is worthwhile or not? Give your answer following the line suggested in the previous problem. (Note that tube wells are not pure social goods. They are excludable as prices can be charged on their use. They are also, strictly speaking, rival as at any one point of time only one individual can use it. However, in poor communities drinking water has to be publicly provided.)

6. Suppose that demand functions of two groups of individuals, A and B, for a mixed good X are given by $X^{da} = a - bP$ and $X^{db} = s - hP$; $a > 0$, $b > 0$, $s > 0$ and $h > 0$. Also assume that Group A individuals purchase X directly, but Group B individuals do not. The latter derive utility from others' consumption of X. Suppose that the supply price of X is constant at $\overline{C}$. Derive the market equilibrium value of X and also the socially optimum value of X. Are they different? Explain your answer. What policies can the government adopt to make the two, if they are different, equal? Explain.

(*Hint:* $X^* = \dfrac{\left(\dfrac{1}{b}a + \dfrac{1}{h}s\right) - \overline{C}}{\left(\dfrac{1}{b} + \dfrac{1}{h}\right)}$, where $X^* \equiv$ the socially efficient level of X.)

7. Consider Problem 6. Suppose that group A consists of N individuals. Demand function of *each* of these individuals is given by $X^{da} = a - bP$. Again group B consists of M individuals and demand function of each of them is given by $X^{db} = s - hP$. Derive the socially optimum quantity of X. What policy should the government pursue to achieve this level of output?

(*Hint:* In case of group A, individual demand functions have to be summed up horizontally. The inverse of this aggregate demand function is the inverse demand function of group A. In case of group B the individual demand functions have to be summed up vertically. For this, inverse of the individual demand function has to be derived and then they have to be added up to derive aggregate demand price as a function of X. This is the aggregate inverse demand function of group B. Then the two inverse demand functions are added up. Equating the aggregate inverse demand function of the two groups to the marginal cost of production of X, we shall get the socially optimum X. Do the rest yourself.)

8. In case of a commodity such as cigarettes, which generate external ill effects or costs, what policies should the government adopt to ensure its socially optimum production? Work out this exercise mathematically using all linear functions and illustrate graphically.

9. Suppose two individuals A and B representing two different groups have an identical demand function for a commodity, X, given by $X = A - BP$, where $P \equiv$ price of X. However, A enters directly into the market for X, but B does not. The latter benefits from A's consumption of X. How do you interpret the demand functions of the two individuals? How will you sum up the two demand functions to derive the socially optimum level of

production of X? Explain. Suppose the cost of production of X is given by the cost function, $C = aX$, where C denotes the total cost of production. How much X will the market produce? What is the socially optimum level of X? Why does the market fail to produce the socially optimum outcome? What are the different ways in which the socially optimum outcome can be achieved? Quantify and explain your answers.

10. Suppose that some firms producing chlorine in competitive markets discharge their effluents into a river damaging output of fish of the fishermen. Per unit of chlorine output denoted by Q, value of fish output declines by d. Demand for chlorine is given by the demand function, $X = H - \alpha P$; $H > 0$ and $\alpha > 0$, where X and P denote demand for and price of chlorine respectively. The supply schedule of chlorine is given by the function, $P = \bar{P}$. Derive the socially optimum level of chlorine output. Explain. What are the different ways in which this outcome can be achieved? Quantify your answer and explain.

    (*Hint:* Marginal social benefit, which equals marginal private benefit of chlorine, is $P = (1/\alpha)(H - X)$. Marginal social cost of chlorine is given by $\bar{P} + d$. Optimum X is therefore, ………. Work out the rest yourself.)

11. Suppose that the government gives each of the dwellers of a slum 10 units of food free of cost every month. Is food a merit good? Answer the question under the assumption that every slum dweller's utility function is given by $U = X^{.4}Y^{.6}$, where food is denoted by X, while all other goods are clubbed together and denoted by Y. Monthly income of each slum dweller is Rs. 200. Prices of both the goods are Rs. 10. Explain your answer and illustrate with graph.

    (*Hint:* In the absence of any kind of assistance from the government, every slum dweller purchases 4 units of X and 16 units of Y. Had the government given the cost of 10 units of food, Rs. 100, as transfer income, every slum dweller would have purchased 6 units of food and 24 units of Y. However, since 10 units of X are given in kind, their optimum consumption is 10 units of X and 20 units of Y. So food is a merit good.)

REFERENCES

For the theory of public goods:

Samuelson, P.A. (1954): The pure theory of public expenditure, *Review of Economics and Statistics,* November, 386–389.

——(1955): Diagrammatic exposition of a theory of public expenditure, *Review of Economics and Statistics,* November, 350–356.

——(1958): Aspects of public expenditure theories, *Review of Economics and Statistics,* **40**, 332–338.

——(1969): Pure theory of public expenditure and taxation, *in*: Margolis J., and Guitton, H., (Eds.), *Public Economics*, St. Martin's, New York.

For survey of the theory of public goods:

Milleron, J.C. (1972): Theory of value with public goods: A survey article, *Journal of Economic Theory,* 5, 419–477.

For mechanisms of preference revelation:

Green, J. and Laffont, J.J. (1977): Characterization of satisfactory mechanisms for the revelation of preferences for public goods, *Econometrica*, **45**, 427–438.

——(1977): On the revelation of preferences for public goods, *Journal of Public Economics*, **8**, 79–93.

For Coase theorem:

Coase, R.H. (1960): The problem of social cost, *Journal of Law and Economics*, October.

For seminal contributions to the endogenous growth theory:

Barro, R.J. (1990): Government spending in a simple model of endogenous growth, *Journal of Political Economy*, **98(5)**, October, Part II, S103–S125.

Lucas, R.E., Jr. (1988): On the mechanics of development planning, *Journal of Monetary Economics*, **22(1)**, July, 3–42.

For a discussion of the distribution of public goods in India:

Banerjee, V.A. (2004): Who is getting the public goods in India? Some evidence and some speculation, *in*: Basu, K.(Ed.), *India's Emerging Economy*, Oxford University Press, New Delhi.

For consumer surplus:

Willig, R. (1976): Consumer's surplus without apology, *American Economic Review*, September, 589–597.

For merit goods:

Musgrave, R.A. (1957): A multiple theory of budget determination, *Finance Archiv*, *New Series*, **17(3)**, 333–343.

——(1958): *The Theory of Public Finance*, McGraw-Hill, New York.

APPENDIX

A.2.1 DERIVATION AND INTERPRETATION OF THE SLOPE OF CPL^A

Equation of PPF is given by

$$X = X(G); \ X' < 0, \ -X' \equiv mrtr_{GX} \text{ and } -X'' > 0 \tag{A.2.1}$$

Equation of the given indifference curve of B

$$X^B = X^B(G); \ X^{B\prime} < 0, \ -X^{B\prime} \equiv mrs^B_{G,X} \text{ and } -X^{B\prime\prime} < 0 \tag{A.2.2}$$

Equation of CPL^A

$$X^A = X(G) - X^B(G)$$

Absolute value of the slope of CPL^A

$$-\frac{dX^A}{dG} = [-X'(G)] - [-X^{B\prime}(G)] = mrtr_{GX} - mrs^B_{G,X} \tag{A.2.3}$$

$$\frac{d}{dG}\left(-\frac{dX^A}{dg}\right) = \frac{d}{dG}[-X'(G)] - \frac{d}{dG}[-X^{B\prime}(G)] \ [-X''(G)] - [-X^{B\prime\prime}(G)] > 0$$

Therefore, CPL^A is concave.

A.2.2 INTERPRETATION OF THE DEMAND PRICE, AREA UNDER THE DEMAND CURVE AND CONSUMER SURPLUS

Here we shall give an interpretation of the demand price and the area under the demand curve. We shall also discuss a measure of the consumer surplus.

Interpretation of the Demand Price

The demand curve shows, a la Marshall, corresponding to any given quantity of X, the maximum price at which it is demanded. This price is called the demand price of X. In what follows we shall develop an interpretation of the demand price.

Note that the price of a commodity is always expressed in terms of another commodity. Price of a commodity states how much of another commodity has to be paid to purchase one unit of the given commodity. This other commodity may be money or any other commodity. Suppose that the price of X is expressed in terms of the commodity Y, which may be money as well. We shall now show that the demand price is nothing but the marginal rate of substitution of X for the commodity in terms of which the demand price is expressed. We shall denote this commodity by Y here. Thus, we shall show that the demand price gives the amount of Y (the commodity in terms of which the demand price is expressed) that each of the buyers of X can sacrifice remaining on the same indifference curve if she gets one additional unit of X. In other words, the demand price of X gives the maximum amount of Y that each of the consumers is willing to sacrifice to have one additional unit of X. To explain this point we focus on

Figure A.2.1, where $\bar{D}\bar{D}$ schedule represents an individual's demand schedule for X. His demand price at $\bar{X}_0$, as shown in the Figure, is P_0^X. This means that the optimum commodity bundle on the individual's budget line that obtains at P_0^X, given his income, contains $\bar{X}_0$. Assuming that Y is the only commodity besides X for simplicity, equation of this budget line is given by $m = P_0^X X + Y$, where $m \equiv$ the given income of the consumer in terms of Y. We get m by dividing the given money income of the consumer by the given money price of Y. This budget line is shown in Figure A.2.2. It is labelled BB. At P_0^X the individual demands $\bar{X}_0$ amount of X. Therefore, the optimum point on the budget line corresponds to $\bar{X}_0$ amount of X. $mrs_{X,Y}$ corresponding to this optimum point equals P_0^X. Therefore, if $\bar{X}_0$ is demanded at P_0^X or

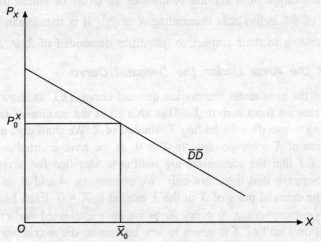

Figure A.2.1: Interpretation of demand price I.

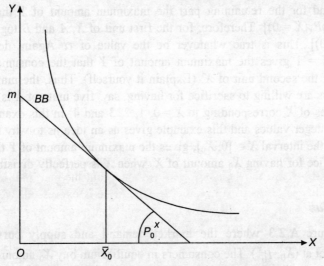

Figure A.2.2: Interpretation of demand price II.

if P_0^X is the demand price corresponding to $\bar{X}_0$, then P_0^X is equal to the $mrs_{X,Y}$ of the consumption bundle containing $\bar{X}_0$ on the consumer's budget line. Thus, demand price of X gives us the marginal rate of substitution of X for the commodity in terms of which the demand price is expressed.

We get the market demand curve by horizontally summing up the individual demand curves. Thus, if there are two individuals A and B and if they demand X_0^A and X_0^B respectively at P_0^X, then the market demand curve will show that the demand for X in the market at P_0^X is the sum of X_0^A and X_0^B. Thus, if corresponding to any given quantity of X, say X_0, the demand price of X as shown by the market demand curve is P_0^X, then this is the demand price of X (or marginal rate of substitution of X for the commodity in terms of which the demand price is expressed) of each of the individuals demanding X at P_0^X. It is the demand price of all these individuals corresponding to their respective quantities demanded of X at P_0^X.

Interpretation of the Area Under the Demand Curve

Let us now focus on the area under the market demand curve, DD, as shown in Figure A.2.3, for the values of X ranging from zero to X_0. This area gives the maximum amount of Y that the consumers are willing to sacrifice for having X_0 amount of X. We shall give a rough explanation of this. Demand price of X corresponding to $X = 0$, as we have pointed out above, gives the maximum amount of Y that the consumers are willing to sacrifice for having the first unit of X. Let us explain. Suppose that there are only two consumers, A and B, in the X market and let $[P_X(X = 0)]$ be the demand price of X in the X market at $X = 0$. Each has the same demand price of X or $mrs_{X,Y}$ corresponding to every X, as we have explained earlier. This implies that if at $X = 0$, an additional unit of X is given to any consumer, the maximum quantity of Y that can be taken away from him without making him worse off is $P_X(X = 0)$. Hence, if $0 < \alpha < 1$ amount of the first unit of X is given to A, the maximum amount of $Y A$ will want to sacrifice is $[\alpha P_X(X = 0)]$ and for the remaining part the maximum amount of Y that B will want to sacrifice is $[(1 - \alpha)P_X(X = 0)]$. Therefore, for the first unit of X, A and B together will want to sacrifice $[P_X(X = 0)]$. This is true whatever be the value of α. Again, demand price of X corresponding to $X = 1$ gives the maximum amount of Y that the consumers are willing to sacrifice for having the second unit of X. (Explain it yourself). Thus, the maximum amount of Y that the consumers are willing to sacrifice for having, say, five units of X is given by the sum of the demand prices of X corresponding to $X = 0, 1, 2, 3$ and 4. In this example, X is discrete and assumes only integer values and this example gives us an idea as to why the area under the demand curve over the interval $X \in [0, X_0]$, gives the maximum amount of Y that the consumers are willing to sacrifice for having X_0 amount of X, when X is perfectly divisible and, therefore, continuous.

Consumer Surplus

Consider now Figure A.2.3 where the market demand and supply curves, DD and SS respectively, intersect at (X_0, P_0^X). The consumers in equilibrium buy X_0 amount of X at the price P_0^X and thereby pay an amount of Y, which is given by the area of the rectangle $O\,P_0^X BX_0$.

However, for having X_0 amount of X the maximum amount of Y that the consumers are willing to sacrifice, as we have pointed out above, is given by the area of the quadrilateral $OABX_0$. Thus the consumers gain. On every intramarginal unit of X the gain is given by the excess of the demand price over the market price of X and, therefore, the total gain is given by the area of the triangle AP_X^0B. This is called consumer surplus. It is often used as a measure of consumer welfare. It should be noted here that the consumer surplus is actually measured by the area between the compensated demand curve and the price line, and not by the area between the ordinary demand curve and the price line. However, if we use the ordinary demand curve to measure the consumer surplus, as we have done here, we get, as shown by Willig (1976), a close approximation of the actual value of the consumer surplus. In what follows, therefore, we shall use the ordinary market demand curve to estimate consumer surplus.

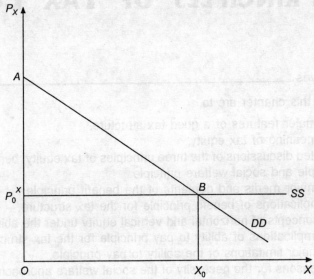

Figure A.2.3: Measurement of consumer surplus.

3 | PRINCIPLES OF TAX EQUITY

Chapter Objectives

The objectives of this chapter are to

 (i) identify the major features of a good tax structure.
 (ii) explain the meaning of tax equity.
(iii) provide detailed discussions of the three principles of tax equity: benefit principle, ability to pay principle and social welfare principle.
 (iv) identify the major merits and demerits of the benefit principle.
 (v) derive the implications of benefit principle for the tax structure.
 (vi) discuss the concepts of horizontal and vertical equity under the ability to pay principle.
(vii) discuss the implications of ability to pay principle for the tax structure.
(viii) identify the major limitations of the ability to pay principle.
 (ix) explain the reasons for the necessity of the social welfare approach, and to discuss its implications regarding the distribution of tax burden.

3.1 INTRODUCTION: PROPERTIES OF A GOOD TAX STRUCTURE

Taxation is a major activity of the ruler or the government and involves exercise of coercive power. Accordingly, political and economic theorists in all ages have spared no efforts in eliminating arbitrariness in taxation. They have developed canons, i.e., identified features, of a good tax structure. The literature specifies the following major conditions that a good tax structure should satisfy. First, *it should be just or equitable*. We shall dwell at length on tax equity in this chapter. Second, *it should be efficient*. The issue of tax efficiency is the subject of discussion of Chapter 4. Third, *it should yield adequate revenue*. Fourth, if a tax is imposed on a group of individuals, they may succeed in transferring the tax burden partly or fully on others. A *good tax structure should make full allowance for that to promote equity*. This issue of the shifting of tax burden has been discussed at length in Chapter 5. Fifth, a *tax structure should be transparent and easily comprehensible* to the taxpayers. Sixth, the *administrative cost of the government, i.e.,* the cost the government has to incur to collect taxes, *and the compliance cost, i.e.,* the expenses the taxpayers have to bear to fulfil all the requirements laid down by the tax laws, *should be low*. Finally, *the tax structure should facilitate use of taxes to meet the fiscal policy objectives of stabilization and growth*.

In what follows we shall focus on the issue of tax equity. There are three major approaches to this aspect of taxation, namely, the benefit principle, the ability to pay principle and the social welfare approach. We shall discuss these principles below.

3.2 BENEFIT PRINCIPLE OF TAXATION AND PUBLIC EXPENDITURE

Public goods, as we have already pointed out in Chapter 2, have to be provided by the government since they are non-excludable as well as non-rival. We have derived there the conditions that are satisfied, when public goods are produced along with private goods in optimum quantities. The questions that immediately arise are, whether it is possible for the government to produce public goods in optimum quantities and how the government should distribute the cost of producing public goods among individuals. The theory that addresses these issues is called the benefit principle of taxation. It applies the market mechanism to resolve the problem. *It states that the government should produce public goods in quantities corresponding to which marginal social benefit of public goods equals marginal social cost of producing public goods. It also recommends that the government should supply the optimum quantities of the public goods to individuals at their respective demand prices, which reflect their marginal benefits from public goods.* The first formal statement of the benefit principle was made by Eric Lindahl and Lief Johansen. We present their model below.

3.2.1 The Model

Assumptions

There are two individuals, A and B. There are only two goods produced in the economy, X and G of which X is a private good and G a public good. Both meet only final demand for goods and services. Production possibility frontier involving X and G is given by

$$\bar{R} = X + 1G \tag{3.1}$$

where 1 gives the marginal and average rate of transformation of G for X or marginal and average cost of producing G in terms of X. Here $\bar{R}$ is a constant. It gives the maximum amount of X that can be produced with the available resources. The government charges A and B prices P_A and P_B respectively for providing the public good, G. These prices are given in terms of X. The government charges the individuals for G just to cover the cost of producing G. Therefore, the aggregate price (sum of prices taken from all the individuals together) the government charges the individuals for G in terms of the private good, X, is 1. Thus $[X + 1G]$ and, therefore, $\bar{R}$ is the GDP of the economy in terms of X. Since the government does not make any profit or loss from the sale of G, the whole value of aggregate production of X and G or the GDP of the economy accrues as gross factor income (factor income inclusive of depreciation) to individuals. Thus, aggregate gross factor income of the individuals in terms of the private good X is $\bar{R}$—see equation (3.1). The model assumes that $\bar{R}$ is optimally distributed between A and B. A's income is $\bar{R}_A$ and B's income is $\bar{R}_B$ so that

$$\bar{R} = \bar{R}_A + \bar{R}_B \tag{3.2}$$

Individuals want to spend their income on X and G in such a manner that their utilities are maximized. Therefore, individuals' demand for G can be derived by carrying out the following optimization exercises:

$$\max_{X^A, G} U^A(X^A, G)$$

subject to

$$\bar{R}_A = X^A + P_A G \tag{3.2a}$$

and

$$\max_{X^B, G} U^B(X^B, G)$$

subject to

$$\bar{R}_B = X^B + P_B G \tag{3.2b}$$

where $U^A(.)$ and $U^B(.)$ are the utility functions of A and B respectively, and X^A and X^B denote amounts of X consumed respectively by A and B. Since G is a pure public good, the whole output of G, denoted by G, is available to both A and B. Hence, the whole output of G is an argument in the utility functions of both the individuals. From (3.2a) we get A's demand for G, denoted G_A, as a function of P_A, given $\bar{R}_A$ and A's utility function. Thus, $G_A = G_A(P_A); G_A{}' < 0$ (assuming G to be a normal good). Inverting the above function, we get A's demand price for G, which is given by

$$P_A = G_A^{-1}(G) \equiv P_A(G); P_A{}' < 0 \tag{3.3}$$

Similarly, from (3.2b) we get B's demand price for G as a function of G. This is given by

$$P_B = P_B(G); P_B{}' < 0 \tag{3.4}$$

Let us illustrate the derivation of the demand price for G of the individuals graphically, considering the case of any one of the two individuals. Focus on A. In the left hand panel of Figure 3.1 the straight line BB represents the budget line of A, as given in (3.2a). The absolute value of its slope is the price of G charged to A, P_A. BB has been drawn for a specific value of P_A, P_A^0. Hence the absolute value of its slope is P_A^0. Its vertical intercept is $\bar{R}_A$. The absolute value of the budget line's slope, P_A^0, measures the amount of X that A has to give up, given his income, if he buys one extra unit of G from the government. $\bar{R}_A$ gives the amount of X that he can purchase with his income if he does not consume any G. From BB the individual will choose that point, which lies on the highest indifference curve. Obviously, the point on the budget line at which one of the indifference curves of A is tangent fulfils the above criterion. I_0 in Figure 3.1 is the indifference curve of A that is tangent to BB at the point (G_0, X_0^A). (G_0, X_0^A) is thus the optimum point on BB. At the optimum point on the budget line, therefore, the absolute value of the slope of the indifference curve, mrs_{GX}, is equal to that of the budget line, P_A^0. As shown in the left hand panel of Figure 3.1, the amount of G chosen or demanded at $P_A = P_A^0$ is G_0. (G_0, P_A^0) is, therefore, a point on A's demand schedule of G, labelled D_A in the right hand panel of Figure 3.1. Alternatively, the demand price of G corresponding to G_0 is P_A^0. P_A^0 in turn, as we have just pointed out, is equal to the mrs_{GX} of the point corresponding to G_0 on the budget line. We denote this mrs_{GX} by $mrs_{GX}(G_0)$. Now $mrs_{G,X}(G_0)$ gives the amount of X that the individual can sacrifice, if he gets 1 unit more G over and above G_0, remaining on the same indifference curve. Thus, at (G, X^A) equal to (G_0, X_0^A), $mrs_{G,X}(G_0)$ amount of X is equivalent to one additional unit of G to the individual, given his tastes and preference. Hence $mrs_{G,X}(G_0)$ may be interpreted as the marginal benefit of G in terms of X at (G_0, X_0^A). *Accordingly, the demand price of G corresponding to any G gives the marginal benefit of G in terms of X to the individual at the given G.*

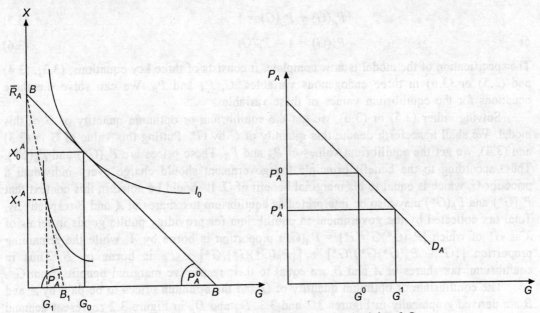

Figure 3.1: Derivation of A's demand schedule of G.

Now, if, given every thing else, P_A is raised to P_A^1, the budget line will be given by BB_1 as shown in the left hand panel of Figure 3.1 and A will choose (G_1, X_1^A) from the budget line. (P_A^1, G_1) is, therefore, another point on A's demand curve of G, D_A, in the right hand panel of Figure 3.1, and P_A^1 is the demand price of G corresponding to G_1. Carrying out this exercise repeatedly, we can derive the whole of A's demand schedule for G.

The marginal and average social cost of producing G in terms of X is unity—see equation (3.1). The government charges the individuals for G just to cover the cost of producing G. Hence in this model government's aggregate supply price of G in terms of X is unity, i.e., the sum of prices at which the government seeks to supply G to the individuals is unity. Thus, government's aggregate supply price of G to the individuals in this model equals the marginal social cost of producing G. The government here seeks to produce G in such a way that individuals' demand for G is satisfied in the best possible manner. This means that the government seeks to produce that level of G corresponding to which aggregate demand price for G is equal to its aggregate supply price. Let us explain the significance of the aggregate demand price for G. Demand price of G in terms of X of an individual gives the marginal benefit of G in terms of X to the individual. Now, if one additional unit of G is produced, it becomes available to all the individuals at the same time. Hence the marginal social benefit of G in terms of X, which is the total additional benefit derived by all the individuals together in terms of X from the production of one additional unit of G, is given by the sum of the demand prices for G in terms of X of all the individuals. Thus, *the government in this model seeks to produce that amount of G corresponding to which marginal social cost of producing G in terms X is equal to its marginal social benefit in terms of X.* In equilibrium, therefore, in this model

$$P_A(G) + P_B(G) = 1 \tag{3.5}$$

or $$P_A(G) = 1 - P_B(G) \tag{3.6}$$

The specification of the model is now complete. It consists of three key equations, (3.3), (3.4) and (3.5) or (3.6) in three endogenous variables, G, P_A and P_B. We can solve the three equations for the equilibrium values of these variables.

Solving either (3.5) or (3.6), we get the equilibrium or optimum quantity of G of this model. We shall henceforth denote this quantity of G by G^*. Putting this value of G in (3.3) and (3.4), we get the equilibrium values of P_A and P_B. These prices are $P_A(G^*)$ and $P_B(G^*)$. Thus, according to the benefit principle the government should charge every individual a price for G, which is equal to his marginal benefit of G. It should be noted in this context that $P_A(G^*)$ and $P_B(G^*)$ may also be interpreted as equilibrium tax shares of A and B respectively. Total tax collected by the government in equilibrium for providing public goods in terms of X is G^* of which $[P_A(G^*)G^*/G^*] = P_A(G^*)$ proportion is borne by A, while the remaining proportion $[\{G^* - P_A(G^*)G^*\}/G^*] = [\{P_B(G^*)G^*\}/G^*] = P_B$ is borne by B. Thus in equilibrium, tax shares of A and B are equal to their respective marginal benefits from G.

The equilibrium or optimum quantity of G and the optimum prices to be paid by A and B are derived graphically in Figures 3.2 and 3.3. D_A and D_B in Figure 3.2 represent demand schedules for G of A and B respectively and ΣD gives the aggregate demand schedule derived through vertical summation of D_A and D_B. The horizontal SS schedule is the supply schedule of G. It gives the supply price of G in terms of X, which is unity, corresponding to every G. The ΣD schedule gives the aggregate demand price corresponding to every G. The equilibrium values of G, P_A and P_B, labelled G^*, P_A^* and P_B^* respectively, correspond to the point of intersection of ΣDD and SS schedules as shown in Figure 3.2.

The equilibrium values of G, P_A and P_B may also be derived graphically using Figure 3.3, where D_A, representing (3.3), gives the demand schedule for G of A and it shows A's demand price for G in terms of X corresponding to every G. The schedule $[1 - P_B(G)]$ gives the government's supply price of G to A when it charges B his demand price for G. The equilibrium values of G, P_A and P_B, as follows from (3.6), correspond to the point of intersection of these two schedules. We denote this equilibrium value of G by G^*. The equilibrium prices of G or tax shares for A and B are labelled $P_A(G^*)$ and $P_B(G^*)$ respectively. For an alternative presentation of the Lindahl–Johansen model, see Appendix to this Chapter.

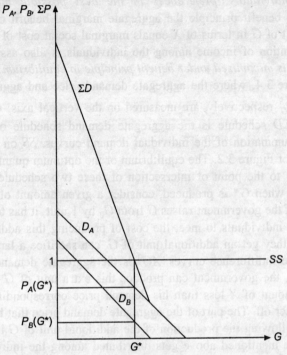

Figure 3.2: Derivation of the optimum prices and the optimum quantity of G.

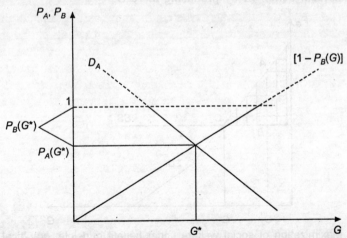

Figure 3.3: Derivation of the optimum prices and the optimum quantity of G.

3.2.2 Benefit Principle and Social Welfare

In equilibrium, in this model the aggregate demand price of G is equal to its aggregate supply price. Hence, individuals' demand for G is fully met, i.e., government produces as much G as individuals want or demand. Each individual also pays his demand price for G. Thus, *under benefit principle production of G and the distribution of the cost of production of G among individuals satisfy individuals' preferences in the best possible manner.* Moreover, in equilibrium under the benefit principle the aggregate marginal benefit of G in terms of X or marginal social benefit of G in terms of X equals marginal social cost of producing G. Finally, the underlying distribution of income among the individuals is also assumed to be optimum. Hence, *social welfare is maximized under benefit principle in equilibrium.* We shall explain this with the help of Figure 3.4, where the aggregate demand price and aggregate supply price of G, denoted P_G^D and P_G^S respectively, are measured on the vertical axis, G is measured on the horizontal axis and ΣD schedule is the aggregate demand schedule of Figure 3.2 derived through the vertical summation of the individual demand curves. SS on the other hand is the supply schedule of G of Figure 3.2. The equilibrium or the optimum quantity of G, denoted G^*, therefore, corresponds to the point of intersection of these two schedules. To see why social welfare is maximized when G^* is produced, consider a given amount of G, say G_0, less than G^*—see Figure 3.4. If the government raises G from G_0 by 1 unit, it has to take away only G^0B amount of X from the individuals to meet the cost of producing this additional unit of G. But the individuals, when they get an additional unit of G, can sacrifice a larger AG^0 amount of X remaining on the same indifference curves. AG^0 is the aggregate demand price for G of the individuals. Therefore, the government can produce this extra unit of G by taking away from each individual an amount of X less than his demand price corresponding to G_0 and thereby making everybody better off. The part of the aggregate demand price that the government leaves with the individuals following the production of the additional unit of G is AB and this amount of X under the scheme mentioned above gets distributed among the individuals making all of them better off. Thus, as long as output of G is less than G^*, it is possible for the government to make every individual better off by producing more G.

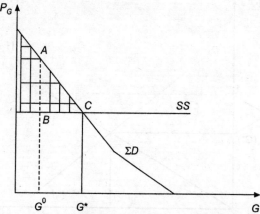

Figure 3.4:   Maximization of social welfare under benefit principle: graphical illustration.

Again, if a larger than G^* amount of G is produced, the aggregate demand price corresponding to such a G will fall short of the marginal social cost of producing G. Therefore, if the government reduces output of G by one unit, its total cost of producing G in terms of X will fall by an amount, which is larger than the aggregate demand price in terms of X. Demand price of G in terms of X of an individual measures the amount of additional X that the individual requires to be on the same indifference curves if availability of G falls by one unit. Hence, the amount by which production of X can be increased if G is reduced by one unit will exceed the total additional amount of X that all the individuals together require to compensate for their loss of one unit of G. Thus, if production of G is reduced by one unit, and the additional amount of X that is produced is distributed among individuals so that everyone gets more X than his demand price of G in terms of X, everyone will be better off. The upshot is that, if more than G^* amount of G is produced, it is possible to make everyone better off by reducing the output of G. Hence society's gain or social welfare is maximized when G^* is produced. At G^* aggregate marginal benefit of G in terms of X is equal to marginal social cost of producing G and total gain to society in terms of X is given by shaded region in Figure 3.4. It should be noted that in equilibrium, as we have already pointed out, the government produces G^* and charges A and B, $P_A(G^*)$ and $P_B(G^*)$ respectively. Hence, for every intramarginal unit of G (i.e., for every unit of G less than G^*) demand prices of both A and B are larger than the prices they respectively pay for G, which are $P_A(G^*)$ and $P_B(G^*)$. Thus, on every intramarginal unit of G they gain, which is given by the excess of their respective demand prices over and above the prices they actually pay. Thus, their total gain corresponding to every intramarginal unit of G is given by the excess of the aggregate demand price of G over the marginal cost of producing G, since the latter equals the sum of prices that individuals actually pay. Their gain is maximized, when G^* amount of G is produced and its amount is given by the shaded region in Figure 3.4.

3.2.3 Benefit Principle and the Problem of Preference Revelation

We shall now show below that, *even though the recommendations of the benefit principle maximize social welfare, it is not possible for the government to implement them. This is due to what we call the problem of 'preference revelation'.* This problem consists in the fact that even though individuals want the government to produce the optimum quantity of G, G^*, which maximizes social welfare, they are unlikely to communicate this information to the government. To get an idea of the problem, consider the case where the government produces a smaller than the optimum quantity of G, say, G_0. At this level of G aggregate demand price for G is higher than its aggregate supply price—see Figure/3.4. Suppose that the government charges all the individuals together the supply price of G in such a way that every individual pays less than his demand price. In this situation, therefore, every individual will gain if he gets more G at the price charged or at any price less than his demand price. Normally, in this situation individuals offer higher prices for G signalling to the producers that they want more of G. This mechanism is referred to as that of preference revelation. This mechanism works for private goods. However, it is unlikely to work in case of public goods. To see why we should consider first the case of a private good, say, X, which is traded in a competitive market. In Figure 3.5, D_AD_A and D_BD_B represent the demand functions for X of two groups of individuals A and B respectively and the DD schedule gives the aggregate demand function, which we have derived through the horizontal summation of the individual demand schedules. It should be noted here that in case of a private good, it is meaningful to sum up the individuals' demand curves horizontally to derive the aggregate demand curve. Let us explain. A private good is excludable and rival. If one unit of a private good is given to one individual, then that same unit cannot be made available to any other individual. Hence, corresponding to any given price, it is meaningful to add up the quantity demanded of the good of every individual to derive the aggregate quantity demanded of the good. If this aggregate quantity is produced, it will be possible to meet every individual's demand for the good at the given price. A smaller quantity will not be able to do so, while a lager quantity will generate excess supply. (*Exercise:* Explain why vertical summation of individual demand schedules is meaningless in case of a private good.)

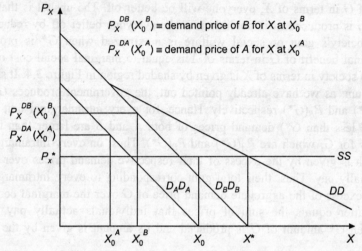

Figure 3.5: Mechanism of preference revelation in case of private goods.

The SS schedule in Figure 3.5 gives the supply schedule of X. The market for X is in equilibrium when aggregate demand for X is equal to its supply. Equilibrium values of price and quantity correspond to the point of intersection of DD and SS schedules. They are denoted by P_X^* and X^*. We shall now show that if producers produce a smaller than the equilibrium quantity of X, the market itself will produce a mechanism whereby the buyers will communicate to the suppliers that they want more X by offering to pay higher prices for X. This mechanism, as we have noted above, is the mechanism of preference revelation. To see how it works consider the situation where some amount of X, say, $X_0 < X^*$, is produced and supplied at P_x^* (see Figure 3.5). Obviously, in this situation demand for X of either of the two groups or of both the groups will remain unfulfilled. In Figure 3.5, A and B have got respectively X_0^A and X_0^B of the total market supply of X_0 and both the groups are dissatisfied. Their respective demand prices labelled $P_X^{DA}(X_0^A)$ and $P_X^{DB}(X_0^B)$ exceed the market price P_x^*. If, at a given price, an individual's demand for a good remains unfulfilled, her demand price for the good will exceed the given price of the good. In this situation, if she gets more of the good at a price less than her demand price for the good, she will be better off. Now, in case of a private good such as X every buyer knows that if she offers a higher price for the good, the sellers will divert their sales from other individuals to her and she will surely get more of the good and thereby will be better off. Hence, every dissatisfied buyer will consider it worthwhile to offer a higher price for the good revealing her preference, i.e., revealing the fact that she wants more of the good. This in turn will make other buyers dissatisfied, as the sellers divert their sales to those who have offered higher prices. As a result these other buyers will also be forced to offer higher prices. Thus, market price of X will move up above P_x^* signalling to the producers that there is an excess demand for X and thereby inducing them to supply more X. This process will go on until production of X expands to X^*.

This process of preference revelation, however, does not operate in the case of public goods. We shall explain this with the help of Figure 3.6, where D_A, D_B and ΣDD schedules represent respectively demand schedules of A and B and the aggregate demand schedule for G. The aggregate demand schedule is obviously obtained through vertical summation of the individual demand schedules. The SS on the other hand gives the supply schedule of G. It shows that the supply price of every quantity of G is constant and it is taken to be equal to unity just for expository reasons. The optimum quantity of G, labelled G^*, therefore, corresponds to the point of intersection of ΣDD and SS schedules. Suppose that the government produces a smaller quantity of G, say, G_0 less than G^*, and supplies it at the aggregate supply price of unity. At this G, the aggregate demand price of G is higher than the aggregate supply price. Hence, price paid by at least one of the individuals for G will be less than his/her respective demand price. In Figure 3.6 both the groups of individuals A and B are paying less than their demand prices. Thus, $P_0^A <$ $P^{DA}(G_0)$ and $P_0^B < P^{DB}(G_0)$, where P_0^A and P_0^B are the actual prices paid by A and B respectively, while $P^{DA}(G_0)$ and $P^{DB}(G_0)$ are A's and B's respective demand prices corresponding to G_0. All these individuals who are paying less than their respective demand prices will be better off if the government provides them with more G at prices less than their respective demand prices. They can signal it to the government by offering to pay higher prices for G. That way they can reveal their preferences, i.e., that way they can reveal it to the government that they want more of G. However, they are unlikely to do so for the following reasons.

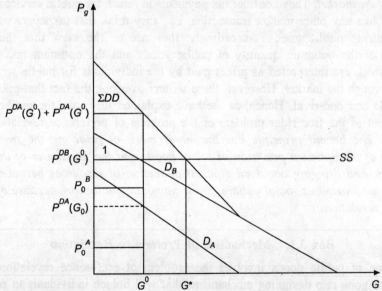

Figure 3.6: Failure of 'preference revelation' in case of public goods.

Consider any individual who is dissatisfied. His demand price for G is higher than the supply price he is facing and he will be better off if he gets more G at any price less than his demand price. He is, however, unlikely to reveal this situation to the government by offering to pay a higher price for G. He knows that, if he offers a higher price for G, the government will not be able to take some amount of G away from other individuals and give it to him. This is because, unlike private goods, G is non-excludable and non-rival. Therefore, if he offers a higher price, other individuals will not be inconvenienced in any manner and they will be under no compulsion to offer higher prices also.

In case of a public good such as G, every individual knows that he will get more of it if and only if the government increases its production. There are usually a large number of consumers of G and the individual knows that, if he offers to pay extra amount for G, it will constitute a negligible proportion of the marginal cost of producing G. Hence, he knows that unless other individuals also offer to pay a larger amount for G, the government will not be able to produce any extra amount of G and thereby make some additional amount of G available to him. Therefore, an individual knows that by offering to pay a higher price for G he can by no means be certain of securing larger supplies of G; but if other individuals offer to pay higher prices for G, then larger supplies of G will be available to him irrespective of whether he offers to pay a higher price or not. Hence, an individual may choose to be a free rider, i.e., instead of offering a higher price to secure more G he might wait for others to offer higher prices and not make a higher offer when others do so. If majority of the individuals choose to be free riders, then preferences will remain unrevealed and the government will not get any signal that it has produced a sub-optimum quantity of G. As a result of this problem of preference revelation, the government cannot implement the benefit principle of taxation.

The proponents of the benefit principle regard the relation between the government and the taxpayers as one of exchange. The government provides the social services, while taxpayers pay for these services by means of taxes. Accordingly, they want this relation to be governed by the rules of the market. They consider tax payments in return for public services as voluntary exchange just like any other market transaction, i.e., they think that taxpayers voluntarily pay taxes for securing public goods. Accordingly, they are of the view that the problem of determination of the optimum quantity of public goods and the optimum tax shares of the individuals (which are interpreted as prices paid by the individuals for public services) should be resolved through the market. However, these writers overlook the fact that public goods are non-excludable and non-rival. Hence, as we have explained just now, the market mechanism fails on account of the free rider problem or the problem of preference revelation in case of public goods. *The benefit principle has the major merit of resolving the twin problem of determination of the optimum provision of social goods and the tax shares of the individuals simultaneously, and bringing about an efficient allocation of resources between private and public goods that maximizes social welfare. But it cannot be put to work because of the problem of preference revelation.*

Box 3.1: Mechanism of Preference Revelation

As provision of public goods involves the problem of preference revelation, a lot of research has gone into designing mechanisms that will induce individuals to reveal their true preferences. One such preference revelation mechanism was designed by Clarke, Groves and Vickery and is referred to as Clarke–Groves–Vickery preference revelation mechanism (CLG). We present it below. Under this mechanism the individuals are to

---

(Contd.)

(Contd.)...

report to the government their demand price for the public good or the marginal rate of substitution of the public good for the private good. For the ith individual this is denoted by $U_i'(G)$. In other words, individuals are to report to the government their inverse demand functions for the public good. On the basis of these announced demand prices the government produces the socially optimum quantity of G corresponding to which

$\sum_i U_i'(G) = c$, where c denotes the constant average and marginal cost of producing the public good. CLG suggests a two-part tax scheme that makes it profitable for the individuals to reveal their true demand prices. The first part of the tax on any individual i is a unit tax in terms of the private good applied at the rate t_i per unit of G supplied. This part of the tax is arbitrary and the only condition that it satisfies is that $\sum_i t_i = c$. Let

us now derive the second part of the tax, $T_i(G)$, to be imposed on the ith individual. For this purpose we have to identify the quantity of G, denoted G_0, that the government would produce if t_j were equal to the announced demand price of the jth individual, U_j', for every j other than i. The value of G_0 is given by the equation $\sum_{j \neq i} U_j'(G) + t_i = c$. The second

part of the tax on the ith individual is then given by

$$T_i(G) = \sum_{j \neq i} [U_j(G_0) - U_j(G)] - \sum_{j \neq i} t_j[G_0 - G];$$

where $\qquad U_j(G) = \int_0^G U_j'(G)dG$ (B.3.1)

Now, $\sum_{i \neq j} \lfloor U_j(G_0) - U_j(G) \rfloor$ is given by the sum of the areas under the announced

inverse demand functions of the individuals other than the ith individual between G_0 and G. Given this tax function, the ith individual will announce her demand price of G in such a manner that her total benefit from G in terms of the private good net of taxes is maximized, i.e., she will report her demand price in such a manner that the G the government produces on the basis of the announced demand price maximizes

$[U_i(G) - t_iG - T_i(G)]$, where $U_i(G) = \int_0^G U_i'(G)dG$. Here, $U_i(G)$ denotes corresponding

to any G the total benefit of G derived by the individual in terms of the private good. The individual knows that the government will choose the socially optimum value of G, which satisfies the equation $\sum_{j \neq i} U_j'(G) + U_i'(G) = c$. In this equation $U_j'(G)$ gives the announced

demand prices of the jth individual for every j other than i. Given these announced demand prices, the ith individual can influence government's choice of G by choosing his demand price of G. He will accordingly choose to announce his demand price in such a

(Contd.)...

(Contd.)...

manner that the amount of G produced by the government maximizes his total post-tax benefit in terms of the private good, $[U_i(G) - t_i G - T_i(G)]$. In other words, the individual, given the announced demand prices of the other individuals, will choose G through his choice of the demand price to be announced. Accordingly, the first order condition for maximization gives us using (B.3.1)

$$U_i'(G) - t_i - T_i'(G) = U_i'(G) - t_i - \sum_{i \neq j} t_j + \sum_{i \neq j} U_j'(G)$$

$$= U_i'(G) + \sum_{i \neq j} U_j'(G) - c = 0 \quad \because \quad \sum_i t_i = c \qquad (B.3.2)$$

From (B.3.2) it follows that corresponding to any given announced demand prices by other individuals, it is profitable for the ith individual to report her true demand price, so that the government produces the quantity of G that maximizes her net benefit from G. She knows that, if she announces a different demand price, the government will produce a G, which will not satisfy (B.3.2) and, therefore, will not maximize her utility. If, for example she reports $\tilde{U}_i'(G)$ as her demand price instead of $U_i'(G)$, which is her true demand price, the government will produce that level of G, which satisfies the equation

$$\tilde{U}_i'(G) + \sum_{i \neq j} U_j'(G) - c = 0$$

and not (B.3.2). Hence, her utility will not be maximized. Therefore, every individual will choose her true demand price.

One problem with the CGV mechanism is that the total tax proceeds exceeds the cost of producing G by $\sum_i T_i(G)$, since $\sum_i t_i = c$. If $\sum_i T_i(G)$ is given back to the individuals, then the mechanism will not work. If, for example, every individual gets S_i from $\sum_i T_i(G)$ so that, $S_i = S_i(\sum_i T_i(G)) \equiv S_i(G)$, then the individual will maximize $[U_i(G) - t_i(G) - T_i(G) + S_i(G)]$. The first order condition will, therefore, be

$$U_i'(G) + \sum_{i \neq j} U_j'(G) - c + S_i'(G) = 0 \qquad (B.3.3)$$

In this case the individual knows that, if she reports her true demand price, the government will produce that level of G, which will satisfy (B.3.2) and not (B.3.3), since the government's objective is to produce the socially optimum quantity of G, which is given by the solution of (B.3.2). But this G will not satisfy (B.3.3) and, therefore, will not maximize her utility. Hence, she will be tempted to state such a demand price that, if the government produces the socially optimum G on the basis of that demand price, it will, at her true demand price, satisfy (B.3.3) but not (B.3.2).

3.2.4 Benefit Principle and the Tax Structure

Tax structure is progressive if tax liability as a proportion of income rises with income. Under a progressive tax structure, therefore, the rich pay a larger proportion of their income as tax. (There are, however, other definitions of progression—see the chapter on personal income tax for these definitions). *If proportion of tax liability in income is independent of income, the tax structure is proportional. However, if tax liability as a proportion of income falls with a rise in income, the tax structure is regressive.* There is more or less a consensus that the tax structure should be progressive. The question that we now turn to is what kind of tax structure is implied by the benefit principle. There is, however, no unambiguous answer to this. Every individual's tax share in the total cost of provision of social goods under this principle, as we have seen above, should be equal to his marginal benefit from the social goods. How is this marginal benefit likely to vary across different income classes? It may be argued that the larger the wealth of an individual, the greater is his need for protection against natural and man-made factors and therefore the greater is the benefit that he derives from public services such as administration, defence, flood control facilities, drainage, sanitation, facilities to forecast weather, earthquakes etc. In fact most of the early supporters of the benefit principle subscribed to this line of thought. However, most of them, with the notable exceptions of Rousseau and Sismondi, were in favour of a proportional tax structure as they thought that benefits from public services rise in proportion to income and wealth. Rousseau and Sismondi were of the view that benefits from public services increase more than proportionately with respect to income and wealth. Hence they supported a progressive tax structure. But, like Mill, one may also argue that the poor are in much greater need of protection from both man and nature than the rich. The rich can arrange for their own security against both human and natural factors, but the poor cannot. Moreover, in modern societies government also provides such services as education, health, drinking water, low-cost housing etc. and the poor benefit a lot from public provision of these services. The rich on the other hand are not as much dependent as the poor on public provision of these services. Hence benefits from public services may fall with a rise in income and wealth. Benefit principle under this condition suggests a regressive tax structure. This is the reason why Mill never supported the benefit theory. Obviously, this debate can never be resolved as benefits are subjective and imperceptible. For a historical account of the benefit principle see Musgrave (1959) and Seligman (1908). In fact, whether the rich or the poor benefit more from public goods also depends a lot on government's policy stance. If the government has a pro-poor policy stance and provides public services that improve living conditions of the poor, they reap more benefits from public goods. If, for example, public services such as sanitation, drinking water, administration, drainage, educational institutions, health centres etc. are concentrated mainly in areas inhabited by the poor, they will benefit more from public goods than the rich. Thus, whether the rich or the poor benefit more from public services depends on a host of factors and cannot be settled apriori.

Box 3.2: Examples of Benefit Tax

For reasons we have already specified (problem of preference revelation) a general benefit tax is infeasible. However, there are examples of specific benefit tax. Take the case of the cess on petrol and diesel in India. The revenue from this cess is used to maintain, improve and construct highways. The tax burden on account of this cess on a vehicle owner varies directly with the distance travelled. This is justified on the ground that benefit from roads increases proportionately with the distance travelled.

Another example of specific benefit tax is the property tax raised by the corporations and municipalities in India. Proceeds from these taxes are used to improve the civic amenities of the localities covered by these local government bodies. Property taxes vary directly with the property values. Justification of this kind of taxation is that benefits of civic amenities of a municipal area rise proportionately with the values of properties located in the area.

3.3 ABILITY TO PAY PRINCIPLE

The ability to pay principle, unlike the benefit principle, does not regard the problem of determination of the optimum levels of government's expenditure and tax revenue as one that is to be resolved through the market mechanism. *The proponents of this principle are of the view that the public expenditure and tax revenue should be determined through a process of planning. They thus take the total amount of tax revenue to be collected as given and recommend that the given amount of total tax burden be distributed among individuals in accordance with their ability to pay. There are two concepts of equity enshrined in this principle: horizontal and vertical. The former states that individuals having the same ability to pay should pay the same amount of tax over their lifetime, while the latter implies that the individuals having higher ability to pay should pay larger amounts of tax over their lifetime.* Before proceeding further it is important to explain precisely and clearly what we mean by an individual's ability to pay.

3.3.1 Ability to Pay

Individuals derive their satisfaction from a variety of sources: consumption, gifts to friends and relatives, bequests to children, holding of wealth and enjoyment of leisure. *Two individuals should be regarded as having the same ability to pay if they have the capacity to enjoy the same, neither more nor less, level of satisfaction from all these different sources over their lifetime.* Such a comprehensive and inclusive definition of ability to pay is, however, difficult to implement in practice since valuation of leisure is extremely problematic. Hence, for all practical purposes, ability to pay of an individual is defined as the present value of her lifetime income. Here of course income is to be comprehensively defined to include all kinds of accretion or addition to wealth. Thus, income should include not only factor income but also transfer income and capital gains or losses. It should also include imputed income from different sources such as owner-occupied houses. Imputed value of leisure should also be a part of income. However, because of the problem of valuation noted above, the definition of income that is normally used as an index of ability to pay does not include the imputed value of leisure. Clearly, non-inclusion of leisure is a major drawback of this index of ability to pay. Obviously, if two persons have the same present value of lifetime income (excluding leisure), but if one of them enjoys a much larger amount of leisure, that person must be having a much higher ability to pay and can convert leisure into income, if he wants to do so. However, because of the practical difficulties associated with the valuation of leisure, we have to make do with this narrow index of ability to pay. For more on this issue, see Box 3.3. Thus, individuals who have the same present value of lifetime income have the same ability to pay. Individuals who have the same present value of lifetime income can choose from the same set of lifetime consumption streams, when consumption is defined to include gifts given to friends and relatives, bequests passed on to children and imputed consumption from different sources such as owner-occupied houses. Let us illustrate the point below. Suppose that an individual lives for two periods, period 1 and period 2. His incomes in periods 1 and 2 are given by Y_1 and Y_2 respectively. There is no uncertainty and the individual has perfect foresight, i.e., he knows the future with certainty. His wealth (W) is defined as the present value of his lifetime income. Thus, $W = Y_1 + Y_2/(1 + r)$, where $r \equiv$ interest rate in period 1. Set of lifetime consumption streams the individual can choose from when consumption includes gifts and bequest, is given by the equation

$$W = C_1 + \frac{C_2}{1+r} \tag{3.7}$$

where C_1 and C_2 denote consumption expenditures of the individual in periods 1 and 2 respectively. Since a part of income may be used to give gifts to friends and relatives and make bequests to children, equation (3.7) holds if and only if consumption includes gifts and bequests. Obviously, when there is no uncertainty and the individual has perfect foresight, he will choose C_1 and C_2 in such a manner that the present value of C_1 and C_2 equals W. (When there is uncertainty and the individual is uncertain of his lifespan and future income, he can never *choose* his lifetime consumption in such a manner that it exactly equals his lifetime income). All possible combinations of C_1 and C_2, which satisfy the above equality, (3.7), lie on the line WW in Figure 3.7. All the individuals whose present values of lifetime incomes equal W can choose from the set of all the combinations of C_1 and C_2 lying on WW, i.e., they can choose from the same set of lifetime consumption streams, even if values of Y_1 and Y_2 vary from one individual to another. All these individuals, therefore, have the same ability to pay. (The above proposition is true if the capital market is perfect. We shall dwell on this point at length later. For the time being we assume the capital market to be perfect. Another point is that, since income is defined comprehensively to include imputed income, consumption must also be comprehensively defined to include imputed consumption. Otherwise the equality, (3.7), will not hold. Thus, if imputed income from owner-occupied houses is included in income, it should also be included in consumption. Otherwise, income and consumption cannot be equal. Imputed income from the owner-occupies house is nothing but the imputed value of the service rendered by the house to its owner. Obviously, this income is consumed at the same time it is produced). Horizontal equity requires all the individuals having the same present value of lifetime income to pay the same amount of tax over their lifetime.

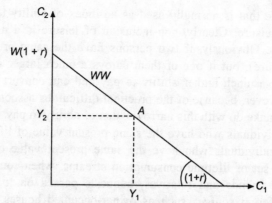

Figure 3.7: Set of all possible lifetime consumption streams individuals having the same lifetime income can choose from.

The question that automatically arises in this context is how to ensure horizontal equity or, more precisely, what variable is to be used as tax base to bring about horizontal equity. Two tax bases have been suggested in the literature, income and consumption. The former has always been used as tax base in the personal income tax. The latter, however, never existed as tax base in the realm of personal taxation. Consumption expenditure has always been taxed through taxes on goods or in rem taxes such as excise or sales taxes. To ensure horizontal equity under conditions of certainty, however, consumption has to be used as a tax base for personal taxation. In what follows we shall treat both income and consumption as bases for personal taxation and compare the two from the point of view of horizontal equity under conditions of certainty.

3.3.2 Horizontal Equity

Choice of Tax Base: Income or Consumption

To serve as the basis of taxation under the ability to pay principle both income and consumption, as we have noted above, have to be comprehensively defined. *An individual earns income from various sources, namely, sale of factor services, transfers, imputed income (for example, from owner-occupied houses) and appreciation in the value of the assets both realized and unrealized. Income from each of these sources contributes to an individual's ability to pay. Hence each of these categories of income should be included in income.* Consider, for example, two individuals earning exactly the same amount of income except for the fact that one lives in an owner-occupied house, while the other in a rented one. Obviously, ability to pay of the former is greater than that of the latter. Hence imputed income from owner-occupied houses and other sources has to be included in income. Again, consider two individuals earning exactly the same amount of income except for the fact that the value of one's assets has appreciated, while that of other's has not. Clearly, the former has greater ability to pay irrespective of whether he realizes the capital gain or not. Whether an individual will realize his capital gain or not is a matter of his choice. Hence income, if it is to serve as the basis of taxation, should include both realized and unrealized capital gains or losses.

Similarly, consumption has to be defined comprehensively also, if it is used as a tax base. Thus, *consumption should include not only value of purchases made by individuals for purposes of consumption but also imputed consumption such as values of services yielded by owner-occupied houses, part of output kept for self-consumption by farmers etc. We also include in consumption here gifts and bequests.* The difference between a consumption tax and an income tax is that the former excludes saving from the tax base.

Consumption as the Tax Base

Let us first focus on consumption as the tax base. Suppose that consumption expenditures of all individuals having the same ability to pay, i.e., having the same present value of lifetime income, are taxed at the same rate, t, in every period of their life. Assume for simplicity that every individual lives for two periods, period 1 and period 2, and consider the ith individual having a given present value of lifetime income, W^i. Hence

$$W^i = Y_1^i + \frac{Y_2^i}{1+r} \tag{3.8}$$

where Y_1^i and Y_2^i denote individual i's incomes in periods 1 and 2 respectively.

Lifetime tax of the ith individual, denoted by T is, therefore, given by

$$T = (C_1^i.t) + \left(\frac{C_2^i t}{1+r} \right) \tag{3.9}$$

where C_1^i and C_2^i denote individual i's consumption expenditures in periods 1 and 2 respectively. Since consumption includes both bequests and gifts given, the following equation must hold

$$W^i = (C_1^i + C_1^i.t) + \left[\frac{C_2^i}{1+r} + \frac{C_2^i t}{1+r} \right] \tag{3.10}$$

$$\Rightarrow \quad C_1^i(1 + t) + (1 + t) \frac{C_2^i}{1+r} = W^i$$

$$\Rightarrow \quad C_1^i + \frac{C_2^i}{1+r} = \frac{1}{(1+t)}.W^i \tag{3.11}$$

Putting (3.11) into (3.9), we get

$$T = \frac{t}{1+t} W^i \tag{3.12}$$

Equation (3.12) implies that the lifetime tax of the ith individual is a function of only t and W^i and of nothing else. It should also be noted in this context that, if an individual belonging to the same ability group as i, i.e., having the same present value of lifetime income as i, lives for more or less than two periods, even then the present value of his lifetime tax will be given by (3.12). (Prove this point yourself). From the above it follows that, *if consumption inclusive of gifts and bequests of every individual having the same ability to pay or W is taxed at the same rate in every period, their lifetime tax burdens will be the same ensuring horizontal equity.*

Income as the Tax Base

Let us now consider a tax at the rate t on the ith individual's income in every period. Lifetime tax in this case, denoted T, is given by

$$T = (tY_1^i) + \left(\frac{tY_2^i}{1+r}\right) + \frac{[(1-t)Y_1^i - C_1^i]rt}{(1+r)}$$

$$= t\left[Y_1^i + \frac{Y_2^i}{1+r}\right] + \frac{S^i rt}{(1+r)}$$

$$= tW^i + \frac{S^i rt}{(1+r)} \tag{3.13}$$

Note that $(S^i r) \equiv [(1-t)Y_1^i - C_1^i]r \equiv$ interest income on saving. It is a part of income in the second period and, therefore, taxed in the second period.

From (3.13) it follows that T is a function not only of t and W^i but also of S^i. This implies that, *if incomes of all individuals having the same ability to pay or W are taxed in every period at the same rate, their lifetime tax burdens do not become the same. Those who save more also pay more violating horizontal equity.*

Comparison of Income and Consumption as the Tax Base

From the above it follows that consumption inclusive of gifts and bequests is superior to income as tax base from the point of view of horizontal equity. However, certain points to the contrary are to be noted. To implement the consumption tax scheme delineated above the tax authority has to identify the individuals having the same present value of lifetime income and tax their consumption expenditures at equal rates. But reality is characterized by uncertainty and individuals' lifespans and their future incomes, are all uncertain. Therefore, it may be impossible to classify them on the basis of their ability to pay or present value of lifetime income. This means that *the consumption tax scheme that ensures horizontal equity cannot be implemented.* Under conditions of uncertainty, future incomes and future consumptions are uncertain, but current income and current consumption are known with certainty. Hence, if individuals having the same current income or the same ability to pay in the current period pay income tax at the same rate, horizontal equity is ensured in the current period. Under conditions of uncertainty this is the best we could do, since by no means we could ensure horizontal equity in the long run. If, however, consumption expenditures of individuals having the same current income or same ability to pay in the current period are taxed at the same rate, savers are favoured and horizontal equity is violated even in the current period. For the above reason, therefore, superiority of consumption as a tax base over income cannot be unambiguously established.

One point should be noted here. If consumption expenditure of every individual inclusive of gifts and bequest is taxed at the same rate irrespective of his ability to pay or present value of lifetime income, W, individuals having the same ability to pay or W will end up paying the same lifetime tax, T, even under uncertainty. This is because (3.7), (3.9), (3.10) and, therefore, (3.12) will hold always for *actual* income and *actual* consumption levels, since consumption here includes gifts and bequests and thereby encompasses all possible uses of an individual's income. However, if consumption expenditure of every individual is taxed at the same rate, the rate at which lifetime tax, T, will increase with ability to pay, W, becomes endogenous and will be given by (3.12). In fact, as is clear from (3.12), T will increase in the same proportion as W. This, as will be clear later, may violate vertical equity.

Another reason why superiority of consumption over income as tax base cannot be established unambiguously is that credit market is usually imperfect. We explain this point below. From our above discussion we get the following results. When we do not know individuals' lifetime incomes with certainty, taxing consumption expenditures of all individuals at the same rate will ensure horizontal equity. Again, when it is possible to know individuals' lifetime incomes with certainty, taxing consumption expenditures of individuals having the same present value of lifetime income at the same rate will ensure horizontal equity. These results will not hold, when credit market is imperfect. Let us explain. We first prove the point that, when credit market is imperfect, individuals having the same present value of lifetime income have different abilities to pay. Note that under the conditions of credit market imperfection, even when individuals are similarly placed, i.e., have the same present value of lifetime income, those who derive their income principally from labour have less access to credit than those who earn their income from assets. Obviously, even though present values of lifetime incomes of both the groups are equal, the former has less ability to pay than the latter. To understand the point clearly, consider the extreme case where the former group has no access to credit. In such a scenario consumption of each individual belonging to the former group in period 1 can at the most equal Y_1. Hence the set of lifetime consumption streams they can choose from is only a sub set of the set available to the latter group. Let us explain with the help of Figure 3.7. If an individual in the former group chooses to consume the whole of Y_1 in the first period, C_2 will be equal to Y_2. If lending by the individuals of the former group at the rate of interest r is possible, but borrowing is not, all the combinations of (C_1, C_2) on WW only to the left of A including A will be available, but the remaining points on WW will not be available. This explains our point. (*Exercise*: Describe in Figure 3.7 the consumption set of an individual of the former group, when she can neither borrow nor lend.)

Box 3.3: Horizontal Equity: Utility Approach

Given the difficulties of having a satisfactory measure of ability to pay, as we have pointed out in the text, some economists such as Feldstein (1976) have conceived of horizontal equity in terms of utility. According to this approach there is horizontal equity if (i) individuals having the same levels of utility in the pre-tax situation continue to enjoy equal levels of utility in the post-tax situation and (ii) taxes do not affect utility ranking of the individuals, i.e., individuals enjoying higher levels of utility before tax should

---

(Contd.)...

(Contd.)...

continue to enjoy higher levels of utility after tax. This definition of horizontal equity or ability to pay is obviously infeasible, as utilities of the individuals cannot be perceived.

However, the utility definition of horizontal equity has certain significant implications. First, it has been shown by the proponents of this approach that every existing tax structure ensures horizontal equity, provided there are no restrictions on individuals' choice, all prices are perfectly flexible and all individuals have the same tastes and preferences. We shall explain this with an example. Suppose two groups of individuals derived the same levels of utility before tax, but they were engaged in two different lines of economic activities. Suppose the tax that is imposed falls more heavily on one line of activity than the other reducing the after-tax incomes of one group of people more than that of the other. Obviously, according to the traditional approach the tax violates horizontal equity. But, if the individuals are free to choose, they will migrate from the more heavily taxed sector to the other sector until the after-tax incomes of the two sectors become equal through the adjustments in the wage rates. (*Exercise:* Take the case of an income tax that gives concessions to saving. Explain why horizontal equity will not be violated in this case, if utility definition of ability to pay is adopted.)

However, if the existing tax structure induces individuals to make some commitments or expenditures that are irreversible, a change in the tax law will violate horizontal equity. Let us elaborate with an example. Suppose that the existing tax laws give substantial tax concessions on interest payments on housing loans. This induces some individuals to take long-term loans and acquire houses. Now, suppose that the concessions are withdrawn. These individuals will then be worse off. It is not possible for them to sell off the house and repay the loan forthwith without any cost. But the individuals who were in the same position before the change in the tax laws, but who did not take the housing loan will not be adversely affected. Hence horizontal equity is violated. To redress this problem, proponents of the utility approach have suggested provision of a sufficiently long adjustment period before the change in the tax laws take effect so that the individuals who are adversely affected by the change get sufficient time to adjust to those changes. It is believed that if the individuals get sufficient time they will be able to take corrective measures to minimize their losses due to the changes.

Now, for every individual belonging to both the groups of individuals the present value of lifetime income equals W. Therefore, if consumption expenditures of individuals belonging to both the groups are taxed at the same rate, say, t, the following equation must hold for every individual belonging to both the groups:

$$W = (1 + t)\left[C_{1c} + \frac{C_{2c}}{1 + r}\right]$$ where C_{1c} and C_{2c} denote consumption levels chosen in periods

1 and 2 respectively. Therefore, lifetime tax T is given by

$$T = t\left[C_{1c} + \left\{\frac{C_{2c}}{(1 + r)}\right\}\right] = \left(\frac{t}{1 + t}\right)W$$

for every individual belonging to both the groups. Therefore, if consumption expenditures of all individuals belonging to both the groups are taxed at the same rate, individuals of both the groups will end up paying the same amount of lifetime tax even though individuals of one group have less ability to pay than those of the other. Thus, *when credit market is imperfect, taxing consumption expenditures of individuals having the same present value of lifetime income at the same rate will violate horizontal equity. This is another problem of choosing consumption as the tax base.* The problem is clearly due to the fact that in the presence of credit market imperfection, present value of lifetime income may not be a satisfactory index of ability to pay. For all these reasons *superiority of consumption over income as tax base is not clearly established.* Therefore, in what follows we shall regard income as the tax base.

3.3.3 Vertical Equity

Ability to pay principle conceives vertical equity in terms of 'equal sacrifice rule', which states that distribution of tax burden conforms to vertical equity when sacrifices due to taxation made by individuals having different abilities to pay are equal. Unfortunately, there is no unanimity among the proponents of the ability to pay principle regarding the meaning of this rule. In the literature there are three alternative interpretations of equal sacrifice, namely, equal absolute sacrifice, equiproportional sacrifice and equimarginal sacrifice. We shall discuss the implications of each of these rules in turn below.

Equal Absolute Sacrifice Rule

According to this rule there is vertical equity when distribution of tax burden is such that each of the individuals having different abilities to pay sacrifices the same absolute quantity of welfare. We shall examine the implications of this rule under the assumption that every individual has the same utility function and there is diminishing marginal utility of income. Given these assumptions, this rule is satisfied if, for every Y the tax burden, T, is such that

$$U(Y) - U(Y - T) = \bar{A} \ \forall \ Y \tag{3.14}$$

where $U(\cdot)$ is the utility function giving the amount of utility derived by every individual from her income. This utility function is the same for every individual by assumption. It is also assumed that $U' > 0$ and $U'' < 0$ for every Y. In (3.14), $U(Y)$ gives the utility from pre-tax income, while $U(Y - T)$ gives the amount of utility from post-tax income. Thus, the LHS gives the absolute amount of sacrifice of welfare of an individual having the income Y due to payment of the tax, T. Equation (3.14) states that for every Y the amount of tax, T, must be such that the absolute amount of welfare sacrificed equals a constant amount, $\bar{A}$. Taking total differential of (3.14), we can see how T will vary with Y under this rule. Thus,

$$U'(Y).dY - U'(Y - T)d(Y - T) = 0$$

$$\Rightarrow \qquad \frac{d(Y - T)}{dY} = \frac{U'(Y)}{U'(Y - T)} \ \text{ and } \ 0 < \frac{U'(Y)}{U'(Y - T)} < 1 \tag{3.15}$$

Let us now examine (3.15). Since there is diminishing marginal utility of income by assumption, $U'(Y - T) > U'(Y)$. Equation (3.15) implies that when tax structure conforms to the equal absolute sacrifice rule and marginal utility of income falls with a rise in income, an increase in Y (pre-tax income) is accompanied by a smaller amount of increase in post-tax income, $(Y - T)$, i.e., T increases with a rise in Y, but the increase in T is less than that in Y. The reason why T increases with an increase in Y may be explained as follows. Marginal utility of income corresponding to a higher level of income, given the assumption of diminishing marginal utility of income, is less. Hence the amount of utility or welfare sacrificed per unit of tax paid from a higher level of income is less. Therefore, to sacrifice a given amount of welfare a larger amount of tax is to be paid out of a higher level of pre-tax income. (*Exercise:* Explain why T does not increase as much as Y.) (*Hint:* From (3.14) it follows that for the total absolute amount of sacrifice of welfare to be equal following an increase Y, both $U(Y)$ and $U(Y - T)$ must increase by the same quantity. When Y rises by dY, pre-tax utility rises by $U'(Y)\, dY$. Hence, it should be accompanied by such a change in $(Y - T)$ that the increase in post-tax utility, given by $U'(Y - T)\, d(Y - T)$, equals $U'(Y)\, dY$. When both $U'(Y)$ and $U'(Y - T)$ are positive, which is the case here by assumption, for this equality to hold $d(Y - T)$ has to be positive, when dY is so. This explains why post-tax income increases, i.e., T increases less than Y, when Y rises.)

From the above it follows that, *if marginal utility of income diminishes with an increase in income, a richer person will pay a larger amount of tax under the equal absolute sacrifice rule.* But does the rule imply a progressive tax structure, given the assumptions made here? To this question we now turn. This question is important because in most of the countries structure of personal income tax is progressive. Tax structure is progressive, proportional or regressive according as

$$\frac{d\left(\dfrac{T}{Y}\right)}{dY} \left\{ \begin{matrix} > \\ = \\ < \end{matrix} \right\} 0 \quad \text{or} \quad \frac{d\left(1 - \dfrac{Y-T}{Y}\right)}{dY} \left\{ \begin{matrix} > \\ = \\ < \end{matrix} \right\} 0$$

or

$$\frac{d\left(\dfrac{Y-T}{Y}\right)}{dY} \left\{ \begin{matrix} < \\ = \\ > \end{matrix} \right\} 0$$

or

$$\frac{1}{Y^2}\left[Y\frac{d(Y-T)}{dY} - (Y-T) \right] \left\{ \begin{matrix} < \\ = \\ > \end{matrix} \right\} 0 \quad \Rightarrow \quad \frac{Yd(Y-T)}{(Y-T)dY} \left\{ \begin{matrix} < \\ = \\ > \end{matrix} \right\} 1 \qquad (3.16)$$

Substituting (3.15) into the above inequality, we find that the tax structure is progressive, proportional or regressive according as

$$\frac{Y.U'(Y)}{(Y-T)\, U'(Y-T)} \left\{ \begin{matrix} < \\ = \\ > \end{matrix} \right\} 1 \qquad (3.17)$$

Now, the product of marginal utility of income and income falls, remains the same or rises according as the elasticity of marginal utility of income with respect to Y is greater than or equal to or less than unity. If elasticity of marginal utility of income with respect to income is equal to unity, for example, an increase in income will lead to an equiproportionate decline in marginal utility of income. Hence, the product of the two will remain the same with changes in Y. Similarly, if elasticity of marginal utility of income with respect to income is greater (less) than unity, an increase in income will lead to a more (less) than proportionate decline in marginal utility of income and hence the product of the two will fall (rise) with a rise in Y. Therefore, from (3.17) it follows that *the tax structure under the rule is progressive, proportional or regressive according to as the elasticity of marginal utility of income with respect to income is greater than, equal to or less than 1.*

Let us now explain the intuition behind the result with the help of Figure 3.8. Consider any two individuals A and B having incomes Y_A and Y_B respectively and $Y_B = k.Y_A$; $k > 1$. Suppose that government collects T_A amount of tax from A. Then the absolute amount of utility that A sacrifices is $U'(Y_A)T_A$, assuming T_A to be small. Suppose that the government follows the equal absolute sacrifice rule and, therefore, chooses T_B in such a way that B also sacrifices the same absolute amount of utility as A. Now, suppose that B's income is, for example, twice as much as A's and elasticity of marginal utility of income is unity. Then $U'(Y_B)$ will be half of $U'(Y_A)$ and B therefore has to pay twice the amount of tax paid by A, (i.e., T_B has to equal $2T_A$), to sacrifice the same absolute amount of utility as A. The tax structure will, therefore, be proportional. In more general terms suppose B's income is k times as much as A's and elasticity of marginal utility of income is unity. Then $U'(Y_B)$ will be $(1/k)$ of $U'(Y_A)$ and B has, therefore, to pay k times the amount of tax paid by A to sacrifice the same absolute amount of utility as A. The tax structure will, therefore, be proportional. If the elasticity of marginal utility of income with respect to income is greater (less) than unity, $U'(Y_B)$ will be less (greater) than $(1/k)$ of $U'(Y_A)$ and B has, therefore, to pay more (less) than k times the amount of tax paid by A to sacrifice the same absolute amount of utility as A. The tax structure will, therefore, be progressive (regressive).

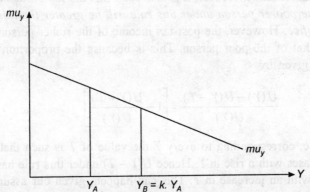

Figure 3.8: Tax structure and income elasticity of the marginal utility of income schedule under equal absolute sacrifice rule.

Equiproportional Sacrifice Rule

Distribution of tax-burden conforms to this rule when taxes paid by individuals having different abilities to pay are such that everyone sacrifices the same proportion or percentage of total utility from his pre-tax income. Formally, under this rule T corresponding to every Y is such that

$$\frac{U(Y) - U(Y - T)}{U(Y)} = \bar{A} \qquad (3.18)$$

Taking total differential of (3.18), we get

$$\frac{d(Y - T)}{dY} = \frac{U'(Y)/U(Y)}{U'(Y - T)/U(Y - T)}$$

and
$$0 < \frac{U'(Y)/U(Y)}{U'(Y - T)/U(Y - T)} < 1 \qquad (\because \quad U' > 0 \text{ and } U'' < 0) \quad (3.19)$$

Equation (3.19), just as in the earlier case, implies that, under this rule an increase in pre-tax income is accompanied by an increase in post-tax income, but by a smaller amount, when there is diminishing marginal utility of income. This means that the amount of tax increases with pre-tax income, but by a smaller amount than the pre-tax income. Intuition behind (3.19) is fairly simple. When there is diminishing marginal utility of income, marginal utility of pre-tax income of a richer person is less than that of a poorer person. If both these individuals pay the same amount of tax, the richer person sacrifices a smaller absolute amount of utility. This is because marginal utility of every unit of tax paid by the richer person is less than the marginal utility of the corresponding unit of tax paid by the poorer person. Therefore, to make the richer person sacrifice the same absolute amount of utility as the poorer person, a larger amount of tax has to be collected from the former. In the present case, however, the richer person has to sacrifice the same proportion of his pre-tax utility as the poorer person. Since the richer person's pre-tax utility is larger, he has to sacrifice under this rule a larger absolute amount of welfare than the poorer person. For both the reasons, therefore, the richer person has to pay a larger amount of tax. Moreover, it is also clear that *the tax burden on the richer person relative to that of the poorer person under this rule will be greater than that under the rule of equal absolute sacrifice.* However, the post-tax income of the richer person under this rule has to be greater than that of the poor person. This is because the proportion of utility sacrificed by an individual is given by

$$\frac{U(Y) - U(Y - T)}{U(Y)} = \left[1 - \frac{U(Y - T)}{U(Y)} \right]$$

Thus, under this rule, corresponding to every Y the value of T is such that $[U(Y - T)/U(Y)]$ is constant. $U(Y)$ increases with a rise in Y. Hence $U(Y - T)$ under this rule has to rise in the same proportion as $U(Y)$ with an increase in Y. This can happen, given our assumptions, if and only if $(Y - T)$ rises with Y.

Does this rule imply a progressive tax structure? We shall focus on this question now. We have already seen that the tax structure is progressive, proportional or regressive according as, see (3.16),

$$\left(\frac{Y}{Y - T} \right) \frac{d(Y - T)}{dY} \begin{Bmatrix} < \\ = \\ > \end{Bmatrix} 1 \qquad (3.20)$$

Substituting (3.19) into the above equation, we find that the tax structure is progressive, proportional or regressive according as

$$\left(\frac{Y}{Y-T}\right)\left(\frac{U'(Y)/U(Y)}{U'(Y-T)/U(Y-T)}\right) \begin{Bmatrix} < \\ = \\ > \end{Bmatrix} 1$$

$$\Leftrightarrow \quad \left[\frac{U'(Y)}{\left\{\left(\frac{U(Y)}{Y}\right)\right\}}\right] \begin{Bmatrix} < \\ = \\ > \end{Bmatrix} \left[\frac{U'(Y-T)}{\left\{\left(\frac{U(Y-T)}{(Y-T)}\right)\right\}}\right] \qquad (3.21)$$

From (3.21) it follows that *the tax-structure is progressive, proportional or regressive according as the ratio of the marginal utility to the average utility of income falls, stays unchanged or rises with income along the marginal utility of income schedule.* The intuition behind the result is quite simple. The amount of utility sacrificed by an individual as he pays T amount of tax is given by $[U'(Y)T]$ (assuming T to be small). Therefore, the amount of utility sacrificed as a proportion of the total amount of utility from pre-tax income is given by

$$\left[\frac{\{U'(Y).T\}}{U(Y)}\right] = \left[\frac{U'(Y)}{U(Y)/Y}.\frac{T}{Y}\right]$$

Therefore, to make the sacrifice of utility as a proportion of total pre-tax utility same for every Y (i.e., for every individual), (T/Y) has to be raised, kept constant or lowered according as the ratio of marginal to average utility of income falls, remains unchanged or rises with Y.

Equimarginal Sacrifice Rule

According to this rule tax structure conforms to vertical equity when every individual is taxed in such a manner that marginal utility of post-tax income is the same for every individual. This rule presupposes diminishing marginal utility of income. When individuals have identical utility functions, the rule calls for levelling off of income from the top. Let us illustrate the point with an example. Suppose that an economy consists of three individuals, A, B and C, with annual income levels equal to Rs. 300, Rs. 400 and Rs. 500 respectively. Also suppose that they have identical utility functions and, therefore, identical marginal utility of income schedules. Clearly, equalization of marginal utilities of post-tax incomes, when utility functions are identical, implies equalization of post-tax incomes. Suppose that the government wants to collect a given tax revenue of Rs. 330. To equalize post-tax incomes in this case the government should collect Rs. 210 from A, Rs. 110 from B and Rs. 10 from C. If the government wants to collect tax revenue of Rs. 100 or less, the tax burden under this rule should fall entirely on C. B under this rule will be taxed if and only if the amount of tax revenue to be collected by the government exceeds Rs. 100. If it is, for example Rs. 101, tax on C should be Rs. 100.5, while that on B should be Rs. .5. There should not be any tax on A. Government under this rule should tax A only when the total tax revenue that it plans to collect exceeds Rs. 300. *This rule therefore, when individuals have identical utility functions, calls for maximum degree of progression.* The reason why this rule calls for levelling off of income from the top will be explained shortly.

While the rationale of the two earlier interpretations of equal sacrifice rule is self-evident, that of the present one is not all that obvious. *The rationale of equimarginal sacrifice rule is that, when distribution of tax burden among individuals conforms to this rule, total sacrifice of utility by all the individuals together as they pay a given amount of tax revenue to the government is minimized. This happens when all individuals have identical utility functions and there is diminishing marginal utility of income.* Let us prove this point mathematically. Suppose that there are two individuals A and B. The government wants to collect $\bar{T}$ amount of tax from them. It wants to distribute $\bar{T}$ between A and B in such a manner that the total amount of utility sacrificed by A and B together is minimized.

Thus the government's optimization programme, when total taxes collected from A and B are denoted by T_A and T_B respectively, is given by

$$\min_{T_A}[\{U(Y_A) - U(Y_A - T_A)\} + \{U(Y_B) - U(Y_B - (\bar{T} - T_A))\}]$$

The FOC is given by

$$- U'(Y_A - T_A)(-1) - U'(Y_B - T_B) = 0$$

$$\Rightarrow \qquad U'(Y_A - T_A) = U'(Y_B - (\bar{T} - T_A)) \qquad (3.22)$$

We can solve (3.22) for T_A. (3.22) shows that minimization of aggregate sacrifice of welfare entailed by a given amount of tax-collection implies equimarginal sacrifice rule. When there is diminishing marginal utility, the second-order condition for minimization of utility is also satisfied. (Check this point yourself). Thus, when $U'' < 0$, and individuals have identical utility functions, equimarginal sacrifice rule implies minimization of aggregate sacrifice of welfare corresponding to any given amount of tax-collection. Let us illustrate the point graphically with the help of Figure 3.9.

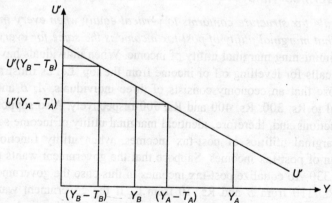

Figure 3.9: Minimization of aggregate sacrifice of welfare entailed by a given amount of tax-collection implies equimarginal sacrifice rule.

Suppose that the government wants to collect $\bar{T}$ amount of tax from A and B. Also suppose that it has distributed $\bar{T}$ between A and B in such a manner that $U'(Y_B - T_B) > U'(Y_A - T_A) \neq$ —see Figure 3.9. In this situation by lowering T_B and raising T_A by the same amount, the government will be able to reduce total sacrifice of welfare by A and B. Suppose that the government lowers T_B by 1 unit. Then the amount of utility that B will gain is $U'(Y_B - T_B)$. To compensate for the loss in tax revenue, if the government raises T_A by 1 unit, A will lose $U'(Y_A - T_A)$ amount of utility, but $U'(Y_A - T_A) < U'(Y_B - T_B)$. Thus, A and B together will gain or their total sacrifice will fall by $[U'(Y_B - T_B) - U'(Y_A - T_A)]$. Thus, as long as $U'(Y_A - T_A) \neq U'(Y_B - T_B)$, it will be possible to reduce aggregate sacrifice just by redistributing the given tax burden between the two individuals.

We are now in a position to explain why this rule calls for levelling off of income from the top. Recall that this rule presupposes identical utility functions and diminishing marginal utility of income. Suppose that there are two persons in an economy, a rich person and a poor person. The government wants to collect tax revenue of $\overline{T}$ from them. Since the objective of this rule is to minimize total sacrifice of welfare of these two individuals together as they pay the given amount of tax, the government should collect the whole of $\overline{T}$ from the rich as long as his income exceeds the poor person's by $\overline{T}$ or more. This is because, if under this condition even a single unit of tax is transferred from the rich person to the poor person, the gain of welfare to the former will be less than the loss in welfare of the latter. Hence the total sacrifice made by the two will increase. Therefore, if $\overline{T}$ exceeds the difference between the two person's income, then only the poor person is to be taxed. In this case only half of the excess of $\overline{T}$ over the difference between the two persons' incomes has to be collected from the poor person. Otherwise, the sacrifice of total utility by the two will not be minimized. (Explain this point yourself.)

3.3.4 Shortcomings of the Ability to Pay Principle

To implement the ability to pay principle, or more precisely, to implement the equal sacrifice rule, it is necessary to know the marginal utility of income functions of the individuals. It is, however, impossible to derive these schedules. Moreover, equal sacrifice rule is based on the assumption that the utilities derived by different individuals are homogeneous and, therefore, their quantities are comparable. Welfare economics, however, does not support such a view. These problems call for a different approach for designing an equitable tax structure. We shall now turn to such an approach.

3.4 SOCIAL WELFARE APPROACH

Optimum Income Tax

This approach presupposes the existence of a social welfare function or social evaluation of the total and marginal utility derived by the individuals from income. The objective of this approach is to design a tax structure that maximizes social welfare. We shall examine the implications of such an approach under the assumption that such a welfare function or evaluation exists. Assume that there are only two individuals A and B, with given incomes, Y_A and Y_B. Let $U(Y)$ be the utility function of income for every individual as perceived by the society. $U(Y)$ also has the property that marginal utility of income is positive and diminishes with a rise in Y. Clearly, $U(Y_A)$ and $U(Y_B)$ give the social utilities derived by A and B respectively from their pre-tax incomes. The social welfare function, according to this approach, is given by

$$\Omega = U(Y_A) + U(Y_B)$$

Maximization of social welfare as follows from the above social welfare function calls for equalization of individuals' incomes, given the assumption of diminishing social marginal utility of income. Let us explain the point with the help of Figure 3.9. Suppose that the social marginal utility of income schedule of the individuals is given by the U' line in Figure 3.9 and $Y_A > Y_B$. This implies that $U'(Y_A) < U'(Y_B)$, given the assumption of diminishing social marginal utility of income. Clearly, if one unit of income is transferred from A to B, social welfare will increase by $[U'(Y_B) - U'(Y_A)] > 0$. This proves the point.

Similarly, if the government wants to raise a given amount of tax revenue from the individuals, maximization of social welfare calls for equalization of post-tax incomes of all individuals. The optimization exercise in this case is given by

$$\max_{T_A, T_B} \Omega = U(Y_A - T_A) + U(Y_B - T_B)$$

subject to $\overline{T} = T_A + T_B$

where $\overline{T}$ is the given amount of tax to be collected and T_A and T_B denote the amounts of taxes to be collected from A and B respectively. Incorporating the constraint into the objective function, we can rewrite the optimization exercise as

$$\max_{T_A} \Omega = U(Y_A - T_A) + U(Y_B - (\overline{T} - T_A))$$

The FOC for maximization in this case is clearly given by

$$U'(Y_A - T_A) = U'(Y_B - T_B)$$

Given the assumption of diminishing social marginal utility of income, the second-order condition for maximization is automatically satisfied. Thus maximization of social welfare calls for equalization of marginal utilities of post-tax incomes of the individuals. Since the social utility functions are the same for all the individuals, it implies equalization of post-tax incomes. In fact, it calls for taxing the rich first. If after bringing the incomes of the rich to the levels of those of the poor through taxation, the tax revenue falls short of the required amount, the remaining tax burden has to be distributed equally among all the people, rich and poor. Thus the social welfare approach implies a marginal tax rate, i.e., tax on the last unit of income, of hundred per cent on the rich. Let us explain these points with the help of Figure 3.9, where A is the rich and B is the poor, with $Y_A > Y_B$. If $\overline{T} \leq (Y_A - Y_B)$, maximization of social welfare requires collection of the whole of the tax from A. It is quite easy to explain. As long as post-tax income of A is greater than the pre-tax income of B, marginal utility of post-tax income of A is less than the marginal utility of pre-tax income of B. So if A's tax burden is raised by 1 unit instead of B's, social welfare will decline by a smaller quantity, which is the social marginal utility of post-tax income of A. In the opposite case social welfare would fall by the social marginal utility of income of B, which is a larger quantity. To maximize social welfare, i.e., to minimize the loss in total utility due to the loss of the taxed amount, the whole of the tax is to be collected from A as long as excess of A's income over B's is greater than or equal to the amount of the given tax revenue to be collected. If, however, the given tax revenue exceeds this amount, the excess has to be allocated equally between the two, so that post-tax incomes of both are equal. This follows from the fact that if marginal utility of post-tax income of one exceeds that of the other, raising the tax burden of the one having lower social marginal utility of post-tax income and lowering that of the other by the same amount will raise social welfare. This point, as you should be able to recall, we have explained earlier.

The theory presented above, therefore, recommends a marginal tax rate, tax on the last unit of income, of hundred per cent on the rich and calls for complete income equalization. Let us illustrate with an example. If the annual income of the rich is Rs. 2000, while that of the poor is Rs. 1000, the tax on the 2000th unit or rupee of income of the rich, which is the marginal tax rate on the rich, according to this theory, is hundred per cent. This is true of every unit of income of the rich above Rs. 1000. Studies undertaken in recent years on optimum income taxation have, however, substantially cushioned this radical result. We shall briefly summarize the major results of these studies below. One major assumption of the theory presented above is that incomes of the individuals are constant and independent of taxes. Modern theories have questioned that assumption. They have pointed out that individuals derive utility not only from income but also from leisure. In such a situation a tax on income will produce an incentive effect. It will, as we have explained in detail in the chapter on tax efficiency, induce the individuals to substitute leisure for income and the consequent fall in labour supply will reduce the full employment level of output. If wages and prices are market clearing in an economy, it will operate with full employment level of output. In such an economy, therefore, aggregate output will fall following the imposition of a tax on the income of the rich. This will reduce the income not only of the taxpayers but also of a large number of other individuals. Let us explain. Following the imposition of the tax, taxpayers reduce labour supply creating labour shortage at the prevailing real wage rate. So the real wage rate will rise inducing producers to reduce output and employment. This fall in aggregate output reduces not only employment but also profit, interest and rental income. Profit, interest and rent earners who are adversely affected need not necessarily be those on whom the tax is imposed. Again, the workers who lose jobs on account of the fall in aggregate output need not necessarily be the taxpayers. A tax on the rich, therefore, reduces the taxpayers' income not just by the amount of the tax, but by a larger amount through its impact on aggregate output. Incomes of other individuals will also fall. Thus, the loss in social welfare due to a tax on the income of the rich may be much larger than what the theory presented above captures. To illustrate with a simple example how a tax on the rich can reduce the welfare of the poor, suppose that a tax is imposed on the income of a rich person, A. Following this A revises her labour–leisure choice and decides to sack her driver and drive her car herself. In this case clearly the loss in social welfare will include not only the loss of welfare of A but also that of her driver. Thus, the loss in utility impinging on the imposition of a tax on the rich may be much larger than what is suggested by the social welfare approach. There is another reason for this. We explain it below.

In the social welfare approach presented above, the loss in utility of a taxpayer following the imposition of a tax is due to income effect alone, i.e., it is simply due to the loss in the taxpayers' income by the amount of the tax. However, when taxpayers choose the allocation of their labour endowments between work and leisure, the tax not only reduces taxpayers' income by the amount of the tax but also lowers price of leisure in terms of income. The latter produces a substitution effect, which also decreases taxpayers' welfare. Thus, when taxpayers make work–leisure choice, imposition of a tax on income reduces taxpayers' income not only by the income effect due to the loss in their income by the amount of the tax but also by the substitution effect. This latter loss is referred to as the excess burden. We have discussed the concept of excess burden in detail in the chapter on tax efficiency. Thus, the loss in social welfare due to an income tax on the rich is larger than what is captured by the original version of the social welfare approach because of the excess burden also. As a result, modern studies (see, for example, Stern (1976)) show that the marginal tax rate on the rich that maximizes social welfare may be much less than hundred per cent. However, if labour supply is not much sensitive to real wage rate, the costs pointed out above are unlikely to be significant.

3.5 CONCLUSION

Both benefit and ability to pay principles have major merits and demerits. The former resolves the problems of optimum provision of social goods and the optimum distribution of the tax burden simultaneously and brings about optimum allocation of resources between private and the public goods. But it ignores completely the issue of taxation necessary for achieving an optimum distribution of income. *Its most important drawback is that it seeks to apply the market mechanism to resolve the problem of efficient allocation of resources between private and the public goods. But in the case of public goods the exclusion principle does not apply and hence the market mechanism fails to resolve the problem.* More specifically, government's provision of social goods through the market gives rise to the problem of preference revelation or the free rider problem and thereby frustrates government's attempt at achieving an optimum allocation of resources between private and public goods.

The ability to pay principle on the other hand completely ignores the problem of efficient provisioning of social goods and takes the amount of tax revenue to be collected as given. It seeks to suggest an optimum or equitable distribution of the given tax burden. This policy cannot be implemented either. *To design the tax structure on the basis of this principle, the government has to know the marginal utility of income schedules of all the individuals. The government has no means of knowing them.* The marginal utility of income schedules of individuals may be different and it is impossible to know these schedules. Even the equimarginal sacrifice rule cannot yield any definite tax structure when the marginal utility of income schedules of individuals are different. *Modern welfare economics does not consider it justifiable to compare utility of one individual to that of another.* Hence equal sacrifice rule in terms of which ability to pay principle conceives vertical equity becomes meaningless. Under these conditions, obviously, the ability to pay principle cannot provide any guideline regarding the construction of an equitable tax structure.

To design an equitable tax structure, therefore, what is required is a social evaluation of the marginal utility of income derived by the individuals. If such a social marginal utility of income schedule exists, *maximization of social welfare calls for equalization of post-tax incomes of all the individuals when individuals' incomes may be regarded as independent of taxation. However, the latter condition is not always met. When taxation affects individuals' incomes by affecting, for example, individuals' labour–leisure choice, maximization of social welfare allows for considerable amount of inequality.*

SUMMARY

1. A good tax structure has the following major characteristics. It is equitable or just, efficient, transparent, involves low administrative and compliance costs, allows for shifting of tax burden by the economic agents on whom the tax is imposed and facilitates use of fiscal policy for stabilization and growth.

2. There are two major principles of tax equity, benefit principle and ability to pay principle. The former is a theory of both public expenditure on the provision of social goods and equitable distribution of the tax burden required to meet this expenditure. The latter is, however, a theory of tax equity only.

3. The benefit principle recommends that the government produces that level of public goods at which marginal social cost of producing public goods is equal to its marginal social benefit, which is given by the aggregate demand price of the individuals for public goods. The benefit principle also suggests that the government charges the individuals their respective demand prices for public goods. Thus, under this principle there occurs efficient allocation of resources between private and the public goods and maximization of social welfare.

4. The benefit principle applies the market mechanism to resolve the problem of optimum provision of social goods and the distribution of the costs involved among individuals. Since exclusion principle does not apply to social or public goods, the solution fails. The government cannot apply the benefit principle as it gives rise to the problem of preference revelation or the free rider problem. The other major problem is that the benefit principle does not throw any light on the optimum procedure of taxation for achieving a just distribution of income. It presumes the distribution of income to be optimum.

5. The ability to pay principle on the other hand ignores the problem of optimum provision of social goods and takes the total amount of tax revenue to be collected as given and focuses exclusively on the issue of optimum distribution of the given tax burden among the individuals. It suggests taxation of individuals in accordance with their abilities to pay.

6. The 'ability to pay' is defined as the capacity to derive utility. In determining this, one should take into account all the different economic activities, which yield utility to an individual, namely, consumption, passing on bequests to children, giving gifts to friends and relatives, holding of wealth and enjoyment of leisure. Construction of such a comprehensive measure of ability to pay is, however, extremely difficult. Valuation of leisure is particularly problematic. Hence, ability to pay of an individual is usually viewed in terms of his income, which is defined comprehensively to include all kinds of accretion to his wealth, namely, factor and transfer income, imputed income and appreciation in the value of assets, realized or unrealized.

7. The principle of ability to pay enshrines two concepts of equity: horizontal and vertical. Horizontal equity states that individuals having the same ability to pay should pay the same amount of tax, while vertical equity means that individuals having higher abilities to pay should pay a larger amount of tax.

8. Both income and consumption can serve as tax base. If ability to pay is defined in terms of present value of lifetime income, then if consumption expenditures of all individuals

having the same ability to pay are taxed at the same rate, they end up paying the same amount of tax over their lifetime. On the other hand, if incomes of all these individuals are taxed at the same rate, those who save more pay more in tax over their lifetime violating horizontal equity. Thus, consumption seems to be a better base for taxation. However, in reality, lifespans and future incomes of individuals are uncertain. Hence it is not possible to apply the present value of lifetime income criterion to determine an individual's ability to pay. The tax scheme, therefore, is infeasible. As a result superiority of consumption over income cannot be established. If income is used as tax base, horizontal equity is established at least in the short run, i.e., individuals earning the same income in any period pay the same amount of tax in that period.

9. The ability to pay principle is based on the equal treatment of equals rule. It states that there is vertical equity if sacrifices of all the individuals having different abilities to pay are the same. There are three interpretations of this equal sacrifice rule, namely, equal absolute sacrifice rule, equiproportional sacrifice rule and equimarginal sacrifice rule. When all the individuals have the same marginal utility of income schedule and there is diminishing marginal utility of income, the richer people pay larger amounts of tax under all the three rules. However, the tax structure under the first two need not necessarily be progressive. It may be proportional or regressive as well depending on the specific shape of the marginal utility of income schedule. However, the equimarginal sacrifice rule implies equalization of post-tax incomes calling for maximum degree of progression. This rule also leads to minimization of the aggregate sacrifice of utilities due to taxation of all the individuals together.

10. The ability to pay principle is also infeasible. Marginal utility of income schedules of the individuals may be different and it is impossible to know these schedules. Even the equimarginal sacrifice rule cannot yield any definite tax structure when the marginal utility of income schedules of individuals are different. Modern welfare economics does not consider it justifiable to compare utility of one individual to that of another. Under these conditions, obviously, the ability to pay principle cannot provide any guideline regarding the construction of an equitable tax structure.

11. To construct an equitable tax structure, therefore, an alternative approach is used: the social welfare approach. It presupposes a social welfare function that evaluates the marginal utility that individuals derive from income. Such an approach calls for equalization of post-tax incomes to maximize social welfare, if individuals' incomes may be regarded as independent of taxation. However, modern studies show that, if incomes are not independent of taxation, maximization of social welfare may call for considerable level of inequality.

═══════════════════ **KEY CONCEPTS** ═══════════════════

- ✓ Tax equity
- ✓ Aggregate demand price for the public good
- ✓ Efficient allocation of resources between private and public goods

- ✓ Benefit principle
- ✓ Marginal social benefit of the public good
- ✓ Optimum prices or tax shares of public goods

✓ Progressive, proportional and regressive tax structure
✓ Ability to pay principle
✓ Vertical equity
✓ Equiproportional Sacrifice Rule
✓ Interpersonal comparison utility
✓ Problem of preference revelation or free rider problem
✓ Horizontal equity
✓ Equal Absolute Sacrifice Rule
✓ Equimarginal Sacrifice Rule
✓ Social welfare approach

REVIEW QUESTIONS

1. What are the major features of a good tax system?
2. Explain why vertical summation of individual demand schedules is meaningless in case of a private good, while horizontal summation is meaningful.
3. Explain why horizontal summation of demand functions for the public good is meaningless, while vertical summation is meaningful.
4. Distinguish between marginal private benefit and marginal social benefit in case of a public good.
5. Explain the objectives of the benefit principle
6. How does the benefit principle resolve the problems of optimum provision of social goods and the optimum distribution of the cost of providing social goods among individuals?
7. Does the benefit principle recommend production of as much public goods as is demanded by the people?
8. Does the benefit principle maximize social welfare? Explain.
9. What are the major shortcomings of the benefit principle? Explain in this context the problem of preference revelation or the free rider problem.
10. Explain the concept of ability to pay.
11. What is meant by horizontal and vertical equity?
12. Which one, income or consumption, serves as a better tax base from the point of view of horizontal equity?
13. What is the relation between vertical equity and equal sacrifice?
14. What are the different interpretations of the equal sacrifice rule?
15. Does a richer person pay larger than a poorer person under every interpretation of the equal sacrifice rule? Explain.
16. When there is diminishing marginal utility of income, the difference between the tax payment of a rich person and that of a poor person is larger under the equiproportional sacrifice rule than that under the equal absolute sacrifice rule. It is, however, the largest under the equimarginal sacrifice rule. Do you agree? Explain.
17. What kind of tax structure is implied by each of the equal sacrifice rules?
18. What are the major demerits of the ability to pay principle?
19. Explain the social welfare approach. What is its recommendation regarding an equitable tax structure?

PROBLEMS AND APPLICATIONS

1. Show that the larger the benefit an individual derives from public goods, the greater will be his tax share under the benefit principle.

   (*Hint:* The greater the benefit the higher is the demand price. If the demand function of an individual shifts upward, more G will be produced. Others will, therefore, pay less as their demand prices fall with a rise in G. Hence this individual whose demand price has risen will have to pay more.)

2. If, as a result of better public management and greater sense of responsibility on the part of the government, quality of public services improves, how will it affect the optimum quantity of production of public goods and the optimum tax shares under the benefit principle?

   (*Hint:* Demand prices will rise leading to upward shifts in individual demand schedules. So, output of public goods will rise. To examine how tax shares are affected, assume that there are only two individuals, A and B. Tax share of A is given by $P_A/(P_A + P_B)$, as $(P_A + P_B)$ equals the average cost of production of the public good. Tax share of A will, therefore, rise if P_A/P_B rises, i.e., if $(\hat{P}_A - \hat{P}_B) > 0$. Assume that the inverse demand function of the ith individual is given by $P_i\left(\underset{-}{G}, \underset{+}{q}\right)$, where $q \equiv$ quality and $i = A, B$. Then

$$(\hat{P}_A - \hat{P}_B) = \left[\frac{1}{\eta_{P_A}} + \frac{1}{\eta_{qA}}\right] - \left[\frac{1}{\eta_{P_B}} + \frac{1}{\eta_{qB}}\right]$$

   where $\eta_{P_i} \equiv$ price elasticity of demand for G of the ith individual and $\eta_{qi} \equiv$ elasticity of demand for G of the ith individual with respect to quality. Proceed on this line.)

3. Do all public goods cater to the rich and the poor alike? Explain.

   (*Hint:* Public goods which mainly benefit the areas, which are inhabited mainly by the poor people, improve principally the lot of the poor and vice versa. Poor people depend much more than the rich on publicly provided education, health services, drinking water etc. Provision of these services, therefore, benefits the poor more. Since the rich has considerable amount of wealth, defence and administration may benefit them more.)

4. How will a shift in the composition of G in favour of the poor affect the optimum quantity of G and optimum tax shares of the rich and the poor under the benefit principle? Explain.

   (*Hint:* Demand price for G of the poor will rise and those of the rich will fall. Hence tax shares of the poor will rise and that of the rich will fall.)

5. Suppose that because of better public management cost of producing public goods falls. How will it affect the optimum tax shares, output of public goods and social welfare under the benefit principle?

   (*Hint:* Assume that average cost of provision of public goods is constant. Also assume that there are only two individuals A and B. Hence average cost of production equals $(P_A + P_B)$. Share of A in the total cost of production is, therefore, $P_A/(P_A + P_B)$. What happens to this accordingly depends upon how (P_A/P_B) is affected. Following the fall in the cost, with demand remaining unchanged, equilibrium value of G rises. Now

$$\frac{d\left(\frac{P_A}{P_B}\right)}{\left(\frac{P_A}{P_B}\right)} = \hat{P}_A - \hat{P}_B = \frac{\frac{dP_A}{dG}dG}{P_A} - \frac{\frac{dP_B}{dG}dG}{P_B} = \frac{dP_A}{dG}\frac{P_A}{G}\frac{dG}{G} - \frac{dP_B}{dG}\frac{P_B}{G}\frac{dG}{G} = \left(\frac{1}{\eta_B} - \frac{1}{\eta_A}\right)\hat{G}$$

where $\eta_i \equiv -\dfrac{dG}{dP_i}\dfrac{P_i}{G}$ = own price elasticity of demand of the ith good, $i = A, B$. Hence,

if $\eta_A > \eta_B$, $(\hat{P}_A - \hat{P}_B) > 0$, i.e., P_A/P_B rises. This means that tax share of A rises.)

6. Examine the implications of deterioration in the Indo-Pak relation for the benefit principle in Indian context.

   (*Hint:* Need for protection against foreign invasion and terrorist activities at home will rise. Demand prices for administration and defence will rise. It is quite likely that the demand prices of the wealthy who have perhaps more to lose, will rise more than those of others. Provision of social goods will rise and tax shares of the wealthy may rise too.)

7. When all the individuals are alike, the optimum tax share of every individual under the benefit principle is $(1/N)$, where N gives the total number of individuals in the economy. Prove.

   (*Hint:* Suppose that the demand price of every individual for the social good, since all individuals are identical, is $P(G)$. Therefore, in equilibrium $NP(G) = C(G)$, where $C(G)$ ≡ the average cost of producing G. Suppose that G^* solves the above equation. Total tax revenue of the government is, therefore, $C(G^*)G^* = NP(G^*)G^*$ and total tax burden on every individual is $P(G^*)G^*$. Therefore, tax share of every individual is $(1/N)$).

8. Suppose that there are two individuals having the same utility function, $U_i = X_i^{.5}G^{.5}$, where U_i ≡ utility of the ith individual, X_i ≡ the quantity of the private good consumed by the individual and G ≡ output of the public good. GDP in terms of the private good is 100 and the social transformation schedule is given by $100 = X + G$, where X ≡ aggregate output of the private good. The GDP is equally distributed between the two individuals. Derive the optimum quantities of G and X and the optimum tax shares of the two individuals. Explain why social welfare is maximized in equilibrium in this model. Examine the impact of (i) a change in the distribution of income so that one individual gets 10 units more income and the other ten units less, (ii) a rise in the power of G in the utility function to 0.8 and fall in the power of X to 0.2, and (iii) technological progress that raises the GDP from 100 to 120. Explain the results and their significance in each of the three cases.

   (*Hint:* $G = 50$, $P_A = P_B = 1/2$. (i) Assuming A gets more, $P_A = 3/5$, $P_B = 2/5$ since A's demand price at every G rises and that of B falls. (ii) $G = 80$, $P_A = P_B = 1/2$. As people get more benefit from G, demand price of every individual at every G is higher. So, aggregate demand schedule shifts upward raising equilibrium G. As demand functions of the two individuals are identical, price charged to every individual is also the same.

(iii) $G = 60$, $X = 60$, $P_A = P_B = 1/2$. Since public and private good are of equal importance to the individual, given his utility function, an increase in aggregate income leads to an equal increase in the output levels of the two goods.)

9. Suppose that two individuals have identical shares in GDP and also identical tastes and preference. How will a change in the distribution of income in favour of one at the expense of the other will affect the tax shares under the benefit principle, when (i) G is a normal good and (ii) G is an inferior good? Examine the implications for the tax structure in each of the two cases.

   (*Hint:* (i) When the good is normal, rich person's demand curve shifts up and the poor person's shifts down by the same amount. Hence the former's tax share rises and that of the latter falls, making the tax structure progressive. (ii) Just the opposite happens making the tax structure regressive).

10. Suppose that income corrupts so that larger income whets the appetite for having more. What kind of tax structure will each of the equal sacrifice rules imply in such a situation? Explain your results.

    (*Hint:* In this case marginal utility of income rises with income. Equal absolute sacrifice rule, therefore, implies larger tax payment by the poor. $U'(Y)T$ is the utility sacrificed. For the poor U' is smaller and so T larger. So the tax structure is regressive. In case of equiproportional sacrifice rule, the tax structure is regressive too and that too to the maximum possible extent. Under equimarginal sacrifice rule, maximization of social welfare calls for taxation of income starting with that of the poorest of the poor and then moving upward along the income scale. The tax structure is, therefore, the most regressive.

11. Will economic growth alter the tax structure under the equal absolute or equiproportional sacrifice rule? Explain:

    (*Hint:* If elasticity of the marginal utility of income with respect to income and the behaviour of the ratio of marginal utility of income to the average utility of income with respect to changes in income are independent of levels of income, economic growth will not affect the tax structure.)

12. Suppose that the utility function of the individuals is given by $U = Y^{.5}$. Also suppose $Y_A = 200$, $Y_B = 150$ and $\overline{T} = 70$. Calculate T_A and T_B, when the government wants to minimize total sacrifice of welfare. Does it imply equimarginal sacrifice rule? How will an increase in Y_A to 250 affect T_A and T_B? Explain.

    (*Hint:* $\max_{T_A} [\{(200 - T_A)^{0.5}\} + \{150 - (70 - T_A)^{0.5}\}]$. If T_A as yielded by the above optimization exercise, with $Y_A = 250$ is greater than 70, then T_A should be taken to be equal to 70. Explain all the results yourself.)

13. Suppose that the government follows equimarginal sacrifice rule to raise a given amount of tax revenue. Also suppose that all individuals have identical utility functions. There is also diminishing marginal utility of income. There occurs economic growth. Can it, total tax revenue to be collected remaining fixed, (i) improve the economic lot of everyone, (ii) make any one worse off, (iii) improve some one's lot indirectly, even though it does not give any benefit to the person directly? Answer this question using a simple framework.

(*Hint:* Consider a simple economy where there are only two individuals A and B. Economic growth can benefit either both of them or just any one of them. Suppose that it benefits both of them. If in the post-growth situation income of the richer person exceeded that of the poorer person by the given amount of tax revenue or more, the entire burden fell only on the richer person. If in the pre-growth situation the excess of the richer person's income over poor person's income was less than the given amount of tax revenues, some burden fell on the poor person too. The point is that, to examine how growth affects the distribution of the given tax burden between the two persons, one has to focus on how it affects the excess of the richer person's income over the poor person's income. If the excess is unaffected, the distribution is also unaffected. The distribution can change only if this excess is affected. Assuming B to be the poor person, $T_B = (1/2)[\overline{T} - (Y_A - Y_B)]$ for $\overline{T} > (Y_A - Y_B)$, $T_B = 0$ for $\overline{T} < (Y_A - Y_B)$. Thus, as long as growth leaves $(Y_A - Y_B)$ unaffected, distribution remains unchanged. If $(Y_A - Y_B)$ rises, T_B will fall provided the new $(Y_A - Y_B) > \overline{T}$. Build on these lines.)

REFERENCES

For comprehensive definition of income for tax purposes:

Goode, R. (1977): The economic definition of income, *in*: Pechman, J. (Ed.), *Comprehensive Income Taxation*, Brookings, Washington, D.C.
Simon, H. (1938): *Personal Income Taxation*, University of Chicago Press, Chicago.

For the debate over income versus consumption as tax base:

Bradford, D. (1980): The case for a personal consumption tax, *in*: Pechman, J. (Ed.), *What should be Taxed: Income or Consumption?* Brookings, Washington, D.C.
Kaldor, N. (1955): *An Expenditure Tax*, Chapter 1, Allen, London.

For vertical equity and progression:

Blum, W.J. and Calven, H. Jr. (1953): *The Uneasy Case for Progressive Taxation*, Chicago University Press, Chicago.
Mill, J.S. (1921): *Principles of Political Economy*, Book V, Chapter II, Longman's, London.
Pigou, A.C. (1928): *A Study in Public Finance*, Part II, Chapters 1 and 2, Macmillan, London.

For historical account of the benefit principle:

Musgrave, R.A. (1959): *The Theory of Public Finance*, Chapter 4, McGraw-Hill, New York.
Seligman, R.E. (1908): *Progressive Taxation in Theory and Practice*, 2nd edition, Part II, Princeton, University Press, Princeton.

For the classics on a good tax structure:

Mill, J.S. (1921): *Principles of Political Economy*, Book V, Chapter II, Longman's, London.
Pigou, A.C. (1928): *A Study in Public Finance*, Part II, Macmillan, London.
Smith, A. (1910): *The Wealth of Nations*, Book V, Chapter II, Part II, "On Taxes", Everyman's Library, London, especially the earlier part dealing with his famous canons of good taxation.

For benefit principle:

Johansen, L. (1965): *Public Economics*, Rand McNally, Chicago.

——(1963): Some notes on the Lindahl theory of determination of public expenditure, *International Economics Review*, **4**, September, 346–358.

For modern studies on income tax design:

Stern, N.H. (1976): On the specification of models of optimum incomer taxation, *Journal of Public Economics*, **6** (1, 2), July–August, 123–162.

For the utility definition of ability to pay:

Feldstein, M.S. (1976): On the theory of tax reform, *Journal of Public Economics*, **6**, 77–104.

APPENDIX

AN ALTERNATIVE PRESENTATION OF THE LINDAHL–JOHANSEN MODEL

In Lindahl–Johansen model, as you recall, the marginal and average cost of production of G in terms of X is unity and the government charges such prices to A and B that the cost of production of G is just covered. Accordingly, if the government charges A the price P_A, it charges B the price $(1 - P_A)$. Thus, $(1 - P_A)$ is the government's supply price of G to B. Substituting $(1 - P_A)$ for P_B in B's budget constraint, as given in (3.2b), we can rewrite it as

$$\bar{R} - \bar{R}_A = (1 - P_A) G + X^B$$

or
$$X^B = \bar{R} - \bar{R}_A - (1 - P_A) G \qquad (A.3.1)$$

Again, we can rewrite A's budget constraint, see (3.2a), as

$$X^A = \bar{R}_A - P_A G \qquad (A.3.2)$$

Substituting (A.3.1) and (A.3.2) into the utility functions of A and B respectively, we can rewrite them as

$$U^A = U^A(\bar{R}_A - P_A G, G) \qquad (A.3.3)$$

and
$$U^B = U^B(\bar{R} - \bar{R}_A - (1 - P_A) G, G) \qquad (A.3.4)$$

We get demand functions of A and B for G by carrying out the following optimization exercises:

$$\max_{G} \ U^i \ (.) \ i = A, B$$

These demand functions are given by

$$G^A = G^A(P_A); \ G^{A'} < 0 \text{ and } G^B = G^B(P_A); \ G^{B'} > 0 \qquad (A.3.5)$$

where G^A and G^B denote respectively A's and B's demands for G.

Putting A's and B's demand functions for G in their respective budget constraints, we get their demand functions for X. Clearly, there is equilibrium in this model if the government sets that value of P_A corresponding to which A and B demand the same amount of G and the government produces as much G as demanded by A and B at the given P_A. It should be noted here that, when this is the case demand for X of A and B is also equal to its supply. Let us explain. In this model by assumption production is always on the production possibility frontier. Hence production of X, as follows from the production possibility frontier, in the equilibrium specified above is given by $[\bar{R} - G^A(P_A^*)] = [\bar{R} - G^B(P_A^*)]$, where P_A^* denotes the equilibrium value of P_A. Aggregate demand for X of A and B in equilibrium as follows from their budget constraints is given by $[\bar{R}_A - P_A G^A(P_A^*)] + [\bar{R} - \bar{R}_A - (1 - P_A)G^A(P_A^*)] = \bar{R} - G^A(P_A^*)$. This establishes our proposition. Thus, in equilibrium we have

$$G^A(P_A) = G^B(P_A) \qquad (A.3.6)$$

Solving the above equation, we get the equilibrium value of P_A. Putting this equilibrium value of P_A in (A.3.5), we get the equilibrium value of G. Substituting this equilibrium value of G in the equation of the production possibility frontier, we get the equilibrium value of X. Graphical solution of (A.3.6) is shown in Figure A.3.1, where G^A and G^B schedules represent demand schedules of A and B for G. The equilibrium values of P_A and G, which are labelled P_A^* and G^* respectively, correspond to the point of intersection of these two schedules. Let us now explain how we derive G^A and G^B graphically. Equation of an indifference curve of A is given by

$$\bar{U}^A = U^A(\bar{R}_A - P_A G, G) \tag{A.3.7}$$

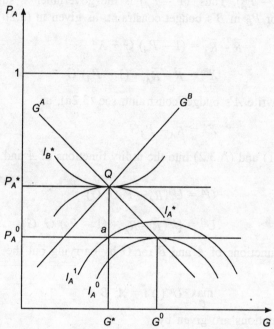

Figure A.3.1:   Equilibrium in the Lindahl–Johansen model.

This indifference curve of A is represented by the concave downward curve I_A^0 in the (G, P_A) plane in Figure A.3.1. Its shape may be explained as follows. Start from any (G, P_A) satisfying (A.3.7). Now, suppose G rises by one unit. It will lower the amount of X available to A, given his budget constraint, by P_A. However, if G is sufficiently small, mrs_{GX}, which measures the amount of X that A can sacrifice remaining on the same indifference curve following the unit increase in G, is larger than P_A and hence A will move over to a higher indifference curve. To keep A on the same indifference curve, therefore, P_A has to be raised, so that the amount of X available to A falls by mrs_{GX} corresponding to the initial (G, P_A) following the unit increase in G. Thus, for low values of G indifference curve of A is upward sloping in the (G, P_A) plane. As G and P_A rise from their low values along the indifference curve, mrs_{GX} falls. This rise in P_A and the fall in mrs_{GX} obviously reduce the slope of the indifference curve. Eventually, a (G, P_A) is reached at which $mrs_{GX} = P_A$. Clearly, at this point the slope of the indifference curve is zero. When G rises beyond this value, $mrs_{GX} < P_A$ and P_A has to be reduced following an increase in G to keep A on the same indifference curve. Hence, the indifference curve is downward sloping for such high values of G. Thus, the slope of the indifference curve of A in the (G, P_A) plane falls monotonically from positive values to negative ones with the rise in G. Hence, it is concave upward as shown in Figure A.3.1.

Two more points should be noted regarding the indifference curves of A. First, a higher indifference curve represents a lower level of utility, since a smaller amount of X corresponds to any given G on a higher indifference curve. Second, the zero slope corresponds to a lower G on a higher indifference curve. The point may be explained as follows. The amount of X corresponding to any given G on a higher indifference curve is smaller. Hence, mrs_{GX} is less, but P_A is higher. Thus following a unit increase in G from a given level, the amount of increase in P_A required to keep A on the same indifference curve is less on a higher indifference curve, i.e., the slope of a higher indifference curve corresponding to any given G is less. Moreover, the slope falls monotonically with an increase in G along any given indifference curve. If corresponding to any given G the slope of a lower indifference curve is zero, it is negative at the same G on a higher indifference curve. Hence on a higher indifference curve the slope is zero at a lower G.

Let us now explain how we derive A's demand curve for G. Suppose that the price of G charged to A is P_A^0. The horizontal line corresponding to P_A^0 in Figure A.3.1 is the supply curve of G to A. It gives the supply price of G to A corresponding to every G. Note that the points on this horizontal line correspond to the largest bundles of (G, X^A) available to A, given A's budget constraint, when price for G charged to A is P_A^0. Let us explain. Consider any point, say, a, on this horizontal line. Corresponding to this point there is a unique (G, X^A) that satisfies A's budget constraint. It lies on the indifference curve, I_1^A. Take a point vertically below it. Given the budget constraint of A, the (G, X^A) that corresponds to this lower point contains the same amount of G, but a larger amount of X and hence the bundle is larger than the one that corresponds to a, since P_A at the lower point is less than that at a. Obviously, this larger bundle is not available to A when A is charged P_A^0 for G. Thus, the bundles below the horizontal line are not available to A. Now consider any point vertically above a. Such a point corresponds to the same G but a higher P_A. Hence (G, X^A) corresponding to such a point, given A's budget constraint, is smaller than the one that corresponds to a. Clearly, therefore, to the individual A bundles lying above the horizontal line are smaller than those lying on the horizontal line. Thus, when the price of G charged to A is P_A^0, A will choose from this horizontal line and he will choose that bundle, which gives him the highest utility. Thus, A will choose from this line that point, which lies on the lowest indifference curve. The lowest indifference curve that A can attain remaining on this horizontal line is the one, which is tangent to it. This indifference curve is labelled I_A^0. At the point of tangency the slope of the indifference curve is zero and the optimum G, as shown in Figure A.3.1, is G_0. The demand for G of A at P_A^0 is, thus, G_0. Hence (P_A^0, G_0) is a point on G^A, A's demand schedule for G. Repeating this exercise, we get A's demand schedule. Since the higher the indifference curve the less is the value of G at which its slope is zero, A's demand schedule for G is downward sloping.

Let us now focus on B. B's indifference curve is given by the equation

$$\bar{U}^B = U^B(\bar{R} - \bar{R}_A - (1 - P_A)G, G) \tag{A.3.8}$$

Let us examine its shape. Start from a (G, P_A) that satisfy (A.3.8). Consider an increase in G by unity from its given value, with P_A remaining unchanged. It will reduce supply of X to B by $(1 - P_A)$, as B has to pay $(1 - P_A)$ to get the additional unit of G. If the initial level of G is sufficiently small, mrs_{GX} corresponding to the initial (G, P_A) will be larger than $(1 - P_A)$. Hence, following the increase in G by unity, the amount of X that the individual can give up remaining on the same indifference curve as before is larger than the amount of X that B has to give up as B pays the price $(1 - P_A)$. Hence, B will be better off. To keep B on the same indifference curve as before, as B is given the additional unit of G, P_A has to be lowered, so that B has to sacrifice mrs_{GX} amount of X. Thus, the indifference curve in the (G, P_A) plane is downward sloping for sufficiently small values of G. With the rise in G the value of mrs_{GX} will fall and $(1 - P_A)$ will rise reducing the excess of the former over the latter. Hence, the absolute value of the slope of the indifference curve will fall. Eventually, when G is sufficiently large, the two will be equal. At this (G, P_A) the slope of the indifference curve is zero. If G is raised beyond this level, mrs_{GX} will fall below $(1 - P_A)$. In such a situation, to keep B on the same indifference curve as before following a unit increase in G, P_A has to be raised. The indifference curve will be upward sloping for such large values of G. The slope of the indifference curve along this upward sloping portion will be rising with the increase in G. (Explain this point yourself). Thus, the slope of an indifference curve of B rises monotonically with G. Hence, B's indifference curves are convex downward in the (G, P_A) plane as shown in Figure A.3.1. Two more points about the indifference curves of B should be noted. First, the higher an indifference curve of B, the greater is the utility of B it represents. Corresponding to any given G the point on a higher indifference curve has a higher value of P_A and, therefore, a lower value of P_B. Hence, a larger amount of X is available to B with the given level of G at such a point. Hence, a higher indifference curve of B represents a higher level of utility. Second, the point with zero slope corresponds to a higher level of G on a higher indifference curve of B. Let us explain. Consider the point with zero slope on a given indifference curve of B. Take a point vertically above the given point. The higher point lies on a higher indifference curve and contains a higher level of X with the given G. At the higher point $(1 - P_A)$ is less and mrs_{GX} is larger. Hence, the former is less than the latter. At this point, therefore, the higher indifference curve is negatively-sloped. $(1 - P_A)$ and mrs_{GX} will be equal on this higher indifference curve and as a result its slope will be zero at a larger value of G. This is because, with a rise in G from its initial value, $(1 - P_A)$ rises and mrs_{GX} falls.

Let us now derive B's demand curve for G. Consider the horizontal line corresponding to P_A^0. This line gives the largest combinations of X and G available to B, when B is charged $(1 - P_A^0)$ for G. Let us explain. Consider a point above this line. At such a point $P_A > P_A^0$. This means that the (X^B, G), that corresponds to such a point, will be available to B if and only if B is charged a price lower than $(1 - P_A^0)$. This means that the (X^B, G), that corresponds to such a point, is larger than the one that corresponds to the one that is vertically below it on the horizontal line. Thus, the points above the horizontal line are not attainable to B when B is charged $(1 - P_A^0)$. For similar reasons the points below the horizontal line correspond to (X^B, G)

that are smaller than the ones that correspond to the points on the horizontal line. Thus, when the government charges B the price $(1 - P_A^0)$ for G, B will choose a point from the horizontal line corresponding to P_A^0. B will choose that point, which lies on the highest indifference curve. Obviously, that point is the one at which an indifference curve of B is tangent to the horizontal line. Indifference curves of B can be tangent to the horizontal line only at their minimum points. Since the minimum point of a higher indifference curve corresponds to a higher level of G, the demand curve of B is upward sloping.

The equilibrium value of G, as follows from (A.3.6), corresponds to the point of intersection of the demand curves of A and B. This point of intersection is labelled Q in Figure A.3.1, where the equilibrium values of P_A and G are labelled P_A^* and G^* respectively. When the government charges A the price P_A^* and produces G^*, demands for G of both A and B are fully satisfied, i.e., the price charged to each individual is equal to his demand price for G, and the cost of production of G is fully met. The marginal social benefit of G in this situation equals marginal social cost of production of G and social welfare is maximized. Two indifference curves of A and B labelled I_A^* and I_A^* in Figure A.3.1 are tangent to each other at Q.

4 ‖ Efficiency of Taxation

The objectives of this chapter are to

(i) explain the concepts of efficiency of taxation, excess burden and deadweight loss.
(ii) show that both direct and indirect taxes involve excess burden in both partial and general equilibrium frameworks.
(iii) discuss the inefficiency associated with subsidies.
(iv) focus on the issue of compatibility of equity and efficiency in a tax structure.

4.1 INTRODUCTION

The objective of this chapter is to discuss different issues related to tax efficiency. A good tax structure, as we have pointed out already, has to be efficient. How is efficiency of taxation defined? How is it to be measured? What are the major sources of inefficiency in taxation? Which taxes are efficient and which are not? Does there exist any conflict between efficiency and equity in a tax structure? These are the questions that this chapter addresses. Efficiency of taxation, as we shall explain at length shortly, is related to the impact of taxation on individuals' or society's welfare. When taxes conform to the benefit principle, social welfare is maximized. Hence benefit taxes are equitable as well as efficient. However, such taxes, as we have pointed out in the Chapter on Principles of Tax Equity, are infeasible. In fact, most of the feasible taxes lead to inefficiency. Moreover, equity and efficiency of a tax structure in the majority of the cases are incompatible with one another. This chapter seeks to provide an explanation of these phenomena.

4.2 EFFICIENCY OF TAXATION: EXCESS BURDEN AND DEADWEIGHT LOSS

Payment of taxes involves transfer of income from the taxpayers to the government. Obviously, such transfers lead to loss in welfare of the taxpayers. However, this loss is often greater than the minimum amount of loss in welfare that this income transfer entails. *The excess of the loss in welfare due to taxation over and above the minimum is referred to as excess burden or deadweight loss. This excess burden measures the efficiency of taxation.* The larger the excess burden of a tax, the less is its efficiency. We shall explain the concept of excess burden in detail below.

4.2.1 Burden of Taxation

However, before going into the concept of excess burden, let us first explain the concept of the burden of taxation, i.e., the burden that a tax imposes on individuals. Is it measured by the amount of tax the individuals pay to the government? The answer is no. Let us illustrate this with a simple example. Suppose that a tax on a commodity, X, is imposed on a unit basis at the rate, t, on the purchase of X. It means that for every unit of the good purchased the buyers have to pay Rs. t to the government. Suppose that $P_X^D = P(X)$ is the inverse demand function of X in the pre-tax situation. It gives the demand price corresponding to any given quantity of X. Demand price corresponding to any given quantity of X is the maximum price at which the buyers are willing to buy the given quantity. Accordingly, following the imposition of the tax, the demand price of the good falls by Rs. t corresponding to every quantity purchased, as buyers will now have to pay Rs. t to the government as tax for every unit of X purchased. The situation is shown in Figure 4.1, where SS and DD give the initial supply and demand curves of X, while DD' represents the new demand schedule. The vertical distance between DD and DD' is Rs. t. Suppose that, as shown in Figure 4.1, the equilibrium value of X falls to zero following this shift. The new demand schedule, DD', is below the supply schedule SS at every X in Figure 4.1.

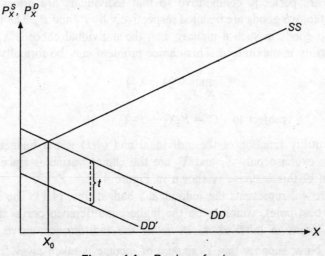

Figure 4.1: Burden of a tax.

Thus the consumers of X evade the tax altogether. Does it mean that the tax has not imposed any burden on them? The answer is obviously no. The consumers now have stopped consuming X, i.e, they have now settled for a different consumption bundle, which they did not choose in the pre-tax situation even though it was available to them then. Clearly, it yields less utility than the one, which they chose in the pre-tax situation. Thus the consumers of X are burdened even though they do not pay any tax. Hence, *the burden of a tax has to be measured in terms of the amount of welfare the individuals lose as a result of the imposition of the tax and not in terms of the amount of tax they actually pay to the government.*

We shall now focus on the concept of excess burden. We shall first examine how excess burden arises in case of an individual, then we shall extend the analysis to the case of the market and finally to that of the community.

4.2.2 Excess Burden and Choice between Goods: Partial Equilibrium Analysis

The Case of an Individual

To examine how excess burden arises in case of an individual we have to first focus on the choice problem that a typical individual solves. She has to decide how much labour to sell in each period, how to allocate her income from the sale of labour between present and future consumption and how to allocate the consumption expenditure of a given period over different kinds of goods and services. Even though all these choice problems are solved simultaneously by the individual, we shall, in what follows, consider them separately one by one for simplicity of exposition.

Allocation of a Given Amount of Consumption Expenditure over Different Goods

Suppose that the individual's given consumption expenditure in a given period is $\bar{C}$, which she allocates between two goods, quantities of which are denoted by X_1 and X_2 respectively. Markets of the two goods are perfectly competitive so that individuals are price takers in both the markets. Prices of the two goods are denoted respectively by P_1 and P_2. The individual allocates $\bar{C}$ between the two goods in such a manner, i.e., the individual chooses X_1 and X_2 in such a manner, that her utility is maximized. This choice problem may be formally stated as follows:

$$\max_{X_1, X_2} U(X_1, X_2)$$

$$\text{subject to} \quad \bar{C} = P_1 X_1 + P_2 X_2 \tag{4.1}$$

where $U(.)$ is the utility function of the individual and (4.1) is her budget constraint. In the above optimization exercise only X_1 and X_2 are the choice variables since prices and $\bar{C}$ are given. The solution of this exercise is shown in Figure 4.2.

$B_1 B_1$ in Figure 4.2 represents the individual's budget line, (4.1). The individual chooses from this line the best point, which is on the highest indifference curve attainable from this budget line. This point is labelled A. It is on the indifference curve I_0. At this point $mrs_{X_1, X_2} = (P_1/P_2)$. Now, suppose that $\bar{T}$ amount of income is taken away from the individual. Alternatively, suppose that a lump sum tax of $\bar{T}$ is imposed on the individual. A lump sum tax on an individual is one which specifies a fixed amount of money to be paid by an individual as tax and this fixed amount is independent of the behaviour of the individual, i.e., it is independent of individual's income, consumption, amounts of different kinds of goods and services purchased or sold etc. Following the imposition of this tax or the loss of $\bar{T}$ amount of income, her budget line is given by $\bar{C} - \bar{T} = P_1 X_1 + P_2 X_2$. This budget line is represented by $B_2 B_2$ in Figure 4.2. It lies below the pre-tax budget line and is parallel to it. The best point to the consumer on this budget line is given by A_1. The highest indifference curve the individual can attain remaining on this budget line is I_1. Thus the individual moves down to a lower indifference curve from I_0 to I_1. This movement from I_0 to I_1 represents the minimum amount of loss in welfare that the individual has to suffer as she parts with $\bar{T}$ amount of income or pays $\bar{T}$ amount of tax to the government. Let us explain. If the individual parts with $\bar{T}$ amount of income, the largest combinations of X_1 and X_2 she can consume are given by the budget line $B_2 B_2$. Bundles those are larger than the ones on $B_2 B_2$ lie above $B_2 B_2$. Value of each such bundle at the given prices exceeds individual's disposable income, $(\bar{C} - \bar{T})$. Hence they are unattainable, given the disposable income of the individual. The point on $B_2 B_2$ that gives the individual the maximum utility, i.e., the point on $B_2 B_2$ that lies on the highest indifference curve of the individual, is A_1. Thus the highest indifference curve that she can attain as she loses $\bar{T}$ amount of income is I_1. Hence, the movement from I_0 to I_1 gives the minimum loss in welfare entailed by $\bar{T}$ amount of tax payment.

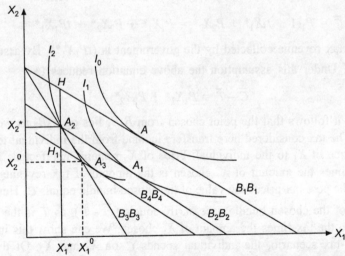

Figure 4.2: Excess burden and individuals' choice over goods.

Excess Burden in Case of a Selective Indirect Tax on a Particular Good

Let us now examine how much welfare the individual will lose if the government takes away from the consumer $\bar{T}$ amount of tax revenue through a selective indirect tax on a good that she consumes. Suppose that the government imposes an ad valorem tax (a tax which is specified as a percentage or proportion of the price) at the rate t on the production of X. This means that, if the producers charge P_1 for X_1, they will have to pay $P_1 t$ as tax to the government. Now P_1

and P_2 denote the supply prices of X_1 and X_2 respectively in the pre-tax situation. The supply price of X_1 in the post-tax situation will be $P_1(1 + t)$, but that of X_2 will remain unchanged. Let us explain. The supply price represents the minimum price at which producers are willing to sell. In the pre-tax situation the minimum price at which producers were willing to sell X_1 was P_1. However, in the post-tax situation the producers have to pay tP_1 as tax for every unit of X_1 produced. Therefore, in the post-tax situation, the minimum price at which they will be willing to supply X_1 to the consumers is $P_1(1 + t)$. This is because if they charge this price to the consumers, they will actually receive P_1. Since no tax is imposed on X_2, its supply price to the consumers remains unaffected. The budget line of the consumer in the post-tax scenario is, therefore, given by

$$\bar{C} = P_1(1 + t)X_1 + P_2X_2 \qquad (4.2)$$

This budget line is represented by B_3B_3 in Figure 4.2. It has the same vertical intercept as the pre-tax budget line, B_1B_1, but the absolute value of its slope is larger. It is given by $[P_1(1 + t)/P_2]$. Hence it is steeper than B_1B_1. We further assume that the government chooses t in such a manner that it collects $\bar{T}$ amount of tax revenue from the individual. From the budget line B_3B_3 the consumer will choose the point A_2, $(X_1{}^*, X_2{}^*)$, at which $mrs_{X_1, X_2} = [P_1(1 + t)/P_2]$. This point lies on the indifference curve I_2, which is tangent to B_3B_3 at A_2. We shall now show that A_2 or $(X_1{}^*, X_2{}^*)$ will necessarily lie on an indifference curve, which is below I_1, i.e., we shall now show that I_2, on which lies A_2, will necessarily be below I_1.

The chosen consumption bundle $(X_1{}^*, X_2{}^*)$ satisfies (4.2). Hence

$$\bar{C} = P_1(1 + t)X_1{}^* + P_2X_2{}^* = P_1X_1{}^* + P_2X_2{}^* + tP_1X_1{}^* \qquad (4.2a)$$

Now, total tax revenue collected by the government is $(tP_1X_1{}^*)$. By assumption t is such that $tP_1X_1{}^* = \bar{T}$. Under this assumption the above equation reduces to

$$\bar{C} - \bar{T} = P_1X_1{}^* + P_2X_2{}^* \qquad (4.3)$$

From (4.3) it follows that the point chosen from B_3B_3 lies on B_2B_2 as well. The reason is not far to seek. The tax considered here transfers income from the individual to the government by raising the price of X_1 to the individual. Price of X_2 remains unaffected. The increment in the price of X_1 times the amount of X_1 chosen is the amount of tax revenue collected by the government. At the post-tax prices the value of the chosen bundle equals $\bar{C}$. Hence at the pre-tax prices the value of the chosen bundle necessarily equals $(\bar{C} - \bar{T})$, as $\bar{T}$ is the increment in the price of X_1 due to the tax times the amount of X_1 chosen. We can show this in a different way also. In the post-tax scenario, the individual spends $\bar{C}$ on X_1 and X_2. Of this $\bar{C}$ amount of expenditure the government gets $\bar{T}$. Obviously, the rest, $(\bar{C} - \bar{T})$, goes to the producers. The producers get the value of the chosen bundle evaluated at the prices they actually receive. These prices are nothing but the pre-tax prices of X_1 and X_2. The value of the chosen bundle at pre-tax prices is, therefore, necessarily equal to $(\bar{C} - \bar{T})$. Thus the chosen bundle will necessarily lie on the budget line, which obtains when prices equal the pre-tax prices and the individual's money income equals $(\bar{C} - \bar{T})$. In other words, the chosen bundle will necessarily lie on the lump sum tax budget line B_2B_2 in Figure 4.2. However, the chosen bundle is not the best bundle on B_2B_2. It is the optimum or best bundle on B_3B_3. Hence marginal rate of substitution corresponding to this bundle equals the absolute value of the slope of B_3B_3, $[P_1(1 + t)/P_2]$. The marginal rate of substitution of the optimum or best bundle on B_2B_2 equals (P_1/P_2). Thus, the bundle chosen by the individual from B_2B_2 under the selective indirect tax is necessarily inferior to the best point on B_2B_2. Hence the bundle chosen by the consumer when the government collects a given amount of tax revenue from the individual by imposing a selective indirect tax on a particular good is necessarily inferior to the bundle, which the individual would have chosen in the pre-tax situation if his income were simply less by the amount of the given tax revenue. Thus, *a selective indirect tax on a particular commodity leads to a larger than the minimum amount of loss in individual's welfare entailed by the transfer of the tax revenue from the individual to the government. In other words such a tax involves excess burden.* The amount of excess burden or deadweight loss in this case is given by the individual's movement from I_1 to I_2.

We can also impute a value to this excess burden by means of what is called *equivalent variation*. This equivalent variation is given by the amount of change in income that will make the individual choose from the selective indirect tax indifference curve, I_2, at pre-tax prices in the absence of any kind of taxation. It is clear from Figure 4.2 that, if the individual is on the budget line B_4B_4 in the absence of taxation, she will choose from I_2. Note that B_4B_4 corresponds to pre-tax prices. Hence it is parallel to the pre-tax budget line B_2B_2. Vertical distance between the two will, therefore, be the same corresponding to every X_1. Vertical distance between the two at X_1^* is HH_1. This means that the income corresponding to B_4B_4 is such that she is able to purchase with X_1^* only $X_1^*H_1$ amount of X_2, which is less than the amount of X_2 she could purchase with her pre-tax income along with X_1^* in the absence of taxation by HH_1. Her pre-tax income in terms of X_2 is $(\overline{C}/P_2)$. Hence she will be on B_4B_4 in the absence of taxation, if her income in terms of X_2 is reduced by HH_1, i.e., if her income in terms of money is reduced from $\overline{C}$ by $(HH_1) P_2$. Again, under the selective indirect tax considered here, when the individual chooses $A_2(X_1^*, X_2^*)$ from I_2, she pays a tax of HA_2 in terms of X_2. This is because under this selective indirect tax she is spending the same $\overline{C}$ amount as before, but this expenditure enables her to purchase with X_1^* amount of X_1 an amount of X_2 which is less than what she could purchase in the absence of taxation by HA_2. The producers are receiving the same prices for X_1 and X_2 as before. The producers are, therefore, getting only the money value of (X_1^*, X_2^*) evaluated at pre-tax prices. This value is clearly less than $\overline{C}$ by the money value of HA_2, which is given by $[(HA_2) P_2]$. Therefore, $[(HA_2) P_2]$ is going to the government as tax from $\overline{C}$, as the individual chooses A_2. From the above it follows that the reduction in income in terms of X_2 that is required in the pre-tax situation to lower the individual's welfare to the level attained under the selective indirect tax is HH_1. It is larger than the tax revenue in terms of X_2 yielded by the selective indirect tax, which is HA_2. The excess of the former over the latter may, therefore, be regarded as a measure of the excess burden. Thus excess burden in terms of X_2 is given by $(HH_1 - HA_2)$. In terms of money it is given by $[P_2 (HH_1 - HA_2)]$. (Work out Problem 3 in this context.)

Let us now explain why the amount of reduction in consumer's income required to make her choose from I_2 in the absence of taxation is larger than the tax revenue yielded by the selective indirect tax. This is because the least cost bundle on I_2 at the pre-tax prices is not A_2, it is the one at which $mrs_{X_1,X_2} = (P_1/P_2)$ whereas at A_2 $mrs_{X_1,X_2} = [P_1(1 + t)/P_2] > (P_1/P_2)$. If from A_2 the consumer raises her consumption of X_1 by one unit, she can give up $mrs_{X_1,X_2}(A_2) = [P_1(1 + t)/P_2]$ amount of X_2 and still remain on I_2, when $mrs_{X_1,X_2} (A_2)$ denotes marginal rate of substitution of X_1 for X_2 at the point A_2. However, to purchase one additional unit of X_1 the amount of X_2 she will have to give up at the pre-tax prices keeping her total expenditure on X_1 and X_2 unchanged is (P_1/P_2). This is because, if the consumer purchases one additional unit of X_1, her expenditure will go up by P_1. Therefore, to keep her total expenditure on X_1 and X_2 unchanged, she will have to reduce purchase of X_2 by such an amount that her expenditure falls by P_1. P_1 amount of money can purchase (P_1/P_2) amount of X_2. So, if the consumer reduces X_2 by (P_1/P_2), her expenditure will go down by P_1 to its initial level. Now, $(P_1/P_2) <$ $[P_1(1 + t)/P_2]$. Therefore, if from A_2 she raises her consumption of X_1 by one unit and lowers purchase of X_2 by $[P_1(1 + t)/P_2]$ to remain on I_2, her expenditure level will go down from its initial level. It will go down by $P_2[P_1(1 + t)/P_2] - P_2(P_1/P_2) = P_2[mrs_{X_1,X_2} (A_2)] - P_2(P_1/P_2)$. Thus, if at any point on I_2 $mrs_{X_1,X_2} > (<) (P_1/P_2)$, the cost of attaining I_2 at pre-tax prices can be reduced by $P_2(mrs_{X_1,X_2}) - P_2(P_1/P_2)$ by raising (lowering) X_1 by 1 unit and lowering (raising) X_2 by mrs_{X_1,X_2}. Therefore, at the pre-tax prices the least cost bundle on I_2 is the one at which $mrs_{X_1,X_2} = (P_1/P_2)$. The value of this least cost bundle at the pre-tax prices, which we denote by Y, is the minimum income that allows the individual to attain I_2 in the pre-tax situation. In other words, in the absence of any kind of taxation, the individual's income has to be reduced by $(\bar{C} - Y)$ to make her choose from I_2. In terms of Figure 4.1, $(\bar{C} - Y) = P_2.HH_1$. Clearly, Y is less than the value of A_2 at the pre-tax prices, which are the prices received by the producers under the selective indirect tax. Let us denote the value of A_2 at the pre-tax prices by Y_1. Since under the selective indirect tax the individual spends $\bar{C}$ on X_1 and X_2, while the producers receive Y_1, $(\bar{C} - Y_1)$ is the tax revenue yielded by the selective indirect tax as the individual chooses A_2. In terms of Figure 4.1 $(\bar{C} - Y_1) = P_2.HA_2$. Now, $(\bar{C} - Y) > (\bar{C} - Y_1)$, since $Y < Y_1$. The magnitude of excess burden is therefore given by $(\bar{C} - Y) - (\bar{C} - Y_1) = P_2.HH_1 - P_2.HA_2$ $= P_2(H_1A_2)$. It also follows from the above that in terms of Figure 4.2 the excess burden is measured by the sum of the excess of $P_2(mrs_{X_1,X_2})$ over $P_2(P_1/P_2) = P_1$ corresponding to every point on the stretch A_2A_3 of I_2. This sum should equal $P_2(H_1A_2)$.

The cause of the excess burden is not far to seek. The selective indirect tax incorporates a distortion in the price system, it raises the price of X_1 in terms of X_2 above its actual price as charged by the producers. Thus, not only does the selective indirect tax transfer $\bar{T}$ amount of tax revenue from the taxpayer to the government, it also makes X_1 dearer in terms of X_2 to the consumer than what it actually is. Thus, *in addition to the income effect due to the loss of $\bar{T}$ amount of consumer's income* indicated in Figure 4.2 by the movement from A to A_1, *the selective indirect tax also produces a substitution effect. The latter is due to the rise in the price of X_1 in terms of X_2 above what is charged by the producers.* This substitution effect is given by the movement from A_1 to A_2 in Figure 4.2. At the chosen points A_2 and A_1 the real income of the consumer, a la Slutsky, is the same, only price ratios faced by the consumer are different. Clearly, *this substitution effect is at the root of the excess burden and the larger this substitution effect, the greater is the excess burden.*

The Case of the Market

Here we focus on the market of a single commodity X and examine how a selective indirect tax on the purchase or sale of this commodity leads to excess burden in the context of this market. We assume that the market is perfectly competitive. We shall carry out our analysis in terms of Figure 4.3 where price of X, denoted by P_X, is measured on the vertical axis and quantities demanded and supplied of X are measured on the horizontal axis. DD and SS represent demand and supply schedules of X respectively in the pre-tax scenario. The marginal private and social costs of production of X are taken to be the same and constant for simplicity. Hence the SS schedule, which gives the marginal private cost of production corresponding to every level of supply of X, is horizontal. DD and SS intersect at (X_0, P_X^0). The consumers in equilibrium buy X_0 amount of X at the price P_X^0 and thereby pay an amount, which is given by the area of the rectangle $OP_X^0BX_0$. However, for having X_0 amount of X the maximum amount that the consumers are willing to sacrifice, as we have pointed out in the Appendix of Chapter 2, is given by the area of the quadrilateral $OA\,B\,X_0$. Thus the consumers enjoy a consumer surplus, which is given by the area of the triangle $A\,P_X^0\,B$. (See Appendix of Chapter 2 for a discussion on consumer surplus). Consumer surplus is used as a measure of consumer welfare.

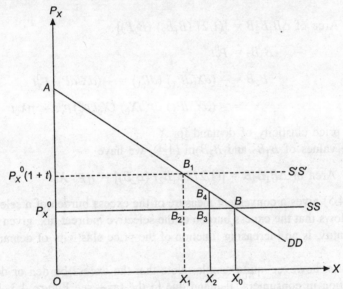

Figure 4.3:   Excess burden of a selective indirect tax: the case of the market.

We shall now examine how a selective indirect tax on the production or sales of X affects consumer welfare as measured by the consumer surplus. Suppose that a selective ad valorem indirect tax at the percentage rate t is imposed on the production or sales of X. Since by assumption the marginal private and social cost of production in the pre-tax scenario is P_X^0, it is the minimum price at which X will be supplied to the consumers in a perfectly competitive market in the absence of any tax. Hence, in the pre-tax scenario the supply price of X is P_X^0. Following the imposition of the tax, the sellers have to pay a tax of (tP_X^0) to the government per unit of X produced or sold. Hence, the minimum price at which they will offer X in the post-tax scenario to the buyers is $P_X^0 + (tP_X^0) = P_X^0(1 + t)$ as the tax raises marginal private cost of production and sale of X to $P_X^0(1 + t)$. The supply schedule of X, which shows the supply price of X to the buyers at every level of X will, therefore, shift upward by (tP_X^0). $S'S'$ is the new supply schedule in Figure 4.3. The demand schedule DD remains unaffected, as the tax does not have any direct impact on the consumers. The post-tax equilibrium corresponds to the point of intersection of DD and $S'S'$. In the post-tax equilibrium, therefore, consumers pay the price $P_X^0(1 + t)$ and buy X_1 amount of X. For every unit of X purchased consumers now pay $(P_X^0 t)$ amount of tax. The total amount of tax they pay to the government via the producers is given by $(X_1 P_X^0 t)$, which is equal to the area of the rectangle $P_X^0 P_X^0(1 + t)B_1B_2$. However, consumers' loss in welfare due to the tax is measured by the amount of decline in consumer surplus. This is given by the area of the quadrilateral $P_X^0 P_X^0(1 + t)B_1B$, which is larger than the amount of tax revenue collected by the government by the area of the triangle B_1B_2B. This excess of loss in consumers' welfare over the amount of tax revenue collected by the government is the excess burden or the deadweight loss, since this excess loss in consumer's welfare is not converted into any gain to the government.

The amount of excess burden or deadweight loss is given by the area of the triangle B_1B_2B. Now,

$$\text{Area of } \Delta B_1B_2B = [(1/2)\,(B_1B_2)\,(B_2B)] \tag{4.4}$$

However,

$$B_1B_2 = P_X^0 t$$

and

$$B_2B = -\,(dX/dP_X)\,(dP_X) = -\,(dX/dP_X)\,P_X^0 t$$

$$= -\,(dX/dP_X)\,(P_X^0/X_0)\,(X_0/P_X^0)\,P_X^0 t = \eta X_0 t$$

where $\eta \equiv$ own price elasticity of demand for X.

Putting the values of B_1B_2 and B_2B in (4.4), we have

$$\text{Area of } \Delta B_1B_2B = [(1/2)\,(B_1B_2)\,(B_2B)] = \eta P_X^0 X_0 t^2 \tag{4.5}$$

Equation (4.5) gives a convenient measure of the excess burden of a selective indirect tax. From (4.5) it follows that the excess burden of the selective indirect tax, given the pre-tax levels of price and quantity, is an increasing function of the price elasticity of demand, η, and the tax rate, t.

The reason is, however, quite simple. Note that the excess burden or deadweight loss is due to the reduction in consumers' demand due to the tax—see Figure 4.3. For every unit of X the consumers cease to buy following the imposition of tax, they lose some consumer surplus. Consider the X_2th unit in Figure 4.2. Following the imposition of the tax, consumers stop buying this unit. As a result they lose the consumer surplus B_3B_4. However, they do not pay any tax on the X_2th unit of X either. They pay tax only on those units of X that they buy. Thus, this loss in consumer surplus of B_3B_4 does not accrue as gain or additional tax revenue to the government. It is just a deadweight loss. This is true of every unit of X that the consumers cease to purchase following the imposition of the tax. In terms of Figure 4.2 this is true of every unit of X lying between X_0 and X_1. Clearly, therefore, the larger the number of units the consumers cease to purchase following the imposition of the tax, the greater is the deadweight loss or excess burden. Given everything else, the higher the value of t, the greater is the rise in the price of X faced by the buyers. Hence the larger is the reduction in the demand for X, i.e., the larger is the number of units the consumers cease to buy, given η and other factors. Again, given t and other factors, the greater the own price elasticity of demand for X, the larger is the fall in demand for X following the rise in the supply price of X to the buyers due to the tax. Hence, excess burden or deadweight loss is an increasing function of, among others, η and t.

4.2.3 Excess Burden and Choice between Goods: General Equilibrium Analysis

The Case of the Community

Let us now consider the general equilibrium framework to examine the issue of excess burden of a selective indirect tax. We develop here a very simple general equilibrium model to capture the major forces that emerge, when we extend our partial equilibrium analysis to the case of the general equilibrium. This simple model suffices for our purpose. We assume that only two goods, X_1 and X_2, are produced in the economy with two inputs, labour and capital. Endowments of labour and capital in the economy are fixed. To simplify our analysis we assume that there are a large number of identical firms and each firm produces X_1 and X_2 with fixed endowments of labour and capital supplied by their owners. There are also a large number of identical individuals. Since firms and individuals are identical, we shall carry out our analysis in terms of a representative individual and a representative firm only. The representative firm, as we have mentioned above, produces two goods X_1 and X_2 with fixed endowments of labour and capital. The production possibility frontier (*PPF*) of the representative firm is given by

$$X_2 = F(X_1); \ F' < 0, \ F'' < 0 \tag{4.6}$$

In this simple economy only X_1 and X_2 are traded and they are traded in perfectly competitive markets. Thus individuals and firms are price takers in both the markets. We denote prices of X_1 and X_2 by P_1 and P_2 respectively. The firm maximizes profit, which is given by

$$\Pi = P_1X_1 + P_2X_2 - A \tag{4.7}$$

where $\Pi \equiv$ profit and $A \equiv$ the fixed cost consisting of the depreciation of the given capital stock of the firm. Substituting (4.6) into (4.7), we can write the profit maximization exercise of the firm as

$$\max_{X_1} \Pi = P_1X_1 + P_2F(X_1) - A \tag{4.8}$$

The FOC for profit maximization is given by

$$-F'(X_1) = \frac{P_1}{P_2} \tag{4.9}$$

Equation (4.9) states that at the profit maximizing (X_1, X_2) the absolute value of the slope of the *PPF*, which gives the marginal rate of transformation of X_1 for X_2 equals the price of X_1 in terms of X_2. This situation is shown in Figure 4.4 where the concave schedule is the production possibility frontier. It is labelled *PPF*. The profit maximizing point on this *PPF* is $A(X_1^0, X_2^0)$, at which the absolute value of the slope of the *PPF* is equal to the given price ratio, (P_1/P_2). Mathematically, we can solve (4.9) for the profit maximizing value of X_1. Putting this value of X_1 in (4.6), we get the profit maximizing value of X_2.

The firm has a large number of owners who supply the given capital and labour. The whole value of the output of the firm, given by $P_1X_1^0 + P_2X_2^0$, accordingly gets distributed among them as profit. Thus the representative individual gets the whole value of output as factor income. It should be noted here that these assumptions are all simplifying ones. They are made only for expository reasons. Results derived here will hold even if we replace these assumptions with more realistic ones. The budget line of the representative individual is, therefore, given by

$$P_1 X_1^0 + P_2 X_2^0 = P_1 X_1 + P_2 X_2 \qquad (4.10)$$

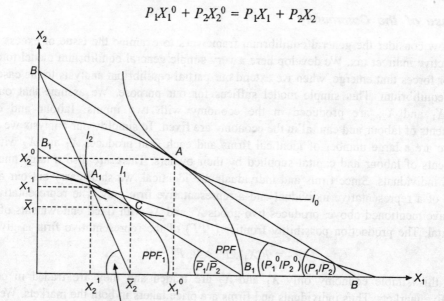

Figure 4.4: Excess burden of a selective indirect tax: general equilibrium.

Clearly, this budget line, labelled BB in Figure 4.4, will pass through A, as (X_1^0, X_2^0) satisfies (4.10) and has (P_1/P_2) as the absolute value of its slope. The individual can choose any point from this budget line. If she chooses any point other than (X_1^0, X_2^0), the economy is not in equilibrium as demand and supply of X_1 and X_2 do not match. Hence prices will change. However, if she chooses (X_1^0, X_2^0), markets for both the goods and, therefore, the economy will be in equilibrium. This equilibrium situation is shown in Figure 4.4. I_0 is the highest indifference curve the individual can attain from BB. We are now in a position to incorporate taxes and to examine how excess burden arises in the general equilibrium framework.

Lump Sum Tax

Let us first introduce a lump sum tax. The impact of a tax in the general equilibrium framework depends crucially on how the government uses the tax proceeds. Here, we assume for simplicity that the government uses the tax proceeds to purchase per force given quantities of K and L at some given prices fixed by itself to produce another good, Z, in a given quantity, $\overline{Z}$. We further assume, again for simplicity, that the cost of the quantities of K and L purchased by the government is $\overline{T}$, which the government collects as lump sum tax from the individual. One implication of the above assumptions is that the PPF involving only X_1 and X_2 in the post-tax scenario will lie below the pre-tax PPF, as the representative firm in the post-tax scenario produces X_1 and X_2 with smaller endowments of labour and capital. This PPF is labelled PPF_1 in Figure 4.4.

As we have explained earlier, the firm will produce from the new PPF, PPF_1, the profit maximizing (X_1, X_2) at which marginal rate of transformation of X_1 for X_2 $(mrtr_{X_1, X_2})$ equals the market price of X_1 in terms of X_2. Suppose that prices of X_1 and X_2 prevailing in the market are $\bar{P}_1$ and $\bar{P}_2$ respectively. At these prices, as shown in Figure 4.4, the firm will produce the output combination, $(\bar{X}_1, \bar{X}_2)$, at which $mrtr_{X_1, X_2} = (\bar{P}_1/\bar{P}_2)$. This output combination is labelled C in Figure 4.4. The whole value of output of the firm as before goes into the hands of the individuals or the owners of the firm as factor income. They also get $\bar{T}$ as factor income from the government. However, they have to pay out $\bar{T}$ as tax as well. Hence the representative individual's disposable income as the firm produces C from PPF_1 is given by $(\bar{P}_1\bar{X}_1 + \bar{P}_2\bar{X}_2)$. Accordingly, her budget constraint is given by

$$\bar{P}_1\bar{X}_1 + \bar{P}_2\bar{X}_2 = \bar{P}_1X_1 + \bar{P}_2X_2 \tag{4.11}$$

It is represented by the line B_1B_1 in the Figure. It passes through the point $(\bar{X}_1, \bar{X}_2)$ and the absolute value of its slope is $(\bar{P}_1/\bar{P}_2)$. If the individual chooses $(\bar{X}_1, \bar{X}_2)$ from her budget line, the economy, as we have explained already, will be in equilibrium. We assume that the individual chooses $(\bar{X}_1, \bar{X}_2)$ from B_1B_1. The indifference curve passing through $(\bar{X}_1, \bar{X}_2)$ and, therefore, tangent to B_1B_1 is labelled I_1. The loss in utility due to the lump sum tax is, therefore, indicated by the movement from I_0 to I_1 in Figure 4.4. In what follows we shall explain that this is the minimum amount of loss in welfare suffered by the individual as $\bar{T}$ amount of tax is taken away from her.

PPF_1 gives the largest bundles of X_1 and X_2 that can be produced in the economy, when the government takes away capital and labour worth $\bar{T}$ to produce $\bar{Z}$ amount of Z. I_1 is the highest indifference curve on PPF_1. Hence the loss in utility indicated by the movement from I_0 to I_1 due to the payment of $\bar{T}$ amount of tax is minimum. Thus, lump sum tax does not involve any excess burden. Let us now consider the case of a selective indirect tax.

Selective Indirect Tax

Suppose that the government imposes a selective indirect tax on the production or sales of X_1 at the rate t on an ad valorem basis. To make the present case comparable to the earlier one it is assumed that the government chooses t in such a manner that it is able to purchase the same given amounts of capital and labour at the same prices as before and produce $\bar{Z}$ amount of Z. In other words, the government chooses t in such a manner that the selective indirect tax yields $\bar{T}$ in tax revenue. The implication of this assumption is that production in the post-tax equilibrium in the present case will take place on the same PPF, PPF_1 in Figure 4.4, as that in the earlier case of the lump sum tax. Moreover, under the present tax regime if the producers actually receive prices P_1 and P_2 for X_1 and X_2 respectively after paying the tax, they have charged to consumers $P_1(1 + t)$ and P_2, as they have to pay tP_1 as tax per unit of X_1 produced or sold. Now, suppose that in the post-tax equilibrium in the present case prices actually received by the producers for X_1 and X_2 after paying the tax are P_1^0 and P_2^0 respectively. Accordingly, individuals face the prices P_1^0 (1 + t) and P_2^0. Thus the tax makes the prices of X_1 as faced by the consumers and producers different. The representative firm in the post-tax equilibrium will produce from the new PPF that (X_1, X_2) at which $mrtr_{X_1, X_2} = (P_1^0/P_2^0)$. This (X_1, X_2) is labelled (X_1^1, X_2^1) in Figure 4.4. Total revenue and profit earned by the representative firm is, therefore, $(P_1^0 X_1^1 + P_2^0 X_2^1)$. The whole of it the firm distributes among its owners. The representative individual, therefore, earns the whole of it as profit or factor income. Besides this, she also gets $\bar{T}$ from the government in return for her sale of labour and capital services. However, the representative individual has to purchase X_1 and X_2 from the market at prices $P_1(1 + t)$ and P_2 respectively. The budget line of the representative individual in equilibrium is, therefore, given by

$$(P_1^0 X_1^1 + P_2^0 X_2^1) + \bar{T} = [P_1^0 (1 + t)X_1] + (P_2^0 X_2) \tag{4.12}$$

In equilibrium in the post-tax scenario, (X_1^1, X_2^1) is produced. Hence, (X_1^1, X_2^1) is also consumed by the representative individual. Therefore, the amount of tax collected by the government is $P_1^0 t X_1^1$ and, as you should be able to recall, in equilibrium t by assumption is such that

$$P_1^0 t X_1^1 = \bar{T} \tag{4.13}$$

If we substitute (4.13) into (4.12), the budget line of the consumer reduces to the following:

$$[P_1^0(1 + t)X_1^1 + P_2^0 X_2^1] = [P_1^0(1 + t)X_1] + (P_2^0 X_2)$$

This equation shows that budget line in equilibrium will pass through (X_1^1, X_2^1), as (X_1^1, X_2^1) satisfies the above equation and the absolute value of its slope will be $[P_1^0(1 + t)/P_2^0]$. This budget line is labelled $B\bar{X}_2$ in Figure 4.4. (Note that the equal vertical intercepts of this budget line and the pre-tax budget line in Figure 4.4 are just an accident). The representative individual chooses (X_1^1, X_2^1) from this budget line. It is obviously the best point on this budget line. Hence, at this point $mrs_{X_1, X_2} = [P_1^0(1 + t)/P_2^0]$. (X_1^1, X_2^1) on the other hand is the profit maximizing (X_1, X_2) on the new PPF, PPF_1, at the producers' prices (P_1^0, P_2^0). At (X_1^1, X_2^1), therefore, $mrtr_{X_1, X_2} = (P_1^0/P_2^0)$. At (X_1^1, X_2^1), therefore, $mrs_{X_1, X_2} > mrtr_{X_1, X_2}$. The situation is shown in Figure 4.4. Clearly, (X_1^1, X_2^1) is not the best point on the new PPF, PPF_1. At the best (X_1, X_2) on PPF_1 $mrs_{X_1, X_2} = mrtr_{X_1, X_2}$. (Explain why any point on PPF at which $mrs_{X_1, X_2} \neq mrtr_{X_1, X_2}$ is not the best point on the PPF). This best point is given by $(\bar{X}_1, \bar{X}_2)$ in Figure 4.4. Equilibrium occurs at this point, as we have seen earlier, in the lump sum tax case. Thus selective indirect tax involves excess burden. The excess burden is indicated by the movement from I_1 to I_2. Obviously, the cause of this excess burden is the distortion in the price system brought about by the selective indirect tax. It drives a wedge between the prices faced by the producers and consumers. Producers produce that bundle at which $mrtr_{X_1, X_2}$ equals the relative price of X_1 they face, while consumers choose that bundle at which mrs_{X_1, X_2} equals the relative price of X_1 they face. Accordingly, in equilibrium at the commodity bundle that is produced and consumed mrs_{X_1, X_2} and $mrtr_{X_1, X_2}$ become different generating excess burden.

Direct Tax and Excess Burden

One should note here that a direct tax in the present case does not involve excess burden. The only direct tax that can be considered in the context of the present choice problem is a consumption tax. A consumption tax can be levied in two ways: by taxing the consumption expenditures of the consumers directly on a personalized basis or by taxing the sales of all consumer goods at the same ad valorem rate. In both the cases, no excess burden arises. We shall show this below.

Partial Equilibrium Analysis: The Case of the Individual

Let us first consider the case of an individual. Suppose that her consumption expenditure is taxed at the rate t so that it yields the tax revenue, $\bar{T}$. The budget line in this case, as follows from (4.1), reduces to

$$\bar{C}(1-t) = (\bar{C} - \bar{T}) = (P_1 X_1 + P_2 X_2) \tag{4.14}$$

This is the same as the lump sum tax budget line, $B_2 B_2$, as shown in Figure 4.2. $B_2 B_2$ or (4.14) in the present case represents the set of largest bundles of X_1 and X_2 available to the individual following her loss of $\bar{T}$ amount of income to the government. She will also choose from this budget line the point at which $mrs_{X_1, X_2} = (P_1/P_2)$, since the absolute value of the slope of her budget line is (P_1/P_2). It is the best point on the budget line. Hence this tax does not give rise to any excess burden.

If, however, both the goods are taxed at the same ad valorem rate, t, consumer's budget line becomes

$$\bar{C} = [P_1(1 + t)X_1] + [P_2(1 + t)X_2]$$

$$\Rightarrow \qquad \frac{\bar{C}}{(1+t)} = (P_1 X_1 + P_2 X_2) \tag{4.14a}$$

This budget line is clearly parallel to the one given by (4.1) and the lump sum tax budget line, $B_2 B_2$, as shown in Figure 4.2. Here also the government chooses t in such a manner that it yields $\bar{T}$ amount of tax revenue to the government. Suppose that at the appropriate t, which yields $\bar{T}$ amount of tax revenue to the government, the consumer chooses (X_1^0, X_2^0). It satisfies (4.14a). Thus

$$\bar{C} = [P_1(1 + t)X_1^0] + [P_2(1 + t)X_2^0] = (P_1 X_1^0 + P_2 X_2^0) + (P_1 t X_1^0 + P_2 t X_2^0)$$

$$= (P_1 X_1^0 + P_2 X_2^0) + \bar{T}$$

$$\Rightarrow \qquad \bar{C} - \bar{T} = (P_1 X_1^0 + P_2 X_2^0)$$

From the above equation it follows that (X_1^0, X_2^0) is a point not only on the budget line representing (4.14a) but also on the lump sum tax budget line, $B_2 B_2$, which is parallel to the budget line representing (4.14a). This is possible if both the budget lines coincide with each other. Therefore, in this case also the individual chooses from the lump sum tax budget line and she chooses its best point at which $mrs_{X_1, X_2} = (P_1/P_2)$. Thus, this tax also does not involve any excess burden.

General Equilibrium Analysis

To compare the present case to those of the lump sum tax and the selective indirect tax we assume that the government through the tax purchases by assumption the same amount of capital and labour as in the cases of the other two taxes to produce $\overline{Z}$ amount of Z. The cost of the services of capital and labour purchased is also as before taken to be equal to $\overline{T}$. Therefore, the representative producer even under the present tax will produce from the production possibility frontier, PPF_1, as shown in Figure 4.4. Suppose that the government taxes consumption expenditure of the individuals by taxing the purchases of X_1 and X_2 at the same ad valorem rate, t. Moreover, t is chosen in such a manner that the government in equilibrium collects $\overline{T}$ amount of tax revenue. Suppose that in the post-tax equilibrium $(\overline{P}_1, \overline{P}_2)$ prevail in the market and the producer produces $(\overline{X}_1, \overline{X}_2)$ at which $mrtr_{X_1, X_{21}} = (\overline{P}_1/\overline{P}_2)$. Then the budget line in equilibrium of the representative individual, as we shall explain below, is given by

$$(\overline{P}_1 \overline{X}_1 + \overline{P}_2 \overline{X}_2) + \overline{T} = [\overline{P}_1(1+t)X_1] + [\overline{P}_2(1+t)X_2] \tag{4.15}$$

The LHS gives individuals' income. The whole value of the output, $(\overline{X}_1, \overline{X}_2)$, evaluated at producers' or market prices, $(\overline{P}_1, \overline{P}_2)$, accrues to the individuals, who are the owners of the firms, as profit. In addition they get $\overline{T}$ amount of factor income from the government. These two components constitute the representative individuals' income. The RHS gives the representative individual's expenditure on X_1 and X_2 evaluated at the prices faced by the individuals. (As they purchase X_1 and X_2 at prices $\overline{P}_1$ and $\overline{P}_2$ respectively, they have to pay a tax of $\overline{P}_1 t$ and $\overline{P}_2 t$ per unit of X_1 and X_2 purchased. Hence effectively prices of X_1 and X_2 faced by the individuals are $\overline{P}_1(1 + t)$ and $\overline{P}_2(1 + t)$ respectively). Hence the two sides should be equal.

Clearly, at the optimum bundle chosen from this budget line $mrs_{X_1, X_2} = (\overline{P}_1/\overline{P}_2)$, since the absolute value of the slope of the budget line equals $(\overline{P}_1/\overline{P}_2)$. In equilibrium, therefore, at the individual's chosen optimum point, which is $(\overline{X}_1, \overline{X}_2)$, $mrs_{X_1, X_2} = mrtr_{X_1, X_2} = (\overline{P}_1/\overline{P}_2)$. Therefore, the optimum point chosen is the best point on PPF_1. (Note that the budget line in equilibrium will pass through $(\overline{X}_1, \overline{X}_2)$, since t by assumption is chosen in such a way that $[t\overline{P}_1\overline{X}_1 + t\overline{P}_2\overline{X}_2] = \overline{T}$ and, therefore, $(\overline{X}_1, \overline{X}_2)$ satisfy (4.15). Moreover, the absolute value of the slope of the budget line is $(\overline{P}_1/\overline{P}_2)$. Thus, the budget line of the representative individual in equilibrium is tangent to PPF_1 at $(\overline{X}_1, \overline{X}_2)$, since at $(\overline{X}_1, \overline{X}_2)$ $mrtr_{X_1, X_2} = (\overline{P}_1/\overline{P}_2)$. It, therefore, coincides with the representative individual's budget line in the lump sum tax case). Hence there is no excess burden. This is the case, as one can easily show, even when the tax is imposed on the consumption expenditure on a personal basis. (Do this yourself. *Hint:* In this case the tax is on consumption expenditure, $P_1X_1 + P_2X_2$. Hence the budget line in equilibrium of the representative individual is given by $(\overline{P}_1\overline{X}_1 + \overline{P}_2\overline{X}_2) + \overline{T} = (\overline{P}_1X_1 + \overline{P}_2X_2)(1+t)$, where t is the rate at which the consumption tax is imposed. This equation is the same as (4.15). The rest of the analysis is exactly the same as that of the case discussed here). Thus direct taxes in the context of the present choice problem do not involve any excess burden. However, as we shall presently show, they do give rise to excess burden in the case of other choice problems of the individuals.

4.2.4 Excess Burden and Choice between Income and Leisure: Partial Equilibrium Analysis

The Case of an Individual

Here we shall focus on the individuals' problem of choice between income and leisure in isolation. An individual has a given endowment of time or labour in any given period. In a day, for example, an individual has 24 hours. In a month an individual has 720 hours etc. The individual has to decide how to allocate the given time or labour endowment between work or earning income and leisure. Obviously, individuals do this allocation in such a manner that their utility is maximized. More precisely, the individual resolves the choice problem carrying out the following optimization exercise:

$$\max_{y,l} \ U(y, l)$$

$$\text{subject to} \quad y = W(\bar{L} - l) \tag{4.16}$$

where $U(.) \equiv$ utility function of the individual, $y \equiv$ income, $l \equiv$ leisure, $W \equiv$ real wage rate and $\bar{L} \equiv$ fixed labour endowment of the individual. The solution of the above optimization exercise is shown graphically in Figure 4.5 where y and l are measured on the vertical and horizontal axes respectively. BB is the individual's budget line as given by (4.16). Its intercepts on the vertical and horizontal axes are $(W\bar{L})$ and $\bar{L}$ respectively. The absolute value of its slope is W. The individual's optimum point on this budget line lies on the highest indifference curve attainable. The highest indifference curve is the one, which is tangent to the budget line, BB. The optimum point is given by the point of tangency. This point is labelled A. It lies on the indifference curve, I_0. At the optimum point $mrs_{l,y} = W$ (Explain the economic reason.)

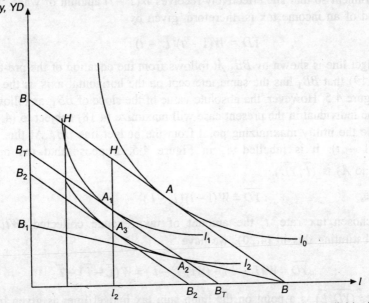

Figure 4.5: Excess burden of a tax on wage income of an individual.

Lump Sum Tax

Now, suppose that a lump sum tax of $\overline{T}$ is imposed on the individual. As a result the individual's budget constraint reduces to

$$YD = W(\overline{L} - l) - \overline{T} \tag{4.17}$$

where $YD \equiv$ disposable income. In the post-tax regime, the individual gets to keep only YD and not Y. Hence the utility function of the individual in the post-tax scenario is given by

$$U(YD, l) \tag{4.18}$$

Under the lump sum tax the individual maximizes (4.18) subject to (4.17). The budget line, (4.17), is represented by $B_T B_T$ in Figure 4.5. It is parallel to BB, but its vertical intercept is less by $\overline{T}$. It gives the largest combinations of YD and l that the individual can choose from, if she loses $\overline{T}$ amount of income, and she chooses the best of these combinations at which $mrs_{l,YD}$ = the absolute value of the slope of the budget line, W. This combination is labelled A_1 in Figure 4.5. It lies on the indifference curve I_1, which is the highest attainable on $B_T B_T$. Thus the movement from I_0 to I_1 indicates the minimum loss in utility that the individual has to suffer if she pays out $\overline{T}$ amount of income as tax. Thus the lump sum tax does not involve any excess burden.

Tax on Wage Income

Let us now suppose that the government imposes a proportional income tax at the rate, t, on wage income. To compare this tax to the lump sum tax considered above we make the assumption that the government chooses t in such a manner that the tax yields $\overline{T}$ amount of tax revenue. Following the imposition of this tax, the individual has to give away (tW) amount from W to the government so that she effectively receives $W(1 - t)$ amount of wage. The budget line under this kind of an income tax is, therefore, given by

$$YD = W(1 - t)(\overline{L} - l) \tag{4.19}$$

This budget line is shown by BB_1. It follows from the equation of the pre-tax budget line, (4.16), and (4.19) that BB_1 has the same intercept on the horizontal axis as the pre-tax budget line, BB, in Figure 4.5. However, the absolute value of the slope of BB_1, as follows from (4.19), is $W(1 - t)$. The individual in the present case will maximize (4.18) subject to (4.19). Therefore, she will choose the utility maximizing point from the budget line BB_1. At this optimum point $mrs_{l,YD} = W(1 - t)$. It is labelled A_2 in Figure 4.5. Suppose that the optimum (l, YD) corresponding to A_2 is $(\overline{l}, \overline{YD})$.

Therefore,
$$\overline{YD} = W(1-t)(\overline{L} - \overline{l}) \tag{4.20}$$

At the chosen tax rate, t, the amount of tax revenue collected, $Wt(\overline{L} - \overline{l}) = \overline{T}$ by hypothesis. Substituting this in (4.20), we have

$$\overline{YD} = W(\overline{L} - \overline{l}) - (Wt)(\overline{L} - \overline{l}) = W(\overline{L} - \overline{l}) - \overline{T} \tag{4.21}$$

Therefore, $(\overline{YD}, \overline{l})$ is a point on the lump sum tax budget line, as given by (4.17), also. It has to be so because in equilibrium under the present proportional tax on wage income the producer is paying the worker the same wage rate as before and the government is taking away $\bar{T}$ amount of tax through the income tax imposed at the proportional rate, t. Therefore, individual's income, inclusive of the tax paid, from the labour supplied, $(\bar{L} - \bar{l})$, should be equal to its pre-tax value, $W(\bar{L} - \bar{l})$, but her income excluding the tax paid should be less than the pre-tax value of the labour supplied by $\bar{T}$. Hence $(\overline{YD}, \bar{l})$ should be a point on the lump sum tax budget line also.

However, at $(\overline{YD}, \bar{L})$, $mrs_{l,YD} = W(1 - t) < W$. Hence, $(\overline{YD}, \bar{l})$ is not the best point on the lump sum tax budget line, as shown in Figure 4.5, since at the best point on the lump sum tax budget line $mrs_{l,YD}$ should equal W. (Explain this point yourself.) Thus, under the proportional tax on wage income yielding the same revenue as the lump sum tax, the individual chooses from the lump sum tax budget line, but she chooses a point, which is inferior to the best point on the lump sum tax budget line. Hence the loss in welfare of the individual as she pays $\bar{T}$ amount of tax revenue to the government under the proportional tax on wage income is greater than the minimum amount of loss that such an income transfer entails. Therefore, *the proportional tax on wage income involves excess burden*. The amount of this excess burden in this case is indicated by the movement from I_1 to I_2 in Figure 4.5.

We can also derive a measure of this excess burden by means of equivalent variation, which is given by such a change or reduction in individual's income that she is just able to attain the post-wage tax indifference curve, I_2, in the absence of any kind of taxation. From Figure 4.5 it is clear that the individual is just able to attain I_2 in the absence of any kind of taxation, if her income is such that she is on the budget line B_2B_2. Since it corresponds to the pre-tax wage rate, it is parallel to the pre-tax budget line BB. Hence the vertical distance between BB and B_2B_2 is the same at every l. It is given by HA_3. Clearly, the individual will be on B_2B_2 in the absence of any kind of taxation, if her income is reduced from its pre-tax level by HA_3, which is larger than the tax revenue of $\bar{T}(=HA_1 < HA_3)$ yielded by the proportional tax on wage income. (Note that HA_1 is the vertical distance between the pre-tax budget line and the lump sum tax budget line. Corresponding to any given l the amount of income on the latter is less than that on the former by $\bar{T}$. Hence the vertical distance between the two, HA_1, equals $\bar{T}$.) Thus, in the absence of any kind of taxation, to make the individual attain the utility level that she attains under the proportional tax on wage income, her income has to be less than its initial level by an amount, which is larger than the tax revenue yielded by the lump sum or the proportional income tax. Hence the excess of the reduction in income required in the absence of any taxes to make the individual attain the utility level attained under the proportional tax on wage income over the tax revenue of the proportional tax on wage income may be regarded as a measure of the excess burden. In terms of Figure 4.5, therefore, excess burden of the proportional income tax is given by A_1A_3.

Let us now explain the reason why the reduction in the individual's income required in the absence of any kind of taxation to make her attain the utility level attained under the proportional tax on wage income is larger than the revenue yielded by the proportional tax on wage income. At the point chosen by the individual under the proportional tax on wage income $mrs_{l,YD} = W(1 - t) < W$. This point is labelled A_2 in Figure 4.5 and it lies on the indifference curve I_2. When the individual is at A_2, she has already given away $\bar{T}$ amount of income to the government and the marginal rate of substitution of leisure for income, denoted $mrs_{l,YD}$ (A_2), equals $W(1 - t) < W$. If she now reduces leisure by one unit from A_2 and thereby raises labour supply by unity, her income in the absence of tax will go up by W, whereas her income need rise by only $mrs_{l,YD}(A_2) < W$ to make her remain on I_2. So, she can sacrifice $[W - mrs_{l,YD}(A_2)]$ amount of income over and above $\overline{T}$ and still remain on I_2 following the substitution. Thus, as long as $mrs_{l,YD} < W$ on I_2, i.e., as long as the individual is to the right of A_3 on I_2, reduction of one unit of leisure for income will take the individual to a higher indifference curve and to make her stay on I_2, an income equal to $(W - mrs_{l,YD})$ has to be taken away from her. $mrs_{l,YD} < W$ at every point on the stretch A_2A_3 on I_2. Hence by adding up $(W - mrs_{l,YD})$ for every point on the stretch A_2A_3 on I_2, we get the maximum amount of income over $\overline{T}$ that can be taken away from her keeping her on I_2, when there are no taxes. This sum should be equal to $HA_3 - HA_1 = A_1A_3$. This explains why in the absence of any taxes the reduction in income that will make the individual just attain the level of utility that she attains under the proportional tax on wage income is larger than the tax revenue yielded by the proportional wage tax. We can derive this result in a more general way also. We describe it below.

We can derive the maximum level of income that can be taken away from the individual to make her choose from the indifference curve I_2 in the absence of taxes by carrying out the following optimization exercise:

$$\max_{l,YD} M = W(\overline{L} - l) - YD$$

$$\text{subject to } \overline{U} = U(YD, l)$$

where M and YD denote respectively the amount of income taken away from the individual and the amount of income left with the individual after M is taken away or the disposable income of the individual, and $\overline{U} \equiv$ the utility level corresponding to I_2. Note that $\overline{U}$ is less than the maximum level of U the individual can attain on the basis of her income $W(\overline{L} - l)$. Forming the Lagrangian expression, we have

$$Z = W(\overline{L} - l) - YD + \lambda[\overline{U} - U(YD, l)]$$

FOCs are given by

$$\frac{\partial Z}{\partial l} = -W - \lambda U_l = 0 \qquad (4.22)$$

$$\frac{\partial Z}{\partial YD} = -1 - \lambda U_{YD} = 0 \qquad (4.23)$$

and

$$\frac{\partial Z}{\partial \lambda} = \overline{U} - U(l, YD) = 0 \qquad (4.24)$$

Substituting the value of λ yielded by (4.23) into (4.22), we get

$$\frac{U_l}{U_{YD}} (\equiv mrs_{l,YD}) = W \qquad (4.25)$$

We can solve (4.24) and (4.25) for the optimum values of l and YD and, therefore, that of M. Let us denote this value of M by M^*. From (4.25) it follows that at the optimum (l, YD)

that maximizes M keeping the individual on a given indifference curve, $mrs_{l,YD} = W$. Thus, if at any point on I_2 we find that $mrs_{l,YD} \neq W$, the amount of income taken away from the individual (M) can be increased keeping her on I_2 either by substituting leisure for income or conversely. Let us illustrate. Consider point A_2 in Figure 4.5. We have seen above that A_2 is chosen from I_2 under the proportional tax on wage income. At $A_{\underline{2}}$, as we have pointed out above, $mrs_{l,YD} = W(1 - t) < W$ and the individual has given away $\bar{T}$ amount of income as tax. We have also explained above that if from A_2 the individual substitutes income for leisure, more income has to be taken away from her to keep her on I_2. This is true of every point on I_2 at which $mrs_{l,YD} < W$. Similarly, if at a point on I_2 we find that $mrs_{l,YD} > W$, more income has to be taken away from her to keep her on I_2 if she substitutes leisure for income from such a point. (Explain this proposition yourself.) It, therefore, follows that in the absence of any kind of taxation an amount of income larger than the revenue yielded by the proportional wage tax has to be taken away from the individual to keep her on the indifference curve she attains under the proportional wage tax, i.e., $M^* > \bar{T}$. Hence $(M^* - \bar{T})$ may be taken as a measure of excess burden.

The reason for this excess burden is again the same as that in the earlier case of the selective indirect tax. *The proportional tax on wage income not only reduces the income of the individual by the amount of the tax revenue but also lowers the wage rate actually received by the individual below what the employers are paying. Therefore, in addition to making the individual poorer by the amount of the tax revenue, the proportional tax on wage income makes leisure cheaper. Thus, the tax produces not only an income effect but also a substitution effect and the latter is the cause of the excess burden.* Let us illustrate this point using Figure 4.5. Note that real income, a la Slutsky, is the same at both A_1 and A_2. Hence the movement from A_2 to A_1 is due to substitution effect. The individual chooses A_2 under the proportional wage tax. If now she is made to face the real wage rate W instead of $W(1 - t)$ and at the same time her income is adjusted so that her real income, a la Slutsky, remains unchanged, then she will make her choice from the budget line $B_T B_T$ that passes through the initially chosen leisure–income combination A_2 and she will choose A_1. The excess burden under the proportional tax on wage income is due to individual's choice of A_2 instead of A_1. Clearly, therefore, the excess burden is due to substitution effect.

The Case of the Market

Let us now focus on the partial equilibrium of a perfectly competitive labour market as shown in Figure 4.6 where the real wage rate is measured along the vertical axis, while labour demand (L^D) and labour supply (L^S) are measured on the horizontal axis. For simplicity of exposition we assume marginal productivity of labour to be constant. This means that the demand price of labour, the maximum price at which producers are willing to employ labour, equals the given marginal productivity of labour. Accordingly, the labour demand schedule is horizontal at the real wage rate, which equals the fixed marginal productivity of labour. The labour supply schedule is, however, assumed to have the usual upward sloping shape. The equilibrium corresponds to the point of intersection of the two schedules. Equilibrium values of wage rate and employment are denoted by W_0 and L_0 respectively. In what follows, we shall derive a measure of the workers' welfare in equilibrium.

Take any (L, W), say, (L^0, W^0), on the labour supply schedule. It means that at the wage rate, W_0, the amount of labour workers are willing to supply is L^0. As we have shown above—recall our discussion on how an individual allocates her labour endowment between leisure and income—for each of the workers willing to supply labour at W_0, $mrs_{l,y}$ equals W_0 at the amount of labour she is willing to supply. To be more precise, suppose that an individual, A, is willing to supply L_A^0 amount of labour at W_0. Then at the leisure–income combination $[\bar{L} - L_A^0,\ y_A^0 = W_0(\bar{L} - L_A^0)]$, which she chooses at W_0, her $mrs_{l,y} = W_0$. Therefore, if A raises her labour supply by one unit from L_A^0, the compensation that she requires to remain on the same indifference curve is W_0 amount of additional income. Therefore, the minimum compensation that each of the workers supplying labour at W_0 will demand for supplying one extra unit of labour over what she is supplying at W_0 is W_0. Note that W_0 is the supply price of labour corresponding to L_0. Thus the supply price of labour corresponding to any given L gives the minimum compensation that the workers need to raise the supply of labour by one unit from the given level. (See the Appendix to Chapter 2 in this context.) At $L^S = 0$, the supply price of labour, as shown by the labour supply schedule in Figure 4.6, is OA_1. Suppose that $OA_1 = W(0)$. This means that the minimum price at which each of the workers participating in the market will be willing to supply the first unit of labour is $W(0)$. Similarly, if the supply price of labour at $L^S = 1$ is $W(1)$, the minimum price at which the workers will be willing to supply the second unit of labour is $W(1)$. Thus the minimum compensation or minimum income for which the workers are willing to supply two units of labour is $[W(0) + W(1)]$. From the above discussion it follows that the area under the labour supply curve over, for example, the closed interval $[0, L_0]$, gives the total minimum income for which workers are willing to supply L_0 amount of labour, when L is continuous instead of being discrete. In equilibrium, workers supply L_0 amount of labour at the wage rate W_0. Their income is, therefore, $(W_0 L_0)$, which is given by the area of the rectangle $OL_0 A W_0$. However, they are willing to supply L_0 amount of labour at the minimum income given by the area of the quadrilateral $AA_1 OL_0$. Hence, their gain is given by the area of the triangle $W_0 A A_1$. We shall use this gain as the measure of workers' welfare. As we have pointed out in the Appendix to Chapter 2, to measure the gain of the workers, one should use income compensated supply schedule. However, here we use the ordinary supply curve for reasons already mentioned in the Appendix to Chapter 2.

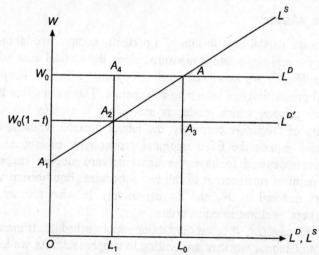

Figure 4.6: Proportional tax on wage income and excess burden in the labour market.

Now, suppose that the government imposes a tax at the ad valorem or proportional rate, t, on wage income. As a result the wage rate actually received by the workers falls from W_0 to $W_0(1 - t)$, since from W_0, which is paid by the producers, workers have to pay $W_0 t$ to the government. Effectively, therefore, in the post-tax scenario the demand price faced by the workers is $W_0(1 - t)$. The demand schedule accordingly shifts downward as shown in Figure 4.6 from L^D to $L^{D'}$. The new equilibrium is given by the point $A_2(L_1, W_0(1 - t))$. Workers' gain accordingly reduces to the area of the triangle $A_2 W_0(1 - t)A_1$. Workers, therefore, lose the area of the quadrilateral $A W_0 W_0(1 - t)A_2$ of which the area of the rectangle $W_0 W_0(1 - t)A_2 A_4$ accrues as tax revenue to the government, but the amount of workers' loss given by the area of the triangle $AA_2 A_4$ does not accrue as gain to any one. Thus this loss is the deadweight loss or excess burden. This loss is not entailed or accounted for by the transfer of the tax revenue from the workers to the government.

Let us now derive a measure of the excess burden given by

The area of the triangle

$$AA_2 A_4 = \frac{1}{2}(A_2 A_4)(A_4 A) = \frac{1}{2}(-dW)\left(\frac{dL^S}{dW}\right)(-dW)$$

$$= \frac{1}{2}(W_0 t)\left(\frac{dL^S}{dW}\frac{W_0}{L^S}\right)\frac{L^S}{W_0}(W_0 t) = \frac{1}{2}(\eta_L t^2 L_0 W_0) \tag{4.26}$$

where $\eta_L \equiv$ own price elasticity of supply of labour. It should be noted here that $dW = -W_0 t$ and the initial equilibrium value of $L^S = L_0$.

The reason for this excess burden is quite easy to explain. It is clearly due to the fall in employment from L_0 to L_1 following the imposition of the tax. On each of the units of labour from L_0 to L_1, excluding L_1, workers were enjoying some gain in the pre-tax situation. The supply price of each of these units was less than the pre-tax equilibrium wage rate. Following the imposition of the tax, workers cease to supply these units and thereby lose their gains on these units of labour. However, they also do not pay any taxes on these units, since they no longer sell them and thereby earn wage income on them. Thus the losses of surpluses on these units are not converted into tax revenue. The losses of gains on these units are, therefore, just deadweight loss or excess burden. The value of excess burden given by (4.26) is, given the initial equilibrium wage rate and employment, an increasing function of both t and η_L. This can be explained following the lines suggested earlier in the context of (4.5). Do this yourself.

4.2.5   Excess Burden and Choice between Income and Leisure: General Equilibrium Analysis

The case of the community.

Firms

We shall now carry out our analysis in the general equilibrium framework under the following assumptions: There are a large number of identical firms each producing a single good (Y) with only one input, labour (L), using the production function

$$Y = F(L); \quad F' > 0 \text{ and } F'' < 0 \tag{4.27}$$

Markets for both labour and the good are perfectly competitive. Every firm is a price taker in each market. The commodity produced is the numeraire. To keep matters as simple as possible, we focus only on the short run here so that the number of firms is fixed. Accordingly, profit in equilibrium may be non-zero. Every firm maximizes profit. Since all the firms are identical, we can carry out our analysis in terms of a single representative firm. Profit maximization exercise of the representative firm is given by

$$\max_{L} \Pi = Y - WL = F(L) - WL \tag{4.28}$$

where $W \equiv$ real wage rate.

First-order condition for profit maximization is given by the equation:

$$W = F'(L) \tag{4.29}$$

Since $F'' < 0$, the second-order condition for profit maximization is satisfied. We can solve (4.29) for the profit maximizing value of L or labour demand of the firm in terms of W. The solution is given by

$$L^D = L^D(W); \ L^{D\prime} < 0 \tag{4.30}$$

where $L^D \equiv$ labour demand or the profit maximizing value of L.

Derivation of (4.30) is shown in Figure 4.7 where we measure W, Y and F' on the vertical axis and L along the horizontal axis. The concave curve $F(.)$ represents the production function. The profit maximizing value of L is given by that point on $F(.)$ at which the slope of the production function equals the given W, W^*. This point is labelled A and the profit maximizing amount of L or labour demand corresponding to A is labelled L^*. At a $W < (>) W^*$ the profit

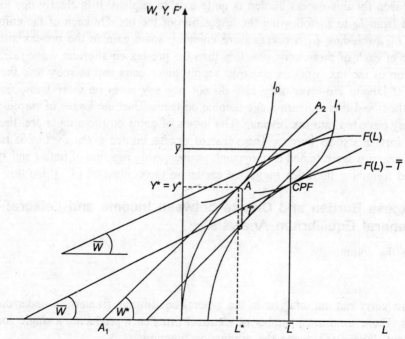

Figure 4.7: Excess burden and labour–leisure choice: general equilibrium.

maximizing value of L will correspond to a point, which is to the right (left) of A, on the production function. This is because marginal productivity of labour falls (rises) along the production function as L rises (falls) and, therefore, marginal productivity of labour on the production function can be equal to a lower (higher) W only at a higher (lower) L. This explains the sign of the derivative of the labour demand function.

Individuals

There are a large number of identical individuals. Every individual sells labour and earns wage income. They also receive profit from firms and they have no control over this profit. This is because here we assume that all the firms are joint stock companies. Accordingly, there is a separation between ownership and management. Thus individuals who own these firms do not have any control over their management and, therefore, on their profit. Individuals also spend all their income on the good produced in the economy. Individuals allocate their given labour endowments in such a manner that their utilities are maximized. Since all the individuals are identical, we shall carry out our analysis in terms of a single representative individual. Since profits of the firms accrue to their owners and since all the owners are represented here by the representative individual, the whole profit of the representative firm is assumed to accrue to the representative individual. A representative individual's optimization exercise may, therefore, be written as follows:

$$\max_{y,L} U(y, \overline{L} - L)$$

$$\text{subject to} \quad y = WL + \Pi \tag{4.31}$$

where $y \equiv$ income earned by the individual, $\overline{L} \equiv$ labour endowment of the individual, $L \equiv$ amount of labour supplied by the individual and $\Pi \equiv$ profit income of the individual, which is the profit earned by the representative firm.

Substituting the constraint into the utility function, we can write it as

$$\max_{L} U(WL + \Pi, \overline{L} - L)$$

In the above optimization exercise only L is the choice variable, since W, Π and $\overline{L}$ are all given to the individuals. W is given to the individual because, as you should be able to recall, both the markets for the good and labour are assumed to be perfectly competitive.

The first-order condition for utility maximization is given by

$$-\frac{\dfrac{\partial U}{\partial l}(WL + \Pi, \overline{L} - L)}{\dfrac{\partial U}{\partial y}(WL + \Pi, \overline{L} - L)} (\equiv mrs_{l,y}) = W \tag{4.32}$$

where $l \equiv \overline{L} - L \equiv$ leisure.

We can solve (4.32) for the utility maximizing value of L, which the individual wants to supply at the given W, given the other exogenous variables. Thus (4.32) yields labour supply as a function of W as shown below:

$$L^S = L^S(W) \tag{4.33}$$

There is equilibrium in the labour market when

$$L^D(W) = L^S(W) \tag{4.34}$$

We have Walras law in this model. To see this write the budget constraint of the representative individual, as given by (4.31), as follows:

$$y^D = W L^S + \Pi \tag{4.35}$$

where $y^D \equiv$ representative individual's demand for the good produced in the economy and $L^S \equiv$ the amount of labour the individual plans to supply. Let us explain (4.35). By assumption the individual here spends all her income on the good, which is also the numeraire. This means that y is expressed in terms of the good. Therefore, $y = y^D$. Again, in (4.31), L actually stands for the amount of labour the individual plans to supply. She carries out the constrained utility maximization exercise to determine the amount of supply of labour that will maximize her utility subject to the budget constraint. As a supplier in a competitive market, she faces a horizontal demand schedule and, therefore, she presumes that she will be able to sell whatever she plans to, while carrying out the optimization exercise. Therefore, in the budget constraint L stands for L^S. Again, Π in the individual's budget constraint represents the profit of the representative firm. In the expression of profit, as shown by (4.28), Y and L stand for the amount of output the firm plans to supply and the amount of labour it plans to employ. As a player in competitive markets the firm presumes that it is able to supply as much output as it produces and employ as much labour as it demands at the prevailing price and wage. Hence its profit equation has to be written as

$$\Pi = Y^S - WL^D \tag{4.36}$$

where $Y^S \equiv$ planned supply of output and $L^D \equiv$ planned demand for labour.

Putting the value of Π, given by $(Y^S - WL^D)$, in the individual's budget constraint we have

$$y^D = WL^S + Y^S - WL^D$$

$$\Rightarrow \qquad \underbrace{(y^D - Y^S)}_{\substack{\text{Excess demand in} \\ \text{goods' market}}} + \underbrace{W(L^D - L^S)}_{\substack{\text{value of excess demand} \\ \text{in labour market}}} = 0 \tag{4.37}$$

Equation (4.37) is the Walras law, which states that if the labour market is in equilibrium, so will be the goods market and vice versa. Therefore, to determine the equilibrium values of the endogenous variables of this general equilibrium model, one need not consider both the markets. It will suffice to consider any one of the two markets. Hence we focus explicitly on the labour market alone. Thus (4.34) gives the general equilibrium value of W. Let us denote this value of W by W^*. Putting this value of W in (4.33), we get the general equilibrium value of employment, which we denote by L^*. This equilibrium situation is shown in Figure 4.7 where (L^*, Y^*) is the equilibrium combination of L and Y. Let us explain. The pair (L^*, Y^*) maximize firm's profit as at (L^*, Y^*), $F'(L^*) = W^*$.

The budget constraint of the individual at W^* is given by

$$y = W^* L + \Pi(W^*) \tag{4.38}$$

where $\Pi(W^*) \equiv$ profit earned at W^*, which is given by $(Y^* - W^* L^*)$. This budget constraint in the (L, y) plane has the slope (W^*). Moreover, if we substitute L^* for L in the budget equation, we find that $W^* L^* + \Pi(W^*) = Y^*$. Therefore, (L^*, Y^*) is a point on the individual's budget line. In other words, it passes through the point (L^*, Y^*) in Figure 4.7. This budget line is represented by A_1A_2 in Figure 4.7.

In equilibrium the individual maximizes her utility given by $U(y, \bar{L} - L)$ subject to the budget constraint, (4.38). Indifference curves underlying the utility function are upward sloping and convex downward in the (L, y) plane as shown by the curve I_0 in Figure 4.7. They are upward sloping because an increase in L lowers the amount of leisure and thereby reduces utility. To compensate for this loss, y has to rise. They are convex downward because as the amount of labour supply rises and, therefore, the amount of leisure falls, the amount of increase in income required to compensate for a unit loss in leisure goes up by assumption. Since the slope of the indifference curve gives the amount of increase in y that compensates for one unit increase in L or one unit decrease in l, it is nothing but $mrs_{l,y}$, which rises as L increases and, therefore, l decreases. The other point about the indifference curves is that the higher an indifference curve, the larger is the income corresponding to any given L or leisure on the indifference curve and hence the greater is the utility level that it represents.

From her budget line the individual chooses the (L, y) that lies on the highest indifference curve. At the chosen or the optimum point the slope of the indifference curve, $mrs_{l,y}$, equals that of the budget line, W. In equilibrium the budget line of the individual, as we have noted above, passes through (L^*, Y^*) and has the slope W^*. It is represented by A_1A_2 in Figure 4.7. The individual obviously chooses (L^*, Y^*) from this budget line in equilibrium. The indifference curve I_0 is tangent to the individual's budget line at (L^*, Y^*). This point of tangency, (L^*, Y^*), is labelled A. Clearly, at A individual's planned demand for goods and services, y, equals planned supply of goods and services, Y^*, and individual's planned supply of labour equals firm's planned demand for labour. Thus at W^* both the markets are in equilibrium.

Let us now focus on some important properties of (L^*, Y^*). At this point, as we have noted above, $mrs_{l,y} = W^* = F'(L) = mrtr_{l,y}$, where $mrtr_{l,y}$ stands for marginal rate of transformation of leisure into income, which is, obviously, nothing but marginal productivity of labour. This is the best point on the production function. Social welfare is maximized at this point. If at any point on the production function $mrs_{l,y} \neq mrtr_{l,y}$, social welfare is not at its maximum. Consider a point to the left (right) of A. At such a point an indifference curve of the individual cuts the production function from above (below). Hence $mrs_{l,y} < (>) mrtr_{l,y}$ at such a point. If L is raised (lowered) by one unit from such a point, the increase (decrease) in income that the individual requires to compensate for (to offset the effect of) the unit decrease (increase) in leisure is less (greater) than the increase (fall) in income that will take place. Hence the individual will be better off. Thus, the point on the production function that maximizes social welfare is the one at which $mrs_{l,y} = mrtr_{l,y}$. We shall now incorporate tax in this general equilibrium framework and examine the issue of excess burden. We shall start with the case of the lump sum tax.

Lump Sum Tax

Suppose that the government imposes a lump sum tax $\bar{T}$ on the individuals. To examine its impact in the simplest possible framework without any loss of generality we assume that the government uses $\bar{T}$ to purchase Y. Accordingly, the consumption possibility frontier (CPF) to the individuals comes to be given by $[F(L) - \bar{T}]$ and not by $F(L)$. However, the slope of the

CPF at every L, for obvious reasons, is the same as that of $F(L)$, $F'(L)$. The CPF is shown in Figure 4.7. As before at any given W producers will produce that Y at which $W = F'(L)$, since the profit function and the profit maximization exercise of the firm are the same as those in the pre-tax situation. The tax is collected from the individuals. Hence firms are not directly affected. Suppose that the equilibrium value of the real wage rate in the post-tax situation is $\overline{W}$. Accordingly, the firm at $\overline{W}$ will produce $(\overline{L}, \overline{Y})$ so that $F(\overline{L}) = \overline{Y}$ and $F'(\overline{L}) = \overline{W}$. The situation is shown in Figure 4.7.

The budget constraint of the representative individual at $\overline{W}$ is given by

$$y = \overline{W}L + \Pi(\overline{W}) - \overline{T} \tag{4.39}$$

where $\Pi(W) \equiv$ profit earned by the firm in the post-tax equilibrium where $W = \overline{W}$. Hence $\Pi(\overline{W}) = \overline{Y} - \overline{W} \, \overline{L}$. Clearly, this budget line has the slope $\overline{W}$. Again, if we substitute the value of $\Pi(\overline{W})$ into (4.39), we find that $y = \overline{Y} - \overline{T}$. Therefore, $(\overline{L}, \overline{Y} - \overline{T})$ satisfies (4.39). Hence the budget line given by (4.39) passes through the point $(\overline{Y} - \overline{T}, \overline{L})$, which is on the CPF, $[F(L) - \overline{T}]$. From this line the individual chooses $(\overline{Y} - \overline{T}, \overline{L})$ so that the goods market and labour market are in equilibrium. At the optimum point chosen, $(\overline{Y} - \overline{T}, \overline{L})$, the indifference curve, I_1, is tangent to the individual's post-tax equilibrium budget line at $(\overline{Y} - \overline{T}, \overline{L})$. Hence the slope of the indifference curve, $mrs_{l,y}$, equals that of the budget line, $\overline{W}$, at $(\overline{Y} - \overline{T}, \overline{L})$. Now, the CPF gives the maximum value of Y that the individuals can enjoy corresponding to every L, if they lose $\overline{T}$ amount of produced goods and services. The best point on this CPF, as we have already explained, is the one at which $mrtr_{l,y}$ ($\equiv F'(L)$), is equal to the $mrs_{l,y}$. Under the lump sum tax individuals and firms face the same W, which is $\overline{W}$ in the present case. Accordingly, at the equilibrium $(L, Y - \overline{T})$, $(\overline{L}, \overline{Y} - \overline{T})$, $mrs_{l,y} = mrtr_{l,y}$. Hence this condition is satisfied at $(\overline{L}, \overline{Y} - \overline{T})$. From the CPF, which gives the largest Y the individuals can enjoy corresponding to every L, when $\overline{T}$ amount of goods and services is taken away, the individuals choose its best point. Thus the loss in utility indicated by the movement from I_0 to I_1 is the minimum amount of loss in welfare that the transfer of $\overline{T}$ amount of income and goods and services from the individuals to the government entails. Thus the lump sum tax does not involve any excess burden.

Proportional Income Tax on Wage Income

Let us now focus on the case where the government imposes a proportional tax at the rate, t, on individuals' income. The tax rate, t, is chosen in such a manner that the government gets $\overline{T}$ amount of tax revenue, which it uses, as before, to purchase Y. This assumption is made obviously to compare the proportional wage tax to the lump sum tax.

This tax, as it is imposed directly on the workers' income, does not affect the optimization exercise of the firm. It continues to be given by (4.28). Accordingly, the FOC for profit maximization as given by (4.29) is the same in this case also.

The budget line of the representative individual will, however, be affected. It will be given by

$$y = W(1 - t)L + \Pi \tag{4.40}$$

The individual will maximize $U(y, \bar{L} - L)$ subject to (4.40). The FOC in this case will, therefore, be given by

$$mrs_{l,y} = W(1 - t) \tag{4.41}$$

Suppose that in this case equilibrium occurs at (Y_0, L_0) and W_0. Obviously, $Y_0 = F(L_0)$ and $W_0 = F'(L_0)$. Otherwise (Y_0, L_0) would not be chosen by the firms.

The budget line of the representative individual in the present case at W_0 is given by

$$y = W_0(1 - t)L + (Y_0 - W_0L_0) \tag{4.42}$$

where $(Y_0 - W_0L_0)$ is the profit earned by the representative firm in equilibrium. It, therefore, accrues as profit income to the representative individual. From this budget line the individual chooses to supply L_0, since this budget line obtains in equilibrium by assumption. Moreover, t by hypothesis is such that W_0tL_0, which gives the total amount of tax paid by the individual in equilibrium, is $\bar{T}$. Therefore, if we substitute L_0 for L in (4.42), the value of y turns out to be $(Y_0 - \bar{T})$. Hence the point $(L_0, Y_0 - \bar{T})$ satisfies (4.42). Thus in equilibrium the budget line, as given by (4.42), has the slope $W_0(1 - t)$ and passes through the point $(Y_0 - \bar{T}, L_0)$. The individual chooses this point from the budget line. Clearly, at this point $mrs_{l,y} = W_0(1 - t)$. The situation is shown in Figure 4.8. Note that in this case also the equilibrium occurs on the lump sum tax CPF, $[F(L) - \bar{T}]$. This is because here also the government takes away in equilibrium $\bar{T}$ amount of tax from the individuals and buys with it $\bar{T}$ amount of goods and services so that corresponding to the equilibrium L, the amount of goods and services available to the individuals is less than the aggregate output by $\bar{T}$. The concave curve labelled CPF in the Figure is the lump sum tax CPF. The slope of the CPF, $[F(L) - \bar{T}]$, at $(Y_0 - \bar{T}, L_0)$ is the same as that of the PPF at (Y_0, L_0). Hence the slope of the CPF at $(Y_0 - \bar{T}, L_0)$ is W_0. The individual's budget line in equilibrium, as we have explained above, passes through $(Y_0 - \bar{T}, L_0)$ and has the slope $W_0(1 - t)$. tt represents this budget line. It obviously cuts the CPF at $(Y_0 - \bar{T}, L_0)$, as its slope is less than that of the CPF at the point, $(Y_0 - \bar{T}, L_0)$, which is labelled A_1 in Figure 4.8. For expository convenience the production function is not shown. The individual chooses point A_1 from this budget line and attains the highest indifference curve attainable, I_1. A_1 lies on the lump sum tax CPF, $[F(L) - \bar{T}]$, but at A_1 $mrs_{l,y} = W_0(1 - t) < W_0 = mrtr_{l,y}$. Hence A_1, as we have explained above, is not the best point on the CPF. (Explain this point yourself.) The best point is A, which obtains in equilibrium in the lump sum tax case. Thus the proportional income tax involves excess burden, which is indicated in Figure 4.8 by the movement from I_0 to I_1. The excess burden is obviously due to the wedge the proportional income tax drives between the prices of leisure faced by the producers and the workers, which are W and $W(1 - t)$ respectively. Accordingly, $mrtr_{L,Y}$ and $mrs_{l,y}$ are equated to W and $W(1 - t)$ respectively leading to the choice of a sub-optimum point from the lump sum tax CPF. Thus, the tax not only transfers $\bar{T}$ amount of income from the workers to the government; it also distorts the price system by making the price of leisure received by the workers different from that paid by the producers. This is the main reason for the excess burden.

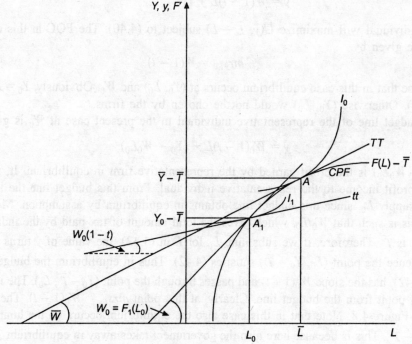

Figure 4.8: Excess burden, proportional income tax, choice between income and leisure: general equilibrium.

Box 4.1: Optimum Commodity Tax

The objective here is to discuss the issue of optimum commodity taxation, which is defined as a commodity tax structure that yields a given amount of revenue to the government without giving rise to excess burden. We have seen earlier that a lump sum tax does not create any excess burden. It is, however, grossly iniquitous and therefore not available as an option. Examples of lump sum taxes are few and far between. In the eighties the Thatcher government in UK introduced a lump sum property tax, which was independent of property value. The tax created a furor and the people voted the Thatcher government out of power in the election that came up following the imposition of the tax. What kind of commodity taxes does not generate inefficiency, when it is not possible to resort to lump sum taxes? This is the question which we shall discuss here.

We have seen above that the basic cause of excess burden is the distortion the taxes incorporate in the price system. The distortion consists in the differences in the price ratios faced by the buyers and sellers. If a tax at an ad valorem rate, t, is imposed on, say, the sales of the ith commodity, then, if P_i be the sellers' price, the price actually received by the sellers, the buyers pay the price $P_i(1 + t)$. Accordingly, if commodities

(Contd.)...

(Contd.)...

are taxed at different rates or if some commodities are taxed and some are not, price ratios or relative prices faced by buyers and sellers become different leading to deadweight losses. The problem can obviously be solved by taxing all commodities at the same ad valorem rate. The problem with this scheme is that consumers consume leisure along with other goods and services. Hence, to avoid excess burden leisure has to be taxed at the same ad valorem rate as the other goods. Otherwise, marginal rate of substitution of leisure for any other good will be different from the marginal rate of transformation of leisure into the other good, giving rise to inefficiency. But, given the problems of valuation of leisure, taxation of leisure is infeasible. Hence we have to look for a commodity tax structure that minimizes excess burden, when lump sum tax and taxation of leisure are not possible.

Inverse Elasticity Rule and Ramsey Rule

Here we shall formally derive a commodity tax structure that minimizes the excess burden of raising a given amount of tax revenue through commodity taxation, when lump sum taxes and taxation of leisure are not feasible. Consider two unrelated goods, X and Y, for simplicity. Two goods are unrelated if demand for neither good depends upon the price of the other good. They are neither substitutes nor complements. Amounts of excess burdens created by taxes at the ad valorem rates, t_x and t_y, as we derived above, are given by $(\eta_x P_x X t_x^2)$ and $(\eta_y P_y Y t_y^2)$ respectively. When two goods are unrelated, a change in the tax rate on one good and the consequent changes in the price and quantity of the good in question have no impact on the market of the other good. Hence the excess burden created in the other market remains unchanged too. In other words, markets of two unrelated goods are completely independent of one another. Accordingly, excess burdens generated in the two markets are also unrelated to each other. Under these circumstances total excess burden generated in the two markets by t_x and t_y is simply the sum of the excess burdens in the two markets and the amount of excess burden in each market is independent of that in the other. Denoting the aggregate excess burden by Z, we have

$$Z = (\eta_x P_x X t_x^2) + (\eta_y P_y Y t_y^2) \tag{B.4.1}$$

We shall first derive the values of t_x and t_y that yield a given amount of tax revenue, $\bar{R}$, to the government and at the same time minimize Z. We shall do this by carrying out the following optimization exercise:

$$\min_{t_x, t_y} Z = (\eta_x P_x X t_x^2) + (\eta_y P_y Y t_y^2)$$

$$\text{subject to} \quad \bar{R} = P_x t_x X + P_y t_y Y$$

Forming the Lagrangian expression, we have

$$L = (\eta_x P_x X t_x^2) + (\eta_y P_y Y t_y^2) + \lambda(\bar{R} - P_x t_x X - P_y t_y Y)$$

(Contd.)...

(Contd.)...

The FOCs for minimization is given by

$$\frac{\partial L}{\partial t_x} = 2\eta_x P_x X t_x - \lambda P_x X = 0 \tag{B.4.2}$$

$$\frac{\partial L}{\partial t_y} = 2\eta_y P_y Y t_y - \lambda P_y Y = 0 \tag{B.4.3}$$

$$\frac{\partial L}{\partial \lambda} = \bar{R} - P_x t_x X - P_y t_y Y = 0 \tag{B.4.4}$$

We can solve the three equations, (B.4.1), (B.4.2) and (B.4.3) for the three unknowns, t_x, t_y and λ. Eliminating λ from (B.4.2) and (B.4.3), we have

$$\eta_x t_x = \eta_y t_y \tag{B.4.5}$$

or

$$\frac{\eta_x}{\eta_y} = \frac{t_y}{t_x} \tag{B.4.6}$$

*When the tax structure is optimum, (B.4.6) is satisfied. It is referred to as the **inverse elasticity rule**. It states that, when the tax structure is optimum, tax rates on commodities are inversely proportional to their elasticities.* If η_x is twice η_y, the tax rate on X, t_x, should be half t_y. The intuition behind this rule is not far to see. We have found above that, the larger the price elasticity of demand, the greater is the excess burden corresponding to any given tax rate. Therefore, to minimize excess burden, commodities having lower price elasticities have to be taxed at higher rates. This is, however, highly inequitable. Price elasticities of necessities are very low, while those of luxuries quite high. Thus, the inverse elasticity rule recommends taxation of necessities at high rates and that of luxuries at low rates. We shall explain later in the Chapter on Tax Incidence that such a tax is highly regressive and, therefore, unjust. Thus there is a contradiction between equity and efficiency.

We shall now focus on (B.4.5) and interpret it. Following the imposition of the tax on the sales of X at the ad valorem rate, t_x, price of X faced by buyers, as we shall explain in Chapter 5 in the section on ad valorem tax, rises by $(P_x t_x)$. Hence $t_x[= (P_x t_x)/P_x]$, gives the proportional increase in the price of X faced by the buyers following the imposition of the tax. η_x on the other hand measures the proportional fall in demand for X per unit of proportional increase in the buyers' price of X. Therefore, $(t_x\eta_x)$ gives the total proportional decline in demand for X following the imposition of the tax. Let us explain with a numerical example. Suppose $t_x = 1/2$ or 50%, which we get by multiplying 1/2 by 100. This means that, following the imposition of the tax, buyers' price of X rises in the proportion (1/2), i.e., $(\Delta P_x/P_x) = (1/2)$. (Thus, if $P_x = 2$, consumers' price rises by (1/2) of 2 = 1, i.e., by $(\Delta P_x/P_x)P_x$). Now $\eta_x = -(\Delta D_x/D_x)/(\Delta P_x/P_x)$. If it is 2, it means that per unit of proportional increase in buyers' price of X, the proportional decline in demand for

---

(Contd.)...

(Contd.)...

X is 2. In percentage terms it means that, if buyers' price of X rises by one percentage point, demand for X falls by two percentage points. If price rises by 2 percentage points, then demand falls by $\eta_x(\Delta P_x/P_x)100 = 2(.02) \times 100 = .04 \times 100 = 4$ percentage points. Therefore if t_x, i.e., total proportional increase in buyers' price $= 0.5$, and $\eta_x = 2$, total proportional fall in demand for X is $2(.5) = 1$. In percentage terms, total fall in demand for X following the imposition of the tax is one hundred percentage points.

Thus (B.4.5) tells us that, *if commodity tax structure is optimum, tax rate on each commodity is such that the proportional or percentage decrease in the demand for every good is the same. This is referred to as the Ramsey rule.*

The point to note here is that, even though we derived the inverse elasticity rule and Ramsey rule under the assumption that the goods are unrelated, those rules will hold even when the goods are related.

4.2.6 Excess Burden and Choice between Present and Future Consumption: Partial Equilibrium Analysis

Individual

Here we focus on the individual's problem of allocating a given amount of lifetime income over lifetime consumption. We shall carry out the analysis in the simplest possible framework under the following assumptions. There is no uncertainty and all the individuals have perfect foresight. They live for two periods. A typical individual earns Y_1 in period 1 and Y_2 in period 2. She also operates in a perfectly competitive loan market, where she is a price taker. The market interest rate, which is the same for both the borrowers and lenders, is denoted by r. There are no restrictions on borrowing and lending. Under these conditions the present value of lifetime income of the individual discounted at r, referred to as her wealth and denoted by W, is given by

$$W = Y_1 + \frac{Y_2}{1+r} \tag{4.43}$$

Individual's consumption expenditures in period 1 and period 2 are denoted by C_1 and C_2 respectively. C_1 and C_2 are assumed to include the individual's gifts and bequest as well. The individual chooses C_1 and C_2 in such a manner that her lifetime utility is maximized subject to the constraint that the present value of her lifetime income discounted at the market rate of interest equals the present value of her lifetime consumption discounted at the market rate of interest. Thus a typical individual carries out the following optimization exercise:

$$\max_{C_1, C_2} U(C_1, C_2)$$

$$\text{subject to} \quad W = C_1 + \frac{C_2}{1+r} \tag{4.44}$$

where $U(.) \equiv$ the utility function of the individual. It should be noted that (4.44) holds because C_1 and C_2 include gifts and bequests as well. Thus C_1 and C_2 include all the different ways in which the individual can spend her income over her lifetime. If C_1 and C_2 had not included gifts and bequests, the RHS would have been less than the LHS. The assumption of perfect foresight implies that the individual knows her lifespan and future income with certainty. We show the solution of the above optimization exercise graphically in Figure 4.9 where C_1 and C_2 are measured on the horizontal and vertical axes respectively. BB represents the budget constraint, (4.44) with slope $- (1 + r)$ and vertical intercept, $[W(1 + r)]$. The individual chooses from this budget line the point that maximizes her utility. At such a point an indifference curve of the individual is tangent to the budget line and hence the absolute value of the slope of the indifference curve, $mrs_{C_1, C_2} = (1 + r)$, the absolute value of the slope of the budget line. (Explain why other points on the budget line are not optimum using economic logic.) Individual's optimum point on BB is labelled A in the figure.

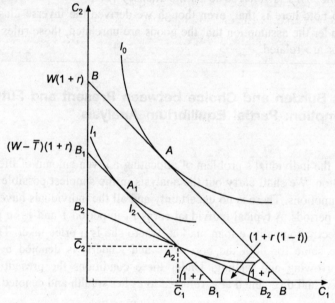

Figure 4.9: Individual's choice between present and future consumption and excess burden.

Lump Sum Tax

Let us now incorporate a lump sum tax, $\overline{T}$, which the government collects from the individual in the first period of her life. The individual, therefore, in the post-tax scenario maximizes her utility subject to the following budget constraint:

$$W = (C_1 + \overline{T}) + \frac{C_2}{1+r} \tag{4.45}$$

This budget constraint is shown by the line $B_1 B_1$ in Figure 4.9. It is parallel to the pre-tax budget line, but its vertical intercept, $(W - \overline{T})(1 + r)$, is less. The individual chooses from this budget line the point that lies on the highest indifference curve. The optimum point is labelled A_1 and it lies on the highest indifference curve, which is labelled I_1. At the optimum point, just as in the earlier case, $mrs_{C_1, C_2} = (1 + r)$. The loss in the individual's welfare indicated by the movement from I_0 to I_1 is the minimum entailed by the transfer of $\bar{T}$ amount of wealth from the individual to the government. Let us explain.

Points on the B_1B_1 line represent the largest combinations of (C_1, C_2) that the individual can choose from following the loss in $\bar{T}$ amount of wealth and she chooses the best of these combinations. So, she loses the minimum possible amount of welfare following the loss of $\bar{T}$ amount of wealth. Thus a lump sum tax does not involve any excess burden.

Proportional Income Tax

Suppose that the government chooses to raise the lifetime tax of $\bar{T}$ from the representative individual through a proportional income tax applied at the rate, t. The tax rate, t, is chosen in such a manner that the present value of lifetime tax of the individual discounted at the market rate of interest, r, equals $\bar{T}$. This assumption is made obviously to compare this tax with the lump sum tax. Suppose that the tax applies to both the lender and the borrower equally. This means that the lender pays tax on the interest income received at the rate t. Similarly, borrowers get tax concession at the rate t on the amount of interest charges on loans. Thus lenders have to pay rt amount as tax from the interest income of r from every unit of the loan. Therefore, the interest rate effectively faced by the lender is $r(1 - t)$. Similarly, the borrower gets a tax deduction of rt amount on the r amount of interest paid on every unit of loan taken, i.e., as she pays r amount of interest for every unit of loan taken, her tax liability goes down by rt. Therefore, both the borrowers and lenders effectively pay and receive respectively the same interest rate, $r(1 - t)$. Hence the budget line of the consumer is given by

$$C_2 = [Y_1(1 - t) - C_1][1 + r(1 - t)] + Y_2(1 - t) \qquad (4.46)$$

Let us explain. $Y_1(1 - t)$ is the individual's disposable income in period 1 from which she saves $[Y_1(1 - t) - C_1]$ (dissaves $[C_1 - Y_1(1 - t)]$) in period 1. This saving (dissaving) is lent out (met with borrowing), as we have already explained, effectively at the rate of interest, $r(1 - t)$. Therefore, the individual earns (pays) in period 2 an interest income of $[Y_1(1 - t) - C_1]$ $r(1 - t)]$ (interest charges of $[C_1 - Y_1(1 - t)]$ $r(1 - t))$. Accordingly, in period 2 the amount of disposable income of the individual is given by $(Y_1(1 - t) - C_1)$ $r(1 - t) + Y_2(1 - t)$. Besides this disposable income, the individual in period 2 has her savings or wealth, $[Y_1(1 - t) - C_1]$ (debt, $[C_1 - Y_1(1 - t)]$), which she has carried over from period 1. Thus, in period 2 her total expenditure, C_2, which includes gifts and bequest also, should equal her disposable income plus (minus) wealth (debt), since she knows and everyone else also knows that period 2 is the last period of her life. Thus (4.46) gives the budget equation of the individual. It gives the largest combinations of C_1 and C_2 that she can enjoy, given her total lifetime income, interest rate and the proportional income tax. Rearranging the terms, we can rewrite (4.46) as

$$C_2 = [Y_1(1 - t) - C_1][1 + r(1 - t)] + Y_2(1 - t)$$
$$= (Y_1 - C_1 - Y_1t)(1 + r - tr) + Y_2(1 - t)$$
$$= (Y_1 - C_1)(1 + r) - (Y_1 - C_1)\,tr - Y_1t(1 + r - tr) + Y_2 - Y_2t$$
$$= (Y_1 - C_1)(1 + r) + Y_2 - Y_1t(1 + r) + Y_1t(tr) - (Y_1 - C_1)\,tr - Y_2t$$
$$= (Y_1 - C_1)(1 + r) + Y_2 - Y_1t(1 + r) - [Y_1(1 - t) - C_1]\,tr - Y_2t$$

Dividing both the sides of the above equation by $(1 + r)$ and rearranging terms, we have

$$\frac{C_2}{1+r} + C_1 = Y_1 + \frac{Y_2}{1+r} - \left[Y_1 t + \frac{Y_2 t}{(1+r)} + \frac{(Y_1(1-t) - C_1)rt}{1+r} \right]$$

$$\Rightarrow \quad C_2 = -(1+r) C_1 + W(1+r) - \left[Y_1 t + \frac{Y_2 t}{(1+r)} + \frac{(Y_1(1-t) - C_1)rt}{1+r} \right] (1+r) \qquad (4.47)$$

$$\Rightarrow \quad C_2 = -(1 + r(1-t)) C_1 + W(1+r) - \left[Y_1 t + \frac{Y_2 t}{(1+r)} + \frac{(Y_1(1-t))rt}{1+r} \right] (1+r) \qquad (4.48)$$

From (4.48) it follows that the budget line is flatter than the original budget line. The absolute value of its slope is $[1 + r(1 - t)] < (1 + r)$, the absolute value of the slope of the original budget line. Its vertical intercept, as follows from (4.44) and (4.48), is also smaller than that of the original budget line. Its horizontal intercept, as follows from (4.47), is less than that of the original budget line. It is shown by B_2B_2 in Figure 4.9.

Let us suppose that the individual in the post-tax equilibrium chooses from B_2B_2 in Figure 4.9 the point $A_2(\bar{C}_1, \bar{C}_2)$. Clearly, $mrs_{C_1, C_2} = (1 + r (1 - t))$ at the given point.

By hypothesis

$$\bar{T} = Y_1 t + \frac{Y_2 t}{1+r} + \frac{(Y_1 - Y_1 t - \bar{C}_1)rt}{1+r} \qquad (4.49)$$

$(\bar{C}_1, \bar{C}_2)$ satisfy (4.47). Therefore,

$$\bar{C}_2 = -(1+r)\bar{C}_1 + W(1+r) - \left[Y_1 t + \frac{Y_2 t}{(1+r)} + \frac{(Y_1(1-t) - \bar{C}_1)rt}{1+r} \right](1+r)$$

$$\Rightarrow \quad \bar{C}_2 = -(1+r)\bar{C}_1 + W(1+r) - \bar{T}(1+r)$$

$$\Rightarrow \quad \frac{\bar{C}_2}{1+r} + \bar{C}_1 = W - \bar{T}$$

Thus, $(\bar{C}_1, \bar{C}_2)$ is a point on the lump sum tax budget line also. However, at $(\bar{C}_1, \bar{C}_2)$, clearly, $mrs_{C_1, C_2} = [1 + r(1 - t)] < (1 + r)$. Thus it is not the best point on the lump sum tax budget line as shown in Figure 4.9. (Explain this point yourself.) Hence the proportional income tax involves excess burden as indicated by the individual's movement from I_1 to I_2 in Figure 4.9.

The result is quite obvious. The government here is choosing t in such a manner that the present value of lifetime tax discounted at the market rate of interest, r, is $\bar{T}$. Thus the present value of the individual's lifetime disposable income discounted at the market rate of interest is $(\bar{W} - \bar{T})$. Clearly, therefore, the $(\bar{C}_1, \bar{C}_2)$ the individual chooses must be such that its present value discounted at the market rate of interest, r, equals $(\bar{W} - \bar{T})$. Hence the chosen $(\bar{C}_1, \bar{C}_2)$ must lie on the lump sum tax budget line. However, in the proportional income tax case the rate at which the individual can exchange C_1 for C_2 is $1 + r(1 - t)$ and not $(1 + r)$. Hence she chooses that point from the lump sum tax budget line at which $mrs_{C_1, C_2} = 1 + r(1 - t)$. Accordingly, the chosen point is not the best point on the lump sum tax budget line. This is the source of the excess burden. Here also the excess burden is due to the distortion that the proportional income tax incorporates in the price system. It makes the interest rate actually faced by the borrower and lender, $r(1 - t)$, different from the market rate of interest, r. As a result, in addition to the wealth effect due to the reduction in the individual's wealth by $\overline{T}$, the proportional income tax produces a substitution effect by making current consumption cheaper in terms of future consumption. The individual, therefore, is induced to choose from the lump sum tax budget line, not the point that he chooses under the lump sum tax, but a point at which the current consumption is larger and future consumption is less. The excess burden is due to this substitution effect. In terms of Figure 4.9, at both A_1 and A_2 the real income of the individual, a la Slutsky, is the same, but the effective interest rates faced by the individual are different. Thus the movement from A_2 to A_1 is due to substitution effect. Consider the individual under the proportional income tax. She chooses A_2 under this tax. If now the effective interest rate faced by the individual is raised from $r(1 - t)$ to r and at the same time her income is adjusted so that her real income, a la Slutsky, remains unchanged so that she is just able to choose her initial consumption bundle, she will face the budget line B_1B_1 and choose the point A_1. Thus the movement from A_2 to A_1 and, therefore, the excess burden are due to substitution effect.

The Case of the Market

The choice between current and future consumption, i.e., between consumption and saving in the current period is related to the market for loanable funds, where saving constitutes the supply side. While saving gives the supply of new loans in any given period, demand for new loans comes from the necessity for financing investment. Demand for new loans can also come from the need to finance additional working capital requirements for increased production, but that source of demand is ignored here for simplicity. We shall, therefore, analyse the issue of excess burden of income tax in the market for loanable funds. We shall do this with the help of Figure 4.10 where interest rate, r, is measured along the vertical axis and saving and investment are measured along the horizontal axis. For simplicity, investment schedule, labelled DD, is taken to be horizontal. The saving schedule is positively sloped as usual. The equilibrium interest rate, saving and investment correspond to the point of intersection of the two schedules. The equilibrium values of interest rate, saving and investment are labelled r^*, S^* and I^* respectively.

The saving schedule gives the supply price of new loans corresponding to every S. Thus, any given point on the saving schedule indicates the minimum price or interest rate at which the corresponding quantity of new loans or savings is supplied. As in the earlier case of the labour market, the area under the saving schedule over the set of values of S ranging from 0 to, say, S^*, gives the minimum interest income that the savers require to supply S^* amount of savings. It is given by the area of the quadrilateral: $A_3OS^*A_1$. In equilibrium the interest rate is r^* and the interest income of the savers is (r^*S^*). It is given by the area of the rectangle $r^*OS^*A_1$. Hence the gain to the savers is given by the area of the triangle $r^*A_1A_3$.

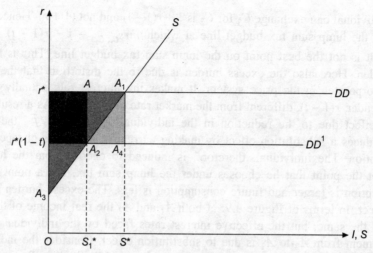

Figure 4.10: Excess burden of a proportional income tax on interest income.

Now, suppose that the government imposes a proportional income tax at the rate t. It does not affect the investors, as it falls not on them but on the savers' interest income. The demand schedule, therefore, remains unaffected. Hence, following the imposition of this tax, the equilibrium interest rate in the market remains unchanged at r^*, since the demand schedule is perfectly elastic at r^*. But for the savers or lenders the rate of interest comes down effectively to $r^*(1 - t)$ as they have to pay from r^* the amount, (r^*t), as tax. Hence the demand schedule, which gives the demand price corresponding to every given level of loan, as faced by the suppliers of loans shifts down to $r^*(1 - t)$. Equilibrium values of saving and investment, therefore, fall from S^* to S_1^*. Savers' gain now reduces to the area of the triangle $r^*(1 - t)A_2A_3$. Of the total loss of savers' welfare given by the area of the quadrilateral $r^*(1 - t)A_2A_1r^*$, the area of the rectangle $r^*(1 - t)A_2Ar^*$, is accounted for by the transfer of tax revenue paid by the savers to the government. Thus the loss in savers' welfare measured by the area of the triangle AA_2A_1 does not accrue as gain to anyone. It is therefore the excess burden or the deadweight loss, which is in excess of the loss accounted for by the transfer of the tax revenue from the taxpayers to the government.

The reason for this excess burden is exactly the same as that in the earlier case. It is due to the reduction in saving brought about by the fall in the interest rate effectively faced by the savers. On every intramarginal unit of loan supplied in the pre-tax equilibrium, i.e., on every unit of loan less than the S^*th unit, the savers made some gain given by the excess of the pre-tax equilibrium interest rate over the minimum interest rate at which they were willing to supply the given unit. Following the imposition of the tax, they cease to supply some of the units they were supplying before. They, therefore, lose the gains they were making on these units in the pre-tax equilibrium. However, they do not pay any tax on the units of loans they cease to supply. Hence, corresponding to the losses of the gains on these units, there is no tax payment to the government. Thus these losses are deadweight loss or excess burden.

Let us now derive a measure of the excess burden. It is given by the area of the triangle

$$A_2AA_1 = (1/2)(A_2A_4)(AA_2) = (1/2)(-dS)(r^*t) \qquad (4.50)$$

Now, $- dS = (dS/dr)(- dr) = (dS/dr)(r*t)$

Because $-dr$ ($\equiv$ fall in interest rate effectively faced by savers) $= r*t$ (4.51)

Again, $\dfrac{dS}{dr} = \dfrac{dS}{dr} \dfrac{r*}{S*} \dfrac{S*}{r*} = \eta_S \dfrac{S*}{r*}$ (4.52)

where $\eta_S \equiv$ elasticity of savings with respect to r.
Substituting (4.52) into (4.51), we have

$$-dS = \eta_S \frac{S*}{r*} (r*t) = \eta_S S*t$$ (4.53)

Substituting (4.53) into (4.50), we have

The amount of excess burden $= (1/2)\eta_S S*r*t^2$ (4.54)

Thus, the amount of excess burden in this case is an increasing function of interest elasticity of savings and the tax rate. Explain this result following lines suggested in earlier cases yourself.

4.2.7 Excess Burden and Choice between Present and Future Consumption: General Equilibrium Analysis

Firms

We shall now extend our analysis to the general equilibrium framework. We shall work under the simplest possible assumptions for expository convenience. The results we shall derive here will, however, hold under more general and realistic conditions. The assumptions that we make here are the following: There are a large number of identical firms and identical households. Each firm is owned by a large number of individuals who supply it with fixed endowments of labour and capital. Firms make factor payments only to its owners, i.e., the firms pay profit only and the whole of its output is profit in terms of the good produced. Credit market is perfectly competitive. Hence interest rate is given to every individual firm and household and borrowing and lending rates are the same. Firms use their given endowments of factors of production to produce one consumer good for both the current period and the future period. These are the only two periods considered here. The consumer good produced in the economy is used as the numeraire. If production of the consumer good in the current period is reduced, the resources released are used to augment productive capacity and more of the consumer good than what has been sacrificed is produced in future. The production possibility frontier (*PPF*) of the representative firm is given by

$$Y_2 = C(Y_1); \quad C' < 0, \; C'' < 0 \quad \text{and} \quad -C' > 1$$ (4.55)

where Y_1 and Y_2 denote outputs of the consumer good in the current and future period respectively. Equation (4.55) states that the amount of output of the consumer good in the future period depends upon how much of the consumer good is produced in the current period. If more is produced in the current period, smaller amount of the given amount of productive resources can be used to produce the consumer good in the next period. Hence Y_2 falls following an increase in Y_1. Moreover, $C'' < 0$ implies that the amount of Y_2 that is sacrificed per unit increase in Y_1 rises with an increase in the production of Y_1. The representative firm maximizes the present value of its profit discounted at the market rate of interest, r. It is given by

$$\Pi = Y_1 + \left[\frac{Y_2}{(1+r)} \right] \tag{4.56}$$

The firm determines Y_1 and Y_2 in such a manner that Π is maximized. The optimization exercise carried out by the firm may, therefore, be stated as follows:

$$\max_{Y_1} \Pi = Y_1 + \left[\frac{C(Y_1)}{(1+r)} \right]$$

The first-order condition for profit maximization is given by

$$- C'(Y_1) = (1 + r) \tag{4.57}$$

Given the assumption that $C'' < 0$, the second-order condition is automatically satisfied. Equation (4.57) implies that corresponding to any r the representative firm produces from the *PPF* that (Y_1, Y_2) at which $mrtr_{Y_1, Y_2} [\equiv - C'(Y_1)] = (1 + r)$. (Explain why yourself.) From (4.55) and (4.57) we get Y_1 and Y_2 as functions of r. Thus

$$Y_1 = Y_1(r) \quad \text{and} \quad Y_2 = Y_2(r) \tag{4.58}$$

In Figure 4.11 where the concave curve labelled *PPF* represents (4.55), we show that when $r = r_0$, at the point A (Y_1^0, Y_2^0), $mrtr_{Y_1, Y_2} (A)(\equiv -C'(Y_1^0)) = (1 + r_0)$. Hence the firm will produce (Y_1^0, Y_2^0) at r_0. This point can be explained using iso-profit lines as well. An iso-profit line gives all combinations of (Y_1, Y_2), each of which yields a given level of profit. Thus the iso-profit line corresponding to the given level of profit, Π_0, is given by the equation:

$$\Pi_0 = Y_1 + \left[\frac{Y_2}{(1+r)} \right]$$

$$\Rightarrow \qquad\qquad Y_2 = - Y_1(1 + r) + \Pi_0(1 + r) \tag{4.59}$$

Clearly, the iso-profit line corresponding to Π_0 in the (Y_1, Y_2) plane is a straight line with the slope, $- (1 + r)$ and vertical intercept, $\Pi_0(1 + r)$. It also follows from (4.59) that a higher iso-profit line corresponds to a larger amount of profit and vice versa. The point on the *PPF* that maximizes the representative firm's profit lies on the highest iso-profit line. Such a point must be a point of tangency between the *PPF* and an iso-profit line. The profit maximizing point on the *PPF*, when $r = r_0$, is labelled A in Figure 4.11. At A an iso-profit line corresponding to r_0 is tangent to the *PPF*. Clearly, every other point on the *PPF* lies on a lower iso-profit line, when $r = r_0$. Accordingly, at the profit maximizing point the absolute value of the slope of the *PPF*, $mrtr_{Y_1, Y_2}$, equals the absolute value of the slope of the iso-profit line, $(1 + r)$, which is $(1 + r_0)$, when $r = r_0$.

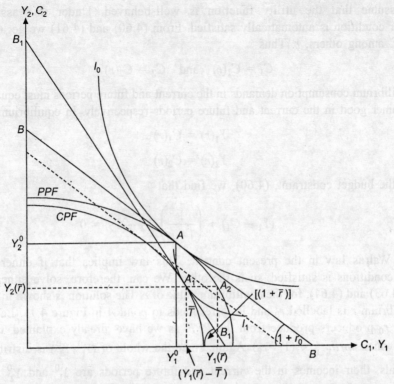

Figure 4.11: Excess burden, lump sum tax, choice between present and future consumption: general equilibrium.

Individuals

Individuals own the firms. They supply the firms with fixed endowments of labour and capital, which the firms use to produce the consumer good. Hence the whole value of output of the firms in each period goes into the hands of their owners as profit income. Thus Y_1 and Y_2 may be taken as the incomes of the representative individual in the current and the future period respectively. The representative individual maximizes

$$U(C_1, C_2)$$

$$\text{subject to} \quad Y_1 + \frac{Y_2}{1+r} (\equiv W) = C_1 + \frac{C_2}{1+r} \tag{4.60}$$

where $U(.) \equiv$ utility function of the individual, $C_1 \equiv$ demand for the consumer good in the current period and $C_2 \equiv$ demand for the consumer good in the future period.

The first-order condition for profit maximization is given by

$$\left[\frac{U'(C_1)}{U'(C_2)} \right] \equiv mrs_{C_1, C_2} = (1+r) \tag{4.61}$$

We assume that the utility function is well-behaved. Under this assumption the second-order condition is automatically satisfied. From (4.60) and (4.61) we get C_1 and C_2 as functions of, among others, r. Thus

$$C_1 = C_1(r) \quad \text{and} \quad C_2 = C_2(r) \tag{4.62}$$

In equilibrium consumption demands in the current and future periods must equal production of the consumer good in the current and future periods respectively. In equilibrium, therefore,

$$Y_1(r) = C_1(r) \tag{4.63}$$

and

$$Y_2(r) = C_2(r) \tag{4.64}$$

From the budget constraint, (4.60), we find that

$$(Y_1 - C_1) + \left(\frac{1}{1+r} \right)(Y_2 - C_2) = 0 \tag{4.65}$$

This is the Walras law in the present context. This law implies that if either of the two equilibrium conditions is satisfied, so is the other. We can, therefore, solve either of the two equations, (4.63) and (4.64), for the equilibrium value of r. The solution is shown in Figure 4.11, where equilibrium r is labelled r_0 and it corresponds to point A in Figure 4.11. Let us explain.

At $r = r_0$ producers produce from the *PPF*, as we have already explained, that (Y_1, Y_2), (Y_1^0, Y_2^0), at which $mrt_{Y_1, Y_2} = (1 + r_0)$. Again, since the whole of (Y_1^0, Y_2^0) is distributed among the individuals, their incomes in the current and future periods are Y_1^0 and Y_2^0 respectively. Accordingly, at r_0 the budget line of the representative consumer is given by

$$Y_1^0 + \frac{Y_2^0}{(1+r_0)} = C_1 + \frac{C_2}{(1+r_0)}$$

This budget line is represented by BB in Figure 4.11. The absolute value of its slope is $(1 + r_0)$ and it clearly passes through (Y_1^0, Y_2^0), as (Y_1^0, Y_2^0) satisfies the budget constraint. The representative individual chooses from this budget line (Y_1^0, Y_2^0) in equilibrium. If she had chosen a different (C_1, C_2) from her budget line, the economy would have been in disequilibrium. If at any r, $C_1 > Y_1^0$ and therefore, as follows from (4.65), $C_2 < Y_2^0$, then the individual dissaves in the current period and, therefore, there is excess demand for loans. Let us explain. Every individual here is identical. So, if at any r any one individual dissaves in the current period, then everyone else also does so. Everyone, therefore, requires loans in the current period to finance the excess of her consumption demand over her income. Hence there will be excess demand for loans in the current period. So r will rise. Similarly if $C_1 < Y_1^0$, r will tend to fall.

Lump Sum Tax

Suppose that the government now imposes a lump sum tax, $\bar{T}$, and uses the proceeds to purchase the consumer good worth $\bar{T}$ in the current period itself. This assumption is made just for expository convenience. It will not scuttle the generality of the result in any manner, but enable us to carry out the analysis in the simplest possible framework. As a result of this assumption, the set of all the combinations of Y_1 and Y_2 available to the individual, which we shall refer to as the consumption possibility frontier (CPF), will lie below the PPF, which is given by (4.55). To derive the former from the latter we have to write the latter in the inverse form as given by

$$Y_1 = C^{-1}(Y_2) \equiv \tilde{C}(Y_2); \ \tilde{C}'\left(\equiv \frac{1}{C'}\right) < 0 \quad \text{and} \quad \tilde{C}'' < 0 \qquad (4.66)$$

The CPF can, therefore, be written as

$$Y_1 = \tilde{C}(Y_2) - \overline{T} \qquad (4.67)$$

It is clear from (4.67) that corresponding to every Y_2 the amount of Y_1 on the CPF will be less than that on PPF by $\overline{T}$. It is also obvious that the slopes of CPF and PPF corresponding to every Y_2 are the same.

This tax, as it is imposed on individuals and not on firms, will not affect the profit function, (4.56), or the FOC for profit maximization, (4.57), of the representative firm. Hence supply functions of Y_1 and Y_2 as given by (4.58) remain unaffected.

The tax will, however, affect the household's budget, which in the pre-tax situation was given by (4.60). It will now be given by

$$Y_1 - \overline{T} + \frac{Y_2}{(1+r)} = W - \overline{T} = C_1 + \frac{C_2}{1+r} \qquad (4.68)$$

As the individual's present value of lifetime disposable income is less than that of the pre-tax situation, W, by $\overline{T}$, the individual in the post-tax situation will choose from this budget line. As a result chosen values of C_1 and C_2 will be less than their pre-tax values corresponding to every r, provided they are normal goods.

Suppose that the equilibrium occurs at $\overline{r}$ so that demand for and supply of Y_1 and Y_2 are equal at $\overline{r}$. Producers in equilibrium will produce from the PPF, $[Y_1(\overline{r}), Y_2(\overline{r})]$, at which $mrtr_{Y_1, Y_2} = (1 + \overline{r})$. The point, $(Y_1(\overline{r}), Y_2(\overline{r}))$, on the PPF is labelled A_2 in Figure 4.11. The representative individual, therefore, in equilibrium earns, $[Y_1(\overline{r})$ and $Y_2(\overline{r})]$, in the current and the future period respectively from which in the current period she has to pay $\overline{T}$ as tax. Thus, the present value of lifetime disposable income of the individual is given by

$$\left[Y_1(\overline{r}) - \overline{T} + \frac{Y_2(\overline{r})}{(1+r)} \right]$$

and the budget equation of the individual in equilibrium is

$$Y_1(\overline{r}) - \overline{T} + \frac{Y_2(\overline{r})}{(1+r)} = W - \overline{T} = C_1 + \frac{C_2}{(1+\overline{r})} \qquad (4.69)$$

The slope of this budget line, as one can deduce easily, is $[-(1 + \overline{r})]$ and its vertical intercept is $(W - \overline{T})(1 + \overline{r})$. Moreover, if we substitute $[(Y_1(\overline{r}) - \overline{T}]$ and $Y_2(\overline{r})$ for C_1 and

C_2 respectively, (4.69) is satisfied. Thus the budget line in equilibrium will pass through the point $(Y_1(\bar{r}) - \bar{T}, Y_2(\bar{r}))$ on the CPF and have the slope $[-(1 + \bar{r})]$. This budget line is represented by B_1B_1 in Figure 4.11. As we have pointed out already, the slope of the CPF at $[Y_1(\bar{r}) - \bar{T}, Y_2(\bar{r})]$, which is labelled A_1 in Figure 4.11, is the same as that at the point $[Y_1(\bar{r}), Y_2(\bar{r})]$, labelled A_2 in Figure 4.11, on PPF. Thus the slope of the CPF at A_1 is $[-(1 + \bar{r})]$. Hence the budget line B_1B_1 is tangent to the CPF at A_1. Since there is equilibrium at $\bar{r}$, the individual chooses $[Y_1(\bar{r}) - \bar{T}, Y_2(\bar{r})]$ as (C_1, C_2) from her budget line so that demand for and supply of Y_1 and Y_2 are equal at $\bar{r}$. Since $[Y_1(\bar{r}) - \bar{T}, Y_2(\bar{r})]$ is the optimum point on the budget line having the slope $[-(1 + \bar{r})]$, the indifference curve on which the point $[Y_1(\bar{r}) - \bar{T} + Y_2(\bar{r})/(1 + r)]$ lies, which is labelled I_1 in Figure 4.11, is tangent to the budget line at the chosen point and, therefore, $mrs_{C_1, C_2} = (1 + \bar{r})$ at the chosen point. Thus the indifference curve is tangent to the CPF also at the chosen point.

From the above it follows that at the point chosen from the CPF, the slope of the CPF, which gives the $mrtr_{Y_1, Y_2}$ of the corresponding point on PPF, equals the marginal rate of substitution of C_1 for C_2. Hence the chosen point is the best point on the CPF to the individual. Prove this point yourself. Since CPF gives the largest bundles of Y_1 and Y_2 available to the consumer when $\bar{T}$ amount of the consumer good is taken away from the individual in the current period, and since the chosen point is the best point on the CPF, the loss in the individual's welfare due to the transfer of $\bar{T}$ amount of income from the individual to the government is minimum under the lump sum tax case. This minimum loss in welfare is indicated by the movement from I_0 to I_1 in Figure 4.11.

Proportional Income Tax

Let us now compare the lump sum tax with a proportional personal income tax applied at the rate, t. Since it is a personal income tax, it does not apply to firms. Hence the tax does not affect the profit function, (4.56), or the FOC for profit maximization, (4.57), of the representative firm. The representative firm therefore, as before, chooses from the PPF that point at which $mrtr_{Y_1, Y_2} = (1 + r)$. The supply functions of Y_1 and Y_2 as given by (4.58) therefore remain unaffected. The government by assumption chooses the tax rate, t, in such a manner that it ends up collecting the same $\bar{T}$ amount as tax and uses it to purchase the consumer good in period 1. This assumption is made to make the proportional income tax comparable to the lump sum tax. This proportional personal income tax, as we have pointed out above, applies equally to the lender and the borrower. The whole of Y_1 and Y_2, which denote the amounts of the consumer good produced in the current and future periods respectively, accrues as current and future incomes to the individuals. Therefore, the budget line of the representative individual under the proportional income tax is given by

$$C_2 = Y_2(1 - t) + [Y_1(1 - t) - C_1][1 + r(1 - t)] \tag{4.70}$$

The above equation can be explained the same way as (4.46). We can rewrite (4.70) as

$$C_2 = Y_2 + Y_1(1 + r) - C_1(1 + r) - [Y_1(1 - t) - C_1] rt - Y_1 t(1 + r) - Y_2 t$$

$$\Rightarrow \quad C_2 + C_1(1 + r) = Y_2 + Y_1(1 + r) - \{[Y_1(1 - t) - C_1]rt + Y_2 t + Y_1 t(1 + r)\}$$

$$\Rightarrow \qquad C_1 + \frac{C_2}{1+r} = Y_1 + \frac{Y_2}{1+r} - \left[Y_1 t + \frac{\{[Y_1(1-t) - C_1] \, rt + Y_2 t\}}{1+r} \right] \qquad (4.71)$$

The individual under the proportional personal income tax chooses from the budget line, (4.70). Hence at the chosen point $mrs_{C_1, C_2} = 1 + r(1 - t)$. Suppose that the equilibrium in this case occurs at $\tilde{r}$, with $(Y_1, Y_2) = (\tilde{Y}_1, \tilde{Y}_2)$. Clearly, the absolute value of the slope of PPF at $(\tilde{Y}_1, \tilde{Y}_2)$, $mrtr_{Y_1, Y_2} (\tilde{Y}_1, \tilde{Y}_2)$, is $(1 + \tilde{r})$. The situation is shown in Figure 4.12 where the point of production on PPF is labelled A.

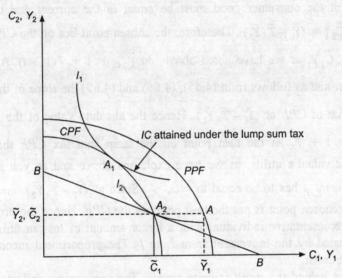

Figure 4.12: Excess burden, proportional income tax, choice between present and future consumption: general equilibrium.

The budget line of the individual in this case, as follows from (4.70), is given by

$$C_2 = \tilde{Y}_2(1 - t) + [\tilde{Y}_1(1 - t) - C_1](1 + \tilde{r}(1 - t)) \qquad (4.72)$$

or, as follows from (4.71), by

$$C_1 + \frac{C_2}{1+\tilde{r}} = \tilde{Y}_1 + \frac{\tilde{Y}_2}{1+\tilde{r}} - \left[\tilde{Y}_1 t + \frac{\{[\tilde{Y}_1(1-t) - C_1] \, \tilde{r}t + \tilde{Y}_2 t\}}{1+\tilde{r}} \right] \qquad (4.73)$$

This budget line is represented by BB in Figure 4.12. At the chosen point from this budget line, as follows from (4.72), $mrs_{C_1, C_2} = 1 + \tilde{r}(1 - t)$. This point is labelled $A_2(\tilde{C}_1, \tilde{C}_2)$ in Figure 4.12. CPF in Figure 4.12 is the same as that of Figure 4.11. It is the lump sum tax CPF representing (4.68). $A_2(\tilde{C}_1, \tilde{C}_2)$ lies on CPF. Let us explain why. The present value of lifetime tax, denoted by T, paid in equilibrium is accordingly

$$T = \left[\tilde{Y}_1 t + \frac{\{[\tilde{Y}_1(1-t) - \hat{C}_1] \, \tilde{r}t + \tilde{Y}_2 t\}}{1+\tilde{r}} \right] = \overline{T} \quad \text{(by hypothesis)} \qquad (4.74)$$

$(\tilde{C}_1, \tilde{C}_2)$ satisfies (4.72) and therefore (4.73). Substituting $(\tilde{C}_1, \tilde{C}_2)$ and (4.74) into (4.73), we have

$$\tilde{C}_1 + \frac{\tilde{C}_2}{1+\tilde{r}} = \tilde{Y}_1 + \frac{\tilde{Y}_2}{1+\tilde{r}} - \left[\tilde{Y}_1 t + \frac{\{[\tilde{Y}_1(1-t) - \tilde{C}_1]\tilde{r}t + \tilde{Y}_2 t\}}{1+\tilde{r}} \right] = \tilde{Y}_1 + \frac{\tilde{Y}_2}{1+\tilde{r}} - \overline{T} \qquad (4.75)$$

Now $(\tilde{Y}_1, \tilde{Y}_2)$ is a point on the *PPF*. Hence $(\tilde{Y}_1 - \overline{T}, \tilde{Y}_2)$, as follows from (4.67), is a point on the *CPF* under the lump sum tax, $\overline{T}$. Since the situation is one of the equilibrium, demand for and supply of the consumer good must be equal in the current and the future period. Therefore, $(\tilde{C}_1, \tilde{C}_2) = (\tilde{Y}_1 - \overline{T}, \tilde{Y}_2)$. Therefore, the chosen point lies on the *CPF* under the lump sum tax. At $(\tilde{C}_1, \tilde{C}_2)$, as we have noted above, $mrs_{C_1, C_2} = 1 + \tilde{r}(1 - t)$. Again, as we have pointed out earlier and as follows from (4.55), (4.66) and (4.67) the slope of the *PPF* at $(\tilde{Y}_1, \tilde{Y}_2)$ is the same as that of *CPF* at $(\tilde{Y}_1 - \overline{T}, \tilde{Y}_2)$. Hence the absolute value of the slope of the *CPF* at $(\tilde{Y}_1 - \overline{T}, \tilde{Y}_2) = 1 + \tilde{r}$. At the best point on the lump sum tax *CPF* that maximizes the representative individual's utility, as we have explained above and as you should be able to argue yourself, $mrtr_{Y_1, Y_2}$ has to be equal to mrs_{C_1, C_2}. Since at $(\tilde{Y}_1 - \overline{T}, \tilde{Y}_2)$ $mrtr_{Y_1, Y_2}$ and mrs_{C_1, C_2} are different, the chosen point is not the best point on the *CPF*. Hence the proportional income tax saddles the representative individual with a larger amount of loss in utility than the lump sum tax as indicated by the movement from I_1 to I_2. The proportional income tax, therefore, involves excess burden.

The intuition behind the result is quite simple. The government collects from individuals even under the proportional income tax $\overline{T}$ amount of tax, which it uses wholly to purchase the consumer good in the current period only. Thus, if $(\tilde{Y}_1, \tilde{Y}_2)$ is produced in the economy, $(\tilde{Y}_1 - \overline{T}, \tilde{Y}_2)$ will be available to the representative individual under the proportional income tax also. Thus the individual's choice even in the present case will lie on the lump sum tax *CPF* in equilibrium. It should also be noted here that the slope of the *PPF* at any (Y_1, Y_2) is equal to that of the lump sum tax *CPF* at the corresponding point, $(Y_1 - \overline{T}, Y_2)$. Now the producers pay the market interest rate, r. To them one additional unit of Y_1 is equivalent to $(1 + r)$ additional amount of Y_2. Hence at the point the producers will choose from the *PPF* $mrtr_{Y_1, Y_2}$ has to be equal to $(1 + r)$. Explain it yourself. The absolute value of the slope of the corresponding point on the *CPF* is also $(1 + r)$.

The representative individual on the other hand faces the interest rate, $r(1 - t) < r$. Accordingly, the rate at which she can substitute C_1 for C_2 is $[1 + r(1 - t)]$, i.e., if she consumes one additional unit of C_1, her wealth and income in the future period will fall by 1 and $r(1 - t)$ respectively and hence she has to give up $[1 + r(1 - t)]$ amount of C_2. Accordingly, at the point she chooses mrs_{C_1, C_2} has to be equal to $[1 + r(1 - t)]$. Therefore, $mrtr_{Y_1, Y_2} > mrs_{C_1, C_2}$ at the point chosen in equilibrium from the *CPF*. Thus, under the proportional income tax the individual does not choose the best point from the lump sum tax CPF giving rise to excess burden. The above discussion also suggests the reason for the excess burden. It is clearly due to the wedge the proportional income tax drives between the interest rates faced by the producers and the consumers.

SUMMARY

1. The excess of the loss in welfare due to taxation over and above the minimum that is entailed by the transfer of the tax revenue from the taxpayers to the government is referred to as *excess burden or deadweight loss*. This excess burden measures the efficiency of taxation. The larger the excess burden of a tax, the less is its efficiency.

2. The burden of a tax has to be measured in terms of the amount of welfare the individuals lose as a result of the imposition of the tax and not in terms of the amount of tax they actually pay to the government.

3. Consider the individual's choice problem of allocating a given amount of expenditure over different goods. In the context of this choice problem a selective indirect tax on a commodity gives rise to excess burden in the case of every individual consumer of the commodity. Every individual consumer has to pay a given amount of tax revenue to the government under the selective indirect tax as she buys the taxed commodity. However, under this tax the loss in her welfare is larger than the minimum amount of loss in welfare entailed by the transfer of the tax revenue from the individual to the government. The excess burden is measured by the excess of the reduction in income that will in the absence of any kind of taxation make the individual choose from the indifference curve attained under the selective indirect tax over the tax revenue yielded by the selective indirect tax. The selective indirect tax produces not only an income effect by transferring the tax revenue from the consumer to the government but also a substitution effect by making the relative price of the taxed commodity higher to the consumer. The excess burden is due to the substitution effect. A direct tax on the consumer's consumption expenditure, however, does not produce any substitution effect. Hence it does not generate any excess burden in the context of the present choice problem.

4. If we focus on the market of a single good, then also we find that a selective indirect tax on the sale of the commodity leads to excess burden. In the context of a market the excess burden is given by the excess of the loss in consumer surplus due to the tax over the revenue yielded by the tax. It, therefore, gives us the part of the loss in consumer welfare that is not converted into any gain to the government. It, therefore, represents the excess burden or deadweight loss. The magnitude of this excess burden is found to be $\eta P_X^0 X_0 t^2$, where $\eta \equiv$ own price elasticity of demand of the taxed commodity, X, and $t \equiv$ the ad valorem tax rate on the sales of X, and P_X^0 and X_0 denote the initial equilibrium price and quantity of X respectively.

5. Selective indirect tax involves excess burden in the case of the general equilibrium also. In the present context, in the general equilibrium, individuals spend all their income earned from the production of the goods on the purchase of the goods. The source of the

excess burden consists in the distortion in the price system that the tax produces by making the prices received by the producers different from those paid by the consumers. Accordingly, at the commodity bundle produced and consumed *mrs* and *mrtr* become different leading to inefficiency. Obviously, the commodity bundle chosen by the producers and consumers is inferior to the best bundle on the *PPF* available to the producers in the post-tax scenario.

6. If we focus on the leisure–income or labour–leisure choice of the individual, then we find that even a direct tax involves excess burden. If a proportional tax on wage income is imposed, the loss in the welfare of the individual will be greater than that under an equal yield lump sum tax. The reason for this excess burden is again the same as that in the earlier case. The proportional tax on wage income not only reduces the income of the individual by the amount of the tax revenue but also lowers the wage rate below what the employers are paying. Therefore, in addition to making the individual poorer by the amount of the tax revenue, the proportional tax on wage income makes leisure cheaper. Thus the tax produces not only an income effect but also a substitution effect and the latter is the cause of the excess burden.

7. In the context of the labour market also we find that a proportional tax on wage income gives rise to excess burden. This is because on every intramarginal unit of labour supplied in the pre-tax scenario workers enjoy some surplus given by the excess of the actual wage rate received over the minimum price at which the workers are willing to supply the given unit of labour. Workers' welfare is measured by the sum of these surpluses. Following the imposition of the tax, employment falls. Therefore, workers cease to supply some of the units of labour they were supplying before. They accordingly lose the surpluses they were enjoying on all these units. Their welfare, therefore, falls by the sum of these surpluses. However, they also do not pay any taxes on the units of labour they no longer supply. Thus the welfare losses on the units that the workers stop selling following the imposition of the tax do not correspond to any tax collection by the government. Thus these welfare losses constitute a deadweight loss or excess burden.

8. Even when we extend our analysis to the general equilibrium framework, we find that a lump sum tax does not produce any excess burden, but a proportional income tax on wage income does. Under both the lump sum tax and an equal yield proportional income tax, the individual chooses from the same set of labour–income combinations, but the proportional income tax makes the wage rates faced by the producers and workers different. As a result in equilibrium at the labour–income combination chosen $mrs_{l,y}$ becomes different from $mrtr_{l,y}$ or marginal productivity of labour. Hence the combination chosen becomes different from the best of the available combinations.

9. When we consider the individual's choice problem over present and future consumption and focus on the individual's behaviour alone in the partial equilibrium framework, we find that a lump sum tax does not involve excess burden, but a proportional income tax does. If we compare a lump sum tax to an equal yield proportional income tax, then we find that both produce the same income effect as the individual loses the same amount of wealth under both. However, the proportional income tax in addition produces a substitution effect by making current consumption cheaper in terms of future consumption. This leads to excess burden.

10. The problem of choice between present and future consumption is related to the market for loanable funds, where saving gives the supply of loans and investment constitutes demand for loans. A proportional income tax reduces saving and thereby leads to excess burden or deadweight loss. On every intramarginal unit of saving the saver in the pre-tax situation enjoyed a surplus of the actual price over her supply price. Sum of these surpluses measured her welfare. Following the imposition of the tax, she ceases to supply some of the units of saving in the loan market and thereby loses the surpluses on these units. However, she also does not pay any tax on these units. Thus this loss in welfare is not converted into any gain to the government. Hence this loss in welfare is deadweight loss or excess burden.

11. In the general equilibrium case also proportional income tax produces excess burden by making the interest rates paid by borrowers and received by lenders different.

═══════════════ KEY CONCEPTS ═══════════════

✓ Burden of a tax
✓ Measure of excess burden
✓ Efficiency of a tax
✓ Ad valorem tax
✓ Distortion in the price system

✓ Excess burden of a tax
✓ Equivalent variation
✓ Selective indirect tax
✓ Unit tax
✓ Proportional income tax

═══════════════ REVIEW QUESTIONS ═══════════════

1. How should the burden of a tax be measured? Explain and illustrate with an example.
2. How is the efficiency of a tax measured? Explain.
3. Consider an individual spending a given amount of money, $\bar{C}$, on two goods, X_1 and X_2. If now the government imposes a lump sum tax $\bar{T}$ on the individual, what is the minimum amount of welfare the individual loses as a result of the tax? Explain. If instead of the lump sum tax the government imposes a selective indirect tax at the rate t on X_1 and chooses t in such a manner that it yields $\bar{T}$ amount of tax revenue, will it lead to any excess burden? If your answer is yes, then suggest a measure of the excess burden and identify the cause of the excess burden.
4. Does a direct tax on the consumption expenditure of the individual considered in the previous problem lead to any excess burden? Explain and illustrate graphically.
5. Consider the general equilibrium framework where the individuals spend all their income on consumption in the current period. Does a selective indirect tax generate excess burden in this framework? If your answer is yes, what is the source of this excess burden? Does a direct tax lead to excess burden? Explain.
6. Why does a lump sum tax not involve excess burden in the context of the labour–leisure choice of an individual? Explain fully.
7. Does a proportional tax on wage income lead to excess burden in the context of labour–leisure choice of an individual? Explain your answer fully.

8. Does a proportional tax on wage income give rise to excess burden or deadweight loss in the context of the labour market? If your answer is yes, identify the source of this excess burden. In this context, explain why the amount of excess burden is an increasing function, among others, of the tax rate and the own price elasticity of labour supply.

9. Does a proportional tax on wage income lead to excess burden in the general equilibrium framework? What is the cause of this excess burden?

10. Does a proportional income tax lead to excess burden in the context of an individual's problem of choice over present and future consumption, when we focus on the individual alone in the partial equilibrium framework? What is the source of this excess burden? Does such a tax lead to excess burden in the case of the market? Does it give rise to excess burden in the general equilibrium framework also?

═══ PROBLEMS AND APPLICATIONS ═══

1. Suppose that the government wants to stop production and consumption of liquor and it estimates the inverse demand and supply functions of liquor, which are given by $P^D = 100 - .5\,X$ and $P^S = 90$. X denotes quantity of liquor. At what rate/rates should the government impose a unit tax on the purchase of X to achieve its objective? Illustrate your answer graphically. Does this tax impose any burden on the individuals? Explain your answer.

   (*Hint:* $t \geq 10$.)

2. Suppose that an individual spends Rs.100 on two goods, X_1 and X_2, which are traded in competitive markets. Prices of the two goods are Re. 1 and Rs. 2 respectively. The utility function of the individual is given by $U = X_1^{0.8} X_2^{0.2}$. If now the government imposes a lump sum tax of Rs. 10, what is the minimum loss in welfare the individual will suffer? Explain your answer.

   (*Hint:* Minimum loss in welfare will be $[80^{0.8}\ 10^{0.2}] - [72^{0.8}\ 9^{0.2}]$.)

3. Consider Problem 2. Suppose that the government instead of the lump sum tax imposes a selective indirect tax on the sales of X_1 at the unit rate t and chooses t in such a manner that it yields Rs. 10 in tax revenue. Derive the optimum post-tax (X_1, X_2). Illustrate this case graphically measuring X_1 and X_2 on the horizontal and vertical axis respectively. Does the vertical distance of the post-tax budget line from the pre-tax budget line corresponding to the optimum point of the post-tax budget line give the tax revenue in terms of X_2. Does the post-tax optimum point lie on the lump sum tax budget line, when the amount of the lump sum tax is Rs. 10? Explain. If your answer is yes, then is it the best point on the lump sum tax budget line? If not, then what conclusion do you draw regarding the efficiency of the selective indirect tax? What is the utility level attained by the individual in the post-tax situation? What is the minimum level of income that will enable the individual attain this level of utility in the absence of any kind of taxation. Explain. Plot the budget line corresponding to this level of income. Does it lie below the lump sum tax budget line of the previous problem? What does the vertical distance between this budget line and the pre-tax budget line measure? Explain. If the selective indirect tax involves excess burden, then derive a measure of the excess burden. Explain the measure.

(*Hint:* $\max\limits_{X_1, X_2} U = X_1^{0.8} X_2^{0.2}$, subject to $100 = (1 + t)X_1 + 2X_2$. This yields X_1 as a function of t. Optimum $(X_1, X_2, t) = (70, 10, 1/7)$. $(X_1, X_2) = (70, 10)$ at the pre-tax prices is clearly on the lump sum tax budget line. However, it is above and to the left of the best point. To derive the minimum income needed to attain the indifference curve attained under the selective indirect tax in the absence of any kind of taxation, carry out the following optimization exercise: $\min\limits_{X_1, X_2} X_1 + 2X_2$, subject to $70^{.8} \, 10^{.2} = X_1^{.8} X_2^{.2}$. This will yield the cost minimizing (X_1, X_2) on the indifference curve corresponding to $\bar{U} = 70^{.8} \, 10^{.2}$. Excess of the lump sum tax, 10, over the value of this cost minimizing (X_1, X_2) at the pre-tax prices is the measure of the excess burden.)

4. Suppose that an individual, with a given income of Rs. 100, consumes only two goods, X_1 and X_2. Her utility function is given by $U = X_1^{.5} X_2^{.5}$. The price of each of the two goods is Re. 1. Suppose that the government imposes a selective indirect tax at the rate of 10% on X_1. Show that the tax involves excess burden. Also derive a measure of the excess burden.

(*Hint:* Post-tax $X_1 = 12.99$ and $X_2 = 35.71$ and tax revenue = Rs. 1.3. If a lump sum tax of Rs. 1.3 is imposed, equilibrium values of X_1 and X_2 become 78.96 and 19.74 respectively. Check that the utility level corresponding to the latter bundle is higher than that corresponding to the former bundle. The utility level corresponding to the former bundle is $(12.99)^{.5} (35.71)^{.5}$. To find out a measure of the excess burden, carry out the following optimization exercise: $\min\limits_{X_1, X_2} X_1 + X_2$, subject to $(12.99)^{.5} (35.71)^{.5} = X_1^{0.8} X_2^{0.2}$. Compute the value of the optimum bundle. Suppose that it is M. Now $(1.3 - M)$ is the measure of excess burden.)

5. Consider a commodity X that is traded in a competitive market. Its pre-tax inverse demand and supply functions are given by $P^D = 100 - 0.5X$ and $P^S = 10$. Suppose that an ad valorem tax at the percentage rate of 10% is imposed on the sale or purchasec of X. How much excess burden does it generate? What happens to the amount of excess burden if (i) the tax is imposed at the rate of 20% and (ii) the rate of fall in the demand price with respect to X is $- 0.8$ instead of $- 0.5$. Illustrate your answers graphically and explain them fully. (Work it out yourself.)

6. Consider the market for food grains of the rich. Food grains are a necessity. Accordingly, demand for food grains of the rich is perfectly inelastic. If now a selective indirect tax is imposed on these food grains, will it generate any excess burden? Illustrate the situation graphically and explain your answer fully.

(*Hint:* Excess burden in this case is zero. Explain yourself.)

7. Consider the market for mango and that for the fruits as a whole. From the point of view of tax efficiency which of the following two taxes—(i) indirect tax on the sales of mangoes only and (ii) a selective indirect tax at the same rate on all fruits—will you prefer? Explain your answer fully.

(*Hint:* Own price elasticity of mangoes is likely to be much higher. Hence excess burden will be larger too.)

8. Consider the labour–leisure choice problem of an individual. Suppose that the utility function of the individual is given by $U = y^5 l^5$. Suppose that the real wage rate is 1 and the labour endowment is 10 hours. Derive the optimum values of l and y. Suppose that a proportional tax at the rate of 10% is imposed on the wage income. How much revenue does the tax yield? If the same amount is raised by means of a lump sum tax, will the individual lose less utility? Does the proportional wage tax involve excess burden? If yes, then derive a measure of this excess burden. Show that the excess burden is solely due to the substitution effect produced by the proportional wage tax. (Work out the problem yourself.)

9. Consider the individual of the previous problem. Suppose that the government imposes a proportional income tax on the individual's wage income at the rate, t. Derive the tax collection of the government as a function of t. Plot it in a graph. Suppose that the government wants to collect 1 unit as tax revenue from this tax. What value of t should the government choose? How much utility does the individual derive in this case? Suppose that she is made to face the pre-tax real wage rate, but her real income, a la Slutsky, is adjusted in such a manner that it remains unchanged. How will her choice change in such a case? Will she make the same choice under a lump sum tax of 1? Does the proportional tax on wage income that yields 1 in tax revenue involve excess burden? If your answer is yes, then how do you explain it?

   (*Hint:* Optimum value of $l = 5$. So it is independent of proportional income tax rate, t, but the optimum value of $y = 5(1 - t)$. Since the optimum labour supply and, therefore, before-tax wage income is 5, total tax revenue is given by $T = 5t$. Therefore, $t = 1/5$. Her chosen (y, l) under the proportional income tax is ($y = 4, l = 5$). If now the proportional income tax is removed so that she again receives the real wage rate of unity, to keep her real income unchanged a la Slutsky, her income is to be reduced so that it just enables her to choose ($y = 4, l = 5$). This happens when her income is reduced by unity or a lump sum tax of unity is imposed on the individual. Her budget equation will therefore become $y = (10 - l) - 1$. Optimum $(y, l) = (4.5, 4.5)$. Under the proportional income tax she attains the utility level 4.48. To ascertain the maximum reduction in income that will allow her to attain 4.48 utility level, carry out the following maximization exercise: $\max\limits_{y,l} U = y^5 l^5$ subject to $y = (10 - l) - M$. From this we get $l = y = (10 - M)/2$. Put these values in 4.48 $= y^5 l^5$ and solve for M. Work out the rest yourself.)

10. You find that a lump sum tax does not involve excess burden, but a non-lump sum tax whose amount varies with incomes or expenditures generates excess burden. Will you therefore recommend lump sum tax? Explain your answer.

11. Suppose that the labour supply function is given by the equation $L^S = 10 + .5W$ and demand price of labour is given by $W^D = 30$. What is the level of welfare enjoyed by the workers in the pre-tax scenario? How much excess burden will a 10% tax on wage income generate? Can you attribute this excess burden to the reduction in employment that the tax causes? Explain your answer.

12. Suppose that an individual lives for two periods. She has perfect foresight and operates in a perfectly competitive credit market where both borrowing and lending rates are the same. Her income in each of the two periods is Rs. 100. Price level is unity in each period.

Her utility function is given by $U = C_1^{.8} C_2^{.2}$. The market interest rate is 10%. What is the maximum utility she attains in this scenario? If the government collects a lump sum tax of Rs. 10 in period 1, how much utility does she lose? Is it the minimum loss in utility due to reduction in wealth by Rs. 10? Suppose that the government now imposes a proportional tax at such a rate that the present value of lifetime tax that it yields is Rs.10. What is the tax rate? What is the level of utility she attains under this tax? Does it involve excess burden? If your answer is yes, how do you explain it?)

REFERENCES

For non-lump sum taxes involving excess burden:

Diamond, P.A. and McFadden, D.L. (1974): Some uses of the expenditure function in public finance, *Journal of Public Economics*, 3.

Harberger, A.C. (1974): Taxation, resource allocation and welfare, *in*: Harberger, A.C. (Ed.), *Taxation and Welfare*, Little Brown, Boston.

For measurement of excess burden when supply curve is upward sloping:

Bishop, R.L. (1968): The effects of specific and ad valorem taxes, *Quarterly Journal of Economics*, May.

For situations where secondary effects cannot be taken to be weak:

Fullerton, D. and Rogers, D.L. (1993): Who Bears the Lifetime Tax Burden? Brookings Institution, Washington, DC.

For problems of estimating excess burden:

Browning, E.K. (1985): A critical appraisal of Hauseman's welfare cost estimates, *Journal of Political Economy*.

5 | TAX INCIDENCE

Chapter Objectives

The objectives of this chapter are to

(i) explain the concepts of statutory and economic incidence.
(ii) analyse economic incidence of direct and indirect taxes in partial and general equilibrium frameworks under competitive conditions.
(iii) extend the analysis of economic incidence to imperfectly competitive market structures.
(iv) analyse the incidence of profit tax.
(v) discuss the incidence of tax on immobile factors.

5.1 INTRODUCTION

Distribution of the burden of any given tax is an important issue in any discussion of taxation. Unless the tax authority has a fair idea about how the burden of a given tax is distributed among individuals, it cannot ascertain whether and to what extent the tax is equitable, given the ethical position of the society. The question that immediately comes to mind is why should there be any ambiguity regarding the distribution of the burden of a given tax. Every tax is collected from a specific group of individuals. Should not the burden of any given tax be borne by those from whom the tax is collected? The answer is often no. Let us illustrate with a simple example. Suppose that the government imposes a unit tax of Re. 1 per cigarette on cigarette sales. The tax is to be paid by the sellers. They have to pay Re. 1 as tax to the government for every cigarette sold. Before tax the sellers were selling cigarettes at Rs. 2 a piece. If now they succeed in raising the price by the whole amount of the unit tax of Re. 1 to Rs. 3, the whole burden of the tax will be borne by the buyers of cigarettes. This is because they now pay Re. 1 extra per cigarette bought. The sellers, however, continue to receive the same price of Rs. 2 as before after paying the tax. In this case, therefore, the sellers are able to shift the entire burden of the tax on the buyers. If, however, the sellers fail to raise the price, the entire burden of the tax falls on them. If the price is raised only by half of the unit tax to Rs. 2.5, the burden of the tax is borne equally by the buyers and the sellers. The sellers in this case are able to shift only half the burden on to the buyers. Thus the issue of the distribution of the burden of a given tax is much more complicated than it seems. It gives rise to a host of questions: Under what conditions is it possible for the people on whom the government imposes the tax to shift the burden to the others and to what extent? Since the burden of a tax may be shifted, how will one ascertain whether a given tax is equitable or not? Can the burdens of all kinds of taxes be shifted? The objective of this chapter is to discuss these questions.

Distribution of tax burden among individuals is referred to as tax incidence. *There are two concepts of tax incidence, namely, statutory incidence and economic incidence. The former is defined as the distribution of the tax burden as specified by the tax authority or the statute of the tax.* Thus the statutory incidence of the unit tax on the sales of cigarettes considered above falls on the sellers of cigarettes. By the statute of the tax they are to pay the tax to the government. *The economic incidence on the other hand is defined as the actual distribution of tax burden.* The two, as we shall show below, usually differ. The chapter is arranged as follows. In Section 5.1 we carry out the analysis of tax incidence in perfectly competitive markets in the partial equilibrium framework. Section 5.2 extends the analysis to the general equilibrium framework. Incidence of taxes on factor income is discussed in Section 5.3. Section 5.4 examines the issue of tax incidence in markets characterized by imperfect competition. Section 5.5 explores the implications of profit tax. The final section, Section 5.6, analyses the incidence of taxes on immobile factors.

5.2 TAX INCIDENCE ON PRODUCED GOODS IN A PERFECTLY COMPETITIVE MARKET: PARTIAL EQUILIBRIUM ANALYSIS

The individuals on whom a tax is imposed by law, as we have pointed out above, are usually able to shift their burden at least partly to other individuals. Let us illustrate this point first in the case of a perfectly competitive market in a partial equilibrium framework. Consider a commodity X, which may be a final good or factor service such as labour or service of capital. Let P be its price, which is to be interpreted as wage rate in case of labour and rental in case of service of capital. The market for commodity X, which is perfectly competitive, is given by the following equations:

Inverse Demand Function of X:

$$P^d = P^d(X); \; P^{d'} < 0 \tag{5.1}$$

Inverse Supply Function of X:

$$P^S = P^S(X); \; P^{S'} > 0 \tag{5.2}$$

Equilibrium Condition:

$$P^d(X) = P^S(X) \tag{5.3}$$

Equations (5.1) and (5.2) give respectively the demand price and supply price of X corresponding to every X. The market is in equilibrium when the two prices are equal. This explains the equilibrium condition. The three equations contain three endogenous variables, P^S, P^d and X. We can solve these three equations for their equilibrium values. We can solve (5.3) for the equilibrium value of X. Substituting it in (5.1) and (5.2), we get the equilibrium values of P^d and P^S respectively. The solution of these three equations is shown in Figure 5.1 where P^d and P^S are measured on the vertical axis and X on the horizontal axis. DD and SS schedules represent (5.1) and (5.2) respectively. Clearly, the equilibrium values of X, P^d and P^S correspond to the point of intersection of these two schedules. These are labelled X_0 and P_0 respectively.

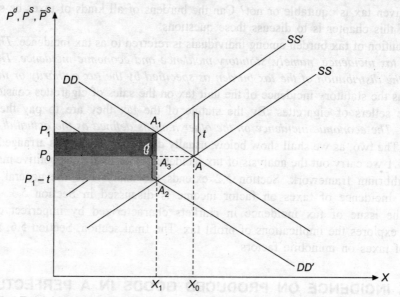

Figure 5.1: Tax incidence in the partial equilibrium framework under competitive conditions.

5.2.1 Unit Tax or Specific Tax on the Sales or Production of X

We focus on the unit or specific tax first. When a tax on a good or factor service is defined as a given sum to be paid as tax per unit of the commodity bought or sold, the tax is a unit tax or a specific tax. When the statute of a tax on, for example, petrol states that the sellers have to pay Rs. 10 for every litre of petrol sold, the tax is a unit or specific tax. Let us suppose that a unit tax or a specific tax at the rate, t, is imposed on the sales or production of X and the sellers of X have to pay this tax to the government by the statute of the tax. The sellers are, therefore, responsible for the tax by law. Hence the statutory incidence falls on the sellers of X. The sellers of X, however, will not remain passive to the imposition of this tax. Let us now examine how they will respond to it.

The inverse supply function of X shows the minimum price at which the suppliers are willing to sell any given quantity of X. Following the imposition of tax, the sellers or suppliers have to pay Rs. t amount of tax per unit of X sold or produced. Accordingly, the producers or suppliers will supply X to the buyers at a price, which is higher than their supply price of the pre-tax situation by Rs. t so that after paying the tax to the government, they get the pre-tax supply price. Since the pre-tax supply price is the minimum price at which X is supplied, the suppliers of X will not settle for anything less. Denoting the supply price of the post-tax situation by $\bar{P}^S$, we have

$$\bar{P}^S = P^S(X) + t; \ P^{S\prime} > 0 \tag{5.4}$$

The supply price to the buyer in the post-tax situation corresponding to every X is, therefore, higher than the pre-tax supply price by Rs. t. The situation is shown in Figure 5.1 where the SS schedule shifts upward by Rs. t corresponding to every X following the imposition of the tax. The new SS schedule is labelled SS'. Vertical distance between the two schedules is Rs. t at every X. Since the tax is not imposed on the buyers, they are not directly affected. They need not pay anything to the government. Therefore, the demand price is not affected. Thus the inverse demand function continues to be given by (5.3) and, therefore, by the DD schedule in Figure 5.1. The market for X is, therefore, in equilibrium, when the demand price equals the new supply price, i.e., when the following equation is satisfied:

$$P^D(X) = P^S(X) + t \tag{5.5}$$

In Figure 5.1 the new equilibrium values of X, P^d and $\bar{P}^S$ correspond to the point of intersection of the demand schedule, DD and the new supply schedule, SS'. These are labelled X_1 and P_1 respectively.

5.2.2 Unit Tax or Specific Tax on the Purchase of X

If the unit or the specific tax at the rate t is imposed on the buyers in place of the sellers, the former have to pay Rs. t for every unit of X purchased. Hence the demand function will be affected and not the supply function. Demand price corresponding to any given quantity gives the maximum price the buyers are willing to pay to purchase the given quantity. Following the imposition of the tax, the buyers of X have to pay Rs. t to the government per unit of X purchased. Clearly, therefore, the maximum price that they will be willing to pay to the producers is less than their pre-tax demand price by Rs. t. Thus the inverse demand function in the post-tax situation will be

$$\bar{P}^D = P^D(X) - t \tag{5.6}$$

where $\bar{P}^D \equiv$ the post-tax demand price. The suppliers are not affected directly as they do not pay the tax. Hence the inverse supply function continues to be given by (5.2). The equilibrium condition is, therefore, given by

$$P^D(X) - t = P^S(X) \tag{5.7}$$

Equations (5.5) and (5.7) are the same. Thus, in both the cases equilibrium values of price and quantity are the same in the post-tax situation. This yields the following result: *A unit tax at a given rate on a good or factor service has the same effect on its equilibrium quantity and price irrespective of whether the tax is imposed on buyers or on sellers.*

Let us explain this result with the help of Figure 5.1. Following the imposition of the unit tax on the buyers, the demand price to the suppliers corresponding to every X falls by Rs. t. Thus the demand schedule to the producers in the post-tax scenario is given by the line DD', which is below the pre-tax demand schedule, DD, and the vertical distance between the two is Rs. t. The post-tax equilibrium price and quantity correspond to the point of intersection of the SS and DD'. This point of intersection is labelled A_2. In the earlier case where the tax is imposed on the sellers the equilibrium price and quantity correspond to the point of intersection of SS' and DD. This point is labelled A_1. It corresponds to the amount of X, X_1. We now show that SS and DD' will also intersect at X_1. Note that the vertical distance between SS' and SS, which lies below SS', is Rs. t. At X_1, therefore, SS lies below SS' at the vertical distance of Rs. t. DD' also lies below DD at a vertical distance of Rs. t at X_1. Since SS' and DD intersect at X_1, therefore, SS and DD', which lie below SS' and DD respectively at a vertical distance of Rs. t, must also intersect at X_1. In both the cases the buyers in equilibrium pay the price, P^d (X_1), which is labelled P_1 in the figure and the sellers receive the price, $[P^d(X_1) - t] \equiv (P_1 - t)$. This establishes the proposition.

5.2.3   Ad Valorem Tax

Ad valorem tax, as distinct from the unit tax, is expressed as a percentage or proportion of the price. Let us first consider the case where an ad valorem tax at the rate, t, is imposed on the suppliers. In the pre-tax situation supply price corresponding to every X is given by $P^S(X)$. It is the minimum price at which the suppliers are to supply any given X to the buyers. Following the imposition of the tax, we assume here that the suppliers declare to the tax authority $P^S(X)$ as their price[1]. Accordingly, for every level of X supplied, the suppliers have to pay a tax of $[P^S(X)t]$ per unit of X supplied. They will, therefore, add the per unit tax of $[P^S(X) \, t]$ to $P^S(X)$ and offer X to the buyers at that price. $[P^S(X) \, (1 + t)]$ is clearly the minimum price at which they will be willing to supply X to the buyers in the post-tax scenario. Thus corresponding to every X the supply price to the buyer rises by $[P^S(X)t]$. The situation is shown in Figure 5.2 where DD and SS represent the demand and supply schedules of X in the pre-tax scenario. The post-tax supply schedule to the buyer will lie above SS and the vertical distance between the two will be $[P^S(X)t]$. The new supply schedule is labelled SS_1. The demand schedule DD, however, remains unaffected. Equilibrium occurs when the supply price to the buyers equals the demand price. In equilibrium, therefore,

$$[P^S(X)(1 + t)] = P^d(X) \tag{5.8}$$

In terms of Figure 5.2, the equilibrium values of X and the demand price correspond to the point of intersection of SS_1 and DD. Hence, *just as in the case of unit tax, the equilibrium value of X will fall and the equilibrium demand price will rise. However, the price received by the suppliers, as is clear from the Figure, will be less.*

Consider now the case where the ad valorem tax is imposed on the purchases of X at the rate, $\bar{t}$. This means that, if the buyers purchase X at the price, P_X, they will have to pay a tax of $P_X \bar{t}$ to the government for every unit of X purchased. This tax will distort the demand price

---

[1]Alternatively we could assume that the tax applies to the price suppliers actually charge to the buyers. Let us denote this price by P_S'. Suppliers, therefore, have to pay tP_S' to the government and hence they actually receive $(1 - t)P_S'$. Since the pre-tax supply price P_S is the minimum price at which suppliers are willing to supply X to the buyers, $(1 - t)P_S' = P_S$. This implies that $P_S' = P_S/(1 - t)$. The post-tax inverse supply function is accordingly $P_S' = P_S(X)/(1 - t)$.

in the following manner. $P^d(X)$ is the pre-tax demand price. It is the maximum price that the buyers are willing to pay for any given X. In the post-tax scenario, the buyers, just in line with the earlier case, will declare, by assumption, $P^d(X)$ as the price they are paying for X to the tax authority[2]. Accordingly, they will have to pay a tax of $\bar{t}P^d(X)$ to the government. Hence, the maximum price that the buyers will be willing to pay to the producers for any given X following the imposition of the tax is $P^d(X)(1 - \bar{t})$. Thus, following the imposition of the ad valorem tax, the demand schedule, labelled DD, in Figure 5.2, will shift downward and the magnitude of this displacement is given by $[P^d(X)\bar{t}]$. The new demand schedule is labelled DD_1. The pre-tax supply schedule, labelled SS in the Figure, remains unchanged, as the suppliers are not directly affected by the tax. Equilibrium occurs when the demand price to the producers equals their supply price, i.e., when

$$[P^d(X)(1 - \bar{t})] = P^S(X)$$

$$\left[\frac{P^S(X)}{(1 - \bar{t})}\right] = P^d(X) \tag{5.9}$$

or

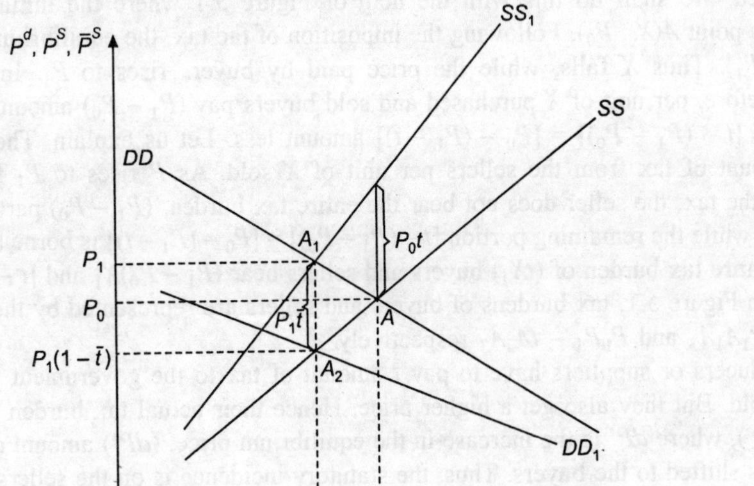

Figure 5.2: Ad valorem tax on a commodity or factor service in a partial equilibrium framework.

In terms of Figure 5.2 equilibrium occurs at the point of intersection of DD_1 and SS. Thus, *following the imposition of the ad valorem tax on the buyers, just as in the case of the unit tax, equilibrium value of X falls and so does the supply price. However, the demand price rises in the post-tax equilibrium, since equilibrium X is less.*

[2]Alternatively, we could assume that the tax applies to the price buyers actually pay to the suppliers. Let us denote that price by P_1^d. They have, therefore, to pay $P_1^d t$ as tax per unit of X purchased. Now the maximum price they are willing to pay for X is the pre-tax demand price P^d. Hence $P_1^d(1 + t) = P^d$. The post-tax demand price faced by the suppliers will, therefore be, $P_1^d = P^d/(1 + t)$.

Despite the similarities in the results drawn, there is an important difference between these two taxes. It follows from (5.8) and (5.9) that they are not the same. This means that they are likely to yield different equilibrium values of X in the situation where $t = \bar{t}$. This is, however, not the case when we have a unit tax. Thus the equilibrium price and quantity in case of the ad valorem tax at any given rate will depend upon on which side of the market the tax is imposed. Not much of this difference should be made though. Corresponding to every tax rate imposed on the buyers, there will usually be a unique tax rate, which, if imposed on the sellers, will yield the same equilibrium situation.

Prove this point graphically and also mathematically using linear demand and supply functions.

In Figure 5.2 t and $\bar{t}$ are chosen in such a manner that they yield the same equilibrium outcome.

5.2.4 Distribution of Tax Burden

We shall explain here how the burden of a unit tax at the rate, t, on the sales or production of X is distributed. We shall do this with the help of Figure 5.1 where the initial equilibrium corresponds to point $A(X_0, P_0)$. Following the imposition of the tax, the equilibrium shifts to the point $A_1(X_1, P_1)$. Thus X falls, while the price paid by buyers rises to P_1. In the post-tax situation, therefore, per unit of X purchased and sold buyers pay $(P_1 - P_0)$ amount extra, while sellers receive $[t - (P_1 - P_0)] = [P_0 - (P_1 - t)]$ amount less. Let us explain. The government collects t amount of tax from the sellers per unit of X sold. As P rises to P_1 following the imposition of the tax, the seller does not bear the entire tax burden. $(P_1 - P_0)$ part of t is borne by the buyers, while the remaining portion $[t - (P_1 - P_0)] = [P_0 - (P_1 - t)]$ is borne by the sellers. Thus, of the entire tax burden of (tX_1) buyers and sellers bear $(P_1 - P_0)X_1$ and $[t - (P_1 - P_0)]X_1$ respectively. In Figure 5.1, tax burdens of buyers and sellers are represented by the areas of the rectangles $P_0P_1A_1A_3$ and $P_0P_1 - tA_2A_3$ respectively.

The producers or suppliers have to pay t amount of tax to the government per unit of X produced or sold. But they also get a higher price. Hence their actual tax burden per unit of X is only $(t - dP^e)$, where dP^e is the increase in the equilibrium price. (dP^e) amount of tax burden per unit of X is shifted to the buyers. Thus, the statutory incidence is on the sellers entirely, but the economic incidence is on both buyers and sellers.

Let us now identify the factors that determine the distribution of tax burden. There is distribution or shifting of tax burden if P increases following the imposition of the tax. If P remains unchanged, the entire burden of the tax is with the sellers and the statutory incidence and economic incidence are the same. We shall, therefore, examine which factors determine the increase in the equilibrium price, dP^e, following the imposition of the tax. We shall work it out mathematically first. For this purpose we have to use the equilibrium condition, (5.5). Substituting the equilibrium value of X, denoted X^e, into (5.5), we rewrite it as the following identity:

$$P^D(X^e) \equiv P^S(X^e) + t$$

Taking total differential of the above identity, we have

$$P^{D'}(X^e)dX^e \equiv P^{S'}(X^e)dX^e + dt \qquad (5.10)$$

Let us now explain the above equation. Demand price of X should be equal to the supply price of X to the buyers in equilibrium in both the pre-tax and post-tax situations. The only determinants of these two prices that change from the pre-tax equilibrium to the post-tax equilibrium are X and t. The former changes by the unknown quantity, dX^e, while the latter changes by the known quantity, dt. The demand price changes because of the change in the former, while the supply price to the buyers changes because of both. Thus the LHS and the RHS of (5.10) give the changes in the demand price of and supply price to the buyers respectively from the pre-tax equilibrium to the post-tax equilibrium. Hence the two sides are equal. Equation (5.10) contains only one unknown, dX^e. We can, therefore, solve it for dX^e. Solving (5.10), we have

$$dX^e = \frac{dt}{(P^{D'}(X^e) - P^{S'}(X^e))} \tag{5.11}$$

Let us explain (5.11). Following the increase in the tax rate by dt, the supply price to the buyers at the initial equilibrium X rises by dt, while the demand price remains unchanged. The market achieves the new equilibrium when X from its pre-tax equilibrium value falls by such an amount that the two prices become equal again. When X falls by 1 unit, supply price falls by $P^{S'}$, while the demand price increases by $-P^{D'}$. Hence, per unit fall in X the excess of supply price over demand price falls by the sum of the two, $P^{S'} - P^{D'}$. Clearly, therefore, the excess of supply price over demand price will fall by dt to zero, when X falls by $dt/[(P^{S'} - P^{D'})]$. This gives the absolute value of fall in X. The actual value of change in X is given by (5.11). Let us now derive the value of dP^e. This is given by the change in P^D due to the change in X as given by (5.11). Taking total differential of (5.1), we have

$$dP^e = P^{D'}(X^e)dX^e$$

Substituting (5.11) into the above equation, we get

$$dP^e = \left[\frac{P^{d'}(X^e)}{(P^{d'}(X^e) - P^{S'}(X^e))}\right]dt = \left[\frac{1}{1 + \{P^{S'}(X^e)/-P^{d'}(X^e)\}}\right]dt \tag{5.12}$$

If we assume that in the initial equilibrium, $t = 0$, then initial equilibrium values of P^S and P^d, as follows from (5.5), are equal. Using this result, we can rewrite (5.12) as

$$dP^e = \left[\frac{1}{\left(1 + \cfrac{P^{S'}(X^e)\cfrac{X^e}{P^S}}{-P^{d'}(X^e)\cfrac{X^e}{P^d}}\right)}\right]dt = \left[\frac{1}{\left(1 + \cfrac{\cfrac{1}{\eta_S}}{\cfrac{1}{\eta_d}}\right)}\right]dt = \left[\frac{1}{\left(1 + \cfrac{\eta_d}{\eta_S}\right)}\right]dt \tag{5.13}$$

where η_d and η_S are own price elasticities of demand for and supply of X respectively.

From (5.13) it follows that *the higher the price elasticity of demand relative to that of supply, the less is the increase in price and hence the less is the burden of the tax borne by the buyers.* This is illustrated quite clearly in Figure 5.3, which shows that, given the post-tax and pre-tax supply schedules (or, given the price elasticity of supply at the initial pre-tax price–quantity configuration), the flatter the demand schedule, (or, the greater the price elasticity of demand at the pre-tax price–quantity configuration), the less is the increase in P.

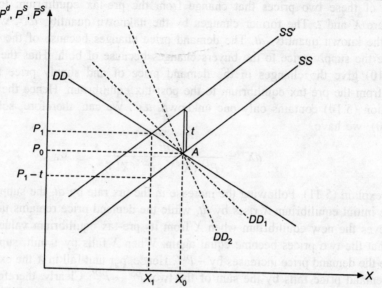

Figure 5.3:   Incidence of a unit tax on the sales of X: given supply elasticity and varying demand elasticities.

Figure 5.4 shows that, given the demand schedule (or, given the price elasticity of demand at the initial pre-tax price–quantity configuration), the flatter the supply curve (or, the greater the price elasticity of supply at the initial price–quantity configuration), the larger is the increase in the price level.

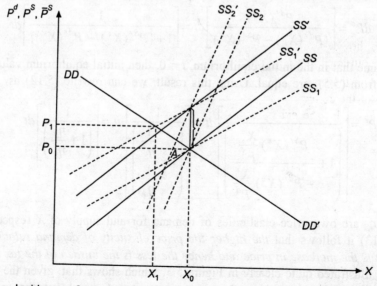

Figure 5.4:   Incidence of a unit tax on the sales of X: given demand elasticity and varying supply elasticities.

Let us now explain the result derived above. Elasticity of demand (supply) is a measure of the ease with which buyers (sellers) can reduce demand (supply) following a given increase (decline) in price and conversely. Therefore, (η_D/η_S) may be regarded as an indicator of the bargaining strength of the buyers relative to that of the sellers. Let us elaborate. Following the imposition of the unit tax, suppliers immediately raise the supply price of X to the buyers by the amount of the unit tax rate at the pre-tax equilibrium value of X. Buyers respond to this by reducing demand for X and thereby creating a situation of excess supply. The larger the price elasticity of demand, the greater is the amount of excess supply created at this higher supply price of X and hence the supply price of X will fall from this higher value to restore equality between demand and supply. The larger the η_d, the greater is the amount of excess supply created at the initial higher supply price of X to the buyers and hence, given other factors including η_S, the larger is the fall in this price required to restore equilibrium and hence the smaller is the ultimate increase in this supply price to the buyers. Accordingly, the less is the burden shifted on to the buyers. Consider two extreme examples. Suppose that $\eta_d = 0$. In this case buyers cannot reduce their demand when the suppliers raise the supply price at the initial equilibrium quantity by the rate of the unit tax. In this case they have no bargaining strength vis-à-vis the suppliers. They cannot do without the initial equilibrium quantity of X whatever be the price. Hence demand and supply remain equal at this higher supply price. As a result buyers end up paying the whole of the tax. If, on the other hand, η_d is infinitely large at the pre-tax equilibrium supply price to the buyers, demand for X will fall to zero as soon as the supply price rises. In this case, if η_S is finite, buyers have infinitely larger bargaining strength vis-à-vis the suppliers, since they can do without X altogether if supply price of X is even slightly raised above its pre-tax equilibrium level, whereas suppliers of X cannot reduce their supply to zero if they receive a price, which is lower than the one they were receiving in the pre-tax equilibrium. If, therefore, the supply price to the buyers is raised even slightly above its pre-tax equilibrium level, there will emerge excess supply of X. Hence equilibrium is restored in the market only when the supply price to the buyers falls back to its pre-tax equilibrium level. In this case, therefore, price received by the suppliers falls by the whole amount of the unit tax rate and, therefore, they bear the entire burden. They are unable to shift any part of the burden on to the buyers. (*Exercise:* Illustrate the two extreme cases discussed above graphically.)

Let us now focus on η_S. Following the imposition of the tax, as we have pointed out already, the immediate change that occurs is that the suppliers raise the supply price to the buyers at the initial equilibrium quantity of X by the rate of the unit tax leading to excess supply of X, if η_d is positive. This price, therefore, begins to fall to restore equilibrium. With the fall in this price demand rises and supply falls reducing excess supply and thereby moving the market towards equilibrium. To what extent the price will fall depends upon the value of η_S, given η_d and other factors. The higher the η_S, the greater will be the fall in supply per unit decline in the supply price of X and hence the less will be the fall in this price required to restore equilibrium. In the extreme case where η_S is infinitely large, supply will fall to zero, if the supply price to the buyers falls even slightly from the level where it rose to immediately after the tax was imposed. In this case, if η_d is finite, suppliers are infinitely more powerful than the buyers. They are in a position to withdraw all their supply if they receive a price even slightly less than what they were getting in the pre-tax equilibrium. But the buyers cannot reduce their demand to zero, when they are offered X at a price, which is higher than what they were paying in the pre-tax equilibrium. In this case, therefore, at every supply price to the buyer less than the level where it rose to immediately after the tax was imposed there will emerge excess demand for X. At every such price supply is zero, as suppliers receive a price lower than the pre-tax equilibrium price, but demand is positive. As a result the supply price to buyers will not fall at all from where it rose to immediately after the tax was imposed and the buyers will end up bearing the entire tax burden. (*Exercise:* Illustrate this case graphically.)

There are two sides to the market of X: the uses side and the sources side. The former refers to the people who use the good, i.e., the buyers of X. The sources side on the other hand refers to the people who are engaged in the production and sale of X, i.e., the owners of factors of production that are engaged in the production and sale of X. We have shown above how the burden of a unit tax on the production or sales of X imposed on the suppliers of X is distributed between the sellers and buyers. We have shown that the suppliers of X on whom the statutory incidence of the tax falls may be able to shift the burden of the tax partly or fully on to the buyers. We have also identified the factors that determine the distribution of the tax burden between the buyers and the sellers, i.e., between the sources and the uses side. But how is the part of the tax burden borne by any one side of the market distributed among the people engaged on that side? That question we have not yet discussed, i.e., we have not discussed yet how the part of the tax burden borne by the buyers (sellers) is distributed among the buyers (sellers). We shall now discuss this question.

Suppose that X is a consumption good. Let us now examine how the part of the burden of the tax borne by the buyers is distributed among them. More precisely, let us examine whether the distribution of the tax burden among the buyers is progressive, proportional or regressive. As we have noted in the chapter on personal income tax, there are considerable ambiguities surrounding the definitions of the terms progressive and regressive. Here we shall stick to one definition. We shall say that the distribution of the tax burden is progressive, proportional or regressive depending upon whether the tax burden as a proportion of income rises, stays unchanged or falls with income. Given these definitions, we shall show below that the distribution of the tax burden among the buyers will be progressive, proportional or regressive depending upon whether the income elasticity of demand for X is greater than, equal to or less than unity. Let us explain. Consider two buyers A and B having incomes Y_A and Y_B and $Y_B = KY_A$; $K > 1$. At the post-tax equilibrium price demand for X of A and that of B are, say, X_A and X_B respectively. Tax burdens of A and B are, therefore, dP^eX_A and dP^eX_B respectively, when dP^e denotes the increase in the equilibrium price paid by the buyers. If income elasticity of demand for X is greater than unity, demand for X, given the prices, rises more than proportionately with respect to income. Hence $\left(\dfrac{X_A}{Y_A}\right) < \left(\dfrac{X_B}{Y_B}\right)$. More generally,

$$\left(\frac{X_A}{Y_A}\right)\begin{Bmatrix}<\\=\\>\end{Bmatrix}\left(\frac{X_B}{Y_B}\right) \text{ according as income elasticity of demand for } X \text{ is } \begin{Bmatrix}>\\=\\<\end{Bmatrix}1$$

Hence,

$$\left(dP^e \frac{X_A}{Y_A} \right) \begin{Bmatrix} < \\ = \\ > \end{Bmatrix} \left(dP^e \frac{X_B}{Y_B} \right) \text{ according as income elasticity of demand for } X \text{ is } \begin{Bmatrix} > \\ = \\ < \end{Bmatrix} 1$$

This establishes our proposition. Goods are classified into luxuries and necessities on the basis of their income elasticities of demand. Goods whose income elasticities of demand are greater (less) than unity are called luxuries (necessities). Thus, *if a unit tax is imposed on a luxury, the part of its burden that falls on the buyers will be progressively distributed. Just the opposite will happen in case of necessities. How is the burden that falls on the suppliers distributed among them cannot be ascertained in the partial equilibrium framework. For that we have to extend our analysis to the general equilibrium framework.*

5.3 TAX INCIDENCE: GENERAL EQUILIBRIUM FRAMEWORK

Let us now consider the general equilibrium framework to examine the issue of tax incidence of a unit tax on the sales of a consumer good, X. We shall consider a very simple general equilibrium framework here to identify only the major forces that emerge as the partial equilibrium framework is extended to the framework of general equilibrium. We assume for simplicity that only two goods, X and Y, are produced in the economy with two inputs, labour and capital. Endowments of labour and capital in the economy are fixed. To simplify our analysis we assume that there are a large number of identical firms and each firm produces X and Y with fixed endowments of labour and capital, which are owned by their owners. There are also a large number of identical individuals. Since firms and individuals are identical, we shall carry out our analysis in terms of a representative individual and a representative firm only. The representative firm, as we have mentioned above, produces the two goods X and Y with fixed endowments of labour and capital, which are supplied by the owners of the firm. The production possibility frontier (*PPF*) of the representative firm is given by

$$Y = F(X); \ F' < 0, \ F'' < 0 \tag{5.14}$$

In this simple economy only X and Y are traded and they are traded in perfectly competitive markets. Thus, individuals and firms are price takers in both the markets. The firm maximizes profit, which is given by

$$\Pi = P_x X + P_y Y - A \tag{5.15}$$

where $\Pi \equiv$ profit and $A \equiv$ the fixed cost consisting of the depreciation of the given capital stock of the firm. Substituting (5.14) into (5.15), we can write the profit maximization exercise of the firm as

$$\max_X \Pi = P_x X + P_y F(X) - A \tag{5.16}$$

The FOC for profit maximization is given by

$$F'(X) = \frac{P_x}{P_y} \tag{5.17}$$

One can easily check that, given the characteristics of the production possibility frontier, the second-order condition for profit maximization is automatically satisfied. The FOC states that at the profit maximizing point on the *PPF* the marginal rate of transformation of X for Y, $F'(X)$, equals the price of X in terms of Y, (P_x/P_y). We illustrate this situation in Figure 5.5 where the concave schedule is the production possibility frontier. It is labelled *PPF*. The profit maximizing point on this *PPF* is $A(X_0, Y_0)$ at which the absolute value of the slope of the *PPF* is equal to the given price ratio, (P_x/P_y). Explain this using economic logic yourself. Mathematically, we can solve (5.17) for the profit maximizing value of X. Putting this value of X in (5.14), we get the profit maximizing value of Y.

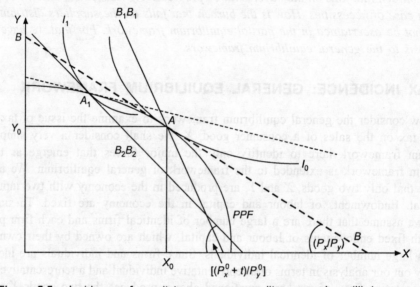

Figure 5.5: Incidence of a unit tax on a commodity: general equilibrium case.

The firm has a large number of owners who, by assumption, supply the given capital and labour. The whole value of output of the firm accordingly gets distributed among them as profit. It should be noted here that these assumptions are all simplifying ones. They are made only for expository reasons. Results derived here will hold even if we replace these assumptions with more realistic ones. This simple model helps us identify the major forces that emerge as the partial equilibrium analysis is extended to the case of general equilibrium.

As the representative individual gets the whole value of output, $P_x X_0 + P_y Y_0$, as factor income, the budget line of the representative individual is given by

$$P_x X_0 + P_y Y_0 = P_x X + P_y Y \tag{5.18}$$

Clearly, this budget line will pass through A, as (X_0, Y_0) satisfies (5.18), and have the slope (P_x/P_y). This budget line is labelled *BAB* in Figure 5.5. The individual can choose any point from this budget line. If she chooses any point other than (X_0, Y_0), the economy is not in equilibrium as demand and supply of X and Y do not match. Hence prices will change. However, if she chooses (X_0, Y_0), markets for both the goods and, therefore, the economy will be in equilibrium. This equilibrium situation is shown in Figure 5.5 where the indifference curve, I_0 of the individual is tangent to *BAB* at A.

We are now in a position to incorporate the unit tax on the sales or production of X and examine what changes it brings about to prices and quantities. We shall do this in the simplest possible framework. Hence we assume that the government redistributes the tax revenue collected as lump sum transfers. The individuals, however, do not perceive this link. Following the imposition of the unit tax on X at the rate t, producers will produce (X_0, Y_0) at the price $[(P_x + t)/P_y]$, since in the post-tax scenario when they charge $[(P_x + t)/P_y]$ to the consumers, they actually get (P_x/P_y). When producers receive prices, P_x and P_y, produce (X_0, Y_0) and charge to the consumers $(P_x + t)$ and P_y, the budget line of the representative individual is given by

$$P_x X_0 + P_y Y_0 + \overline{T} = (P_x + t)X + P_y Y \qquad (5.19)$$

where $\overline{T}$ denotes the amount of the lump sum transfer that the representative individual receives from the government and by assumption $\overline{T} = tX_0$. However, the individual, by assumption, does not perceive the link between $\overline{T}$ and tX_0. Let us explain (5.19). The producers produce (X_0, Y_0) and charge $(P_x + t)$ and P_y to the consumers. However, they receive P_x and P_y. Their profit is, therefore, $P_x X_0 + P_y Y_0$, which is distributed among the owners. The representative individual receives it as income. In addition, the individual receives $\overline{T}$ from the government as transfer income. Thus, the LHS of (5.19) gives the total disposable income of the representative individual. She, however, has to pay $(P_x + t)$ for X and P_y for Y. The RHS, therefore, gives the value of her purchases of X and Y. The two sides should be equal. This explains (5.19). Since $\overline{T} = tX_0$ by assumption, (X_0, Y_0) satisfy the budget equation, (5.19) and it has the slope $[(P_x + t)/P_y]$ in the (X, Y) plane. This budget line thus passes through the point (X_0, Y_0) with the slope $[(P_x + t)/P_y]$ in Figure 5.5. It is labelled $B_1 B_1$. Since X is now more expensive to the consumer in terms of Y, she will no longer choose (X_0, Y_0) from the budget line. She will substitute Y for X and choose some point above A on the budget line. There will thus be an excess supply of X and excess demand for Y. P_x will fall and P_y will rise. With the fall in P_x and rise in P_y producers will reduce X and raise Y along PPF. The individuals will also demand more X and less Y. Thus, equilibrium will occur at some point to the left of A on the PPF, with lower P_x and higher P_y. We label this point A_1. We denote the new equilibrium P_x and P_y by P_x^0 and P_y^0 respectively. At $A_1(X_1, Y_1)$ marginal rate of transformation of X for Y, $F'(X)$, equals (P_x^0/P_y^0). The consumer faces the prices $(P_x^0 + t)$ and P_y^0, and as before her budget line passes through A_1 with the slope $[(P_x^0 + t)/P_y^0]$. This budget line is labelled $B_2 B_2$ in Figure 5.5. From this budget line she chooses A_1.

From the above it follows that following the imposition of the unit tax on the sale of X, price of the taxed good to the consumers rises relative to the prices of other goods. Hence, demand shifts from the taxed good to other goods. As a result prices of other goods to both the producers and consumers rise, while the price of the taxed good to the producers falls. This induces the producers to shift resources from the taxed good to the non-taxed ones. Production of the former will, therefore, fall and that of the latter will rise. These changes have the following implications for tax incidence in the general equilibrium framework:

(i) Rise in the prices of the non-taxed goods shifts the burden on to the consumers of these goods as well.

(ii) With the fall in the production of the taxed good, prices of the factors used intensively in its production fall and prices of the factors used intensively in the production of the non-taxed goods rise as their production rises.

The effect or the result yielded by the partial equilibrium analysis is called primary effect, while the changes (i) and (ii) specified above, which we derive from the general equilibrium analysis, are called secondary effects. Let us illustrate. Suppose that the taxed good is a luxury. We find from our partial equilibrium analysis that the burden of the tax on the luxury good is progressively distributed among the buyers. This is the primary effect of a tax on a luxury good. If the non-taxed goods are mostly luxuries too, the burden of the increase in their prices, as specified in (i), will also be distributed progressively among the buyers. Again, if the non-taxed goods are also labour-intensive relative to the taxed good, prices of labour, in accordance with (ii), will rise relative to that of capital. This will tend to raise the workers' (poor people's) income relative to the capital owners', who are rich. Hence, in this case, secondary effects, (i) and (ii), reinforce the primary effect derived from the partial equilibrium analysis and the burden of the tax will be progressively distributed. On the other hand, if the non-taxed goods are necessities and relatively more capital-intensive, the secondary effects on burden distribution will tend to offset the primary effect. Under these conditions distribution of the burden of a tax even on a luxury good may turn out to be regressive because of the secondary effects.

There is, however, a view that the secondary effects yielded by the general equilibrium analysis are quite weak and hence the results derived from the partial equilibrium analysis will hold. Let us explain. Consider first the secondary effect, (i), which consists in the rise in the prices of non-taxed goods following the imposition of the tax. It is more likely than not that some of the non-taxed goods will be luxuries and others necessities and hence the impact of the secondary effect (i) on burden distribution will be quite weak. The burden of the rise in the prices of luxuries will be progressively distributed among buyers, while the burden of the increase in the prices of the necessities will be regressively distributed among the buyers. Hence, the distribution of the burden among buyers due to the secondary effect, (i), is unlikely to show any tendency to be either progressive or regressive. The partial equilibrium result will, therefore, dominate and the burden of the tax will be progressively distributed among the buyers.

Now focus on the secondary effect, (ii). It is quite likely that some of the non-taxed goods will use less intensively the factors which are used more intensively in the taxed goods, while the other non-taxed goods will use these factors more intensively than the taxed good. As a result the secondary effect, (ii), on factor prices is likely to be quite weak.

For the above mentioned reasons the *result derived from the partial equilibrium analysis is likely to hold, i.e., the burden of an indirect tax on a luxury good (necessity) is likely to be progressively (regressively) distributed.*

5.4 INCIDENCE OF A TAX ON FACTORS OF PRODUCTION: PARTIAL EQUILIBRIUM ANALYSIS

Analysis of the incidence of a tax on a factor of production can also be carried out in terms of Figure 5.3. Suppose that X is a factor of production, labour service or service of capital,

P denotes the wage rate or the rental rate and P^d and P^S denote respectively demand price and supply price of labour service or service of capital. If a unit tax at the rate t is imposed on the income from capital or labour, the supply schedule as in the earlier case will shift. The suppliers of the factor service have to pay Rs. t to the tax authority per unit of the factor service sold and, therefore, charge the producers $P^S(X) + t$. The demand price and, therefore, the demand schedule are obviously not affected. Thus the analysis of incidence of a tax on factor of production is similar to that of a selective indirect tax on a commodity. Accordingly, distribution of the tax burden between the owners of factors of production and the producers in the partial equilibrium framework will depend upon the elasticity of demand relative to that of supply. In general, if elasticities are positive and finite, price of the taxed factor to the producers will rise. Thus on the uses side the producers will be burdened. Again, the price of the taxed factor as received by its owners will fall. On the sources side, therefore, the owners of the taxed factor of production will be burdened. Work out the details yourself. Now, if the taxed factor of production is labour, the wage rate as received by the workers will fall. Since workers are poorer than the owners of capital, the burden of the tax on labour services is likely to be regressively distributed among the owners of factor services. Just for the opposite reason burden of a tax on capital services is likely to be progressively distributed among the owners of factor services.

5.4.1 Tax on Factors of Production: General Equilibrium Analysis

When we extend the analysis to the general equilibrium framework, we have to reckon with two other forces. First, on the sources side with the fall in the price of the taxed factor of production to the owners, supply of the taxed factor declines and its price to the producers rises leading to a rise the intensity in the use of other factors relative to the taxed factor. As a result marginal productivity of other factors falls precipitating a decline in the prices of the other factors as well. Thus owners of the non-taxed factors of production are also burdened. Second, on the uses side, with the rise in the price of the taxed factor to the producers, prices of the goods using the taxed factor more intensively rise relative to the others and thereby burden the consumers of these goods.

From the above it follows that the analysis of the distribution of the burden of a factor tax is fairly complicated. A tax on capital services, which is likely to be progressive on the sources side in the partial equilibrium framework, may not be so. This is because, as follows from the first of the above two effects, it burdens the owners of other factors of production as well. Moreover, consumers of goods using the taxed factor intensively are also burdened and these goods may be necessities. Hence nothing definite can be said about the nature of the burden distribution of a factor tax. However, as we have mentioned above, there is a view that the secondary effects, which we observe when we extend the analysis to the general equilibrium case, are likely to be weak so that the result of the partial equilibrium framework holds. This may be explained as follows. Focus on the sources side. A tax on capital services, for example, will lower prices of both land and labour. While workers belong to the relatively poorer sections of the population, landlords may be rich. Hence both the rich and the poor face the brunt of the fall in the prices of the non-taxed factor services. Therefore, the distribution of the burden among the factor owners due to the fall in the prices of the non-taxed factors is unlikely to show any pronounced tendency of being either regressive or progressive. Thus the impact of this secondary effect on the distribution of income on the sources side is likely to be quite weak and the impact of the partial equilibrium analysis on the sources side will determine the nature of the distribution of the burden of the factor tax on this side. Again, on the uses side prices of goods using the taxed factor intensively rise. However, one cannot say a priori that these goods will be either necessities or luxuries. Chances are that some of them will be luxuries and others necessities. In that case both the rich and the poor will be burdened on account of this secondary effect. As a result the distribution of burden on the uses side due to this secondary effect is unlikely to show any strong tendency to be either progressive or regressive. Hence the impact of this secondary effect on the distribution of the tax burden on the uses side will also be quite weak. If this argument is true, the result of the partial equilibrium analysis will hold and therefore there is a high probability that a tax on capital services will be progressive, while that on the labour service will be regressive.

Box 5.1:   Incidence of Government Expenditure: Subsidy

Subsidies are just the opposite of taxes. Subsidies are paid by the government to the economic agents. However, their benefits may not remain confined just to their direct recipients. They may spill over to others as well. In other words, statutory and economic incidence of subsidies may differ substantially. In India there are subsidies on many items including food, fertilizer, power etc. Let us illustrate how statutory and economic incidence of subsidies differ by considering the example of a unit subsidy at the rate s on the sales of a commodity, X, which is traded in a competitive market. Its inverse demand and supply functions are given by $P^D = P^D(X)$ and $P^S = P^S(X)$ respectively. Producers will now get s for every unit of X sold. The unit subsidy will, therefore, reduce the supply price corresponding to every X by s. This is because, if the producers charge the buyers $P^S(X) - s$, they will get $P^S(X)$, which is the minimum price at which the suppliers are willing to supply any given X. The demand function will, however, remain unaffected. Thus, as we have seen before, if both price elasticities of demand and supply are finite, price of X will fall benefiting the buyers also. Distribution of benefits between buyers and sellers will depend upon the magnitude of price elasticity of demand relative to that of supply. Work out the result yourself following the line suggested in the context of a unit tax on the production or sale of a good or factor service.

5.5 TAX INCIDENCE UNDER MONOPOLY

So far we focused on the issue of tax incidence in competitive markets where neither sellers nor buyers have any market power. There is a general belief that the producers with market power shift the entire burden of any tax imposed on them to the buyers. We shall now take up the case of a monopolist and examine to what extent this general belief is true. We shall first examine this issue mathematically and then illustrate graphically. Let us suppose that a unit or a specific tax at the rate t is imposed on the sales of a commodity, X, produced by a monopolist. Monopolist's inverse demand function and cost function are given by $P(Q)$ and $C(Q)$ respectively. Following the imposition of the tax, the cost function becomes $C(Q) + tQ$, as for every unit of Q produced or sold the producer has to pay t to the government as tax. Profit of the monopolist denoted by Π in the post-tax situation is, therefore, given by

$$\max_{Q} \Pi = P(Q)Q - [C(Q) + tQ]$$

The monopolist chooses Q in such a manner that her profit is maximized. The FOC for profit maximization is given by

$$[P'(Q)Q + P(Q)] - [C'(Q) + t] = 0 \qquad (5.20)$$

The first and the second term within third brackets on the LHS of (5.20) give the marginal revenue and marginal cost respectively. We can solve (5.20) for the profit maximizing value of Q as a function of, among others, t. We can, therefore, use (5.20) to determine how an increase in t affects the profit maximizing Q. Denoting the profit maximizing Q by Q^* and substituting it in (5.20), we convert it into the following identity:

$$P'(Q^*)Q^* + P(Q^*) - [C'(Q^*) + t] \equiv 0$$

Taking total differential of the above identity, we get the following equation:

$$[P''(Q^*)Q^* + 2P'(Q^*)]dQ^* = [C''(Q^*)dQ^* + dt]$$

Let us explain the above equation. At both the initial and new profit maximizing positions of the monopolist corresponding respectively to the initial t and the new higher t marginal revenue and marginal cost are equal. Hence, the change in marginal revenue from the initial equilibrium to the new one should be equal to that of marginal cost. Only two of the determinants of marginal revenue and marginal cost change from one equilibrium to the other. These are Q^* and t. They change by dQ^* and dt respectively. Marginal revenue changes because of dQ^* alone. The change in marginal revenue due to dQ^* is given by the LHS of the above equation. Marginal cost changes because of both dQ^* and dt. Its change due to dQ^* and dt is given by the RHS of the above equation. Clearly, dQ^* and dt are such that the two sides are equal. This explains the above equation. Now, dt is known. We have changed t by a given amount to find out how it affects Q^*. So in the above equation, there is only one unknown, dQ^*. We can, therefore, solve it for dQ^*. It is given by

$$dQ^* = \frac{-dt}{(C'' - P''Q^*) + (-2P')} < 0$$

(since from the second-order condition for profit maximization it follows that the denominator is positive). (5.21)

Substituting Q^* into the inverse demand function, we get the profit maximizing value of P. Denoting it by P^*, we get

$$P^* = P(Q^*)$$

Taking total differential of the above equation and substituting into it (5.21), we get

$$dP^* = \frac{(-P')dt}{(C'' - P''Q^*) + (-2P')} > 0 \qquad (5.22)$$

We assume that t was equal to zero initially. Hence $dt = t$.

Let us now examine the implications of (5.22). Note that, if $dP^* = t$, the monopolist is able to shift the whole of the burden of the tax on to the consumers. However, that will not normally be the case. Suppose, for example, that the demand function and the cost function are linear. In that case, $C'' = P'' = 0$ and therefore, as follows from (5.22), $dP^* = (1/2)t$. Hence the monopolist will be able to shift only half the tax burden to the buyers. More generally, it follows from (5.22) that

$$dP^* < t \quad \Leftrightarrow \quad P' < C'' - P''Q^* \tag{5.23}$$

This condition is likely to be met normally. Usually, the larger the output of a good, more scarce are the inputs most suitable for its production and hence the higher is the cost of raising its output. In other words marginal cost of production rises with an increase in output, i.e., $C'' > 0$. Again, the larger the use of a good, the harder it becomes to substitute the given good for other goods. So, the larger the use of a good, the weaker is the substitution effect produced by a unit decline in its price. This means that the larger the use of a good, the smaller is the increase in its demand brought about by a unit decline in its price. In other words, the larger the use of a good, the greater is the fall in its price required to raise its demand by unity. Hence $d(-P')/dQ = -P'' > 0$ in normal circumstances. Thus (5.23) will normally be satisfied. Hence, monopolists in most cases will not be able to shift the entire tax burden on to the consumers.

Let us now illustrate the incidence of a unit tax on a monopolist graphically with the help of Figure 5.6 where DD, MR and MC_0 schedules are the pre-tax demand, marginal revenue and marginal cost schedules respectively. Pre-tax equilibrium quantity corresponds to the point of intersection of MC_0 and MR. It is labelled Q_0. The pre-tax equilibrium P is labelled P_0. It corresponds to Q_0 on DD. Following the imposition of the unit or specific tax at the rate, t, the

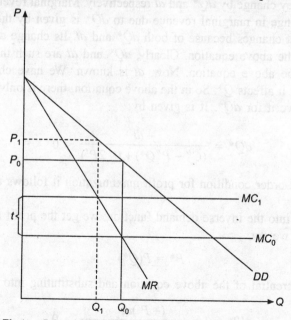

Figure 5.6: Incidence of a unit tax on a monopolist.

MC schedule shifts upward by t. The post-tax MC schedule is labelled MC_1. DD and MR schedules remain unchanged. Accordingly, the post-tax equilibrium Q labelled Q_1 is less than Q_0 and post-tax price, labelled P_1, is higher than its pre-tax equilibrium level, P_0. However, it is higher than P_0 by an amount smaller than t.

5.6 PROFIT TAX

Profit tax refers to tax on economic profit, which is nothing but supernormal profit or excess of profit over its normal level. It is appealing on grounds of equity, as profit income accrues principally to the rich. It is attractive, as we shall presently show, on grounds of efficiency also. If a proportional tax at the rate t is imposed on profit, denoted by Π, post-tax profit of a producer will be given by $(1 - t)\Pi$. Clearly, maximization of post-tax profit implies maximization of pre-tax profit, since t is given to the producer. Thus pre-tax profit maximizing output and price will maximize post-tax profit also. This is the case in all market structures. Thus the burden of profit tax remains entirely on profit earners. They cannot shift it as price faced by buyers remains unchanged. The profit tax leaves price and output of the pre-tax situation unaffected. Only profit goes down by the amount of the tax.

However, profit tax is not popular, as it is very difficult to measure economic profit in practice. The major problem relates to measuring normal profit. What is the normal rate of return on investment? There is no satisfactory answer to that. Sometimes the return on riskless government securities is taken as the normal rate of return. But investments, unlike government securities, are risky. Hence the normal rate of return on investment should be higher than that on government securities to allow for the risk premium. There is no objective criterion for measuring risk or risk premium associated with any given kind of investment. Different investments differ in the degrees of risk they involve. Hence normal rates of return on different types of investment must also be different. For these problems profit tax despite its non-distortionary nature and appeal on grounds of equity is not popular.

5.7 INCIDENCE OF A TAX ON IMMOBILE FACTOR AND CAPITALIZATION

We shall discuss here the effect of a tax on a factor, which is immobile, i.e., which cannot move from one place to another or from one use to another to escape the taxes imposed on it. One important example is land. If the Government of West Bengal, for example, imposes a tax on land, land cannot move away from West Bengal to escape the tax. The effect of a tax on an immobile factor is discussed with the help of Figure 5.7 where price of the immobile factor denoted P is measured on the vertical axis, while quantities demanded and supplied are measured along the horizontal axis. Since an immobile factor is immobile not only across space but also across alternative uses, the supply of the immobile factor is inelastic. Hence the vertical line SS represents the supply curve of the factor. The downward sloping schedule, DD, represents the demand schedule. Equilibrium price and quantity correspond to the point of intersection of the two schedules. Like land, labour may be immobile as well, if substitution of leisure for labour is not possible. This is the case when, for example, a worker, if he sells labour, has to work for an institutionally fixed number of hours daily. If Government of India, for example, imposes a tax on labour income, labour cannot usually move away from India to escape the tax. If in addition substitution of leisure for labour is not possible in India for institutional or other reasons, labour will be immobile in India and accordingly its supply will be perfectly inelastic. Now suppose that the factor considered in Figure 5.7 is labour. Following the imposition of the tax, the workers cannot change the supply of labour by substituting leisure for work. Demand schedule of the producers is, however, not affected since the tax does not fall on them directly. Thus the equilibrium price remains unaffected. Workers, therefore, fail to pass on any burden of the tax to the producers. In this case, therefore, the entire burden of the tax is borne by the workers or the owners of the labour service.

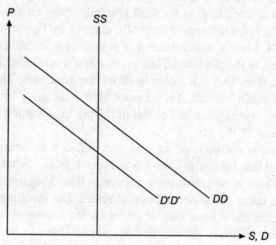

Figure 5.7: Tax on an immobile factor.

Suppose that the factor of production is land and the tax at the rate, t, is imposed on income from land. We know that in case of land or any other asset, purchase of which entitles the owner to a stream of future incomes, the price offered for the asset, i.e., the demand price of the asset equals the present value of the expected future income stream from the asset discounted at the market rate of interest, denoted r. Thus in the post-tax scenario the demand price of the asset, under the assumption that the asset yields income for T periods, equals

$$P^D = \frac{Y_1(1-t)}{1+r} + \frac{Y_2(1-t)}{(1+r)^2} + \dots + \frac{Y_T(1-t)}{(1+r)^T} = \frac{Y_1}{1+r} + \frac{Y_2}{(1+r)^2} + \dots$$

$$+ \frac{Y^T}{(1+r)^T} - \frac{t}{1+r} + \frac{t}{(1+r)^2} + \dots + \frac{t}{(1+r)^T} = Y - A$$

where $Y \equiv \dfrac{Y_1}{1+r} + \dfrac{Y_2}{(1+r)^2} + \dots + \dfrac{Y^T}{(1+r)^T}$, $A \equiv \dfrac{t}{1+r} + \dfrac{t}{(1+r)^2} + \dots + \dfrac{t}{(1+r)^T}$,

$Y_i \equiv$ expected income of the ith period; $i = 1, 2, \dots, T$

Thus, the demand price corresponding to every given level of the quantity demanded falls bringing about a downward shift in the demand schedule. In Figure 5.7 the new demand schedule is represented by $D'D'$. Thus, the price of land falls making the existing owner, i.e., the seller of the land, worse off. The point to note here is that even though the tax falls on the future incomes from land, the burden of the tax is borne fully by the seller even though the tax will be paid by the buyer. This is because the loss in income due to the future taxes is already factored into in the reduction in the price. In fact the reduction in the price is exactly equal to the present value of the future taxes. This process by means of which future taxes are incorporated into the price of an asset is called *capitalization*. The point to note is that if a factor is immobile across space and alternative uses and therefore inelastic in its supply, a tax on the income from such a factor will be borne by the owners. In case the factor is an asset such as land, ownership of which entitles the owner to a stream of future incomes, the taxes reduce the price of the asset exactly by the amount of the present value of the future expected taxes putting thereby the entire burden of all the future taxes on the existing owners of the asset, even if the asset is sold off and the taxes as a result are paid in future by the buyers who buy them at the time the tax is imposed.

Another important point to be noted here is that the above analysis holds for factors and assets that are truly immobile, i.e., which are immobile not only across space but also across uses. In that case the supply of the factor is inelastic. However, if following the imposition of a tax on the income of a factor or asset, it can move to non-taxed areas or uses, the supply of the factor in the taxed area or use will be elastic and the owners will be able to escape the burden partly or fully. Work it out yourself. Thus, if labour can be converted into leisure, and if leisure is not taxed, supply of labour may be elastic even if it is immobile across space. Similarly, if only land used for non-agricultural uses is taxed, supply of land to these uses will be elastic, even if land is immobile across space.

SUMMARY

1. Statutory incidence of a tax refers to the distribution of the burden of the given tax among individuals as specified by the statute of the tax. Economic incidence on the other hand refers to the actual distribution of the burden of the tax among individuals. Usually the two differ, as the individuals on whom the statutory incidence falls are able to shift the burden on to others.

2. A unit tax or a specific tax on a good or factor service is defined as an absolute amount of tax per unit of the good or factor service traded. A unit tax on a commodity will reduce its quantity traded, raise the price paid by the buyers and lower the price received by the sellers. A unit tax at a given rate on a good or factor service has the same effect on its equilibrium quantity and price irrespective of whether the tax is imposed on buyers or on sellers.

3. An ad valorem tax on a good or factor service is specified as a percentage or proportion of its price. An ad valorem tax has the same kind of impact as a unit tax on the quantity and price of the taxed commodity. However, the quantitative magnitudes of the impact of an ad valorem tax on a commodity at a given rate will depend upon on which side of the market the tax is imposed.

4. Partial equilibrium analysis of tax incidence shows that how the burden of a unit or ad valorem tax on the purchase or sale of a commodity traded in a competitive market will be distributed between the buyers and sellers will depend upon the value of price elasticity of demand relative to that of supply. The higher the price elasticity of demand relative to that of supply, the less is the increase in price and hence the less is the burden of the tax borne by the buyers. The burden on buyers of a unit or ad valorem tax on the purchase or sale of a consumption good is progressively, proportionally or regressively distributed among them according as income elasticity of demand for the good is greater than, equal to or less than unity. Thus the burden of a tax on a luxury good is progressively distributed among buyers, while the burden of a tax on a necessity will be regressively distributed among them.

5. Partial equilibrium analysis of a tax on the purchase or sale of a factor of production traded in competitive markets shows that the distribution of the burden of the tax between the suppliers and producers depend again on the price elasticity of demand for the factor relative to that of its supply. The higher the former relative to the latter, the less is the burden borne by the producers. A tax on capital service is likely to be progressive, while that on labour service may be regressive.

6. Extension of the analysis to the general equilibrium framework shows that the analysis of tax incidence is extremely complicated. However, there is a view that the forces that emerge as we extend our analysis to the general equilibrium case are quite weak and hence the results of the partial equilibrium analysis are likely to hold.

7. There is a general belief that producers with market power are able to shift the burden of taxes imposed on them entirely to the buyers. However, there seems to be no ground for this belief. If a tax is imposed on the sales or output of a monopolist, then under normal circumstances she has to bear at least a part of the burden.

8. The burden of a tax on economic profit cannot be shifted. It leaves prices and outputs unchanged. Hence a profit tax is non-distortionary and therefore quite appealing. However, it is not popular because it is extremely difficult to measure economic profit in practice.

9. If a tax is imposed on the income of an immobile factor, its burden is borne entirely by the owners of the immobile factor. If a tax is imposed on the future income from an immobile factor such as unimproved land and if it is sold in a given period, the burden of the tax on future incomes from the land sold will be borne entirely by the sellers even though the taxes will be actually paid by the buyers in future periods. The process by means of which future taxes get built into the current prices of an asset is called capitalization.

KEY CONCEPTS

✓ Statutory incidence
✓ Unit tax or specific tax
✓ Expenditure incidence
✓ Capitalization

✓ Economic incidence
✓ Ad valorem tax
✓ Immobile factor

REVIEW QUESTIONS

1. Distinguish between statutory incidence of a tax and its economic incidence.
2. Distinguish between a specific or a unit tax and an ad valorem tax.
3. How does a unit tax on the purchase or sale of a good or factor service affect its equilibrium price or quantity? Does this effect depend upon on which side of the market the tax is imposed?
4. How does an ad valorem tax on the purchase or sale of a good or factor service affect its equilibrium price or quantity? Does this effect depend upon on which side of the market the tax is imposed?
5. Examine the incidence of a unit tax on a good or factor service, which is traded in a competitive market in the partial equilibrium framework. How is the burden of a tax on a consumption good distributed among its consumers?
6. How does the extension of the analysis of tax incidence to the general equilibrium case modify the partial equilibrium results in case of a good and in the case of a factor service.
7. Is a monopolist able to shift the entire burden of a tax imposed on his sales or production on to the buyers? Explain.
8. How does a tax on economic profit of a firm affect its output and price? What is the source of its appeal? Why is it not popular?
9. How is the burden of a tax imposed on an immobile factor such as land distributed? What is meant by capitalization?

PROBLEMS AND APPLICATIONS

1. Inverse demand and supply functions of a commodity, X, is given by $P^D = 100 - 0.5X$ and $P^S = -20 + 0.5X$ respectively. Find out the impact of a unit tax at the rate of Rs. 10 on the sale of X. Show that a unit tax at the same rate on the purchase of X will have the same impact.

   (*Hint:* In the pre-tax scenario $X = 120$ and $P = 40$. When the tax is imposed on buyers, in the post-tax scenario, the equilibrium condition is: $100 - 0.5X - 10 = -20 + 0.5X \Rightarrow X = 110$, $P^D = 45$ and $P^S = 35$. When the unit tax is imposed on the sellers, the equilibrium condition is: $100 - 0.5X = -20 + 0.5X + 10 \Rightarrow X = 110$, $P^D = 45$ and $P^S = 35$)

2. Inverse demand and supply functions of a commodity, X, is given by $P^D = 100 - 0.5X$ and $P^S = -20 + 0.5X$ respectively. Find out the impact of an ad valorem tax at the rate of 10% on the sellers of X. Show that an ad valorem tax at the same rate on the buyers of X will not have the same impact. At what rate should the ad valorem tax on the buyers be imposed to achieve the same impact?

   (*Hint: Case 1: Equilibrium condition:*

   $$(100 - 0.5X) = (-20 + 0.5X)(1.1)$$

   $\Rightarrow \qquad\qquad X = 116.19, \; P^D = 41.9$

   and $\qquad\qquad P^S = 38.95.$

Case 2: Equilibrium condition:

$$(100 - 0.5X)(1 - 0.1) = (- 20 + 0.5X)$$

$$\Rightarrow \qquad X = 115.79, \ P^D = 42.11$$

and $\qquad P^S = 37.895$

Case 3: Equilibrium condition:

$$[100 - 0.5(116.19)](1 - t) = [- 20 + 0.5(116.19)]$$

$$\Rightarrow \qquad t = 0.90908$$

3. Consider the demand and supply functions of Problem 1. Find out (i) the rate of the unit tax and (ii) the rate of the ad valorem tax that will reduce X by 5 units.

   (*Hint: Unit tax: Equilibrium condition:*

$$(100 - 0.5X) = (- 20 + 0.5X) + t$$

$$\Rightarrow \qquad - dX = dt$$

$$\Rightarrow \qquad dt = 5.$$

   Ad valorem tax: Equilibrium condition:

$$(100 - 0.5X) = (- 20 + 0.5X)(1 + t)$$

$$\Rightarrow \qquad - dX = 40dt$$

$$\Rightarrow \qquad dt = 5/40. \text{ (Assuming } X = 120 \text{ and } t = 0))$$

4. Examine the impact of a unit subsidy at the rate s on the purchase of a commodity, X, which is traded in a competitive market in the partial equilibrium framework. How will the benefit of the subsidy be distributed among buyers, if the commodity is a necessity? Illustrate your answer graphically.

   (*Hint:* In this case, the equilibrium condition is given by $P^D(X) + s = P^S(X)$. Now, examine graphically the impact of the subsidy. Show how the subsidy is distributed. Then work out mathematically just the way it has been done in case of an indirect tax.)

5. In India government procures food grains from the producers at a fixed price and sells it to the consumers at a subsidized price so that supply of foodgrains is perfectly elastic at this price. Suppose that the government gives a unit subsidy at the rate, s. Also suppose that the poor consumers have a fixed money income and spend all their money income on food. The rich consumers on the other hand have a completely inelastic demand for food. How is the benefit of the subsidy distributed between the government and the consumers? If now the government increases the rate of the subsidy, who benefit most? How will the incidence change if producers of food grains directly supply food grains to the consumers, when (i) consumers receive a unit subsidy on the purchase of food grains at the rate, s and (ii) when the producers receive the unit subsidy at the rate, s, on their sales?

   (*Hint:* Suppose that P_C is the price at which the government procures food grains. The supply price is, therefore, $P_C - s$. Demand: $(\bar{M}/P) + \bar{R}$, where $\bar{M} \equiv$ fixed money income of the poor and $\overline{R} \equiv$ fixed food demand of the rich. Demand price is, therefore, $\overline{M}/(X - \overline{R})$. In this case consumers pay the price $P_C - s$ and the whole benefit of the subsidy is reaped by them. The poor gets $[\overline{M}/(P_C - s)]s$, and the rich $\overline{R}s$. If s rises, benefit to poor rises more than proportionately. If government withdraws, benefit of subsidy will be shared by consumers and producers, if the latters' supply function is not perfectly elastic. So, benefit to consumers will be less. Effect of subsidy is independent of on which side of the market it is given. Explain all these points in detail mathematically and graphically.)

6. In India almost all goods including medicines are taxed. Analyze the incidence of a unit tax on medicines. Do you support such a tax?

    (*Hint:* Medicine is a necessity. Its demand is highly inelastic. A tax on it is likely to be regressive. Explain in detail. Derive the result mathematically and illustrate graphically.)

7. Suppose that the inverse demand function faced by a monopolist producing a commodity X is given by $P^D = 100 - 0.5X$. Her cost function is given by $C = X$, where $C \equiv$ total cost of production of the monopolist. Analyse the incidence of a subsidy at the unit rate, s, on the consumption of X.

    (*Hint:* It will raise the demand price by s at every X. Work out the rest.)

8. In India there are subsidies on inputs used in the production of food grains. The objective of these subsidies is to benefit the consumers of food grains. Do you think that these input subsidies are better than direct subsidies on production or consumption of food grains?

    (*Hint:* In case of input subsidies it is likely that only a part of the subsidy in the form of lower input prices will accrue to the farmers and this part will be shared by the farmers and consumers of food. In the other case the whole of the subsidy will be shared. Hence, direct subsidy is better from the point of view of the consumers of food.)

9. Suppose that the inverse demand and supply functions in the market for food grains are given by $P^D = A - BX$ and $P^S = C + DX$ respectively, where X denotes quantity of food grains. The government gives a unit subsidy at the rate, s, on the purchase of inputs for food grains. However, the benefit of this subsidy accrues only partly to the farmers producing food grains. Their marginal cost of food grains falls only by half of s. Compare this subsidy to a direct unit subsidy at the rate, s, on the sale or purchase of X.

    (*Hint:* In the first case supply price is given by $C + DX - s/2$, while in the second case it is given by $C + DX - s$. Now proceed.)

10. In India the state governments are empowered by the Constitution to levy taxes on land or income from land. Suppose that the Government of West Bengal imposes taxes on income from land at rates higher than the other states to raise industrial investment in the state. Will the scheme work? Do you consider such a scheme equitable? Explain.

    (*Hint:* It will lower land prices in West Bengal by the present value of the future stream of expected taxes. This will raise profitability of investment including industrial investment, as the cost of land is now less. However, this rise in the profitability of industrial investment is at the cost of the landowners, many of whom might be quite poor, while the investors are likely to be quite rich.)

11. Suppose that you are made the Finance Minister of West Bengal and the Government of West Bengal has the power to impose sales taxes on all goods. Upon assuming office you find that there are sales taxes at high rates on medicines. In the first budget you prepare, will you eliminate taxes on medicines and make up the revenue loss by raising taxes on consumer durables and automobiles? Explain your answer.

(Hint: Taxes on medicines are likely to be regressive as they are necessities, while those on cars and consumer durables are likely to be progressive as they are luxuries.)

REFERENCES

General:

Fullerton, D. and Rogers, D.M. (1993): *Who Bears the Lifetime Tax Burden?* Brookings Institution, Washington DC.

Laurence, K. and Laurence, S. (1987): Tax incidence, Chapter 16, *Handbook of Public Economics*, Vol II, Auerbach, A.J. and Feldstein, M. (Eds.), North Holland.

Pechman, J.A.(1985): *Who Paid the Taxes 1966–85?* Brookings Institution, Washington DC.

On profit tax:

Gillis, M. and McLure, E.C. (1979): Excess profits taxation: Post-mortem of the Mexican experience, *National Tax Journal*, 32(4).

For discussion on optimal taxation:

Sandmo, A. (1976): Optimal taxation—An introduction to the literature, *Journal of Public Economics*, July–August.

6

PERSONAL INCOME TAXATION

Chapter Objectives

The objectives of this chapter are to discuss

(i) the definition of taxable income.
(ii) the properties of an optimum income tax structure and how India's income tax structure deviates from the optimum one.
(iii) the problems of a progressive tax structure and their remedies.
(iv) the problems created by inflation and ways of resolving them.
(v) the effects of income tax on saving, investment, labour supply and risk-taking.

6.1 INTRODUCTION

Personal income tax and corporation income tax are the most important direct taxes in India. In Table 6.1 we find that the contribution of the personal income tax to total tax revenue as well as its proportion in GDP is showing upward trends since the nineties. Currently, a little less than one fifth of the total tax revenue in India comes from personal income tax. This percentage is substantially less than that in the developed countries. The reason for the discrepancy is that quite a large part of the GDP in LDCs like India originates in the unorganized sector consisting of innumerable small production units. It is extremely costly to monitor and tax the incomes of this very large number of small establishments.

The rationale of personal income tax is grounded in the ability to pay principal, which, as we have seen in Chapter 4, recommends income as the basis of taxation for reasons of equity. It is also more or less universally accepted that maximization of social welfare calls for, if not complete equalization of post-tax incomes, at least a progressive tax structure. Accordingly, everywhere the structure of personal income tax is progressive and India is not an exception to this. This chapter discusses how the personal income tax should be designed and how and to what extent India's personal income tax structure deviates from the ideal one. Section 6.2 focuses on the definition of taxable income. Section 6.3 dwells on the problems that the progressive tax structure gives rise to and how they can be circumvented. Section 6.4 delves into the problems engendered by inflation and suggests ways of resolving them. Section 6.5 discusses the effects of income tax on individuals' choices. The final section contains the concluding remarks.

Table 6.1

Tax Revenue as a Percentage of Gross Tax Revenue					
2007–2008	2008–2009	2009–2010	2010–2011	2011–2012	2012–2013

	2007–2008	2008–2009	2009–2010	2010–2011	2011–2012	2012–2013
Personal income tax	17.3	17.5	19.6	17.5	18.6	17.6

Tax Revenue as a Percentage of GDP					

Personal income tax	2.1	1.9	1.9	1.8	1.8	1.9

6.2 DEFINITION OF TAXABLE INCOME

The definition of taxable income that is more or less universally accepted as the benchmark in the designing of the personal income tax structure, was given by Haig and Simons in the first half of the twentieth century. We shall henceforth refer to their definition of taxable income as H–S definition of taxable income. *They define taxable income as the sum of all kinds of incomes that can be used for purposes of consumption. Thus, taxable income includes all the different kinds of factor incomes, viz., wages and salaries, rent and royalty, interest, dividend and profit of proprietorship firms, all kinds of transfer income received from domestic government, domestic business, domestic households and foreigners, incomes received in kind such as imputed rent of owner-occupied houses, services rendered by members of a family working at home, imputed value of services rendered by consumer durables and, finally, capital gains realized or unrealized.*

The rationale of this definition of taxable income stems from the notion of horizontal equity, which states that individuals having the same power to consume should pay the same amount of tax. From this point of view therefore all the different types of income delineated above should be included in taxable income. Transfer incomes add to an individual's ability to consume or consumption potential the same way as factor incomes. Similarly, incomes received in kind also increases individuals' consumption potential. Consider two individuals having the same amount of income in cash. But suppose, unlike the other individual, one individual lives in a house of her own, possesses a number of consumer durables and her spouse performs all the domestic chores. Obviously, this individual's power to consume or consumption potential is far greater than that of the other. Capital gains mean appreciation in the value of assets such as land, houses, precious metals, gems and jewellery, artwork etc. in the possession of an individual. Capital gains may be positive or negative. Obviously, just like any other income, capital gains add to an individual's consumption potential. It should be noted in this context that no distinction should be made between realized or unrealized capital gains in the definition of taxable income. Taxable income should include both and treat them at par with one another. This is because whether an individual realizes her capital gains or leaves them unrealized is a matter of her choice. Consider two individuals having the same amount of income from all the sources including capital gains. Suppose one individual realizes her capital gains, while the other chooses not to do so. Clearly, there is no basis for treating the capital gains of the two individuals differently from the point of view of horizontal equity. The latter could, if she wanted, realize her capital gain and spend it on consumption. Exclusion of unrealized capital gains from taxable income thus violates horizontal equity.

6.2.1 Critique of the H–S Definition of Taxable Income

H–S definition of taxable income has been criticized on grounds of both equity and efficiency. We shall discuss them in turn. As we have pointed out above, H–S definition of taxable income has found wide acceptance on grounds of horizontal equity. Under this definition, taxable income includes all kinds of incomes and every kind of income is taxed at the same rate. Thus, two individuals having the same amount of income irrespective of the source of income have to pay the same amount of tax. This definition, therefore, ensures horizontal equity.

However, it has been pointed out by some (see, e.g., Feldstein (1976)) that, when individuals' skill levels differ, H–S definition may violate horizontal equity instead of ensuring it. Consider two individuals, one skilled and the other unskilled, having the same amount of income. However, the job of the former is more satisfying and substantially less strenuous than that of the latter. Hence the skilled individual is better off than the latter even though income levels of the two are the same. Thus taxing them at equal rates as suggested by the H–S definition violates horizontal equity. Even though the point made here has merit, usually individuals having higher skills or ability also earn larger incomes. Hence H–S definition despite this caveat has enormous appeal as a just definition of taxable income.

Taxes generate inefficiency or excess burden by distorting individuals' behaviour or choice. H–S definition, however, appears to be efficient as it suggests taxation of all kinds of incomes at the same rate. This is unlikely to affect individuals' allocation of resources across different lines of economic activities. If incomes from different sources were taxed at different rates, people would have shifted resources from high-tax areas or occupations to low-tax ones giving rise to excess burden. Hence H–S definition appears to be efficient. The impression is, however, erroneous, since minimization of excess burden, as we have seen in Chapter 4 on Efficiency of Taxation (see Box 4.1), requires tax rates on different commodities to be inversely proportional to their supply elasticities. Thus tax rate on income from unimproved land, whose supply is completely inelastic, should be larger than that on income from labour. Despite this critique, H–S definition has considerable appeal to people on grounds of horizontal equity. Taxing different kinds of income at different rates, though necessary on grounds of efficiency, appear to be grossly unjust. Thus, in every country, H–S definition serves as a useful benchmark in the designing of the income tax structure.

6.2.2   Problem of Implementation of H–S Definition

One of the main features of the H–S definition of taxable income is that it arrives at the figure of taxable income by deducting from the sum of incomes from all sources the expenditure incurred to earn the incomes. This, however, poses considerable problems in reality. Taxable income from business according to the H–S definition has to be calculated by deducting from total revenue all the business expenses. In practice it is very difficult to distinguish between business expenses and consumption. If the owner of a business makes a trip abroad in the interest of her business, it is very difficult to say how much of the expenses are strictly for business and how much of them are for personal pleasure. For example, the number of days she stays abroad might not be necessary for her work. She may spend for her own personal pleasure a few days more than what are strictly necessary for executing her work. This may apply to her other expenditures as well.

Valuation of incomes received in kind also poses considerable problems. It is very difficult to estimate imputed values of services received from consumer durables, as rental markets for most of these goods do not exist. Even in case of owner-occupied houses estimation of the imputed rent of a particular house may be problematic since an identical rented house may be hard to come by. Houses in the same locality having the same floor area may differ widely in many other respects and rental rates may also depend significantly on these differences. Similarly, housework done by the members of families staying at home may be difficult to evaluate.

Capital gains are another problem area. There are certain kinds of assets such as financial assets, which have active markets. Prices of these assets are available always. Thus estimation of capital gains or losses in case of these assets is easy. But there are many assets such as artwork, land, houses etc., which do not have active markets or whose markets are highly imperfect. In case of such assets, valuation of capital gains or losses is almost impossible. In case of land or houses, for example, to evaluate capital gains, it is necessary to identify market transactions where identical houses or pieces of land are traded. But such transactions are few and far between. One can, however, get around the problem by appointing assessors, but their valuations usually contain elements of subjective judgments and, therefore, may vary from one assessor to another.

6.2.3   Taxable Income in India

Income of an individual according to India's Income Tax Act consists of (i) income from salary, (ii) income from house property, (iii) profits and gains from businesses and other professions, (iv) capital gains and income from other sources, which consists of dividend, winnings from lotteries, horse races etc., interest on securities, loans, bank deposits etc., rental income from letting out furniture, machinery, plant etc., if they are not covered under (ii), rent from land and royalty. Certain deviations from the H–S definition of taxable income are noticeable even at this stage. Taxable income in India *omits imputed incomes from consumer durables or imputed values of services rendered by family members working at home.* The omission is, however, understandable in view of the difficulties and costs valuation of these services involves. Before making any further comments on the definition of taxable income of India, we have to go into the details of the different categories of income mentioned above.

Income from Salary

Income from salary consists of the following components: Wages, annuity or pension, gratuity, any fee, commission, perquisite in lieu of or in addition to any salary or wages, any advance of salary, the amount contributed by an employer towards a Recognized Provident Fund (RPF) in excess of 12% of the employee's salary and the interest in excess of 12% on the balance in the RPF, any payment received in respect of any period of leave not availed, the value of any perquisites and benefits to the employee provided by the employer, any profit in lieu of salary, that is, any amount or compensation due to or received by an employee from her employer, or former employer, at or in connection with the termination of her employment or modifications of the terms and conditions of the employment, any taxable amount in the RPF transferred from one employer to the other. With effect from April 1, 2002, salary also includes the value of any other fringe benefit or amenity provided by the employer to his employee.

Income from salary is, thus, quite comprehensively defined to include all kinds of compensations both in cash and kind made by employers to employees. The only exception being the contribution made by the employer to an RPF up to 12% of the employee's salary plus interest income of up to 12% on the employee's balance with the RPF. This exemption cannot be justified in the light of the H–S definition of taxable income.

Income from House Property

The annual value of any property, which is defined as the rental income from any property, owned by an individual is taxable under the head 'income from house property' While there are a few deductions available from this income, income from a property is not taxable under the head 'income from house property' when (a) the property is used for one's own business or profession, (b) the property is self-occupied, (c) it is income from a farmhouse, (d) the property income is of a local authority, (e) it is the property income of a university or an educational institution, (f) it is the property income of a trade union, (g) it is the property held for charitable or religious purposes, (h) it is the property income of a political party, (i) it is the property income of an approved scientific research association. Clearly, omissions of (a), (b) and (c) cannot be justified in the light of the H–S definition. (a) and (b) can be understood in view of valuation difficulties, but it is hard to see any ground for the omission of (c). Actually, it should be regarded as a part of the government's general policy of providing incentive to production and investment in agriculture. Even though in India agriculture contributes only about one fifth of GDP, it supports more than 60% of her population. It is generally believed that faster agricultural growth is the key to the alleviation of the problems of unemployment and poverty. Accordingly, social return from production and investment in agriculture is regarded as much higher than the private returns and the government, therefore, provides tax concessions on incomes from agriculture along with input subsidies to bring about efficient allocation of resources. Other exemptions may be vindicated on the ground that those incomes accrue to non-profit organizations working for the benefit of the society. Hence such exemptions do not violate horizontal equity.

Annual Value of the House Property

There are two concepts of the annual value of house property, gross and net. In case of the property that is rented out, the former is defined as the rental income actually realized during the year under consideration. If the owner fails to realize a part of her rental income, that part will not be included in the gross annual value. This is in consonance with the H–S definition. The net annual value is the gross annual value, net of the municipality taxes paid. However, in case of self-occupied property, both the gross and the net annual values are taken to be nil. This, though justifiable on grounds of valuation difficulties, obviously violates horizontal equity. To estimate the gross annual value of the property let out, four factors are taken into account, namely, (i) rent actually payable by the tenant, (ii) municipal valuation of the property, (iii) fair rental value (market value of a similar property in the same area) of the property and (iv) standard rent payable under the Rent Control Act. In fact, in general the maximum of these four is taken to be the gross annual value of the property to save on the administrative costs of checking on the information provided by the property owner regarding actual amount of rental income received.

The H–S definition is a net concept. It derives the amount of taxable income by subtracting from total revenue or receipts the costs incurred by the taxpayer in earning her income. *In India also two deductions are allowed from the net annual value in the calculation of the taxable income from house property. These are the repair and collection charges and interest on borrowed capital.* The former refers to the costs incurred to maintain and repair the property and to collect the rents from the tenants. The latter on the other hand consists in the interest paid by the owner on the loan taken to acquire the property. Again, to save on administrative costs, repair and collection charges are pegged at 30% of the net annual value. A ceiling has also been put on the interest cost that can be deducted from the net annual value. This ceiling for 2005–2006 was Rs. 1,50,000 for loans taken after 1999 and Rs. 30,000 for loans taken before 1999.

Profits and Gains from Business and Other Professions

This category of income consists of gains from any business carried on by the assessee during the year; income derived from trade, profession or any other similar service; interest, salary, bonus, commission or remuneration due or receivable by the partner from the partnership firm and income from speculative transactions. However, export-oriented units are to be taxed only to the extent of 20% of the total profits spread over five years. This definition covers all kinds of profit incomes. Exporters have been given tax concessions in violation of horizontal equity and H–S definition. This is, however, a part of the government's policy to give fiscal incentives to the export sector on grounds of the positive externalities it generates. There is a general belief that the economic activities in India are constrained by the availability of, among others, foreign exchange. Thus, an increase in exports not only benefits those who buy these exports but also those who gain from the increase in GDP that occurs following the relaxation of the foreign exchange constraint that additional exports bring about. Improved export performance also boosts foreign investors' confidence facilitating inflow of foreign direct and portfolio investments to the benefit of the country. Hence marginal social returns from exports are regarded to be much higher than the private returns. This calls for fiscal incentives to exports to bring about efficient allocation of resources.

Capital Gains

Indian Income Tax Act defines capital gains as follows. It is regarded as the profit from the sale or transfer of capital assets that have appreciated in value. It is clear from this definition that it only includes realized capital gains in the taxable income in violation of the H–S definition and horizontal equity. This omission, as we have pointed out above, is justifiable only on grounds of administrative difficulties involved in estimating unrealized capital gains. Capital asset is defined as property of any kind held by a person, irrespective of whether it is connected with her business. However, this does not include, to name only the major ones: (a) stock-in-trade, raw materials and stores held for business purposes, (b) personal effects, that is, movable property, including clothes and furniture, but excluding jewellery for personal use and (c) rural agricultural land. Omission of (a) is justified as gains from the appreciation in the value of these items will be captured in profits and gains from businesses and professions. The rationale of exclusion of (b) is also quite plain to see. Markets of these items are highly imperfect. Markets of most of these items hardly exist. Hence it is extremely difficult to evaluate capital gains from these items and thereby check on the information provided by the owner of the capital asset. Exclusion of (c) again should be regarded as a part of the government's general policy of providing fiscal incentives to agriculture for reasons we have already discussed.

In India an important distinction is made between short-term and long-term capital assets. A capital asset that is held for less than three years is deemed to be a short-term asset. If sold, it attracts tax at the normal rates. An asset that has been held for more than three years is deemed a long-term asset, and attracts tax at concessional rates when sold. However, in the case of securities such as equity or preference shares, debentures, government issuings, and units of mutual funds and the Unit Trust of India (UTI), the assets are deemed short-term if they are held for less than a year. Conversely, these assets are deemed long-term if they are held for more than a year. This difference in the treatment of capital gains from short- and long-term capital assets is also extremely difficult to justify on grounds of equity. The difference is made perhaps to discourage individuals to engage in speculative activities in shares and securities and encourage them to use these assets as genuine saving instruments.

Indian Income Tax Act treats capital gains and capital losses equivalently. If the owner of a capital asset suffers a loss from the sale of the asset, the loss is referred to as capital loss and it is deductible from the taxable income. Moreover, as we have mentioned above, under the Act capital gains are taxable not only on the sale of the capital assets but also on their transfer. The word transfer means the following:

(a) The exchange or relinquishment of an asset or the extinguishment of any rights in an asset.
(b) The acquisition of an asset.
(c) The conversion of an investment into stock-in-trade. This means that, if one buys, say, shares as an investment, and later wants to trade in them, then on the day one makes the change, one has converted one's asset into stock-in-trade. The difference in the cost and the market price on the date of the conversion is treated as capital gains in one's hand. However, this capital gain is liable to tax not in the year of conversion, but in the year in which the converted asset is sold or transferred.
(d) In the case of immovable property like land or a building, the transfer is complete when possession is handed over to the buyer. Thus, tax is payable on the gains when possession is handed over even if the sale deed has not been executed or the property registered.
(e) Any transaction, which in effect transfers or gives the benefits of immovable property.

Income from Other Sources

This refers to all kinds of incomes not covered under the three categories of income specified above. More precisely, it includes dividend; winnings from lotteries, horse races etc.; interest on securities when the securities are held as investment; interest on bank deposits, loans etc.; rental income from hiring out furniture, machinery etc. when such incomes are not covered under the head profits and gains from business; ground rent and royalty. When securities are held as stock-in-trade, as is the case with the stockbrokers, interest on securities is covered under the head profit and gains from business.

It should be noted here that, *while H–S definition of taxable income requires all the different kinds of incomes to be treated equally, Indian Income Tax Act treats some of the incomes mentioned above differently.* For example, winnings from lotteries etc. are not taxed at normal rates. Excess of all such winnings over Rs. 5000 are taxed at the rate of 30%. The rationale of this policy is hard to fathom because if such incomes were taxed at normal rates, poorer people earning such incomes would have paid less taxes than the rich, since personal income tax in India is progressive. Under the present policy the poor and the rich pay tax at the same rate on such incomes. Incomes from all the different sources mentioned above are added together to derive taxable income. All these different incomes, except for the exceptions noted above, are equally treated. Thus the Government of India seeks to follow the H–S definition as closely as possible. However, given the enormous difficulties involved in the valuation of certain kinds of incomes and the necessity to bring about an efficient allocation of resources, it has to in certain cases deviate from the H–S definition.

Itemized Deductions from Taxable Income

Income Tax Act may allow certain items of income to be deducted on grounds of equity and efficiency. Let us explain. Individuals having the same amount of income may not have the same ability to pay. Consider two individuals with the same amount of income. But suppose one has one handicapped child while the other's child is healthy. Obviously, the former is compelled to make some expenses for the handicapped child, which the latter need not make. Thus the former has less ability to pay than the latter. Similarly, if one of the two individuals having the same amount of income has to make large medical expenses, while the other need not, the former has less ability to pay than the latter. Thus the Income Tax Act may allow deductions of expenses for the upkeep of handicapped children and medical expenses from taxable income.

Similarly, some items of income may be exempted from taxation on grounds of efficiency. The part of income that is spent on activities that generate external benefits may be exempted from taxation to induce individuals to spend more than what they would normally do on such activities so that those activities take place on the socially desirable scale. This kind of exemption is warranted if it is the best way of encouraging the activities noted above. As we have already pointed out in the Chapter on private, public and mixed goods that there are a number of ways in which optimum levels of output of mixed goods can be brought about and exemption of spending on mixed goods from income tax may not always be the best way of doing it.

India's Income Tax Act allowed for a number of deductions up to a maximum of Rs. 1,00,000 from taxable income for the financial year 2005–2006. These are listed below:

(a) *Investment in financial assets issued by the government or public financial institutions:* Investments in certain types of financial assets such as General Provident Fund, Public Provident Fund, Life Insurance Policies of LIC or Unit Trust of India, NSCs, LIC's Pension Scheme, Jeevan Suraksha (up to a maximum of Rs. 10,000) and Health Insurance Policy of GIC, Mediclaim (up to a maximum of Rs. 10,000). Investments in the financial assets noted above are allowed to be deducted from taxable income up to a maximum of Rs.1,00,000. The financial assets noted above, except for Mediclaim, are all long-term saving instruments. Obviously, the rationale of this policy does not lie in the issue of equity. Of the two individuals having the same amount of income, the one making the above-mentioned investments will pay smaller taxes violating horizontal equity. Thus rationale of these deductions lies in the realm of efficiency. These concessions raise the return on saving and thereby encourage people to save and to save in the form of the above-mentioned financial assets, which are issued by the government or by the public financial institutions. In countries like India there is a general belief in the official circle and also outside that the economy's aggregate output is constrained by the available stock of capital and large doses of investment are, therefore, needed for rapid growth. However, since aggregate output is capacity-constrained, investment cannot be raised in a non-inflationary way without stepping up saving. In fact, following Harrod and Domar, it is generally held that growth rate in these countries is given by (s/v) where $s \equiv$ the saving ratio and $v \equiv$ capital output ratio. Saving therefore not only yields return to the savers but also facilitates growth in capital and output. Social return on saving is, therefore, regarded to be higher than the private return. The deductions are, therefore, warranted. Through these deductions the government not only raises return on saving but also encourages people to save in the form of certain safe long-term assets issued by the government and public financial institutions. The motivation behind this may be the following. It promotes these financial assets as merit goods. The deductions discourage people to engage in speculative activities through investments in risky assets and thereby expose themselves to market and other risks. Proceeds from the sale of these assets primarily finance investment in infrastructure, which yields strong external benefits. For all these reasons social returns on these assets are much higher than their private return. Hence, tax exemptions of investments in these assets may be warranted.

(b) *Purchase of new residential house or flat:* We have already seen that all kinds of incomes should be taxed at equal rates irrespective of how they are used on grounds of equity. Accordingly, income spent on acquiring a house should not be treated differently from income that is used for some other purpose. Obviously, the government regards acquisition (as opposed to renting) of house/flat as a merit good and, therefore, gives fiscal concessions to the purchase of houses.

(c) *Tuition fees of education of any two children:* Education, as we have pointed out already, is a mixed good that generates considerable positive externality. This is particularly true in today's society where knowledge and skill increase workers' productivity manifold. This warrants tax concessions on investments in education.

(d) *Medical treatment and deposits made for maintenance of handicapped dependents:* The rationale of this deduction is obviously rooted in equity. Consider two individuals earning the same amount of income, but one for health reasons has to make substantial medical expenditure, which is a matter of compulsion and not of choice. The healthy person, therefore, has much greater ability to pay than the other person. The same is true of persons with handicapped dependents. They have much less ability to pay than those with the same income but no handicapped dependents.

It should be noted that the total amount that can be deducted under (a), (b), (c) and (d) cannot exceed Rs. 1,00,000.

(e) *Exemption of house rent allowance:* There is an exemption for the salaried people living in rented houses. They earn house rent allowances and they can deduct from their taxable income the minimum of the following three items: (i) actual house rent received, (ii) rent paid in excess of 10% of salary, (iii) 50% of salary in metropolitan cities and 40% of salary outside. Fiscal incentive to people living in rented houses is surely warranted in India since imputed rent of owner-occupied houses is not included in taxable income. Consider two individuals in India who have the same taxable income but one is living in a rented house, while the other is living in her own house. Since the imputed income from the self-occupied house is not included in the taxable income of the latter, she has much greater ability to pay than the other. However, since this exemption is allowed only to the salaried persons, others living in rented houses are discriminated against.

6.3   PERSONAL INCOME TAX STRUCTURE

It is more or less universally accepted that income tax should be progressive. In every country, in the interest of administrative convenience, taxable income is divided into tax brackets or slabs and a tax rate is specified for incomes belonging to each such bracket. These tax rates are called marginal tax rates. Let us illustrate with an example. Suppose that in a country incomes are divided into the following tax brackets, namely, Rs. (0–50,000), (50,000–1,00,000), (1,00,000–1,50,000) and so on. Also suppose that the tax rates specified for these tax brackets are 0% for the lowest tax bracket, 10% for the second lowest tax bracket, 20% for the third lowest tax bracket and so on. These tax rates are the marginal tax rates. Tax liability of a person earning, say, Rs. 1,20,000 is calculated in the following manner. For the first fifty thousand rupees of her income, she pays nothing, as the tax rate that applies to that income is zero. The tax rate that applies to the next fifty thousand of her income is 10%. Hence, she has to pay a tax of Rs. 5000 on this income. The tax rate that applies to the next twenty thousand of her income is 20%, as it belongs to the third lowest tax bracket and accordingly, she has to pay a tax of Rs. 4000 on that income. Thus her total tax liability is Rs. 9000. It is more or less universally accepted that the marginal tax rates should rise with income. If marginal tax rates are the same for all tax brackets, every individual pays the same proportion of her income as tax irrespective of the level of her income. The tax structure is accordingly proportional. However, if the marginal tax rate rises with income, proportion of income paid as tax, i.e., the average tax rate, rises with income and the tax structure is progressive. There are of course other definitions of progressive tax structure. We shall discuss them shortly.

6.3.1 Personal Income Tax Structure in India

In India individual is the taxpaying unit. In some countries such as the USA, taxpaying unit is the family. All individuals are not treated equally. Women and senior citizens, defined as individuals who are of the age of sixty five or more at any time during the given financial year, are given favourable treatment. This may be vindicated on grounds of equity as they belong to physically weaker sections of people. Hence they have to make more expenses than others for their safety and/or health. Accordingly, they derive less utility than others from any given amount of income. Income tax structure in India is progressive. Marginal income tax rates for the year 2012–2013 are given in Table 6.2.

Table 6.2 Income Tax Rates for the Assessment Year 2012–13

General

Total annual taxable income slab (Rs.)	Tax rate (as percentage of taxable income) (Rs.)
0–1,80,000	Nil
1,80,001–5,00,000	10%
5,00,000–8,00,000	20%
More than 8,00,000	30%

Women

Total annual taxable income slab (Rs.)	Tax rate (as percentage of taxable income) (Rs.)
0–1,90,000	Nil
1,90,000–5,00,000	10%
5,00,000–8,00,000	20%
More than 8,00,000	30%

Senior Citizens (Individuals aged between 60–80 Years)

Total annual taxable income slab (Rs.)	Tax rate (as percentage of taxable income) (Rs.)
0–2,50,000	Nil
2,50,001–5,00,000	10%
5,00,000–8,00,000	20%
More than 8,00,000	30%

Senior Citizens who are Aged 80 Years or More

Total annual taxable income slab (Rs.)	Tax rate (as percentage of taxable income) (Rs.)
0–5,00,000	Nil
5,00,001–8,00,000	20%
More than 8,00,000	30%

For the general tax payers, as shown in Table 6.2, the tax rate applicable to taxable income in the Assessment year 2012–13 (i.e., for income earned in the financial year 2011–12) up to Rs. 1,80,000 was nil. The tax rate applicable to income in excess of Rs. 1,80,000 up to Rs. 5,00,000 was 10 per cent, tax rate applicable to taxable income in excess of Rs. 5,00,000 up to Rs. 8,00,000 was 20 per cent and the tax rate applicable to income in excess of Rs. 8,00,000 was 30 per cent. In case of women tax payers, as shown in Table 6.2, the tax rate applicable to taxable income up to Rs. 1,90,000 was nil. Tax rates applicable to incomes above Rs. 1,90,000 were the same as those applicable to the general tax payers.

Tax rates applicable to incomes of senior citizens aged between 60 years and 80 years and those who are 80 years old or older are also specified in the above tables.

Measures of Progression

The tax structure is progressive if the average tax rate, i.e., the fraction of total income paid as tax, rises with income. However, not all progressive tax structures are equally progressive. Tax structure of a country may be more progressive than that of another. The question that naturally arises is how to measure the degree of progression in a tax structure. There is, however, no unambiguous answer to this question. Three different measures of progression have been suggested, namely, average rate progression, liability progression and residual income progression. In what follows we shall discuss each of these measures in turn.

Average rate progression: This measure of progression follows directly from the definition of progressive taxation. The degree of progression, according to this measure, is given by the rate at which the average tax rate rises with income. Formally, degree of progression is given by

$$[d(T/Y)/dY] > 0 \qquad (6.1)$$

where T and Y denote total tax revenue and income respectively. Clearly, (T/Y) is the average tax rate and the amount by which it increases per unit of increase in Y measures the degree of progression. If the amount of increase in the average tax rate per unit increase in income is 1.5, the degree of progression is 1.5. This amount can of course vary from one level of income to another. Graphically, the degree of progression is measured by the slope of the line that indicates the level of (T/Y) corresponding to every Y in the $[(T/Y), Y]$ plane. Three possible situations are shown in Figure 6.1. In case of line I the average rate progression falls as income rises, along line II the average rate progression is constant, while along line III average rate progression rises with income.

When income is discrete, the average rate progression is measured by the following formula:

$$[(T_1/Y_1) - (T_0/Y_0)]/(Y_1 - Y_0)$$

where $Y_1 > Y_0$. T_1 and T_0 denote total tax liabilities corresponding to Y_1 and Y_0 respectively. Using it, one can measure the degree of average rate progression of the personal income tax of India. Do it yourself for the year 2006–2007.

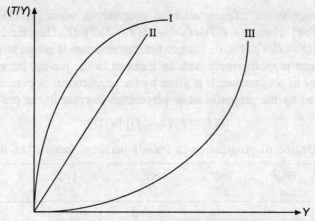

Figure 6.1: Average rate progression.

Liability progression: Tax structure is progressive when fraction of income paid as tax or total tax liability as proportion of income, (T/Y), rises with income. This means that when tax structure is progressive, tax liability, T, rises more than proportionately with respect to income, i.e., $(dT/T) > (dY/Y)$. This suggests a measure of progression. The greater the proportional increase in tax liability relative to proportional increase in income, i.e., the larger the value of $[(dT/T)/(dY/Y)]$, the higher is the degree of progression. If we multiply the numerator and denominator of the above expression by 100, we divide the percentage increase in tax liability by the percentage increase in income. *Thus in percentage terms, the higher the percentage increase in tax liability per 1% increase in income, the greater is the degree of progression. This measure of degree of progression is referred to as the liability progression.* In case of progressive tax structure, it is obviously greater than one. Graphically, liability progression is given by the slope of the line indicating the value of the logarithm of tax liability corresponding to every value of logarithm of Y in the (log Y, log T) plane, as shown in Figure 6.2. Just as in the earlier case degree of progression falls, stays unchanged and rises along lines I, II and III respectively. When income is discrete, liability progression is given by the following formula:

$$[(T_1 - T_0)/T_0]/[(Y_1 - Y_0)/Y_0]$$

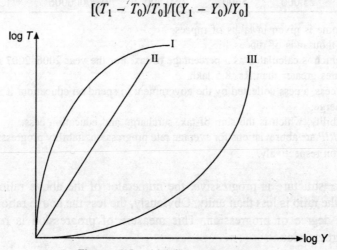

Figure 6.2: Liability progression.

Residual income progression: Tax structure is progressive, when $[d(T/Y)/dY] > 0$. However, $(T/Y) = 1 - [(Y - T)/Y]$. Hence $[d(T/Y)/dY] = -d[(Y - T)/Y]/dY$. Therefore, the tax structure is progressive when $d[(Y - T)/Y]/dY < 0$. Thus, when tax structure is progressive, post-tax income, $(Y - T)$, rises less than proportionately with an increase in the pre-tax income. This suggests a measure of the degree of progression. It is given by the proportional or percentage increase in the post-tax income dived by the proportional or percentage increase in the pre-tax income, i.e., by

$$[d(Y - T)/(Y - T)]/[dY/Y]$$

Table 6.3 Degree of progression in India's personal income tax in 2006–2007

(i)[1] Y	(ii)[2] Tax	(iii)[3] S	(iv)[4] EC	(v)[5] T	(vi)[6] ARP	(vii)[7] LP	(viii)[8] RIP
1.0	0	0	0	0			
1.5	5	0	100	5050	0.00000068	∞	0.899
2.0	15	0	300	15,300	0.00000086	4.06	0.831
2.5	25	0	500	25,500	0.00000050	2.68	0.862
3.0	40	0	800	40,800	0.00000068	3.00	0.773
3.5	55	0	1100	56,100	0.00000048	2.20	0.788
4.0	70	0	1400	71,400	0.00000038	1.90	0.788
4.5	85	0	1700	86,700	0.00000028	1.68	0.845
5.0	100	0	2000	1,02,000	0.00000022	1.60	0.860
5.5	115	0	2300	1,17,300	0.00000018	1.50	0.872
6.0	130	0	2600	1,32,600	0.00000016	1.40	0.891
6.5	145	0	2900	1,47,900	0.00000014	1.40	0.893
7.0	160	0	3200	1,63,200	0.00000010	1.30	0.897
7.5	175	0	3500	1,78,500	0.00000010	1.28	0.909
8.0	190	0	3800	1,93,800	0.00000008	1.26	0.906
8.5	205	0	4100	2,09,100	0.00000008	1.26	0.922
9.0	220	22,000	4840	2,46,840	0.00000058	3.05	0.323
9.5	235	23,500	5270	2,63,770	0.00000006	1.22	0.920
10.0	250	25,000	5600	2,80,600	0.00000006	1.23	0.910

[1]$Y \equiv$ taxable income is given in lakhs of rupees.
[2]Tax is given in thousands of rupees.
[3]$S \equiv$ surcharge which is calculated as a percentage of tax. For the year 2006–2007 it is 10% of tax for taxable incomes greater than Rs. 8.5 lakh.
[4]$EC \equiv$ education cess, a cess collected by the government to spend on education. It is pegged at 2% of tax plus surcharge.
[5]$T \equiv$ total tax liability, which is the sum of tax, surcharge and education cess.
[6,7,8]ARP, LP and RIP are abbreviations for average rate progression, liability progression and residual income progression respectively.

When the tax structure is progressive, the numerator of the above ratio is less than the denominator, i.e., the ratio is less than unity. Obviously, the less the above ratio relative to unity, the greater is the degree of progression. This measure of progression is referred to as the residual income progression.

Graphically, residual income progression is given by the slope of the line indicating the value of $\log(Y - T)$ corresponding to every value of $\log Y$, as shown in Figure 6.3. Residual income progression rises, stays unchanged and falls along lines II, I, and III respectively. When income is discrete, residual income progression is given by

$$\frac{\dfrac{(Y_1 - T_1) - (Y_0 - T_0)}{(Y_0 - T_0)}}{\dfrac{(Y_1 - Y_0)}{Y_0}}$$

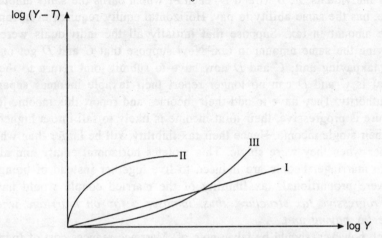

Figure 6.3: Residual income progression.

The values of measures of progression, namely, average rate progression (*ARP*), liability progression (*LP*) and residual income progression (*RIP*) recorded in Table 6.3 against a given level of income indicate the rate of progression, as income rises from the income preceding the given level of income to the given level of income. Thus, the values of *ARP*, *LP* and *RIP* against the taxable income Rs. 1.5 lakh give the degree of progression as taxable income rises from Rs.1 lakh to Rs. 1.5 lakh. Each of the measures shows that the tax structure is progressive as taxable income rises from 1 lakh to 1.5 lakh. Let us first focus on *ARP*. It rises as taxable income increases from Rs. 1.5 lakh to Rs. 2 lakh. This is because the marginal tax rate that applies to the latter is higher than that of the former. It, however, falls as taxable income goes up from Rs. 2 lakh to Rs. 2.5 lakh since the marginal tax rates are the same at the two levels of income. As the marginal tax rate at the taxable income, Rs. 3 lakh, is higher than that at Rs. 2 lakh, *ARP* rises again as taxable income increases from Rs. 2.5 lakh to Rs. 3 lakh. As the marginal tax rate is the same for all income levels in the range of Rs. 3 lakh to Rs. 8.5 lakh, *ARP* falls steadily as income rises from Rs. 3 lakh to Rs. 8.5 lakh. There is a jump in *ARP* as taxable income rises from Rs. 8.5 lakh to Rs. 9.5 lakh since at income levels greater than Rs. 8.5 lakh a surcharge at the rate of 10% of tax is levied. However, since the marginal tax rate and the rate of surcharge remain unchanged at income levels higher than Rs. 9 lakh, *ARP* becomes small and more or less constant. Other measures also display similar pattern for the same reasons.

6.4 PROBLEMS WITH A PROGRESSIVE TAX STRUCTURE

Progressive tax structure gives rise to a number of problems. We shall dwell on them in turn.

6.4.1 Choice of Units

There are problems associated with the choice of the taxpaying unit. The government can choose either the *individual* or the *family* as the taxpaying unit. Problems arise whatever be the taxpaying unit chosen. Suppose that the family is made the taxpaying unit, as in the US. Consider four individuals, *A*, *B*, *C* and *D*, each of whom earns the same amount of income and, therefore, has the same ability to pay. Horizontal equity requires every one of them to pay the same amount in tax. Suppose that initially all the individuals were single and, therefore, paying the same amount in tax. Now suppose that *C* and *D* get married. Since family is the taxpaying unit, *C* and *D* now have to submit joint return to the income tax authority. That is *C* and *D* can no longer report their taxable incomes separately to the income tax authority. They have to add their incomes and report this income jointly. When the tax structure is progressive, their joint income is likely to fall into a higher tax bracket than each of their single income. Hence their tax liability will be larger than what they were paying together when they were single. This violates horizontal equity and also acts as a disincentive to marriage. People are induced to live together instead of being married. If income tax were proportional, tax liability of the married couple would have remained unchanged. *Progressive tax structure, thus, imposes a tax on marriage when family is chosen as the tax paying unit.*

One point, however, should be taken note of. Marriage reduces cost of living. There are economies of scale in living together. Hence the cost of maintaining the standard of living that *C* and *D* had before marriage will come down after marriage raising their ability to pay. Hence after marriage *C* and *D* should pay more tax than what they were paying together before marriage to ensure horizontal equity. Otherwise *A* and *B*, who are single, will be discriminated against. However, under the progressive tax structure the increase in the tax liability of *C* and *D* after marriage may be much larger than what is warranted by the reduction in their cost of living. The tax structure should, therefore, be properly modified to accommodate the problems noted. Thus tax rates applicable to married couples should be suitably raised above those who are living singly to allow for the economies of scale enjoyed by the former. However, the higher tax rates should apply not only to the married couples but also to those who are living together without marriage.

If individual is made the taxpaying unit, different problems arise. In this case no distinction is made between single and married individuals. Every individual single or married has to submit separate statement of taxable income. Therefore, in the example given above *C* and *D* even after marriage continue to file separate income tax returns and pay the same amount of tax as before. However, this, as we have pointed out already, violates horizontal equity and discriminates against single individuals. To resolve this problem tax rates applicable to married individuals or individuals in live-in relationships have to be made higher than those applicable to single individuals to allow for the economies of scale that living together makes possible.

6.4.2   Inflation

In times of inflation, nominal incomes of individuals rise with prices. The additional value of aggregate output that is generated with the increase in prices is distributed as additional factor income among individuals. Let us explain with an example. Suppose that the real NDP is 100 units and the price level is Re. 1. The nominal NDP is Rs. 100. Ignoring indirect taxes and business saving for simplicity, the whole of this is distributed among people as factor income. Ignoring transfers, people's nominal income is also Rs. 100. Now suppose that the price levels doubles, with real NDP remaining unchanged. The nominal NDP, therefore, becomes Rs. 200 and the whole of it again goes into the hands of the people as factor income. Thus real income of the people remains unchanged. However, if the income tax is progressive, nominal incomes of individuals may go into higher tax brackets. Let us explain with an example. Suppose that before the increase in the price level every individual's nominal income was Rs. 10 and the tax rate applicable to income up to Rs. 10 was 10%. After the inflation, however, everyone's income rises to Rs. 20 and suppose that the marginal tax rate applicable to income above Rs. 10 and less than or equal to Rs. 20 is 20%. Thus everyone has to pay 20% of the addition nominal income of Rs. 10 as tax. Thus everyone's tax liability rises three times to Rs. 3 from Re. 1, while the nominal income just doubles. Thus the proportion of income individuals pay out as tax rises on account of inflation. In this example the proportion of tax in income rises to 15% from 10%. In other words, in times of inflation, nominal tax liability of individuals increases more than proportionately with respect to prices. Hence tax liability rises in real terms. In our example nominal tax liability rises 15%, while price level increases 10%. Hence real tax liability rises 5%. This phenomenon is called bracket creep. Inflation thus raises real tax liability of the individual through the bracket creep. Obviously, if the tax were proportional, the tax rate applicable to every level of income would have been 10% and nominal tax liability of everyone would have increased in the same proportion as the nominal income (to Rs. 20 in our example) and, therefore, real tax liability would have remained the same. The problem of an increase in the real tax liability of the people due to inflation, which leaves real income unaffected, arises only when the tax structure is progressive. This problem can be avoided if the widths of the tax brackets are raised in the same proportion as the price level. In our example, to avoid this problem of bracket creep, widths of tax brackets have to be doubled from 0–10 to 0–20, from 11–20 to 21–40 and so on following the doubling of the price level.

Income tax laws of many countries including India allow for standard deduction and itemized deductions. The former refers to an amount that the taxpayers are allowed to deduct from their total income to arrive at the figure of taxable income. The standard deduction is specified in nominal terms. The tax rate that, therefore, applies to the amount of income that is covered by standard deduction is zero. Clearly, if the nominal value of the standard deduction is not raised in the same proportion as the price level in times of inflation, the bracket creep cannot be avoided. Explain this point with an example yourself. Similarly, there are many items of income that the tax laws allow the taxpayers to deduct from the taxable income. In India, for example, the part of income that is invested in certain types of financial assets issued by the government or public financial institutions is allowed to be deducted from the taxable income. These itemized deductions are also specified in nominal terms. Thus the tax rate that applies to the part of income that is covered by the standard and itemized deductions is zero. To avoid bracket creep, therefore, in times of inflation nominal values of both standard and itemized deductions have to be raised in the same proportion as prices. From the above it follows that the tax widths, standard and itemized deductions should be indexed to inflation so that their nominal values rise in proportion with the prices and their real values remain unaffected. In India, however, the aforementioned items are not inflation indexed.

Capital Gains and Inflation

Capital gains mean appreciation in the values of assets owned by individuals. These are a part of taxable income. Capital gains occur because of increases in the prices of assets. In times of inflation, prices of all goods along with those of assets rise. Thus capital gains may be illusory. Suppose that prices of houses and also those of other goods and services double. Thus house owners make a capital gain in nominal terms. Their taxable incomes in nominal terms will go up by the additional values of their houses. However, in real terms values of their houses are unchanged. In real terms, therefore, there are no capital gains. Hence there should not be any tax imposed on this nominal capital gain. Let us explain with an example. Suppose that initially prices were stable. An individual's nominal factor income in this scenario was Rs. 100 and she did not make any capital gain. Now prices of all goods and services including those of assets owned by the individual double. Accordingly, her nominal factor income doubles and she also makes some capital gain. Therefore her nominal income more than doubles, while her real income remains unchanged. In this situation if nominal tax slabs are doubled and no tax is imposed on her capital gain, the individual's real tax liability will remain unchanged, as should be the case. If, however, the nominal capital gain is taxed, her real tax liability will rise, even after doubling of nominal tax slabs. Hence capital gains should be taxed only when there are real capital gains. Real capital gains occur when prices of assets rise more than proportionately with respect to prices of other goods. Let us illustrate with an example. Suppose initially the value of an asset was Rs. 100. Now prices of all goods and services double, while that of the capital asset trebles so that its value rises to Rs. 300. The asset, therefore, appreciates in value because of the increase in its value by Rs. 100 over Rs. 200. Hence tax should be imposed on this increase in its value over Rs. 200 only. This is exactly what is done in India.

6.4.3   Capital Gains Tax in India

We have already pointed out that only realized capital gains are taxed in India because of the difficulties involved in evaluating unrealized capital gains. However, Indian Income Tax Act allows adjustments for inflation in calculating capital gains. To calculate capital gains the Act allows the taxpayer to use the cost of inflation index. Suppose that an individual bought an asset at Rs. 1 lakh in 2000 when cost of inflation was 100. He sold it at Rs. 2 lakh in 2005. However, in 2005 cost of inflation index was 150. This means that compared to the year 2000 prices of goods and services have gone up by 50% in 2005. This implies that the increase in the value of the asset by Rs. 50,000, which is 50% of the value of the asset in the year 2000, does not represent any real capital gain in the year 2005. This is accommodated by the Act. The Act states that the cost of acquiring the asset is to be estimated as [1 lakh (150/100) = 1.5 lakh]. The amount of capital gain according to the Act is therefore Rs. (2 lakh −1.5 lakh) = 0.5 lakh.

6.5 EFFECT OF INCOME TAX ON ECONOMIC DECISIONS

Income tax may affect individuals' decisions significantly. Individuals decide on allocation of their given endowment of time between work and leisure, allocation of their income between consumption and saving and allocation of their wealth over different types of assets involving varying degrees of risk. Income tax reduces income from work by taking away a part of it as tax and thereby reduces incentive to work or makes leisure less costly. It also lowers rate of return on saving, as a part of interest income from saving has to be given away as tax. This reduces incentive to save. Income tax also brings about a decline in expected income from risky assets and thereby makes risk-taking less rewarding. Thus prima facie it seems that income tax may adversely affect labour supply, saving and risk taking. However, economic analysis shows that the effects of income tax on labour supply, saving and risk-taking are much more complex than what they appear to be. We shall examine these issues in detail below.

6.5.1 Income Tax and Labour Supply

Here we shall examine how income tax affects an individual's choice between income and leisure. An individual has a given endowment of time or labour in any given period. In a day, for example, an individual has 24 hours. In a month an individual has 720 hours etc. The individual has to decide how to allocate the given time or labour endowment between work or earning income and leisure. Obviously, individuals do this allocation in such a manner that their utility is maximized. More precisely, individuals resolve the choice problem carrying out the following optimization exercise:

$$\max_{y,l} U(y, l)$$

$$\text{subject to} \quad y = W(\overline{L} - l) \tag{6.2}$$

where $U(\cdot) \equiv$ utility function of the individual, $y \equiv$ income, $l \equiv$ leisure, $W \equiv$ real wage rate and $\overline{L} \equiv$ fixed labour endowment of the individual. In the above optimization exercise, W is given to the individual, as he is assumed to be a player in perfectly competitive goods and labour markets. The solution of the above optimization exercise is shown graphically in Figure 6.4 where y and l are measured on the vertical and horizontal axes respectively. BB is the individual's budget line as given by (6.2). Its intercepts on the vertical and horizontal axes are $(W\overline{L})$ and $\overline{L}$ respectively. The absolute value of its slope is W. The individual's optimum point on this budget line lies on the highest indifference curve attainable from this budget line. This indifference curve is the one, which is tangent to the budget line, BB. The optimum point is given by the point of tangency. This point is labelled A. It lies on the indifference curve, I_0. At the optimum point $mrs_{l,y} = W$.

Tax on Wage Income

Let us now suppose that the government imposes a proportional income tax at the rate, t, on wage income. Following the imposition of this tax, the individual has to give away (tW) amount from W to the government so that she effectively receives $W(1 - t)$ amount of wage per unit of labour supplied. The budget line under this kind of an income tax is, therefore, given by

$$YD = W(1 - t)(\overline{L} - l) \tag{6.3}$$

where $YD \equiv$ disposable income. This budget line is shown by BB_1 in Figure 6.4. It follows from the equation of the pre-tax budget line, (6.2), and that of the post-tax budget line, (6.3), that BB_1 has the same intercept on the horizontal axis as the pre-tax budget line, BB in Figure 6.4. However, the absolute value of the slope of BB_1, as follows from (6.3), is $W(1 - t)$. The individual in the present case will maximize her utility subject to (6.3). Therefore, she will choose the utility maximizing point from the budget line BB_1. At this optimum point $mrs_{l,YD} = W(1 - t)$. It is labelled A_1 in Figure 6.4. From A to A_1 consumption of leisure changes from l_0 to l_1. To identify the factors responsible for this change, we have to decompose the total change of consumption of leisure into substitution and income effects. The substitution effect is given by the change in consumption of leisure that occurs, when the individual makes her choice at the post-tax wage rate, but her income is adjusted in such a manner that her real income remains the same as that in the pre-tax situation. This means that we get the substitution effect from the change in consumer's optimum choice, when, following the imposition of the tax, she faces the post-tax wage rate, but her money income is adjusted so that the highest indifference curve she is able to attain is the one she chose from in the pre-tax situation. In other words, we get the substitution effect from the consumer's optimum choice, when in the post-tax situation her money income is adjusted in such a manner that her post-tax budget line shifts up and becomes tangent to the indifference curve she chose from in the pre-tax situation. In terms of Figure 6.4, therefore, the substitution effect is given by the point of choice of the individual from the budget line B_2B_2, whose slope is $W(1 - t)$ and which is tangent to the pre-tax indifference curve, I_0. The point that is chosen from this budget line is A_2. Thus the change in the consumption of leisure from l_0 to l_2 is due to substitution effect. Hence substitution effect raises consumption of leisure. If the individual operates on a budget line, the absolute value of whose slope is less than that of the pre-tax budget line and if from that budget line she chooses a point lying on I_0, $mrs_{l,y}$ at the chosen point will be less than that of the pre-tax optimum point. Hence the chosen point will be to the right of the pre-tax optimum point of the individual. Thus the substitution effect will unambiguously raise the consumption of leisure.

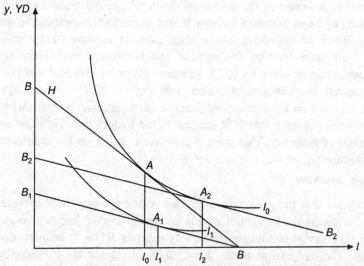

Figure 6.4: Effect of income tax on labour supply.

The intuition is quite simple. Proportional income tax on wage income reduces the real wage rate actually received by the worker and thereby makes leisure cheaper, i.e., now the individual foregoes smaller amount of income if she chooses to enjoy an extra unit of leisure. This induces the individual to substitute leisure for income. Hence the substitution effect raises demand for leisure.

We get the income effect by comparing A_2 and A_1 in Figure 6.4. At both these points the consumer makes her choice at the same post-tax wage rate, but her real incomes at A_2 and A_1 are different and they are equal to her pre-tax and post-tax real incomes respectively. Consumer's real income in the post-tax situation is obviously less as the tax forces the individual to choose from a lower indifference curve. If both leisure and income are normal goods, the fall in real income alone will reduce demand for leisure as well as income because of income effect. As shown in the figure, both l and y are less at A_1 than those at A_2. Thus substitution and income effect on the consumer's demand for leisure work in opposite directions. While the former tends to raise it, the latter tends to lower it. What happens to demand for leisure in the net depends upon the relative strengths of these two effects. If the substitution effect is stronger, as shown in our figure, demand for leisure will go up. In the opposite case, it will go down.

The effect of a proportional tax on wage income on supply of labour is, therefore, ambiguous. If the substitution effect dominates the income effect, supply of labour will fall. It will rise, if the latter is stronger than the former.

From the above it follows that the issue of how income tax affects labour supply has to be resolved empirically. Unfortunately, no such studies are available in Indian context. However, a large number of empirical studies have been carried out in the US. Even though results of these studies vary considerably, most of them *show that income tax has negligible impact on supply of labour of male workers in the age group of 20–60, but it discourages labour supply of married women.*

Laffer Curve

Reagan administration in the US represented a specific school of thought in macroeconomics. It is referred to as supply side economics. This school is of the view that a market economy always operates with full employment level of output. One of the influential members of this school, Arthur B. Laffer, proposed an inverted U-shaped relationship between income tax rate and income tax revenue. He pointed out that an increase in the income tax rate reduces labour supply and thereby lowers the full employment level of output. Hence income tax revenue can move either way following an increase in the income tax rate. (Work out Problem 2 in this context). He posited that at lower levels of the tax rate, an increase in the tax rate leads to a less than proportionate fall in aggregate income and thereby brings about an increase in the tax revenue. However, at higher levels of the income tax rate, an increase in the tax rate is followed by a more than proportionate fall in aggregate income and, therefore, a decline in the tax revenue. This relationship is shown in Figure 6.5. The curve depicting this relationship is called the Laffer curve. Clearly, when the tax rate, t, is zero, tax revenue is zero. Hence the Laffer curve starts from the origin. Then it slopes upward until a critical value of t, labelled t^* in the figure, is reached. For values of t higher than t^* the curve is downward sloping. Clearly, at $t = 1$, labour supply falls to zero, since there is no incentive to work. Supply-siders created a storm during the Reagan era by claiming that the income tax rate in the US was higher than t^* and recommended a cut in the tax rate to raise revenue. The recommendation was implemented. However, it did not yield the desired result.

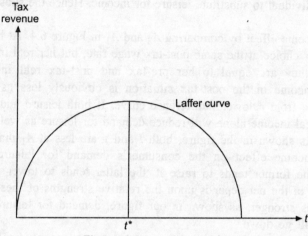

Figure 6.5: Laffer curve.

6.5.2 Effect of Income Tax on Saving

Here we examine how income tax affects an individual's saving. For this purpose we have to focus on the individual's problem of allocating a given amount of lifetime income over lifetime consumption. We shall carry out the analysis in the simplest possible framework under the following assumptions. There is no uncertainty, i.e., all individuals have perfect foresight. They live for two periods. A typical individual earns Y_1 in period 1 and Y_2 in period 2. She also operates in a perfectly competitive loan market, where she is a price-taker. The market interest rate, which is the same for both the borrowers and lenders, is denoted by r. There are no restrictions on borrowing and lending. The present value of lifetime income of the individual discounted at r, referred to as her wealth and denoted by W, is given by

$$W = Y_1 + \frac{Y_2}{1+r} \tag{6.4}$$

Individual's consumption expenditures in period 1 and period 2 are denoted by C_1 and C_2 respectively. C_1 and C_2 are assumed to include the individual's gifts and bequest as well. The individual chooses C_1 and C_2 in such a manner that her lifetime utility is maximized subject to the constraint that the present value of her lifetime consumption discounted at the market rate of interest equals the present value of her lifetime income discounted at the market rate of interest. Thus a typical individual carries out the following optimization exercise

$$\max_{C_1, C_2} U(C_1, C_2)$$

subject to $\quad W = C_1 + \dfrac{C_2}{1+r} \tag{6.5}$

where $U(\cdot) \equiv$ the utility function of the individual. It should be noted that (6.5) holds because C_1 and C_2 include gifts and bequests as well. Thus C_1 and C_2 include all the different ways in which the individual can spend her income over her lifetime. If C_1 and C_2 had not included gifts and bequests, the RHS would have been less than the LHS. The assumption of perfect foresight implies that the individual knows her lifespan and future income with certainty. We show the solution of the above optimization exercise graphically in Figure 6.6 where C_1 and C_2 are measured on the horizontal and vertical axes respectively. BB represents the budget constraint, (6.5), with slope $-(1 + r)$ and vertical intercept, $(W(1 + r))$. The individual chooses from this budget line the point that maximizes her utility. At such a point an indifference curve of the individual is tangent to the budget line and hence the absolute value of the slope of the indifference curve, $mrs_{C_1,C_2} = (1 + r)$, the absolute value of the slope of the budget line. (*Explain:* why other points on the budget line are not optimum using economic logic). Individual's optimum point on BB is labelled A in the figure.

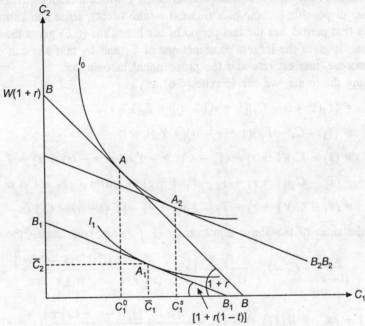

Figure 6.6: Effect of income tax on an individual's saving.

Income Tax

Suppose that the government imposes a proportional income tax at the rate, t, and the tax applies to both the lender and the borrower equally. This means that the lender pays tax on the interest income received at the rate t. Similarly, borrowers get tax concession at the rate t on the amount of interest paid on their loans. Thus lenders have to pay rt amount as tax from the interest income of r from every unit of the loan. Therefore, the interest rate effectively faced by the lender is $r(1 - t)$. Similarly, the borrower gets a tax deduction of rt amount on the r amount of interest paid on every unit of loan taken, i.e., as she pays r amount of interest for every unit of loan taken, her tax liability goes down by rt. Therefore, both the borrowers and lenders effectively pay and receive respectively the same interest rate, $r(1 - t)$. Hence the budget line of the consumer is given by

$$C_2 = [Y_1(1 - t) - C_1][1 + r(1 - t)] + Y_2(1 - t) \qquad (6.6)$$

Let us explain. $Y_2(1 - t)$ is the individual's disposable income in period 1 from which she saves $[Y_1(1 - t) - C_1]$ (dissaves $[C_1 - Y_1(1 - t)]$) in period 1. This saving (dissaving) is lent out (met with borrowing), as we have already explained, effectively at the rate of interest, $r(1 - t)$. Therefore, the individual earns (pays) in period 2 an interest income of $[Y_1(1 - t) - C_1] r(1 - t)$ (interest charges of $[C_1 - Y_1(1 - t)] r(1 - t)$). Accordingly, in period 2 the amount of disposable income of the individual is given by $[Y_1(1 - t) - C_1] r(1 - t) + Y_2(1 - t)$, irrespective of whether the individual is a borrower or lender. Besides this disposable income, the individual in period 2 has her savings or wealth, $[Y_1(1 - t) - C_1]$ (debt, $[C_1 - Y_1(1 - t)]$), which she has carried over from period 1. Thus in period 2 her total expenditure, C_2, which includes gifts and bequest also, should equal her disposable income plus (minus) wealth (debt), since she knows and everyone else also knows that period 2 is the last period of her life. Thus (6.6) gives the budget equation of the individual. It gives the largest combinations of C_1 and C_2 that she can enjoy, given her total lifetime income, interest rate and the proportional income tax.

Rearranging the terms, we can rewrite (6.6) as

$$
\begin{aligned}
C_2 &= [Y_1(1 - t) - C_1][1 + r(1 - t)] + Y_2(1 - t) \\
&= (Y_1 - C_1 - Y_1 t)(1 + r - tr) + Y_2(1 - t) \\
&= (Y_1 - C_1)(1 + r) - (Y_1 - C_1) \, tr - Y_1 t(1 + r - tr) + Y_2 - Y_2 t \\
&= (Y_1 - C_1)(1 + r) + Y_2 - Y_1 t(1 + r) + Y_1 t(tr) - (Y_1 - C_1) \, tr - Y_2 t \\
&= (Y_1 - C_1)(1 + r) + Y_2 - Y_1 t(1 + r) - [Y_1(1 - t) - C_1] \, tr - Y_2 t
\end{aligned}
$$

Dividing both the sides of the above equation by $(1 + r)$ and rearranging the terms, we have

$$\frac{C_2}{(1 + r)} + C_1 = Y_1 + \frac{Y_2}{(1 + r)} - \left[Y_1 t + \frac{Y_2 t}{(1 + r)} + \frac{[Y_1(1 - t) - C_1] rt}{(1 + r)} \right]$$

$\Rightarrow \qquad C_2 = -(1 + r)C_1 + W(1 + r) - \left[Y_1 t + \frac{Y_2 t}{(1 + r)} + \frac{[Y_1(1 - t) - C_1] rt}{(1 + r)} \right] (1 + r) \qquad (6.7)$

$\Rightarrow \qquad C_2 = -[1 + r(1 - t)]C_1 + W(1 + r) - \left[Y_1 t + \frac{Y_2 t}{(1 + r)} + \frac{Y_1(1 - t) rt}{(1 + r)} \right] (1 + r) \qquad (6.8)$

From (6.8) it follows that the budget line is flatter than the original budget line, (6.5). The absolute value of its slope is $[1 + r(1 - t)] < (1 + r)$, the absolute value of the slope of the original budget line. Its vertical intercept, as follows from (6.5) and (6.8), is also smaller than that of the original budget line. Its horizontal intercept, one can easily verify from (6.5) and (6.7), is also smaller. It is shown by $B_1 B_1$ in Figure 6.6.

Let us suppose that the individual in the post-tax equilibrium chooses the point $A_1(\bar{C}_1, \bar{C}_2)$ from B_1B_1 in Figure 6.6. Clearly, $mrs_{C_1,C_2} = [1 + r(1 - t)]$ at the given point. As a result of the tax, current period's consumption changes from C_1^0 to $\bar{C}_1$. To comprehend the reason for this change, we have to decompose it into substitution and income effect. We get the substitution effect by noting the consumer's optimum choice, when the consumer faces the post-tax interest rate, $r(1 - t)$, but her income is adjusted in such a manner that her real income is the same as that in the pre-tax situation, i.e., she is able to choose from the highest indifference curve that she attained in the pre-tax situation. In other words, we get the substitution effect from the optimum choice of the consumer when she operates on the budget line, whose slope is the same as that of the post-tax budget line, but which is tangent to the highest indifference curve attained in the pre-tax scenario, labelled I_0 in Figure 6.6. B_2B_2 is such a budget line in Figure 6.6 and the consumer chooses C_1^s from it and $C_1^s > C_1^0$. This must be the case since at the optimum point chosen from I_0 at the post-tax interest rate, $mrs_{C_1,C_2} = r(1 - t) < r$. Hence the chosen point should be to the right of the pre-tax optimum point on I_0. Thus current consumption rises on account of the substitution effect. Substitution effect, therefore, tends to reduce saving. The intuition behind the result is quite simple. The tax reduces the interest rate to the borrowers and lenders. An additional unit of C_1 in the post-tax scenario reduces C_2 by a smaller amount, $1 + r(1 - t)$, and not by the pre-tax quantity, $(1 + r)$. Hence current consumption becomes cheaper in terms of future consumption inducing the individual to substitute current consumption for future consumption. Hence *current consumption tends to rise and, therefore, saving tends to fall on account of the substitution effect.*

The movement from A_2 to A_1 is the income effect, since at both these points the consumer faces the same interest rate, which is the post-tax interest rate, but real incomes are different. A_2 and A_1 correspond to pre-tax and post-tax real incomes respectively. When C_1 and C_2 are normal goods, the fall in real income from the pre-tax to the post-tax situation reduces both C_1 and C_2. Accordingly, C_1 and C_2 at A_1 are less than those at A_2. Fall in C_1 clearly raises saving.

Thus, substitution and income effect work in opposite directions in case of saving as well. The former tends to lower it, while the latter puts an upward pressure on it. In the net the effect on saving depends on the relative strengths of these two effects. Hence the issue has to be settled empirically. Unfortunately, little empirical work has taken place in this regard in India. Empirical studies carried out in the context of the US economy yield contradictory results. There is now a broad agreement that the effect of tax on saving is negligible. See Hausman and Poterba (1987) in this context.

6.5.3 Effect of Income Tax on Risk-taking

Income tax, as we have shown above, may affect saving and thereby individuals' wealth. A fall in saving leads to a reduction in wealth. It may also affect composition of wealth. Since income tax reduces expected return from risky assets, it makes risk-taking less rewarding. As a result one may expect the income tax to shift the composition of wealth in favour of riskless assets, even though income tax reduces return from riskless assets too. Choice of the composition of wealth is referred to as portfolio choice. Modern studies on portfolio choice of the individuals were pioneered by the path-breaking work of Tobin (1958). We shall, therefore, use Tobin's framework to examine how income tax affects individual's portfolio choice.

Tobin's model is based on the following assumptions. It considers an individual having a given amount of wealth, which is assumed to be unity for simplicity. The individual can hold her wealth in the form of either a risky asset or a riskless asset. Proportions of wealth held in the form of the risky and riskless assets are denoted by A_1 and A_2 respectively. Obviously, $A_1 + A_2 = 1$. The individual has a subjective probability distribution over all possible rates of return on the risky asset. The expected return of the risky asset is denoted by μ. Let us explain. Suppose that possible rates of return on the risky asset or possible incomes from 1 unit of wealth or 1 rupee invested in the risky asset are $r_1, r_2, ..., r_n$, then

$$\mu = \sum_{i=1}^{n} p_i r_i \qquad (6.9)$$

where p_i denotes the probability of occurrence of the ith return, r_i. Standard deviation of the possible rates of return of the risky asset is denoted by σ. Thus

$$\sigma = \sqrt{\sum_{i=1}^{n} p_i (r_i - \mu)^2} \qquad (6.10)$$

From the above it follows that if 1 unit of wealth or Re. 1 is invested in the risky asset, it will yield an expected return of μ. Hence, if A_1 amount of wealth is invested in the risky asset, it will yield an expected income of $\mu A_1 = \sum_{i=1}^{n} p_i (A_1 r_i)$, since in the ith state of nature A_1 amount of wealth invested in the risky asset yields an income of $A_1 r_i$. The riskless asset does not yield any income by assumption. Therefore, denoting expected income from the portfolio where A_1 proportion of wealth is invested in the risky asset and the rest invested in the riskless asset by R, we have

$$R = \mu A_1 + 0 A_2 = \mu A_1 \qquad (6.11)$$

The risk of 1 unit of wealth invested in the risky asset is measured by σ by assumption. Clearly, therefore the risk involved in A_1 amount of wealth invested in the risky asset is σA_1. The risk involved in the portfolio where A_1 proportion of wealth is invested in the risky asset and the rest invested in the riskless asset, denoted ρ, is therefore measured by σA_1. Thus

$$\rho = \sigma A_1 \qquad (6.12)$$

From (6.11) and (6.12) it is clear that the individual can assume different amounts of risk and return by choosing different values of A_1. Solving (6.12) for A_1 and putting this value in (6.11), we get

$$R = \frac{\mu}{\sigma} \rho \qquad (6.13)$$

Equation (6.13) gives all possible combinations of R and ρ that the individual can assume by varying the value of A_1 from 0 to 1. Let us explain. First focus on the slope of (6.13), μ/σ, which gives the amount of increase in R following a unit increase in ρ. From (6.12) it follows that a unit increase in A_1 will raise ρ by σ. Therefore, if A_1 rises by $1/\sigma$, ρ will go up by unity.

However, if A_1 rises by $1/\sigma$, R, as follows from (6.11), will increase by μ/σ. This explains the slope of (6.13). Let us start from the portfolio where $A_1 = 0$ and $A_2 = 1$. Values of R and ρ corresponding to this portfolio are both zero. If now the individual raises A_1 by $1/\sigma$ and, therefore, reduces A_2 by $1/\sigma$, ρ will go up to unity from zero and R will rise to μ/σ from zero. If A_1 is raised further by $1/\sigma$ and, therefore A_2 reduced further by $1/\sigma$, ρ will go up by unity from 1 to 2 and R will rise by μ/σ to $2\mu/\sigma$ from μ/σ. This explains (6.13). It gives all combinations of risk and return the individual can assume by varying the values of A_1 and A_2. Hence it may be regarded as the individual's budget constraint involving risk and return. We plot it in Figure 6.7. It is represented by the line BB, which is a ray through the origin, with the slope (μ/σ).

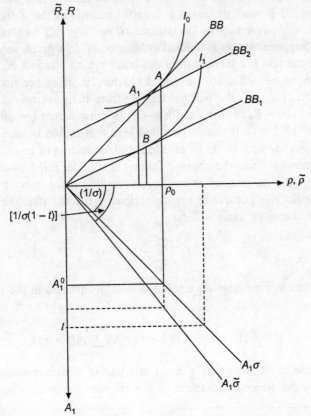

Figure 6.7: Income tax and risk-taking: case of full loss-offset.

Indifference curves of the individual in risk and return are superimposed on the budget constraint in Figure 6.7. Individuals are assumed to be risk-averse. Hence they willingly take more risk if and only if they get more expected return. Hence indifference curves are upward sloping. The amount of increase in R that compensates for a unit increase in ρ is assumed to rise with an increase in ρ. Hence indifference curves are convex downward. The individual is better off, if R is higher corresponding to any given ρ. Hence a higher indifference curve represents a higher level of utility to the individual. Obviously, an individual will choose from her budget line that point, which is on the highest indifference curve. This is clearly the one at which an indifference curve is tangent to the budget line. The indifference curve I_0 in Figure 6.7 is tangent to BB. Hence it is the highest indifference curve attainable from BB. The point of tangency, A, is therefore the optimum point.

In the fourth quadrant the line, labelled A_1P, represents the inverse of (6.12), which indicates the values of A_1 corresponding to different values of ρ. The value of A_1 that corresponds to the optimum point, A, on the budget line, as read off from $A_1\rho$, is A_1^0.

Let us now examine how an income tax applied at the proportional rate t to income affects individual's portfolio choice. *We assume that there is full loss offset, i.e., the tax applies symmetrically to both positive and negative income.* Let us illustrate with an example. Suppose that an individual earns positive income of Rs. Y from an asset. Then she has to pay a tax of Rs. tY on that income. If instead she earns a negative income of Rs. Z from an asset, her tax liability falls by Rs. tZ, when income tax statute allows for full loss offset. Let us give a numerical example. Suppose that an individual holds a bond. In a given year she suffers a large capital loss on the bond and her income from the bond, which consists of interest income and capital loss, turns out to be − Rs. 10, i.e., she loses Rs. 10. Then her tax liability under full loss-offset will be −Rs. $10t$, i.e., she will get Rs. $10t$ from the government. Therefore her loss will fall; it will be Rs. 10 − Rs. $10t$ = Rs. $10(1 - t)$. In other words her after-tax income from the bond will be −Rs. $10(1 - t)$. It should be noted here that Indian Income Tax Act allows for full loss-offset. It allows, as you should be able to recall, deduction of capital losses on financial assets from taxable income. From the above it follows that under full loss-offset after-tax return from the risky asset in the ith state of nature becomes $r_i(1 - t)$ for every i, where $i = 1, 2, ..., n$, irrespective of whether r_i is positive or negative. Hence expected after-tax income from 1 unit of wealth invested in the risky asset will be

$$\mu(1 - t) = \sum_{i=1}^{n} p_i r_i (1 - t)$$

Expected after tax income from A_1 amount of wealth invested in the risky asset, denoted $\tilde{R}$, will therefore be

$$\tilde{R} = R(1 - t) = A_1\mu(1 - t) = A_1\sum_{i=1}^{n} p_i r_i (1 - t) \tag{6.14}$$

Again, the amount of risk involved in Re. 1 or 1 unit of wealth invested in the risky asset, which is measured by the standard deviation of the after-tax returns, is given by

$$\sqrt{\sum_{i=1}^{n} p_i \left[r_i(1 - t) - \mu(1 - t)\right]^2} = (1 - t)\sqrt{\sum_{i=1}^{n} p_i(r_i - \mu)^2} = (1 - t)\sigma$$

The amount of risk involved in A_1 amount of wealth invested in the risky asset, denoted $\tilde{\rho}$, is therefore given by

$$\tilde{\rho} = \rho(1 - t) = A_1\sigma(1 - t) \tag{6.15}$$

Solving (6.15) for A_1 and putting it into (6.14), we get

$$\tilde{R} = \frac{\mu}{\sigma}\tilde{\rho} \tag{6.16}$$

Individual's budget constraint in risk and return in the post-tax scenario is given by (6.16). It can be explained the same way as (6.13) and it is identical with (6.13). In the post-tax scenario, as follows from (6.16), to assume one additional unit of risk, the individual has to raise A_1 by $1/\sigma(1-t)$. Again, if A_1 rises by $1/\sigma(1-t)$, $\tilde{R}$ will increase by $\mu(1-t)[1/\sigma(1-t)] = \mu/\sigma$. This explains why pre-tax and post-tax budget lines in risk and return are identical. *BB* in Figure 6.7, therefore, represents the post-tax budget line as well. *In the post-tax scenario, therefore, the individual will choose the same combination of risk and return as before. A, therefore, remains the optimum point even in the post-tax scenario.* However, the line representing the inverse of (6.15), which is labelled $A_1\tilde{\rho}$ in the figure and which shows the value of A_1 corresponding to every value of $\tilde{\rho}$, lies below $A_1\rho$, since its slope, $1/\sigma(1-t)$, is larger. This means that to assume the same amount of risk as in the pre-tax scenario, the individual in the post-tax scenario has to invest a larger proportion of wealth in the risky asset. Thus, *in the full loss-offset case, even though the individual assumes the same amount of risk as before, she invests a larger fraction of her wealth in the risky asset.*

The intuition of the result is the following. A unit increase in risk in the post-tax scenario leads to as much increase in expected return as in the pre-tax situation. Thus risk-taking remains as rewarding as before. Income tax with full loss-offset, therefore, does not produce any substitution effect. However, any given fraction of wealth invested in the risky asset in the post-tax situation yields smaller amounts of both risk and return. This produces an income effect, which induces the individual to invest larger fraction of their wealth in the risky asset and thereby raise expected return and risk to their respective pre-tax levels.

In some countries there is no provision for loss-offset, i.e., the taxpayers are not allowed to deduct their losses from their taxable income. The tax, therefore, reduces the expected positive incomes of the individual, but leaves expected negative incomes unaffected. Clearly, therefore, the risk involved in any given allocation of wealth between risky and riskless assets goes up, while the expected return goes down. This is, therefore, likely to discourage risk-taking. This of course does not come out clearly in Tobin's model, as corresponding to any (A_1, A_2) both R and ρ go down in the model in the present no loss-offset case. Hence we use a different model, the one developed by Musgrave and Domar (1944), to capture the impact of no loss-offset. This model is presented in the appendix.

6.6 CONCLUSION

Income tax is growing in importance in India. However, its coverage is still quite narrow since quite a large part of India's GDP originates in the unorganized sector. There are no taxes on income derived from agriculture, which constitutes a significant segment of the unorganized sector. This, as we have already pointed out, may be regarded as a part of the government's general policy of giving incentives to agricultural production and investment. It is also enormously costly to monitor the incomes originating in innumerable small production units. It is, therefore, not surprising that less than 2% of GDP is raised as personal income tax. Such a narrow coverage of the personal income tax clearly violates both the ability to pay and benefit principles of tax equity.

One related problem is that of tax evasion. As it is extremely costly to monitor economic activities being carried out in the unorganized sector, concealment and therefore under-reporting of income is quite easy. The probability of being caught is very low. As a result tax evasion is rampant. It is estimated that only about 30 million Indians pay income tax even though the size of India's middle class is 300 million. In fact, in the post-reform period income tax rates have been brought down drastically to reduce tax evasion. It is argued that, the higher the tax rate, the larger is the tax saved from the concealment of any given amount of income and, therefore, the higher is the return from tax evasion. It is widely held in the official circles in India today that high tax rates give strong incentives to tax evasion. Hence low tax rates are recommended to check tax evasion. It is also believed that lowering of tax rates will reduce tax evasion to such an extent that the total tax revenue will rise.

Efforts are also on in recent years to simplify tax laws and procedures to reduce the cost of compliance. If, along with that, penalties on tax evasion are raised; the administrative machinery to detect cases of tax evasion is strengthened; corruption in public administration is reduced and efforts are made to convince the people that the taxes they pay will contribute to supplies of quality social good, tax collection will improve substantially. This is extremely important in view of the acute shortage of infrastructural services, which the government has to provide in the main because of their public good type characteristics, and the large revenue and fiscal deficits, which have seriously impaired government's ability to invest.

=== **SUMMARY** ===

1. Haig and Simons define taxable income of an individual as the sum of incomes of the individual from all sources. It should include all kinds of factor income, transfer income, all kinds of incomes in kind and capital gains both realized and unrealized. This definition is universally accepted and referred to as the H–S definition of taxable income. Incomes from all sources according to this definition have to be taxed at the same rate to ensure horizontal equity.

2. H–S definition of taxable income has been criticized on grounds of both equity and efficiency. Two individuals may be earning the same amount of income, but one's job may be boring and strenuous relative to that of the other. Clearly, the person having the cushy job is better off and taxing his income at the same rate as that of the other will be discriminatory. Again, inverse elasticity rule of optimum commodity taxation states that tax rates applicable to different kinds of income ought to be different.

3. It is difficult to implement the H–S definition of taxable income, as estimation of unrealized capital gains and imputed value of services from consumer durables and houses is extremely difficult to evaluate.

4. In India, definition of taxable income closely follows the H–S definition, but it excludes imputed value of services from owner-occupied houses, consumer durables, income from farm houses, employers' contribution to PPF up to 12% of the employees' income plus interest income on the employee's balance with the PPF. These exemptions cannot be justified in the light of the H–S definition of taxable income. In case of capital gains also capital gains on (a) stock-in-trade, raw materials and stores held for business purposes, (b) personal effects, i.e., movable property, including clothes and furniture, but excluding jewellery for personal use, and (c) rural agricultural land are not included in taxable

income. Moreover, unrealized capital gains are excluded from taxable income and short-term and long-term capital gains are taxed at different rates. These clearly violate the H–S definition.

5. Income Tax Act of a country can have provisions for itemized deduction on ground of equity. Two individuals having the same amount of income may not have the same ability to pay. Thus one may have larger number of dependents, physical handicap or illness and, therefore, lower ability to pay. Income Tax Act, therefore, can provide for deductions of medical expenses, expenditure incurred for the upkeep of handicapped children and expenditure on dependants from taxable income on grounds of equity. India's Income Tax Act for the financial year 2006–2007 allowed for a number of deductions up to a maximum of Rs. 1,00,000 from taxable income. These are listed below: (i) investment in financial assets issued by the government or public financial institutions, (ii) purchase of new residential house or flat, (iii) tuition fees of education of any two children, (iv) medical treatment and deposits made for maintenance of handicapped dependents and, finally, (v) exemption of house rent allowance.

6. In India, individual is the tax-paying unit. Tax structure is progressive. Favourable treatment is given to women and senior citizens. Tax rates applicable to different income slabs in 2006–2007 for the three categories of citizens are summarized in Table 6.2. In 2006–2007, individuals earning more than Rs. 8,50,000 had to pay a surcharge at the rate of 10% of their tax liability. Every taxpayer also had to pay 2% of her tax liability including surcharge as education cess.

7. There are three measures of degree of progression, namely, average rate progression, liability progression and residual income progression. The first one consists in the amount of increase in the fraction of income paid out as tax following a unit increase in taxable income. The degree of progression according to this measure is, therefore, likely to vary from one income level to another. According to liability progression degree of progression is given by the percentage increase in tax liability following 1% increase in taxable income. In case of liability progression, therefore, degree of progression has to be greater than unity for progressive taxation. Residual income progression is given by the percentage increase in post-tax income per 1% increase in pre-tax income.

8. Progressive income tax gives rise to a number of problems. One of them relates to choice of units. If family is made the tax-paying unit, married couples are discriminated against, while if individuals are made tax-paying units, single individuals are discriminated against. In both cases, therefore, there should be separate tax rates for single individuals and individuals in live-in relationships to ensure horizontal equity.

9. Inflation married or leads to an increase in individuals' nominal incomes, even when their real incomes remain unchanged. Under progressive income tax, therefore, individuals' nominal incomes may move into higher tax brackets with inflation, even though their real income remains the same. Thus individuals' nominal tax liability may rise more than proportionately with respect to prices. Hence their real tax liability may rise on account of inflation even though their real income remains the same. This is referred to as bracket creep. To avoid this problem, nominal tax brackets have to be widened in proportion to prices.

10. Taxable income should include both realized and unrealized capital gains. Inflation leads to spurious capital gains. In times of inflation, prices of all goods and services along with those of assets increase. If all these prices increase in the same proportion, real values of assets remain the same, despite their higher nominal values. Thus, there is no capital gain in real terms. Hence, there should not be any tax on capital gains. This practice is followed in India.

11. Proportional income tax has ambiguous effect on income and leisure. It makes leisure cheaper in terms of income foregone and thereby induces individuals to substitute leisure for income. This is the substitution effect. It also reduces real income and thereby tends to reduce both income and leisure, when they are normal goods. This is the income effect. Demand for leisure will rise and, therefore, labour supply will fall if the substitution effect is stronger than the income effect and vice versa.

12. Laffer, an influential supply-sider, proposed an inverted U-shaped relationship between income tax rate and income tax revenue. This relationship is known as Laffer curve.

13. The effect of a proportional income tax on saving is also ambiguous. The tax produces both substitution and income effect and they operate in opposite directions on saving. The former tends to raise it, while the latter tends to lower it, when both current and future consumption are normal goods.

14. A proportional income tax with full loss-offset induces individuals to invest a larger proportion of their wealth in risky assets.

========================== **KEY CONCEPTS** ==========================

✓ Taxable income
✓ Realized capital gains
✓ Short-term capital gains
✓ Itemized deductions
✓ Average rate progression
✓ Bracket creep
✓ Full loss offset

✓ Capital gains
✓ Unrealized capital gains
✓ Long-term capital gains
✓ Taxpaying unit
✓ Liability progression and residual income progression
✓ Laffer curve

========================== **REVIEW QUESTIONS** ==========================

1. State the H–S definition of taxable income. Explain why it ensures horizontal equity. Illustrate your answer with examples.

2. Can the H–S definition of taxable income be criticized on grounds of equity and efficiency? Explain.

3. Assess India's definition of taxable income in the light of H–S definition of taxable income.

4. What are the major itemized deductions allowed for in India's Income Tax Act of 2006–2007? Do you consider them to be justified? Explain.

5. Suppose that Mr. Bose is a citizen of India and his taxable income was Rs. 9,00,000 in 2006–2007. He also bought NSCs worth Rs. 80,000. How much tax did he have to pay in the given year?

6. What are the different measures of degree of progression?

7. Measure the degree of progression of India's personal income tax using liability progression.

8. What problems arise under progressive tax structure regarding the choice of units?

9. Does inflation lead to any problem under a progressive tax structure? Explain.

10. Explain with examples why itemized and standard deductions have to be inflation-indexed?

11. Should there be any tax on capital gains, when asset prices and prices of all other goods and services increase in the same proportion? Does India's Income Tax Act impose tax on nominal capital gains, when there are no capital gains in real terms?

12. How does proportional income tax affect labour supply?

13. What is Laffer curve? Explain it.

14. How does a proportional income tax at the rate, t, affect an individual's saving?

15. How does a proportional income tax affect risk-taking in Tobin's model when there is full loss offset.

═══════ PROBLEMS AND APPLICATIONS ═══════

1. Suppose that the utility function of an individual is $U = Y^{0.5} l^{0.5}$ and $\bar{L} = 24$ hr. Derive the labour supply function of this individual. How is this labour supply function affected if wage income is taxed at the rate of 10%, assuming that the initial hourly wage rate is Re.1? Explain the change in terms of substitution and income effect.

   (*Hint:* In the absence of taxation optimum level of daily labour supply is given by $L^S = 24 - 12/W$. In the post-tax scenario $L^S = 24 - 12/W(1 - 0.1)$. To derive the substitution effect find out on the pre-tax indifference curve attained the point at which $mrs_{l,y} = (1 - 0.1)$.)

2. Suppose that in an economy all firms are identical. There are 100 firms. All firms operate in competitive markets. They are all identical and their production function is given by $Y = L$, where L denotes labour employed. Using the labour supply function of the earlier problem and assuming that there are 200 individuals, derive the full employment level of output. Derive the relationship between income tax rate and income tax revenue. Do you get the Laffer curve?

   (*Hint:* Here marginal productivity of labour and, therefore, equilibrium real wage rate is unity. Full employment output equals full employment level of employment. Total tax revenue is, therefore, $(24 - 12/(1 - t))\, 200t$. Do the rest).

3. Suppose that an individual with a two-period lifespan has the following utility function, $U = 0.5 \log C_1 + 0.5 \log C_2$. She earns in both the periods 100, while the rate of interest is 10% . How will an income tax imposed at the rate of 10% affect her saving? Explain.

4. Suppose that the government wants the individuals to invest more in share markets instead of in bank deposits, government securities with fixed returns etc. Will the government impose a proportional income tax with full loss-offset? Explain.

5. Suppose that an individual's wealth is unity. There are two assets, a riskless asset, money, and a risky asset, bond. There are two possible states of nature. The riskless asset yields zero income in both the states. The other asset yields an income of Rs. 10 in the good state and Rs. –6 in the bad state. Both the states have equal probability of occurrence. Utility function in risk and return of the individual is given by $U = 0.5 \log R - 0.5 \log \rho$, where R and ρ denote return and risk of the portfolio respectively. Derive the individual's optimum portfolio. How will it be affected, if an income tax at the rate of 10% is imposed on the individual's income, with full loss offset?

    (*Hint:* In the absence of taxation, $\mu = 2$, $\sigma = 8$. Optimum values of ρ and R are 4 and 1 respectively. A_1 is, therefore, $(1/2)$. After-tax optimum values of ρ and R will remain unaffected. However, in the after-tax scenario, we shall have the following equation $\rho = A_1 8 \, (0.9)$ in place of the pre-tax equation $\rho = A_1 8$. Hence the optimum $A_1 = 5/9$.)

6. Does the real value of tax on capital gains remain unchanged in the face of inflation in India? If not, then how should India's capital gains tax be revised?

    (*Hint:* Real value of capital gain is $Z = (P_{At}/P_t)A \Rightarrow \hat{Z} = (\hat{P}_{At} - \hat{P}_t) \Rightarrow \dot{Z} = A(P_{At}/P_t)$ $(\hat{P}_{At} - \hat{P}_t)$ where $P_{At} \equiv$ price of the asset at time, t; $P_t \equiv$ average price of goods and services at time, t, $A \equiv$ given quantity of the asset, $\hat{Z} \equiv (dZ/dt)/Z$ and $\dot{Z} \equiv (dZ/dt)$. In India under the capital gains tax amount of capital gains is estimated approximately as $AP_{At}(\hat{P}_{At} - \hat{P}_t) = AP_t \dot{Z}$. The amount of capital gains tax is, therefore, $AtP_t \dot{Z}$. Real value of capital gains tax is, therefore, $At\dot{Z}$. Thus real value of capital gains tax is related only to real value of capital gains.)

7. Individual is the taxpaying unit in India under India's Income Tax Act. There are no separate tax schedules for married and single individuals. Do you consider this arrangement acceptable? Explain.

8. How is inflation likely to affect real value of revenue from personal income tax in India?
    (*Hint:* Since standard deductions and itemized deductions and nominal tax slabs are not inflation indexed and the tax structure is progressive, real value of tax collection is likely to increase with inflation.)

========================= **REFERENCES** =========================

For definition of taxable income:

Bradford, D.F. (1986): *Untangling the Income Tax*, Harvard University Press, Cambridge, MA.

Feldstein, M.S. (1976): On the theory of tax reform, *Journal of Public Economics*, 6.

Simons, H. (1950): *Personal Income Taxation*, University of Chicago Press, Chicago.

For a discussion on choice of units:

Alm, J. and Wittington, L.A. (1993): Marriage and the Marriage Tax, 1992, *Proceedings of the Eighty-fifth Annual Conference on Taxation.* National Tax Association, Tax Institute of America.

For discussion of Laffer curve:

Fullerton, D. (1982): On the possibility of an inverse relationship between tax rates and government revenue, *Journal of Public Economics,* 19(1).

For empirical studies on effect of income tax and saving:

Hausman, J.A. and Poterba, J.M. (1987): Household behaviour and the tax and the Tax Reform Act of 1986, *Journal of Economic Perspectives.*

For effect of income tax on portfolio choice:

Musgrave, R.A. and Domar, E.D. (1944): Proportional income taxation and risk-taking, *Quarterly Journal of Economics,* 58.

Sandmo, A. (1985): The effects of taxation on savings and risk-taking *in*: Auerbach, A. and Feldstein, M. (Eds.), *Handbook of Public Economics,* Vol. 1.

Tobin, J. (1958): Liquidity preference as behaviour towards risk, *Review of Economic Studies,* 25.

APPENDIX

The pioneering study that examines the effect of income tax on the individual's portfolio choice is that of Musgrave and Domar (1944). Even though modern analysis of risk-taking, pioneered by the path-breaking work of Tobin (1958), has become much more sophisticated since their time, the one developed by Musgrave and Domar seems to be more suitable for examining the impact of no loss-offset for reasons explained in the text. In their model, no loss-offset, as should be the case, reduces expected return, but raises risk corresponding to any given allocation of wealth between riskless and risky assets.

Assumptions of the Domar–Musgrave model are the following. An individual has a given amount of wealth, which, as before, we assume to be unity. She invests a fraction, A_1, of it in a risky asset and the remaining part, A_2, in a riskless asset. Clearly, $A_1 + A_2 = 1$. The model examines how the individual chooses A_1 and A_2. There are N states of nature. The return from 1 unit of wealth invested in the risky asset yields a return r_i in the ith state of nature, where $i = 1, 2, ..., N$. Let us suppose that the returns are arranged in descending order, i.e., $r_1 > r_2 > ... > r_N$ and $r_k = 0$. Hence all returns from r_{k+1} to r_N are negative, while all other returns are non-negative. The probability of occurrence of the ith state of nature is p_i. The expected return from 1 unit of wealth invested in the risky asset, denoted r, is therefore given by

$$r = \sum_{i=1}^{k} p_i r_i - \left[- \sum_{i=k+1}^{N} p_i r_i \right] = \bar{R} - g$$

where $\bar{R} \equiv \sum_{i=1}^{k} p_i r_i$ and $g \equiv - \sum_{i=k+1}^{N} p_i r_i$

Hence expected return from A_1 amount of wealth invested in the risky asset, denoted $\bar{\mu}$, is given by

$$\bar{\mu} = A_1(\bar{R} - g) \tag{A.6.1}$$

The risk of 1 unit of wealth invested in the risky asset is here measured by g, the expected absolute value of the negative returns from 1 unit of wealth invested in the risky asset. The risk of A_1 amount of wealth invested in the risky asset, denoted $\bar{\rho}$, is therefore given by

$$\bar{\rho} = A_1 g \tag{A.6.2}$$

From (A.6.1) and (A.6.2) it is clear that the individual can assume different amounts of risk and return by choosing different values of A_1. Solving (A.6.2) for A_1 and putting this value in (A.6.1), we get

$$\bar{\mu} = \frac{(\bar{R} - g)}{g} \bar{\rho} \tag{A.6.3}$$

Equation (A.6.3) gives the budget constraint of the individual in risk and return. It shows the $\bar{\mu}$ the individual can get corresponding to any given $\bar{\rho}$. Its slope is $(\bar{R} - g)/g$. It gives the amount by which $\bar{\mu}$ goes up if $\bar{\rho}$ goes up by unity. From (A.6.2) it follows that if A_1 goes up by unity, $\bar{\rho}$ rises by g. Therefore the individual has to raise A_1 by $1/g$ to assume 1 additional unit of risk. The rise in A_1 by $1/g$ in turn, as follows from (A.6.1), leads to an increase in $\bar{\mu}$ by $(r - g)/g$. This explains the slope of (A.6.3). The slope of (A.6.3) is constant. When A_1 is zero, both $\bar{\mu}$ and $\bar{\rho}$ are zero. If A_1 is raised from zero, for every $(1/g)$ amount of increase in A_1, $\bar{\rho}$ goes up by unity and $\bar{\mu}$ rises by $(r - g)/g$. Thus, if A_1 is raised from zero by, say, $3/g$, $\bar{\rho}$ will be 3 and $\bar{\mu}$ will be $3(r - g)/g$. This explains the budget constraint (A.6.3). We plot it in the $(\bar{\rho}, \bar{\mu})$ plane in Figure A.6.1. It is labelled BB.

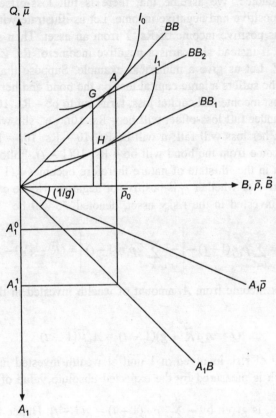

Figure A.6.1: Risk-taking under no loss-offset.

Indifference curves of the individual in risk and return are superimposed on the budget constraint in the figure. Individuals are assumed to be risk-averse. Hence they will willingly take more risk if and only if they get more expected return. Hence indifference curves are upward sloping. The amount of increase in $\bar{\mu}$ that compensates for a unit increase in $\bar{\rho}$ is assumed to rise with an increase in $\bar{\rho}$. Hence the indifference curves are convex downward. The individual is better off, if $\bar{\mu}$ is higher corresponding to any given $\bar{\rho}$. Hence a higher indifference curve represents a higher level of utility to the individual. Obviously, an individual will choose from her budget line that point, which is on the highest indifference curve. This is clearly the one at which an indifference curve is tangent to the budget line. The indifference curve I_0 in Figure A.6.1 is tangent to BB at the point A. Hence it is the highest indifference curve attainable from BB. The point of tangency, A, is, therefore, the optimum point.

In the fourth quadrant the line $A_1\bar{P}$ represents Equation (A.6.2), which indicates the values of A_1 corresponding to different values of $\bar{P}$. The value of A_1 that corresponds to the optimum point, as read off from $A_1\bar{P}$, is A_1^0. The optimum value of A_2 is, therefore, $(1 - A_1^0)$.

Let us now examine how an income tax applied at the proportional rate t to income affects individual's portfolio choice. We assume that there is full loss-offset, i.e., the tax applies symmetrically to both positive and negative income. Let us illustrate with an example. Suppose that an individual earns positive income of Rs. Y from an asset. Then she has to pay a tax of Rs. Yt on that income. If instead she earns a negative income of Rs. Z from an asset, her tax liability falls by Rs. tZ. Let us give a numerical example. Suppose that an individual holds a bond. In a given year she suffers a large capital loss on the bond and her income from the bond, which consists of interest income and capital loss, turns out to be − Rs. 10, i.e., she loses Rs. 10. Then her tax liability under full loss-offset will be − Rs. $10t$, i.e., she will get Rs. $10t$ from the government. Therefore, her loss will fall; it will be Rs. 10 − Rs. $10t$ = Rs. 10 $(1 - t)$. In other words, her after-tax income from the bond will be − Rs. $10(1 - t)$. Following the imposition of the tax, after-tax return in the ith state of nature therefore becomes $r_i(1 - t)$ for every i, where $i = 1, 2, ..., N$, irrespective of whether r_i is positive or negative. Hence expected after-tax return from 1 unit of wealth invested in the risky asset, denoted $\tilde{r}$, will be

$$\tilde{r} = \sum_{i=1}^{k} p_i r_i (1 - t) - \left[- \sum_{i=k+1}^{N} p_i r_i (1 - t) \right] = (\bar{R} - g)(1 - t)$$

Expected after tax income from A_1 amount of wealth invested in the risky asset, denoted Q, will therefore be

$$Q = A_1(\bar{R} - g)(1 - t) = A_1\bar{\mu}(1 - t) \tag{A.6.4}$$

Again, the amount of risk involved in 1 unit of wealth invested in the risky asset in the after-tax scenario, which is measured by the expected absolute value of the after-tax negative returns of the risky asset, is given by $- \sum_{i=k+1}^{N} p_i r_i (1 - t) = g(1 - t)$. Hence the risk involved in A_1 amount of wealth invested in the risky asset in the after-tax scenario, denoted B, is given by

$$B = A_1\bar{P}(1 - t) = A_1 g(1 - t) \tag{A.6.5}$$

Solving (A.6.5) for A_1 and putting it into (A.6.4), we get

$$Q = \frac{\bar{R} - g}{g} B \tag{A.6.6}$$

Individual's budget constraint in risk and return in the post-tax scenario is given by (A.6.6). It can be explained the same way as (A.6.3) and it coincides with (A.6.3). In the post-tax scenario, it follows from (A.6.6) that to assume one additional unit of risk, the individual has to raise A_1 by $1/g(1-t)$. Again, if A_1 rises by $1/g(1-t)$, Q will increase by $(\bar{R}-g)(1-t)/g(1-t) = (\bar{R}-g)/g$. This explains why pre-tax and post-tax budget lines in risk and return are identical. BB in Figure A.6.1, therefore, represents the post-tax budget line as well. In the post-tax scenario therefore, just as in the Tobin's model, the individual will choose the same combination of risk and return as before. A, therefore, remains the optimum point even in the post-tax scenario. However, the line representing (A.6.5), which is labelled A_1B in the figure and which shows the value of A_1 corresponding to every value of B, lies below $A_1\bar{P}$. This means that to assume the same amount of risk as in the pre-tax scenario, the individual in the post-tax scenario has to invest a larger proportion of wealth in the risky asset. Thus in the full loss-offset case, even though the individual assumes the same amount of risk as before, she invests a larger fraction of her wealth in the risky asset.

The intuition of the result is also the same as that in Tobin. A unit increase in risk in the post-tax scenario leads to as much increase in expected return as in the pre-tax situation. Thus risk-taking remains as rewarding as before. Income tax with full loss-offset, therefore, does not produce any substitution effect. However, any given fraction of wealth invested in the risky asset in the post-tax situation yields smaller amounts of both risk and return. This produces an income effect, which induces the individual to invest larger fraction of their wealth in the risky asset and thereby raise expected return and risk to their respective pre-tax levels.

In many countries personal income tax statute does not provide for any loss-offset. This means that losses are not allowed to be deducted from taxable income. Clearly, income tax in this case reduces returns in good states of nature, but leaves unaffected magnitudes of losses in bad states of nature. This tax, therefore, reduces expected return from the risky asset, but does not affect much the risk involved in investment in the risky asset, as the amount of loss in each bad state of nature and the probability of occurrence of each bad state of nature remains unaffected. It is, therefore, likely to discourage investment in risky asset. In what follows we shall examine this issue formally within the framework of the present model. In this case each positive return falls to $r_i(1-t)$, $i = 1, ..., k$. Negative returns remain unaffected. The expected return from 1 unit of wealth invested in the risky asset, denoted q, is therefore given by

$$q = \sum_{i=1}^{k} p_i r_i (1-t) - \left[-\sum_{i=k+1}^{N} p_i r_i \right] = [\bar{R}(1-t) - g]$$

Hence expected income from A_1 amount of wealth invested in the risky asset, denoted $\tilde{Q}$, is given by

$$\tilde{Q} = A_1[\bar{R}(1 - t) - g] \tag{A.6.7}$$

Again, the amount of risk involved in 1 unit of wealth invested in the risky asset remains g. Hence the amount of risk involved in A_1 amount of wealth invested in the risky asset denoted $\tilde{B}$ is given by

$$\tilde{B} = A_1 g \tag{A.6.8}$$

Solving for A_1 from (A.6.8) and substituting its value in (A.6.7), we get

$$\tilde{Q} = \frac{[\bar{R}(1-t) - g]}{g} \tilde{B} \qquad (A.6.9)$$

Equation (A.6.9) is the budget equation involving risk and return in the no loss-offset case. It can be explained the same way as (A.6.6). (Do it yourself). Its slope is less than that of (A.6.6). It means that a unit increase in risk leads to a smaller increase in expected return. Hence (A.6.9) is represented in Figure A.6.1 by BB_1, which is a flatter ray through the origin than BB. The individual chooses H from this budget line. We can decompose the total change in risk and return from A to H into substitution and income effect. The movement from A to G is due to the substitution effect, as the individual chooses G from the pre-tax indifference curve, but at the lower price of risk, $[\bar{R}(1 - t) - g]/g$. Since risk-taking is less rewarding than before, the substitution effect induces the individual to take less risk. The movement from G to H is clearly due to income effect, as at both the points risk-taking has the same reward, but the level of real income at H is less than that at G. The tax actually reduces the amount of expected return corresponding to every value of risk. This induces the individual to take more risk. This is the income effect. The two effects, therefore, work in opposite direction. The individual will, therefore, take more risk if and only if the income effect is stronger than the substitution effect and conversely. In this case the relationship between risk, $\tilde{B}$, and A_1, as given by (A.6.8) is the same as that in the pre-tax situation. Thus (A.6.8) is also represented by $A_1\bar{\rho}$. Hence, if substitution effect is stronger than the income effect, which is the case shown in Figure A.6.1, the individual will take less risk and, therefore, invest a smaller proportion of her wealth in the risky asset. Just the opposite will happen, if income effect is stronger than the substitution effect.

7 CORPORATION INCOME TAX

Chapter Objectives

The objectives of this chapter are to discuss

  (i) the rationale of corporation income tax.
  (ii) the base of corporation income tax and its components, depreciation allowance and its implications.
  (iii) the incidence of corporation income tax.
  (iv) the impact of corporation income tax on investment.
  (v) the implications of corporate tax for corporate finance.
  (vi) the structure of India's corporation income tax.

7.1 INTRODUCTION

Corporation income tax is an important source of tax revenue of the Government of India. It contributes more revenue than the personal income tax and its share in total tax revenue is growing rapidly in recent years. The share of corporation income tax in total tax revenue rose from 9.3% in 1990–1991 to 29.9% in 2005–2006. Its contribution to revenue from direct taxes increased during the same period from 48.69% to 62.42%, while that of the personal income tax fell from 48.69% to 37.37%. The base of corporation tax is the income or profit of the corporations. It is calculated by deducting from the total revenue the business costs incurred. It is an income from capital. But there are other types of capital income also. Profits originating in proprietorship businesses are also capital income. So are interest and rental incomes. Thus the base of corporation tax is only a part of the total income from capital.

    This chapter discusses different aspects of corporation income tax. The most important question that arises in this context is whether there is any ground for taxing incomes of corporations in addition to the incomes of the individuals who own these corporations. The issue is controversial. It is discussed at length in Section 7.2. A review of different arguments seems to support the view that there is no case for separate taxation of corporations' incomes in addition to individuals' incomes. This view clearly calls for integration of corporations' incomes with their owners' incomes. Section 7.3 accordingly discusses different methods of accomplishing this. Income of a corporation, as we have just mentioned, is measured by deducting from the revenue of the corporation all the business costs incurred. Depreciation is an important component of this cost. Hence tax statute of every country allows corporations to deduct depreciation in estimating its taxable income. However, unlike other business costs, the amount of depreciation that a corporation can deduct in any given period is specified by the tax statute and it can differ substantially from the actual depreciation of the corporation in the given period. The amount of allowable depreciation is called depreciation allowance and it is a policy instrument of the government. The government can use it to influence the effective tax rate on corporate income. Section 7.4 is devoted to the analysis of different aspects of depreciation allowance. Perhaps the most important question relating to corporate tax is who bears the burden of the tax. The incidence of corporation income tax is unclear except for the fact that it does not fall on the corporations in any way. Its burden is borne instead by the people, namely, the owners of the corporations, workers, buyers of the products of the corporations, owners of capital in the unincorporated sector and others. The incidence of corporate tax or the distribution of burden of the corporate tax is discussed in Section 7.5. Corporation tax also affects corporate investment. Section 7.6 discusses this issue. Finally, Section 7.7 presents and assesses the structure of India's corporation income tax in the light of the discussions made in the earlier sections.

7.2   RATIONALE OF CORPORATION INCOME TAX

A corporation is a joint stock company. The fund that is required to set up the company is raised partly by selling shares in the market and partly by borrowing. The shares are normally issued at a price of Rs. 10 or Rs. 100. Any one can buy these shares. Every buyer or shareholder becomes an owner of the company. Thus a very large number of individuals come to own the corporations. They, however, do not run the company themselves. They elect from themselves through voting a Board of Directors who manages the company on their behalf. Thus, there is alienation between management and ownership in case of corporations. Even though the whole of the corporations' profit belongs to their shareholders, the Board of Directors reserves the right of not distributing the whole of it among them. Thus, there is a question of whether a corporation's income should be regarded separately from the shareholders' income for tax purposes. This question does not arise in case of proprietorship organizations where there is no alienation between ownership and management. Hence income of such an organization is inseparable from its owner's.

7.2.1   Integrationist and Absolutist Views

The issue of corporation income tax is controversial. *Whether there is any basis for taxing incomes of corporations in addition to incomes of persons owning the corporations is a highly debatable one. There are two opposing views in this regard, the integrationist view and the absolutist view.* We present these views below.

Integrationist View

Integrationist view states that incomes of corporations belong to their owners, the shareholders. Individuals' taxable incomes according to this view should include incomes of all kinds and all these different types of incomes should be taxed at equal rates irrespective of their sources to ensure horizontal equity. Thus, if both incomes of corporations and those of shareholders are separately taxed, individuals' incomes from corporations will be taxed at higher rates than other types of income. Let us illustrate with an example. Suppose that incomes of corporations are taxed at the rate of 20%. Suppose that a joint stock company earned an income of Rs. 100 in one year and the corporation income tax rate was 20% so that it had to pay Rs. 20 as tax to the government. The company distributed the rest among the shareholders who had to pay personal income tax at the rate of 30%. Thus they had to pay Rs. 24 as personal income tax to the government on Rs. 80 they received from the company. In the absence of corporation income tax, they would have received the whole of Rs. 100 and paid a tax of only Rs. 30. Thus, in the presence of corporation income tax the incomes of the shareholders from the corporations in our example are taxed at the rate of 44%, while other types of income are taxed at the rate of 30%. This violates horizontal equity. To bring the issue in sharp relief consider the example of two individuals having the same amount of income. Suppose that one of them earns income only from labour, while the other earns only dividend income. Suppose that the latter holds 10% of the shares of the company cited in the above example. In the absence of corporation income tax, she would have earned dividend of Rs. 10 and would have paid 30% of this income, Rs. 3, as tax. Suppose that the other person also earns Rs. 10 as wage income and pays tax at the rate of 30%. So, both would have paid the same amount of tax in the absence of corporation income tax and there would have been horizontal equity. However, in the presence of corporation income tax, the dividend earner receives only Rs. 8 as dividend as the company pays Rs. 20 out of its total profit of Rs. 100 as corporation income tax. The individual again has to pay from this dividend income Rs. 2.4 as personal income tax. Therefore, the dividend earner actually pays a total tax of Rs. 4.4 from her profit income of Rs. 10. Hence the dividend earner is discriminated against and as a result horizontal equity is violated. According to this view, therefore, corporations' incomes should be integrated with the individuals' incomes and only the individuals' incomes should be taxed to ensure horizontal equity.

Absolutist View

According to the absolutist view corporations in modern economies are very powerful. They are separate entities. Shareholders have very little control over them. *There is a separation between ownership and control and the managers run the companies independently. Thus, according to this view, even though shareholders own the companies, there is ground for taxing corporations' incomes in addition to their owners' incomes.* This position is, however, indefensible because whatever income the corporations earn, it accrues to their owner only, even though most of the shareholders do not have any say in the day to day running of the company. Thus personal income tax adequately covers the income which corporations earn.

There is of course the issue of undistributed profit, which one has to reckon with. Corporations may retain quite a large part of the profit and corporation income tax may be viewed as a way reaching this part of income only. Problem with this view is that retained profit of a corporation belongs to the shareholders and should be treated as a part of the income of the shareholders, even though they do not actually receive it. Moreover, undistributed profit of a corporation, as we shall explain shortly below, raises the value of its shares by the amount of the profit retained. Thus the undistributed profit of a corporation goes into the hands of the shareholders in the form of capital gains. Accordingly, personal income tax that treats incomes from all the sources equally should adequately take care of the undistributed profit.

It is of course true that share markets often function imperfectly and value of shares—even though it should reflect the true value of the corporations—do not always give the true value of the corporation. In such a scenario, following retention of profit by corporations and the consequent increase in the value of the corporation by the amount of the retained profit, value of its shares may not increase by the amount of the retained profit. See Bradford (1981) in this context. There may, therefore, be a case for corporation income tax on this ground, but such a tax should be imposed only on the undistributed profit of corporations. In such an event, however, individuals' capital gains on shares due to retention of profit by corporations should be exempted from personal income tax. This can be done by allowing the shareholders to raise the value of the shares by the amount of the retained earning. If they are allowed to do so, then appreciation in the value of their shares over and above this amount will be reckoned as capital gain.

7.2.2 Benefit Argument

It has been argued that corporations derive considerable benefits from the infrastructural facilities put in place by the government. Thus roads connecting different areas reduce transportation costs and enlarge market size. Communications infrastructures, satellites, regulatory authorities such as TRAI in case of India etc., lower communication costs; financial infrastructure such as the central bank, regulatory authorities such as SEBI in India, reduce costs of financial transactions. *For all these benefits it is argued that corporations should pay taxes.* There are two problems with this line of thought. First, benefits from these services are enjoyed not only by the corporations but also by other firms. Thus there is no case for taxing only incomes earned by corporations. Second, the benefits ultimately accrue in the form of higher incomes to the owners of the corporations only. Actually, these benefits are enjoyed not only by the earners of profit but also by other individuals. Thus personal income tax can adequately and equitably make the individuals pay for these benefits if taxes can be imposed on lines suggested by the benefit principle. There is, however, the benefit of limited liability, which only the owners of corporations enjoy. Unlike proprietorship organizations where every owner has unlimited liability, in a corporation, owners' liabilities are limited. This means that in a proprietorship organization, i.e., an organization that is not a joint stock company or a limited liability partnership organization, every owner is fully responsible for all the outstanding debts of the company, it does not matter how many owners own the company. In case the company goes bankrupt, the creditors can legally seek recovery of their outstanding dues from any single owner, even when the company is owned by many. In case of a corporation, however, an owner is not responsible for her company's debts. If a corporation becomes bankrupt, a shareholder at the most loses the value of her shares and nothing more than that. It has been argued by some that since the privilege of limited liability is enjoyed exclusively by the owners of the corporations, they should be taxed for this benefit over and above the personal income tax they pay and this tax can take the form of the corporation income tax. This argument is untenable on following grounds. The benefit principle states that the government should tax individuals for the benefits they receive from social goods to meet the cost of provision of social goods. To confer the privilege of limited liability on the owners of corporations, the government or the society need not incur any cost. Hence on this ground the benefit principle does not give any support to corporation income tax.

7.2.3 Regulatory Argument

Taxation on corporations may be needed to regulate their behaviour. Corporations are large and tend to monopolize different areas of production. Taxes may be imposed on corporations to curb the growth of monopolies. This argument may have some merit, since, as we shall show below, corporation income tax by reducing return on capital employed in the corporate sector leads to flight of capital from the corporate sector and thereby tends to reduce its size and increase the size of the unincorporated sector.

7.3 Integration

We have seen above that *integration of incomes of corporations with those of the shareholders is called for on grounds of equity. It can be accomplished in two ways, namely, the partnership method and the capital gains method.* In what follows we shall discuss these two methods in turn.

7.3.1 Partnership Method

Under this method shareholders of a corporation are regarded as partners in a partnership organization. Hence the entire profit earned by a corporation, irrespective of whether the whole of it is distributed or not, has to be allocated among its shareholders and each shareholder has to be informed of the amount of profit that has been allotted to her. Let us suppose that a corporation has earned a profit of Rs. 1 crore in a year and it has 1000 shareholders having equal stakes in the company. Under the partnership method, therefore, the company has to allot to each shareholder equal profit share of Rs. 10,000 and notify each shareholder of her profit share. The company, however, may not distribute the whole of the profit to the shareholders. In case the company decides to retain 20% of the profit, each shareholder will get a dividend of Rs. 8000 only. Upon receiving the notification, however, the shareholder will have to add the whole of Rs. 10,000 to her taxable income even if a part is retained by the company and pay tax on her whole profit share, Rs. 10,000 in our example, at the marginal rate that is applicable to her. Thus, if the marginal tax rate applicable to a taxpayer is 30%, she has to pay tax at the rate of 30% on her profit share.

This procedure, however, gives rise to the problem of liquidity. Let us illustrate this problem with an example. Suppose that in the example given above the company retains 80%

of the profit instead of 20%. Each shareholder, therefore, gets Rs. 2000. Shareholders whose marginal tax rate is more than 20% have to pay a tax that exceeds the dividends they receive. As a result they may not have sufficient liquid income to pay this additional tax in excess of Rs. 2000. To circumvent this problem the partnership method has a system called withholding. Under this system the firm pays a tax on its profit at some specified rate. If the tax on the profit share of an individual exceeds the amount of tax already paid by the corporation on the individual's profit share, the individual only pays the excess amount. In the opposite case the individual gets a refund. Let us illustrate with an example. Suppose that the corporation under the system of withholding pays tax at the rate of 20% on its profit. In the above example where every shareholder has a profit share of Rs. 10,000, the corporation pays Rs. 2000 as tax on every shareholder's profit share. Suppose that the marginal tax rate applicable to a shareholder is 25%. Total tax she has to pay on her profit share is, therefore, Rs. 2500. However, Rs. 2000 has already been paid by the corporation. So, she will have to pay only Rs. 500 as tax. If the marginal tax rate applicable to the shareholder were 15%, she would have got a refund of Rs. 500. This system resolves the problem of liquidity to a large extent.

Retention of profit under this approach leads to another problem. The retained earning, as we have mentioned already, raises the value of the shares by the amount of the retained earning. This addition to the value of the shares is again taxable as capital gains. But the shareholders have already paid tax on these retained earnings. This problem can, however, be resolved, as we have already mentioned, by allowing each shareholder to raise the value of her shares by the amount of the part of her profit share retained by the company so that the increase in the value of her shares due to retention of a part of her profit share is not regarded as a capital gain.

This approach has been criticized on grounds of administrative difficulty. It has been pointed out that there exist active secondary markets in shares. Hence profit shares of shareholders change continuously. New shareholders enter and old shareholders leave. Hence it becomes extremely costly to keep a tab on the continuously changing profile of shareholders and profit shares.

7.3.2 Capital Gains Method

This method aims at full integration in the following manner. It repeals corporation profit tax and makes both realized and unrealized capital gains of individuals' taxable. Thus dividend becomes taxable as a component of income of the shareholders and retained earnings also become taxable as a part of the realized or unrealized capital gains of the shareholders. It should, however, be noted that retained earning will lead to an equal amount of increase in the value of shares if and only if the stock market accurately value shares. Bradford (1981) discusses conditions under which retained earning does not bring about an equal increase in the value of shares.

Nowhere, however, full integration has been attempted. In some countries such as India, dividend is excluded from taxable income of individuals. However, addition to the value of shares due to retained earning is nowhere excluded from capital gains. Hence there is double taxation of such earnings everywhere. However, in most countries capital gains get favourable treatment. For example, only realized capital gains are taxed in all countries. Hence it is possible to escape this tax indefinitely. In many countries even realized capital gains attract lower tax rates.

7.4 TAX BASE: SOME OF THE ISSUES

Corporation income tax, as we have already mentioned, *applies to corporations' net income, which is defined as total revenue of the corporations net of all the business costs incurred by corporations including* (i) *interest payments on loans taken by corporations to finance investment and purchase inputs and* (ii) *depreciation of fixed capital.* Exclusion of these two components of business cost from the taxable income of corporations has significant distortionary implications for corporate behaviour. We shall discuss them below.

7.4.1 Depreciation

Depreciation of fixed capital is obviously a component of business cost and the corporation accordingly is allowed to deduct depreciation in reporting its taxable income. However, corporations are not always allowed to deduct the actual amount of depreciation of their fixed capital. Tax authorities often specify a period over which the depreciation is to be calculated. This period is referred to as depreciation period. They also specify the method by means of which depreciation is to be calculated. There are three methods of calculating depreciation, namely, straight-line method, method of declining balance and sum-of-years-digits method. Tax authorities usually choose any one of these three methods.

Methods of Calculating Depreciation

Straight-line method: According to this method capital depreciates at a constant rate over its lifespan, which is specified by the tax authority. This officially specified lifespan of capital or the officially specified period over which depreciation is calculated is referred to as the depreciation period. *According to the straight-line method value of depreciation in each year during the depreciation period is the value of capital divided by the numbers of years in the depreciation period.* Let us illustrate this method with an example. Suppose that depreciation period of a machine is 10 years and its cost is Rs. 10,000. Depreciation of this machine each year according to the straight-line method is, therefore, Rs. 10,000/10 = Rs.1000. Note that the depreciation period specified by the statute of corporation income tax may differ substantially from the actual lifespan of the plant or the machines. Moreover, the amount of depreciation yielded by the depreciation period and the method of calculating depreciation specified by the tax authority may differ widely from the actual depreciation of fixed capital. Depreciation period and the method of calculation of depreciation, as we shall presently see, are, in fact, policy instruments at the disposal of the tax authorities.

Method of declining or reducing balance: Again, suppose that the depreciation period specified by the tax authority is D and the value of the capital good is K. Then *according to this method the rate of depreciation in the first period is twice the rate yielded by the straight-line method.* The rate of depreciation suggested by the straight-line method is $[(K/D)/K]$ = $[1/D]$, i.e., $(1/D)$ fraction of the existing capital stock depreciates in every period during the depreciation period. In the numerical example given in the context of the straight-line method, the depreciation rate is $(1/10)$. Under the declining balance method, the depreciation rate in the first period is $2(1/D)$ or $(2/10)$ in the numerical example. *The same rate applies in every other period, but it applies not to the initial value of the capital good but to its depreciated value,*

which is obtained by subtracting from the initial value of the capital good, the amount that has already been depreciated. Thus in the first period, the rate, $(2/D)$, applies to K, since the amount of K that is already depreciated is zero. Hence the total amount of depreciation in the first period is $(2/D)K = (2K/D)$. In the second period the rate, $(2/D)$, applies not to K, but to $K - (2/D)K$, since $[2/D]K$ is already depreciated. Therefore, in the second period, the amount of depreciation is given by $(2/D)[K - (2/D)K] = (2/D)[1 - (2/D)]K$. In the third period, therefore, the existing amount of capital stock is given by $[1 - (2/D)]K - (2/D)[1 - (2/D)]K = [1 - (2/D)]^2 K$ and the rate of depreciation applies to it. Thus the amount of depreciation in the third period is $(2/D)[1 - (2/D)]^2K$. In the fourth period, therefore, the existing capital stock is $[1 - (2/D)]^3K$—show it yourself—and the depreciation rate, $(2/D)$, applies to it. It is clear that the sum of the amount of depreciation of each year summed over an infinitely long period as given by $(2/D)K + (2/D)[1 - (2/D)]K + (2/D)[1 - (2/D)]^2K + ... = K$. However, corporations are allowed to deduct the whole of their capital cost as depreciation over the depreciation period. To ensure that under the present method, in the last two years of the depreciation period corporations are allowed to apply the straight-line method to the undepreciated part of the capital stock in calculating depreciation. Thus, if $K =$ Rs. 1000 and depreciation period is 4 years, amounts of depreciation in the first two years are $(2/4)1000 = 500$ and $(2/4)(1000 - 500) = 250$. In the third period, therefore, the undepreciated value of the capital stock is Rs. 250 and the corporation is allowed to apply the straight line method to Rs. 250 to calculate the depreciation of the last two years. Thus the amount of depreciation in each of the last two years is Rs. 125.

The point to note here is that under this method the amount of depreciation falls with the passage of time, while under the earlier method the amount of depreciation remains constant over time. Total value of depreciation under both the methods equals the initial value of the capital good. Hence *present value of the stream of depreciations discounted at the market rate of interest under the second method will be larger than that under the first.* The amount of depreciation that the tax statute allows the corporations to deduct from taxable income in each year of the depreciation period is called depreciation allowance. *Under the reducing balance method, therefore, the present value of tax savings due to depreciation allowance will be larger than that under the earlier straight-line method.* To see the logic clearly, consider the following example. Suppose that the depreciation period is two years and the depreciation allowances in the first two years are d_1 and d_2 respectively. If the corporation income tax applies at the rate t to the taxable income of the corporations, tax savings due to the depreciation allowances, which are deducted to calculate taxable income, are td_1 and td_2 respectively. Present value of tax savings due to depreciation allowances is, therefore, $td_1/(1 + r) + td_2/(1 + r)^2$. If now d_1 is raised by Δ and d_2 is also reduced by the same amount so that the sum of d_1 and d_2 remains the same, the present value of tax savings rises by $\Delta/(1 + r)$ on the one hand and falls by $\Delta/(1 + r)^2$ on the other hand. Since $\Delta/(1 + r) > \Delta/(1 + r)^2$, present value of tax savings due to depreciation allowance rises by $[\Delta/(1 + r) - \Delta/(1 + r)^2]$. Thus the larger the depreciation allowance in earlier years, the greater is the present value of tax savings due to depreciation allowance.

Sum-of-years-digits method: *Under this method also a fraction of the initial value of the capital good depreciates every year during the depreciation period. This fraction is calculated in the following manner. The fraction in any given year, say $T < D$, is given by the ratio of the* *number of years remaining, which is defined as D – T + 1, to the sum of years during the depreciation period, which in turn is defined as 1 + 2 + 3 + ... + (D – 2) + (D – 1) + D = (D/2)(D+1).* Thus in the numerical example used to illustrate the straight-line method above, D = 10 years. Sum of years during the depreciation period is, therefore, 1 + 2 + ... + 10 = (10/2) × (10 + 1) = 55. Remaining number of years in the first year, second year etc. are respectively (10 – 1 + 1) = 10, (10 – 2 + 1) = 9 and so on. Thus the fraction of Rs. 10,000 that is depreciated in the first, second and third years etc. are (10/55), (9/55), (8/55) respectively. *Under this method also total amount of depreciation allowed to be deducted during the depreciation period equals the initial value of the capital and the present value of the stream of depreciations is larger than that under the straight-line method.* This is because, just like the reducing balance method, under this method also, while the total amount of depreciation equals the initial value of capital, depreciation allowances in earlier years are larger than those in later years.

7.4.2 Depreciation Allowance and Effective Tax Rate

In the presence of depreciation allowance, statutory tax rate or nominal tax rate may differ substantially from the actual or effective tax rate. We show this below.

Depreciation Period, Economic Depreciation and Accelerated Depreciation

Here we shall explain the concepts of economic and accelerated depreciation and how they are related to the depreciation period. This we shall do with the help of following example. Suppose that the cost of an investment project is C and the tax statute fixes the depreciation period for the project at 10 years and states that the straight-line method should be used to calculate depreciation. The investor will, therefore, be able to deduct $(C/10)$ as depreciation every year to calculate taxable income from the project. It should be noted here, as we have pointed out earlier, that the depreciation period may differ from the actual period over which the project is used before being obsolete or junk. Similarly, the amount of depreciation yielded by the depreciation period in combination with the method of calculation of depreciation as specified by the tax statute may differ from the actual amount of depreciation of the project. *The actual amount of depreciation of an investment project is called its economic depreciation. Tax statute may allow an investment project to depreciate at a faster or slower rate than it actually does. The former case is referred to as that of accelerated depreciation.*

Let us now examine how the tax liability of an investment project that costs C and yields an income (inclusive of depreciation) of R every period for N periods is calculated. Suppose that the tax statute fixes the tax rate for the project at t, depreciation period at $D < N$ and recommends the straight-line method for calculating depreciation. The tax liability of the investment project under these conditions in the initial period, the period in which the project was undertaken, which we refer to as period zero, is given by

$$T = \frac{t\left(R - \dfrac{C}{D}\right)}{(1+r)} + \frac{t\left(R - \dfrac{C}{D}\right)}{(1+r)^2} + \text{......} + \frac{t\left(R - \dfrac{C}{D}\right)}{(1+r)^D} + \frac{tR}{(1+r)^{D+1}} + \text{......} + \frac{tR}{(1+r)^N}$$

$$= tR\sum_{i=1}^{N}\frac{1}{(1+r)^i} - t\left(\frac{C}{D}\right)\sum_{i=1}^{D}\frac{1}{(1+r)^i} \tag{7.1}$$

It follows from the above that the tax liability depends not only on the nominal tax rate, t, but also on the depreciation period, D, and the method of calculation of depreciation. We shall now show that *the shorter the depreciation period, i.e., the smaller the value of D or the larger the amounts of depreciation allowed in the earlier periods, given the length of the depreciation period, the less is the tax liability.* Let us first explain why shorter depreciation period reduces tax liability. Tax liability for the depreciation period, D, is given by (7.1). It shows that the tax saving due to depreciation allowance is given by

$$S(D) = t\left(\frac{C}{D}\right) \sum_{i=1}^{D} \frac{1}{(1+r)^i} \qquad (7.2)$$

where $S(D) \equiv$ tax saving for the depreciation period, D. If now the depreciation period is raised from D to $D + 1$, tax saving due to depreciation allowance becomes

$$S(D+1) = t\left(\frac{C}{D+1}\right) \sum_{i=1}^{D+1} \frac{1}{(1+r)^i} \qquad (7.3)$$

We shall now show that $S(D + 1) < S(D)$. We know that

$$S(D) - S(D+1) = tC\left[\frac{\frac{1}{D} - \frac{1}{D+1}}{(1+r)} + \frac{\frac{1}{D} - \frac{1}{D+1}}{(1+r)^2} + \ldots + \frac{\frac{1}{D} - \frac{1}{D+1}}{(1+r)^D} - \frac{\frac{1}{D+1}}{(1+r)^{D+1}}\right] \qquad (7.4)$$

Now

$$\left[\frac{\frac{1}{D} - \frac{1}{D+1}}{(1+r)} + \frac{\frac{1}{D} - \frac{1}{D+1}}{(1+r)^2} + \ldots + \frac{\frac{1}{D} - \frac{1}{D+1}}{(1+r)^D}\right] >$$

$$\left[\frac{\frac{1}{D(D+1)}}{(1+r)^D} + \frac{\frac{1}{D(D+1)}}{(1+r)^D} + \ldots + \frac{\frac{1}{D(D+1)}}{(1+r)^D}\right] = \frac{\frac{1}{(D+1)}}{(1+r)^D} > \frac{\frac{1}{(D+1)}}{(1+r)^{D+1}} \qquad (7.5)$$

From (7.4) and (7.5) it follows that $S(D) > S(D + 1)$.

Similarly, one can easily show that if amounts of depreciation are raised in earlier periods and those in later periods in the depreciation period are lowered commensurately so that the total amount remains equal to the cost of the investment project, tax saving due to depreciation allowance rises. Suppose that the amount of depreciation in each of the first $m(< D)$ periods is raised by a and that in each of the remaining $(D - m)$ periods is lowered by $[am/(D - m)]$, then $[S(D)/t]$ changes by

$$\left[\frac{a}{(1+r)} + \frac{a}{(1+r)^2} + \ldots + \frac{a}{(1+r)^m}\right] - \left[\frac{\frac{am}{(D-m)}}{(1+r)^{m+1}} + \frac{\frac{am}{(D-m)}}{(1+r)^{m+2}} + \ldots + \frac{\frac{am}{(D-m)}}{(1+r)^D}\right]$$

$$> \left[\frac{a}{(1+r)^m} + \frac{a}{(1+r)^m} + \ldots + \frac{a}{(1+r)^m}\right] - \left[\frac{\frac{am}{(D-m)}}{(1+r)^{m+1}} + \frac{\frac{am}{(D-m)}}{(1+r)^{m+1}} + \ldots + \frac{\frac{am}{(D-m)}}{(1+r)^{m+1}}\right]$$

$$= \frac{am}{(1+r)^m} - (D-m)\left[\frac{\frac{am}{(D-m)}}{(1+r)^{m+1}}\right] = \frac{am}{(1+r)^m} - \left[\frac{am}{(1+r)^{m+1}}\right] > 0 \qquad (7.6)$$

This establishes our proposition. From the above it follows that *if tax statute allows for accelerated depreciation in place of economic depreciation, tax liability is less*. The accelerated depreciation, as we have just shown, can be provided either by shortening the depreciation period or by raising the amounts of depreciation in earlier years and lowering them commensurately in later years within the given depreciation period or by both.

7.4.3 Economic Depreciation and Tax Neutrality

A tax is neutral if it does not distort individuals' choice. A tax on income from investment is neutral if it does not distort the return-wise ranking of the investment projects. If depreciation allowance is based on economic depreciation, corporation income tax is neutral. Present value of the future income stream of an investment project, denoted V, is given by

$$V = \sum_{i=1}^{T} \frac{R_i - d_i}{(1+r)^i}$$

where R_i and d_i denote gross income or gross profit from the investment project and actual depreciation in period i respectively. T gives the actual lifespan of the investment project. If the depreciation allowance is based on economic depreciation only, the present value of the future net income from the investment project in the post-tax scenario, denoted V_T, becomes

$$V_T = \sum_{i=1}^{T} \frac{t(R_i - d_i)}{(1+r)^i} = t \sum_{i=1}^{T} \frac{(R_i - d_i)}{(1+r)^i} = tV$$

where $t \equiv$ the tax rate. Thus, when the depreciation allowance provided in the tax statute is based on economic depreciation only, the present value of the future returns of every investment project becomes the tax rate times the pre-tax present value. Hence ranking of the investment projects remains unchanged. Accordingly, economic depreciation is tax neutral.

Accelerated depreciation may, however, distort rankings and, therefore, may not be neutral. Let us illustrate with an example. Suppose that the depreciation period of every project is the same as that in the economic depreciation case. Accelerated depreciation is provided by raising the amounts of depreciation above their actual values in earlier years and lowering them in later years commensurately. In this scenario long period projects' present values will fall less than the short period projects' and as a result, rankings of the investment projects may be distorted. Let us explain. Consider an investment project with T-period life. Initially, suppose that the tax statute allowed for economic depreciation only. Now the tax statute changes, and the amount of depreciation in each of the first m periods is raised by a fixed amount, a, and the amount of allowable depreciation in each of the remaining $T - m$ periods is lowered by $[am/(T - m)]$ so that the total amount of depreciation over the lifetime of the project remains equal to its cost. As a result the amount of tax savings due to the depreciation allowance changes by

$$\frac{dS(T)}{t} = \left[\frac{a}{(1+r)} + \frac{a}{(1+r)^2} + \ldots\ldots + \frac{a}{(1+r)^m}\right] - \left[\frac{\dfrac{am}{(T-m)}}{(1+r)^{m+1}} + \frac{\dfrac{am}{(T-m)}}{(1+r)^{m+2}} + \ldots\ldots + \frac{\dfrac{am}{(T-m)}}{(1+r)^T}\right] > 0$$

(7.7)

where $[dS(T)/t] \equiv$ change in the tax saving due to depreciation allowance, when T is the depreciation period.

We know from (7.6) that $dS(T) > 0$. Our objective here is to examine how $dS(T)$ changes, if T rises. It is clear from (7.7) that a change in T affects only the second term on the RHS of (7.7). We shall, therefore, focus only on that term, which we denote by $V(T)$ and rewrite as follows:

$$V(T) = \left[\frac{\dfrac{am}{(T-m)}}{(1+r)^{m+1}} + \frac{\dfrac{am}{(T-m)}}{(1+r)^{m+2}} + \ldots\ldots + \frac{\dfrac{am}{(T-m)}}{(1+r)^T}\right]$$

Consider another investment project, which is identical with the earlier one except for the fact that its life is $T + 1$ instead of T. In its case, therefore,

$$V(T+1) = \left[\frac{\dfrac{am}{(T+1-m)}}{(1+r)^{m+1}} + \frac{\dfrac{am}{(T+1-m)}}{(1+r)^{m+2}} + \ldots\ldots + \frac{\dfrac{am}{(T+1-m)}}{(1+r)^{T+1}}\right]$$

$$V(T) - V(T+1) = \left[\frac{\dfrac{am}{(T-m)} - \dfrac{am}{(T+1-m)}}{(1+r)^{m+1}} + \frac{\dfrac{am}{(T-m)} - \dfrac{am}{(T+1-m)}}{(1+r)^{m+2}} + \ldots\ldots \right.$$
$$\left. + \frac{\dfrac{am}{(T-m)} - \dfrac{am}{(T+1-m)}}{(1+r)^T} - \frac{\dfrac{am}{(T+1-m)}}{(1+r)^{T+1}}\right]$$

$$= \left[\frac{\dfrac{am}{(T-m)(T+1-m)}}{(1+r)^{m+1}} + \ldots\ldots + \frac{\dfrac{am}{(T-m)(T+1-m)}}{(1+r)^T}\right] - \frac{\dfrac{am}{(T+1-m)}}{(1+r)^{T+1}}$$

$$> \left[\frac{\dfrac{am}{(T-m)(T+1-m)}}{(1+r)^T} + \ldots\ldots + \frac{\dfrac{am}{(T-m)(T+1-m)}}{(1+r)^T}\right] - \frac{\dfrac{am}{(T+1-m)}}{(1+r)^{T+1}}$$

$$= \frac{\dfrac{am}{(T+1-m)}}{(1+r)^T} - \frac{\dfrac{am}{(T+1-m)}}{(1+r)^{T+1}} > 0$$

(7.8)

From (7.8) it follows that, everything else remaining the same, as T rises to $T + 1$, the second term on the RHS of (7.7) falls. The first term remains unaffected. Hence $dS(T)$ increases. Thus, *tax savings due to depreciation allowance in case of accelerated depreciation is larger for longer period investment projects.* This illustrates why accelerated depreciation lowers present value of net incomes from longer investment projects less than that from the shorter ones. Since accelerated depreciation affects present values of investment projects of different life periods differently, it may alter their ranking. Hence accelerated depreciation may not be neutral.

7.4.4 Statutory Tax Rate and Effective Tax Rate

Here we shall distinguish between statutory and effective tax rates and show that in the presence of depreciation allowance they are usually different. If the tax statute states that income from investments will be taxed at the proportional rate, t, then t is the statutory tax rate. Effective tax rate on the other hand is defined as follows:

$$\text{Effective tax rate} = \frac{r - r_t}{r} \tag{7.9}$$

where $r \equiv$ before-tax rate of return and $r_t \equiv$ after-tax rate of return. Thus, if $r = 10\%$ and $r_t = 5\%$, effective tax rate as yielded by (10.9) is 50%. Let us illustrate how r and r_t are calculated with an example. Consider a T-period investment project, which yields the income stream $(y_i - d_i)$, $i = 1, ..., T$, where $y_i \equiv$ gross income in the ith period and $d_i \equiv$ actual or economic depreciation in the ith period. The before-tax rate of return, r, of this investment project is given by the following equation:

$$C = \frac{y_1 - d_1}{(1 + r)} + \frac{y_2 - d_2}{(1 + r)^2} + ... + \frac{y_T - d_T}{(1 + r)^T}$$

The after-tax rate of return, r_t, on the other hand is given by the following equation:

$$C = \frac{t(y_1 - \overline{d}_1)}{(1 + r_t)} + \frac{t(y_2 - \overline{d}_2)}{(1 + r_t)^2} + ... + \frac{t(y_T - \overline{d}_T)}{(1 + r_t)^T}$$

where $\overline{d}_i$ is the depreciation allowance for the ith period as specified in the tax statute. We know that $\overline{d}_i \forall i$ depends upon C, the depreciation period, D and the method of calculation of depreciation specified in the tax statute. Thus the effective tax rate as given by (7.9) not only depends upon the nominal tax rate, but also on the three factors mentioned above.

7.4.5 Expensing and Initial Allowance

Corporation income tax applies to net income from investment. *Net income from investment in every year during the lifetime of the project is defined as gross revenue (total revenue inclusive of depreciation) in the given year, net of the costs of business in the given year.* Certain costs such as the value of intermediate inputs, cost of hiring labour, land etc. are allowed to be deducted as and when they are incurred from gross revenue to arrive at taxable income or net income. These costs are regarded as 'expensed'. The cost of capital, however, is not allowed to be deducted in full in the period in which it is incurred. It is deducted through the depreciation allowance over the lifetime of the investment project. *What happens if the whole of the capital cost is allowed to be deducted in the period in which it is incurred. If that is done, the government will not get any tax revenue from the investment project.* Let us establish this point below. Suppose that the cost of an investment is I. If the whole of this is allowed to be deducted as 'initial allowance' to arrive at taxable income in the period in which the investment is made, the tax saving in the period will be tI, where the tax rate is denoted by t. Let us explain. Usually the investor will have income from other sources. Let us denote this income by Y. She will have to pay tax on that income. Suppose the tax rate that applies to Y is t. The 'initial allowance' allows her to deduct I from Y to arrive at the taxable income. Hence taxable income falls by I and, therefore, tax liability declines by tI. The investor can use this tax saving to raise her investment in the project by tI, which will lead to a further fall in taxable income by tI from $Y - I$ to $Y - I - tI$. Therefore, tax liability will fall further by $t(tI) = t^2I$, which she can use again to raise her investment in the project in the given period. Thus, because of the initial allowance her investment in the project can be raised by $tI + t^2I + t^3I + \ldots$. Hence in the given period her total investment in the project can be

$$I + tI + t^2I + t^3I + \ldots = \frac{I}{1-t} \tag{7.10}$$

Suppose that future incomes from the investment of I in the project are $Y_1, Y_2, \ldots, Y_T$. Therefore, future incomes from an investment of $[I/(1 - t)]$ are $Y_1/(1 - t), Y_2/(1 - t), \ldots, Y_T/(1 - t)$. In the absence of tax the income stream she receives from her investment of I in the project is $Y_1, Y_2, \ldots, Y_T$. In the presence of the tax and the 'initial allowance', however, the income stream she receives is given by $\{Y_1(1 - t)/(1 - t), Y_2(1 - t)/(1 - t), \ldots, Y_T(1 - t)/(1 - t\} = (Y_1, Y_2, \ldots, Y_T)$. Thus her income stream from the project remains the same as that in the pre-tax situation. Let us now see how much the government gets. Because of the initial allowance the government in the initial period, i.e., the period in which the investment is made, loses tax revenue of $t[I/(1 - t)]$. However, because of the investment of $[I/(1 - t)]$ made in the initial period, investor's future incomes rise to $Y_1/(1 - t), Y_2/(1 - t), \ldots, Y_T/(1 - t)$. Hence investor's tax liability in future periods rises to $tY_1/(1 - t), tY_2/(1 - t), \ldots, tY_T/(1 - t)$. The present value of these future taxes in the initial period is given by $t/(1 - t)[Y_1/(1 + r) + Y_2/(1 + r)^2 + \ldots + Y_T/(1 + r)^T]$. We know that when all markets are perfect, $[Y_1/(1 + r) + Y_2/(1 + r)^2 + \ldots + Y_T/(1 + r)^T] = I$. Let us explain. Suppose that the present value of future income from the given level of investment in the given project discounted at the market rate of interest, r, is greater than I. This means that if the given amount, I, is lent out in the market, it will yield a smaller stream of future income. Hence funds will be withdrawn from the loan market and invested in the given project until the present value of the future income stream from any given level of investment in the project becomes equal to it. It will happen through the rise in r brought about by the withdrawal of funds from the loan market and the decline in the expected income from the project engendered by larger investment in the project. This explains why $[Y_1/(1 + r) + Y_2/(1 + r)^2 + \ldots + Y_T/(1 + r)^T] = I$. Hence $t/(1 - t)[Y_1/(1 + r) + Y_2/(1 + r)^2 + \ldots + Y_T/(1 + r)^T] = [t/(1 - t)]I$. Thus the present value of the additional future taxes received by the government in the initial period exactly equals the loss of tax revenue in the initial period. Hence the government gets no tax at all from the incomes from investment, when there is 'initial allowance'. Usually, in countries where there is initial allowance only a fraction, say α, of the cost of investment project is allowed as 'initial allowance'.

7.5 INCIDENCE OF CORPORATION INCOME TAX

Incidence of corporation income tax is not well-understood. Economic incidence of corporation income tax, as you should be able to recall, refers to the actual distribution of the burden of the corporation income tax. Pioneering study in this area is that of Harberger (1974). We present it below. It carries out the analysis of the incidence of corporation income tax under the assumption that the economy is closed; aggregate capital stock in the economy is fixed; the economy consists of two sectors, corporate sector and unincorporated sector; all markets are perfectly competitive; all prices are market clearing so that the given endowments of labour and capital in the economy are fully employed in every period, and, finally, production functions display constant returns to scale so that marginal productivities of capital and labour depend only upon the ratio in which capital and labour are employed. Now, the tax takes away a part of the income, which is nothing but the profit, of the corporations. Hence the burden falls on the owners of the corporations or the shareholders. This is the story only in the short run. In the intermediate and the long run, the burden of the tax is likely to spread to other sectors and other people. The tax reduces return on the capital employed in the corporations relative to the return on capital in the unincorporated sector. Therefore, if capital is shiftable, it will be shifted to the unincorporated sector from the corporate sector reducing return on capital in the unincorporated sector as well. This movement of capital will continue until after-tax returns on capital in both the sectors become equal. Thus, in the intermediate and in the long run the burden of corporation income tax will not remain confined to the owners of corporations only; it will spread to the owners of other enterprises as well. The point may be explained with the help of Figure 7.1 as well. In the Figure NC and CC give respectively the rate of return in the corporate and that in the unincorporated sector corresponding to every given level of capital employed in the corporate sector, which we denote by K_c. Amount of capital employed in the unincorporated sector, denoted K_{nc}, is given by $(\bar{K} - K_c)$, where $\bar{K}$ denotes the given amount of capital in the economy. Thus, as K_c rises, $(\bar{K} - K_c) = K_{nc}$ falls. There is diminishing return to capital by assumption. Hence CC is downward sloping and NC is upward sloping in the Figure. Equilibrium allocation of $\bar{K}$ between the corporate and the unincorporated sector corresponds to the point of intersection of CC and NC. Following the imposition of the corporate tax at the rate t, after-tax return in the corporate sector falls by tr_c corresponding to every K_c. Accordingly, CC shifts downward by the given amount. The new CC is labelled CC'. The new equilibrium K_c is less than its initial equilibrium value and it corresponds to the point of intersection of CC' and NC. It is labelled K_c^1. After-tax return of the corporate sector therefore falls, but before-tax return is higher. The former and latter are labelled r_c^1 and r_c^{t1} respectively. Corporation tax, therefore, raises the rental rate or price of the service of capital in the corporate sector. In the initial equilibrium, it was r_c^0. Following the imposition of the tax, it rises to r_c^{t1}.

Corporation income tax thus raises the price of the service of capital to the corporations. This will induce a substitution of labour for capital in the corporate sector and thereby tend to raise demand for labour and reduce that of capital. The expansion in the unincorporated sector and contraction in the corporate sector also raises demand for labour, if the former, as is usually the case, is more labour intensive than the latter. Both these forces are likely to raise price of labour. Thus corporation income tax is likely to be beneficial to the workers.

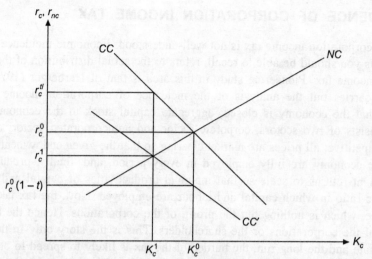

Figure 7.1:   Allocation of a given level of capital between the corporate and the unincorporated sector.

The rise in the supply price of capital also raises the cost of production in the corporate sector. There also takes place, as we have just explained, a contraction in the corporate sector and, therefore, in the supply of goods produced by the corporate sector. Both these factors will raise the prices of the products of the corporate sector. Hence consumers of the corporate sector will also be burdened. The point to note here is that the burden of the corporation income tax is by no means borne by the corporations. It is borne, as we have briefly explained above, by the people: the shareholders of the corporations, the producers of the unincorporated sector and the consumers.

However, Harberger's model has one important shortcoming. It assumes that aggregate capital stock is fixed. This is clearly not true in the intermediate and the long run. The fall in the return on capital due to the tax may lower investment and thereby reduce capital stock and the capital–labour ratio relative to the no-tax situation. This will tend to reduce marginal productivity of labour and thereby real wages. The fall in the real wage rate obviously burdens labour. Again, if we assume that there is perfect international mobility of capital, and the economy we are corned with is small, the return on capital in the domestic economy will be equal to and, therefore, determined by the world rate of interest. In such a scenario, if corporation tax in the domestic economy tends to reduce return on capital in the domestic economy, capital will start moving away from the domestic economy until post-tax return on domestic capital equals the world rate of interest. In such a scenario, no burden of the tax falls on capital. Due to capital flight capital–labour ratio in the domestic economy will fall reducing marginal productivity of labour and, therefore wage rate. Hence labour is burdened. From the above it follows that *the incidence of corporation income tax is at the best ambiguous. It depends upon a large number of factors.*

7.5.1 Corporation Income Tax as Tax on Monopoly Profit

Return to capital consists of two components, namely, normal return to capital and super-normal profit. The latter is also referred to as excess profit or economic profit or monopoly profit.

Corporation income tax applies to both the components. To the extent it applies to the normal return of capital, it raises, as we have mentioned above, the supply price of capital and thereby the cost of production. This in turn gives a cost push to the prices.

Firms with market power and firms in competitive markets in the short run may earn excess profit. To the extent corporation income tax applies to the excess profit, it is neutral. Let us explain. Suppose that Π denotes excess profit. Firms take pricing and output decisions to maximize Π. Under corporation income tax at the rate, t, after-tax excess profit of a firm falls to $(1 - t)\Pi$, as it has to give away $t\Pi$ to the government. Decisions that maximize Π also maximize $(1 - t)\Pi$, since t is given to a firm. Thus, *to the extent corporation income tax applies to economic or monopoly profit, it does not affect firms' prices and outputs.*

7.6 CORPORATION INCOME TAX AND INVESTMENT

We shall discuss here the impact of corporation income tax on investment. There are many theories of investment. Here, we shall use the neoclassical theory of investment for our purpose. According to this theory of investment an investor undertakes an investment project if the expected average income inclusive of interest cost and depreciation from the project per period, i.e. expected average profit from plus interest cost and depreciation of the investment project per period, which we shall denote by R, exceeds the user cost of capital of the investment project. The user cost of capital is calculated as follows. Suppose that the cost of the investment project is C. If the investor finances the project with her own money, she will lose interest income of rC in every period, when r denotes the market rate of interest. If she purchases the project with loan, she will have to pay interest charges of rC to the lenders every period. Also suppose that the project depreciates at the rate δ, i.e., the value of the investment project falls by δC every period due to wear and tear or obsolescence. Hence the cost of using the investment project or the user cost of capital of the investment project in every period is $(r + \delta)C$. All investment projects for which

$$R > (r + \delta)C \qquad (7.11)$$

are profitable and, therefore, will be undertaken. For the marginal investment project $R = (r + \delta)C$.

Following the imposition of the corporation income tax expected average per-period income from the project falls to $R(1 - t)$, when t denotes the corporation income tax rate. Corporation income tax also allows the taxpayer to deduct interest charges and depreciation in computing taxable income from an investment project. Thus taxable income of the investment project is not R, but $R - (r + \delta)C$, when the project is financed entirely with loan. Corporation income tax applies not to R but to $R - (r + \delta)C$. As a result corporation income tax raises the tax liability of the corporation by Rt on the one hand and reduces it by $t(r + \delta)C$ on the other hand. Thus the tax reduces not only the average expected per-period income of an entirely loan-financed investment project to $R(1 - t)$, but also the user cost of capital to $(1 - t)(r + \delta)C$. Therefore, all loan-financed investment projects for which

$$R(1 - t) > (r + \delta)C(1 - t) \qquad (7.12)$$

are profitable in the post-tax scenario. Thus, when investment projects are entirely financed with loans, condition for an investment project to be profitable remains the same even after the corporation income tax is imposed. Hence all the investment projects that were profitable before remain profitable and those that were unprofitable before remain unprofitable after the imposition of the tax. Thus *the level of investment and its composition remain unaffected by the corporation income tax, when investment is financed only with loans and the tax statute allows for economic depreciation. The tax in this situation, therefore, does not distort investment decisions.*

However, if investments are financed not with loans, but with internal resources (reserves of undistributed profits), interest income foregone cannot be deducted from R in calculating taxable income. Only depreciation can be deducted. Hence the corporation tax will apply to $(R - \delta C)$ and not to $[R - (r + \delta)C]$. Thus the tax raises tax liability as before by Rt but lowers it by only δCt. This means that, even though the tax reduces the expected average per-period income from the project to $R(1 - t)$, it reduces the user cost of capital to $rC + \delta C(1 - t)$. Therefore, when investment projects are financed from internal resources, they are profitable in the post-tax scenario if and only if

$$R(1 - t) > Cr + C\delta(1 - t) = C(r + \delta)(1 - t) + Crt \qquad (7.13)$$

Comparison of (7.13) to (7.12) and (7.11) shows that in this case some of the investment projects that were profitable before the imposition of the tax will become unprofitable after the imposition of the tax. Hence level of investment will fall.

From the above it follows that the ranking of investment projects, which are financed with internal resources, will be adversely affected by the tax. Thus to the extent investment is financed with internal resources, corporation income tax will reduce the level of investment. *Corporation income tax will, therefore, reduce the aggregate investment and raise the proportion of loan-financed investment in aggregate investment. The corporation income tax is thus biased against corporations that are credit-costrained and have to finance their investment from their internal resources. These are usually the newly established corporations.*

7.6.1 Investment Allowance or Investment Tax Credit

Indian Income Tax Act allowed for investment allowance in the past. It has now been withdrawn. Suppose that there is an investment allowance, which is also alternatively referred to as investment tax credit, at the rate α. This means that the tax liability of the investor undertaking an investment project that costs C falls by αC. This effectively lowers the cost of the investment project from C by αC to $(1 - \alpha)C$. In the presence of this investment allowance or investment tax credit, taxable income from an investment project that is financed with loan is $R - (r + \delta)C(1 - \alpha)$ and, therefore, it will be profitable if and only if

$$R(1 - t) > (r + \delta)(1 - t)C(1 - \alpha) \qquad (7.14)$$

Similarly, in the presence of investment allowance an investment project that is financed with internal resources will be profitable if and only if

$$R(1 - t) > [r + \delta(1 - t)]C(1 - \alpha) \qquad (7.15)$$

Comparison of (7.14) to (7.12) and (7.15) to (7.13) shows that *investment allowance reduces user cost of capital and thereby encourages investment.*

7.6.2 Accelerated Depreciation

Accelerated depreciation also leads to larger tax savings and encourages investment. Suppose that depreciation allowance exceeds economic depreciation owing to accelerated depreciation and depreciation allowance becomes $\beta\delta$, $\beta > 1$, instead of δ, which denotes economic depreciation. This can happen if, for example, the depreciation period is made shorter than the actual period of use of the investment project and the straight line method is specified for calculating depreciation. Taxable income from an investment project financed entirely with loans then is given by $R - (r + \beta\delta)C$. The tax in this case, therefore, raises tax liability on the one hand by Rt and lowers it on the other hand by $(r + \beta\delta)Ct$. Thus, the tax reduces average expected income of the investment project to $R(1 - t)$ and the user cost of capital to $(r + \delta)C$ $- (r + \beta\delta)Ct = (r + \delta)C(1 - t) - (\beta - 1)\delta Ct$. In this case, therefore, investment projects financed entirely with loans are profitable if and only if

$$R(1 - t) > (r + \delta)C(1 - t) - (\beta - 1)\delta Ct \qquad (7.16)$$

Comparison of (7.16) to (7.12) clearly shows that *accelerated depreciation encourages investment*. Same result will hold for the investment projects that are financed with internal resources. Show this yourself.

We have seen above in Section 7.4.3 that *accelerated depreciation leads to larger tax saving for the long-term investment projects. So, accelerated depreciation also induces investors to switch from short-term investment projects to long-term investment projects.*

7.7 CORPORATE FINANCE

Corporation income tax has important implications for corporate finance. Corporations can finance their expenditure by borrowing as well as by selling shares. Accordingly, the surplus corporations earn over and above costs of intermediate inputs, labour and rent is distributed among the financiers of the corporations in the form of interest and dividend. Corporation income tax in most countries builds a bias against equity finance and thereby distorts corporations' choice between debt finance and equity finance. Let us explain. Corporation income tax excludes interest payments from the taxable income of corporations, but includes dividends paid. Thus corporation income tax applies to dividends, but not to interest payments. Dividends in most countries are a part of the taxable income of the shareholders who receive them. Thus personal income tax applies to the dividends received by shareholders. Thus dividends are taxed twice, while interest payments are taxed only once, since only personal income tax applies to them. Corporations can, therefore, minimize loss in income due to taxation of the individuals who finance corporate expenditure by resorting to debt financing instead of equity financing. Hence *corporation income tax gives a strong incentive to the corporations to prefer debt financing to equity financing and thereby distorts corporations' choice between these two methods of financing.* We shall explain this point below.

Even if corporations resort to equity financing, dividends are not the only way in which corporations can distribute their profit to the shareholders. *There are tax-wise less costly ways of transferring profits to the shareholders. Despite this corporations pay dividends. This apparently irrational behaviour on the part of the corporations is referred to as dividend paradox.* We shall discuss it in the next section.

7.7.1 Dividend Paradox

Corporations can distribute their after-tax profit among shareholders not only in the form of dividends, but also in the form of capital gains. The value of the shares of a corporation reflects the value of the corporation. If a corporation retains its after-tax profit instead of paying it out as dividends, the value of the corporation, i.e., the value of the assets of the corporation, increases by the amount of this retained profit. As soon as people come to know about it, they expect the price of the shares of the corporation to rise. They will, therefore, rush to buy them and thereby raise their price to the expected level. Shares of the shareholders of the corporation will, therefore, appreciate in value and the amount of the capital gain will be equal to the dividend due to them from the corporation. Capital gains in most countries are taxed only when they are realized. Even when realized capital gains are taxed, they are in many countries taxed at a lower rate than other types of income. Thus, if a corporation retains its after-tax profit, shareholders get them in the form of capital gains on their shares and, therefore, can escape the tax on these capital gains altogether by keeping them unrealized. Even though this channel is available, most of the corporations still pay dividends. There are two major theories that seek to explain this dividend paradox. They are presented below.

First, it has been pointed out that firms think that people regard firms that pay dividends regularly as financially sound. Hence firms pay out dividends to give a signal that they are solid financially. This theory, therefore, regards dividend payment as a signaling device that the corporations use to emphasize their financial strength. There are, however, many problems with this line of reasoning. If a corporation communicates to the shareholders that they are distributing their profit as capital gains instead of as dividends so that the shareholders can save on their tax obligations, shareholders will regard it as an act of good management. They will, therefore, value the firm more highly. Moreover, there are many ways in which people can know about the financial position of a corporation. For that purpose they need not rely solely on the record of dividend payments by a firm.

Second, marginal tax rates applicable to different economic agents vary considerably from one economic agent to another. Marginal income tax rates applicable to charitable organizations, universities etc. are almost zero. *Firms, it is argued, try to attract some specific segments of economic agents. Those who want to attract the low-income tax economic agents pay dividends, while others opt for other ways of distributing profit. This phenomenon is referred to as clientele effect.* Empirical studies have shown some evidence of the clientele effect.

7.7.2 Debt Financing versus Equity Financing

Since interest payments are deductible from taxable income, but dividend payments are not, corporation income tax, as we have mentioned above, builds a bias against equity financing. Hence one expects the corporations to finance all their expenditures with borrowing. We can discuss this issue in the light of the *Modigliani–Miller theorem. It states that when returns from all investment projects are certain, and there are no taxes, corporations should be indifferent between debt and equity finance.* The reason may be explained as follows. A corporation distributes its surplus among its financiers either in the form of interest or in the form of dividend. Suppose that investment projects yield a certain future annual return of 10%. Note that under conditions of certainty all investment projects are riskless and therefore yield the same rate of return in equilibrium. Suppose that under conditions of certainty one investment project yields a higher rate of return than the others. Everyone will then plan to invest in the given project in preference to others. Price of the given investment project will therefore rise reducing it return, while prices of others will fall raising their returns. This will continue until the returns become equal. The corporations will, therefore, be willing to borrow at the demand price of 10% to finance their projects. Since demand for loans is perfectly elastic at 10%, market interest rate will settle down to 10% as well. If in this situation corporations borrow to finance their projects, they will pay the income from the investment project solely as interest to the lenders. If they finances the projects by selling equity, they will distribute their income from capital as dividend. Hence corporations should be indifferent between the two modes of financing. The difference between debt finance and equity finance in the absence of taxation lies in the fact that in case of the former, there is a risk of bankruptcy in case the corporation defaults on its debt servicing obligations, i.e., if it fails to pay interest on and repay the loan. In case of the latter there is no such risk. A firm is not declared bankrupt, if it fails to pay dividend to its shareholders, who are its owners. This risk is obviously present when future returns of investment projects are uncertain. When they are certain, there is no risk of default on loan obligation. Hence the difference between debt finance and equity finance disappears and, therefore, a corporation becomes indifferent between the two. However, *under conditions of uncertainty, the risk of default and bankruptcy constitute the crucial difference between the two modes of financing. Even though the corporation income tax builds a bias against equity finance, too much borrowing under conditions of uncertainty expose corporations to the risk of bankruptcy. Hence, despite the bias against equity finance in the corporation income tax structure, corporations do not rely solely on borrowing to finance their expenditures.*

7.8 CORPORATION INCOME TAX: INDIAN SCENARIO

Corporation income tax, as we have noted already, constitutes the most important source of direct tax revenue in India. In what follows we present and assess India's corporate tax structure in the light of what we have discussed above.

7.8.1 Unit of Corporation Income Tax

Indian Income Tax Act regards a corporation as an independent juristic person. Accordingly, it views its income separately from its shareholders'. Corporation income tax applies to the income of the corporations. India's Income Tax Act distinguishes between domestic and foreign corporations and taxes incomes of these two types of corporations at different rates. The former refers to those companies that are incorporated in India and also to those whose control and management are situated wholly in India. The latter refers to all other corporations.

7.8.2 Taxable Income and Tax Rates

India's Income Tax Act, as we just noted, applies to both Indian and foreign companies. We focus on the former first.

Indian Companies

Corporation income tax applies to Indian companies' total income arising out of their worldwide operations. India's Income Tax Act allows deduction of all business expenses (including depreciation and interest on borrowed funds) in the assessment of a corporation's income. The tax rates applicable to corporations' income for the assessment year 2014–15 are 30 per cent for Indian companies and 40 per cent for foreign companies. In addition, there is a surcharge, which is specified as a percentage of total tax to be paid. For Indian companies it is nil for those whose net income does not exceed Rs. 1 crore, 5 per cent for those whose net income is in the range of Rs. 1 crore to Rs. 10 crore and 10 per cent for those whose net income exceeds Rs. 10 crore. For the foreign companies the rates of surcharge for the above-mentioned three categories are nil, 2 per cent and 5 per cent respectively. In addition to the income tax and surcharge, both foreign and domestic companies have to pay an education cess, which is 3 per cent of the tax payable plus surcharge.

Minimum Alternate Tax (MAT)

A company has to calculate its taxable income following the norms laid down in the Indian Income Tax Act. However, it prepares its profit and loss account following the procedure specified in the Companies Act. As a result it is often found that the taxable income of a company is nil even though it has earned positive book profit as revealed by the profit and loss account. These companies are referred to as zero tax companies. To redress this anomaly, Section 115 JA was introduced in the year 1997–98. It imposes a minimum alternate tax (MAT) on the zero tax companies. For the assessment year 2014–15, Indian companies whose book profit does not exceed Rs. 1 crore, have to pay Rs. 19.05 lakh, those whose book profit is in the range of Rs. 1 crore to Rs. 10 crore have to pay a tax of Rs. 20.00775 lakh and those whose book profit exceeds Rs. 10 crore have to pay a tax of Rs. 20.9605 lakh. Foreign companies in the above-mentioned three categories have to pay taxes of 19.055 lakh, 19.4367 lakh and 20.00075 lakh respectively.

Depreciation Allowance

Indian Income Tax Act allows deduction of depreciation in the calculation of the taxable income of the Indian corporations. Depreciation is calculated using the reducing balance method. The Act specifies different depreciation rates for different categories of capital goods. In the year 2006–2007 the rate of depreciation was fixed at 15% for general machinery and plant. However, the initial rate of depreciation, i.e., the rate of depreciation in the period in which the plant and machinery were bought, was fixed at 20%. Thus, attempts were made at providing for accelerating depreciation to encourage investment.

Treatment of Business Losses

Indian Income Tax Act allows for full loss offset. This means that if an Indian corporation incurs a loss in a given financial year, it can set it off against any other kind of income except capital gains in the same year. In case its other incomes are nil or inadequate, it can set off the loss against its profit in any subsequent year during the eight-year period since the year of loss.

If in any financial year the income of the company is too low to avail itself of the depreciation allowance, it can carry forward the depreciation allowance indefinitely and set it off against any future income. Let us illustrate. Suppose that in a given financial year the taxable income of a corporation inclusive of depreciation is nil. Due to depreciation allowance its tax liability falls by Rs.100, say. Since in the given financial year its tax liability is nil without the depreciation allowance, it cannot avail itself of the depreciation allowance in the given year. In such a situation, if in any future year its tax liability is positive, it can deduct the initial year's tax saving due to depreciation allowance from its tax liability of the given year. If its tax liability in the given year falls short of the tax saving, it can carry the unabsorbed part to any future period. Provision of full loss-offset is an important feature of Indian corporate tax structure. In the absence of this provision, weak firms are discriminated against. In the absence of this provision, firms that make losses in any given period do not get any tax rebate or transfer payment on their negative income nor can they avail themselves of the depreciation allowance, but they have to pay tax at the same rate as the strong firms, when they make positive profit. Hence the tax discriminates against the weak firms and they lose out further in competition due to the absence of the full loss offset provision.

Assessment of India's Corporate Tax Structure

India's corporate tax structure has two notable features. First, it adopts an integrationist approach and, therefore, seeks to avoid double taxation of undistributed profit and dividends. However, it taxes dividends at a much lower rate than undistributed profit and thereby violates one basic integrationist principle, which states that incomes from all sources should be taxed at equal rates. However, the lower tax rate on dividends, which cannot be justified on grounds of equity, has been incorporated to induce individuals to participate directly in the share market. Second, the provision for loss offset and the carry forward facility imply equitable treatment of strong firms and firms with temporary difficulties. This provision treats positive and negative income symmetrically, i.e., it taxes positive income and gives tax relief on negative income at equal rates. Let us illustrate. Suppose that the corporation tax rate is t. If a firm's income is y, which is positive, it pays a tax of tY. If, on the other hand, the firm's profit is $-y$, its tax liability is $-tY$, i.e., its tax liability falls by tY. However, if a loss making firm has no other income, its tax liability on income from other sources is zero. Hence it cannot offset its tax saving due to negative profit against any tax liability on other incomes. In such a situation, Indian Income Tax Act allows the corporation to carry forward its tax savings to future periods and offset it against future tax liabilities, whenever they arise. In the absence of this provision, firms with temporary difficulties are discriminated against. This loss offset and carry forward facilities are applicable to depreciation allowances also.

The next question is who bear the burden of the corporation income tax in India. India has a large unincorporated sector, which is more labour-intensive than the corporate sector. There are also restrictions on the international movement of capital, which makes international mobility of capital imperfect. As a result world rate of return on capital differs from domestic rate of return on capital. In such a scenario, following the imposition of corporation income tax, capital will move out to the unincorporated sector reducing return on capital in that sector as well. Reduction in domestic return on capital will induce some capital flight out of the country, but it will not raise the return on domestic capital to its initial level, since international mobility of capital is imperfect. Thus owners of domestic capital will be burdened. As the tax raises supply price of the capital to the domestic corporate sector, corporate prices will rise and, therefore, consumers of corporate sector will be burdened. Effect on labour is, however, ambiguous. Due to the rise in the supply price of capital and the substitution of labour for capital that it gives rise to and the expansion in the unincorporated sector at the expense of the corporate sector, demand for labour will rise tending to raise wage rate and thereby making labour better off. However, if capital stock falls in the intermediate and the long run following reduction in investment due to lower return on capital, capital–labour endowment ratio will fall reducing marginal productivity of labour. It will tend to lower wage rate and thereby make labour worse off. Thus one cannot say apriori whether workers will gain or lose.

Corporation income tax also has efficiency cost. It follows from our discussion above that it distorts allocation of resources between the corporate and unincorporated sectors and also between consumption and investment in the presence of equity-financed investment and accelerated depreciation. It affects composition of investment also. All this reduces social welfare, if initial allocation were optimum. The initial allocation would be optimum in the absence of externalities, imperfect competition and undesirable inequality in the distribution of income and wealth. These conditions are not fulfilled in countries like India. Since the majority of the people live on the unincorporated sector, which is more labour-intensive, the shift in the allocation of resources in favour of the unincorporated sector may be desirable. However, countries like India are capital-poor. The disincentive to investment that the corporation income tax produces on account of equity-financed investment is, therefore, undesirable. Accordingly, provision of accelerated depreciation, which tends to neutralize the dampening effect of corporation income tax on equity-financed investment, is justified.

The other point about India's corporation income tax is that the foreign companies that are engaged in business in India supply technical services, know-how and finance to Indian firms. Most of these firms are global players, while India is a small buyer. Hence she is likely to face perfectly elastic supply of these commodities at world prices. In such a situation, the burden of the corporation income tax on foreign firms will be shifted entirely to the Indian firms.

SUMMARY

1. There is a controversy over whether incomes of corporations should be taxed in addition to individuals' incomes. There are two opposing views on this issue, the integrationist view and the absolutist view.

2. The integrationist view states that there should not be any separate tax on corporations' income. It should be integrated with their owners' or shareholders' incomes and it should be taxed at the same rate as incomes of the individuals from all other sources.

3. The absolutist view states that corporations are separate entities as there is a separation of management and ownership. Hence there is ground for separate taxation of corporations' incomes. The view seems to be untenable, as whatever corporations earn belong to their owners.

4. Benefit argument states that corporations derive considerable benefits from various types of infrastructures built by the government. Hence there is a case for separate taxation of corporations' incomes. This view is, however, untenable, as all other firms and individuals also derive benefits from government-provided infrastructure. Moreover, whatever benefits corporations derive accrue to their owners in the form of additional income.

5. There are two methods of integrating a corporation's income with those of its owners, namely, the partnership method and the capital gains method. Under the former the corporation allots its entire profit to the shareholders and notifies each shareholder her profit share irrespective of whether the corporation pays out its whole profit as dividend or not. The shareholder in turn has to add her profit share to her taxable income and pay income tax on it at the marginal tax rate applicable to her. The problem with this method is that shareholders and their profit shares change continuously as shares are traded all the time in the share market. It is, therefore, extremely difficult to keep track of the shareholders and their profit shares. Balance sheet method on the other hand makes full integration by repealing corporation income tax altogether and making both realized and unrealized capital gains taxable. Thus both dividend income and undistributed profit become taxable.

6. Corporation income is a net concept. It is arrived at by subtracting all its business costs from the revenue of the corporation. Depreciation is a component of business cost. Corporation income tax statute allows for deduction of depreciation. It specifies a lifespan of the machines and the depreciation has to be calculated over this period. This period is referred to as the depreciation period. Depreciation period can, however, differ from the actual period over which the capital good is used. The tax statute also specifies the method by means of which depreciation has to be calculated. Tax authorities usually specify three methods of calculating depreciation, namely, the straight-line method, method of declining balance and sum-of-years-digits method. The actual rate of depreciation, which is called economic depreciation, may, however, differ from the

amount of depreciation yielded by the depreciation period and the method of calculation of depreciation specified by the tax statute. If the tax statute allows for faster rate of depreciation than what happens actually, it is called accelerated depreciation. The tax statute can allow for accelerated depreciation either by shortening the depreciation period below the actual lifespan of the project or by raising the amounts of depreciation above their actual values in early years and lowering the amounts of depreciation below the actual amounts of depreciation in later years so that the total amount of depreciation remains equal to the cost of the project or by both. Everything else remaining the same, accelerated depreciation leads to larger tax saving.

7. Effective tax rate of an investment project is defined as $(r - r_t)/r$, where r and r_t denote before-tax and after-tax returns of the investment project. Effective tax rate and actual tax rate may differ from one another for various reasons. Depreciation allowance is one of them. Effective tax rate depends not only on the tax rate but also, among others, on the depreciation allowance, which in turn depends upon the depreciation period and the method of calculation of depreciation specified in the tax statute.

8. If the statute of corporation income tax allows the corporation to deduct the whole of the capital cost of an investment project in the period in which it is incurred, the government will not get any tax revenue from the investment project. Hence in most countries including India only a fraction of the capital cost is allowed to be deducted in the initial period.

9. The incidence of corporation income tax is unclear. It depends upon a host of factors. One thing that is clear is that it is not borne by the corporations, but by the people. In a country like India, where there are restrictions on international mobility of capital, a part of the burden is surely borne by the owners of capital. Consumers of corporate products are also likely to be burdened. It is not clear, however, whether labour is burdened too.

10. If investment projects are financed with loans only and if tax statute allows only for economic depreciation, corporation income tax is neutral, i.e., it affects neither the aggregate level of investment nor its composition.

11. Accelerated depreciation encourages investment and shifts its composition in favour of long-term investment projects. Tax saving on equity-financed investment projects is less than that on loan-financed investment projects. In the presence of equity-financed investment projects, corporation tax reduces aggregate investment and shifts the composition of aggregate investment in favour of loan-financed investment projects.

12. Corporation income tax applies to both normal profit and economic profit. To the extent it falls on the latter, it is nondistortionary.

13. Corporation income tax builds a bias against dividend payment and equity finance. Still corporations pay dividend and do not rely solely on borrowing. Corporations, it is argued, pay dividends to signal that it is financially sound. It is also argued that corporations often target certain specific segments of economic agents. Thus firms that want to attract low-marginal tax rate economic agents may prefer to pay out their profit as dividends. On

the other hand, corporations that target high-tax economic agents retain their profit instead of distributing it. This phenomenon is referred to as clientele effect.

14. Modigliani–Miller theorem states that in the absence of taxation and uncertainty regarding future returns on investment, corporations are indifferent between debt finance and equity finance. However, corporation income tax builds a strong bias against equity finance by taxing dividends twice and interest payments just once. Despite that corporations do not rely solely on debt finance. This is because under conditions of uncertainty too much reliance on debt finance exposes corporations to the risk of bankruptcy.

15. Indian Income Tax Act distinguishes between Indian and foreign companies. The former are defined as those that are incorporated in India or whose management and control are situated wholly in India. All other companies are regarded as foreign companies. Incomes of these two types of companies are taxed at different rates. Taxes on foreign companies are withholding taxes, i.e., these taxes are deducted at source. This means that the Indian companies making payments to the foreign companies deduct these taxes from the amount payable to the foreign companies and give them to the government.

16. In case of Indian companies, the tax applies to the income that these companies earn from their worldwide operations. As far as foreign companies are concerned, the tax applies to the income that arises or that is deemed to arise out of their Indian operations.

17. Indian Income Tax Act taxes undistributed profit and dividend at different rates. In 2006–2007 the basic rate that was applied to Indian corporations' undistributed profit was 30%. In addition there was a surcharge of 10%. Moreover, 2% of the total tax payable was to be paid as education cess. It taxed dividends at the rate of only 12.5%. To avoid double taxation of undistributed profit and dividends, long-term capital gains and dividends were exempted from personal income tax. Taxation of undistributed profit and dividends at different rates mars government's attempt at integration. In 2006–2007, royalties, dividends and interest income received by foreign companies from Indian corporations were taxed at the basic rate of 20%, while fees for technical services were taxed at the rate of 10%.

18. Indian companies estimate taxable income following the norms of the Indian Income Tax Act. However, they prepare their profit and loss account on the basis of the provisions of the Company Act. As a result many Indian companies show zero taxable income despite positive book profit. MAT applies to these companies. In 2006–2007 Indian companies whose tax liability was less than 7.5% of their book profit had to pay MAT at the rate of 7.5% of their book profit.

19. Indian Income Tax Act allows deduction of depreciation in the calculation of taxable income. It specifies the reducing or declining balance method for the calculation of depreciation. It thereby provides for accelerated depreciation to encourage investment.

20. Indian Income Tax Act also allows for full loss offset and carry forward facility. This is of considerable help to firms passing through a difficult period temporarily.

KEY CONCEPTS

✓ Integrationist view	✓ Absolutist view
✓ Depreciation period	✓ Depreciation allowance
✓ Economic depreciation	✓ Accelerated depreciation
✓ Tax neutrality	✓ Effective tax rate
✓ Statutory tax rate	✓ Minimum alternate tax
✓ Straight-line method	✓ Method of declining or reducing balance
✓ Sum-of-years-digits method	✓ Expensing
✓ Initial allowance	✓ Full loss offset
✓ Dividend paradox	✓ Modigliani–Miller Theorem
✓ User cost of capital	

REVIEW QUESTIONS

1. Present and compare the integrationist view and the absolutist view. Which one do you prefer and why?

2. Present and evaluate the benefit argument in support of separate taxation of corporations' income.

3. Present and evaluate the regulatory argument in support of separate taxation of corporations' income.

4. Explain the partnership method and the capital gains method of integrating corporate income with their owners' income. Which one do you prefer and why?

5. What is depreciation period? What are the methods of calculating depreciation?

6. Distinguish between actual or economic and accelerated depreciation. Which one leads to greater tax saving and why? What are the different ways in which the tax authority can provide for accelerated depreciation?

7. Why does economic depreciation make corporation income tax neutral, while accelerated depreciation make it non-neutral? Explain.

8. Define effective tax rate. Is it affected by depreciation allowance?

9. If the whole of the capital cost of an investment project is allowed to be deducted as depreciation in the period in which it is incurred, the government will earn no income from the investment project. Prove this statement.

10. How is the burden of corporation income tax distributed among economic agents?

11. How does corporation income tax affect the level and composition of aggregate investment?

12. Explain dividend paradox.

13. What is meant by clientele effect? Explain.

14. How does corporation income tax distort corporations' choice between equity finance and debt finance?

15. Present and evaluate the structure of the corporation income tax in India.

═══════ PROBLEMS AND APPLICATIONS ═══════

1. For the sake of equity there should be tax either on undistributed profit of the corporations or on capital gains. Do you agree with this statement? Explain your answer. In case your answer is yes, which of the two taxes will you prefer and why?

   (*Hint:* Unrealized capital gains are extremely difficult to compute and tax.)

2. Construct a numerical example involving two investment projects to show how accelerated depreciation can be non-neutral.

3. Which one of the three methods of estimating depreciation reduces tax burden the most?

4. At the current juncture there is an acute shortage of infrastructural services in India. If corporation tax rates are uniform across all sectors, should investment tax credit be the same also?

   (*Hint:* Investment tax credit or investment allowance should be larger for firms producing infrastructural services. The same effect can be achieved through subsidy.)

5. How will an increase in the depreciation period affect the effective tax rate on an investment project?

6. How should the statute of corporation income tax be modified to remove its bias against equity finance?

   (*Hint:* Allowing deduction of dividends also from the taxable income of corporations.)

7. Is there any bias against dividend payment in the structure of India's corporation income tax?

   (*Hint:* No. It encourages dividend payment and discourages retained earning by taxing dividends at a much lower rate than retained profit.)

8. Business saving constitutes a very small part of total saving in India. Internal source is also an unimportant source of finance for financing investment. Is there any ground to believe that India's corporation tax structure is responsible for this? Explain.

9. If corporation tax is repealed in India and to compensate for the loss in revenue, the government brings dividends and long-term capital gains within the purview of the personal income tax, how will government's tax revenue be affected?

   (*Hint:* It is likely to raise tax revenue, since mostly well-to-do sections of people invest in corporations and their marginal tax rate is higher than the tax rates applicable to dividend and retained earnings of corporations.)

10. In India corporation income tax applies at the rate of 30% to undistributed profit. From the point of view of the integrationist approach at what rate should it be taxed? If there

is a tax on undistributed profit, should capital gains on shares be taxed as well? Is balance sheet method of integration preferable to the kind of corporation income tax we have in India?

(*Hint:* From the point of view of the integrationist approach undistributed profit of corporations should be taxed at the same rate as any other type of income of the individuals. Tax rate applicable to the undistributed profit of corporations should be the marginal tax rate applicable to the individuals owning the company. If the marginal tax rate applicable to the shareholders is more or less the same, there is no problem. However, if it varies, it will create problems. In such a situation balance sheet method is better. It is better for another reason as well. If there is a tax on undistributed corporate profit, there should not be any tax on capital gains on shares due to accumulation of reserves of profit. However, shares appreciate in value due to speculative factors as well. This should be taxed for reasons of equity. The problem with the balance sheet method is that it requires taxation of unrealized capital gains as well. It is extremely costly to do that.)

11. Indian Income Tax Act taxes dividend payments at a much lower rate than undistributed profit of corporations. Dividends are tax exempt in the hands of the shareholders. Do you support this from the point of view of equity?

REFERENCES

For integratation of corporation and personal income tax:

US Department of Treasury (1992): *Integration of the Individual and Corporate Tax Systems,* US Government Printing Office, Washington DC.

For retained earning and value of shares:

Bradford, D.F. (1981): The incidence and allocation effects of a tax on corporate distribution, *Journal of Public Economics,* 15(1).

For incidence of corporate tax:

Harberger, A.C. (1974): The incidence of the corporation income tax, *in:* Harberger, A.C. (Ed.) *Taxation and Welfare,* Little Brown, Boston.

For corporation tax and investment:

Chirinko, R.S. (1993): Business fixed investment spending: A critical survey of modeling strategies, empirical results and policy implications, *Journal of Economic Literature,* 31(4).

For a general discussion of different aspects of corporate tax:

Mervyn, A.K. and Fullerton, D. (Eds.)(1984): *The Taxation of Income from Capital,* Chicago University Press, Chicago.

For a discussion on debt versus equity financing:

Modigliani, F. and Miller, M.H. (1958): The cost of capital, corporation finance and the theory of investment, *American Economic Review*, 48.

Stiglitz, J.E. (1974): On the irrelevance of corporation financial policy, *American Economic Review*, 64.

On dividend paradox:

Stiglitz, J.E. (1973): Taxation, corporate financial policy and the cost of capital, *Journal of Public Economics*, February.

8 | SALES TAX

Chapter Objectives

The objective of this chapter is to give an idea of the structure of sales taxes. More precisely, it purports to discuss the issues such as

(i) units of sales taxes.
(ii) types of sales taxes.
(iii) methods of implementing sales taxes.
(iv) problems of turnover tax.
(v) value added tax (VAT).
(vi) structure of sales taxes and excises in India.

8.1 INTRODUCTION

Sales taxes or excises are imposed on the sales of firms. Income taxes in contrast apply to factor payments made by firms. Sales taxes and excises are an important source of tax revenue in India even though their share in total tax revenue is declining of late (see Table 8.1). The question that emerges naturally in this context is whether there is any rationale of sales taxes in addition to income tax. As we have explained in Chapter 2, *sales taxes are warranted on goods that generate negative externalities such as cigarettes, alcoholic beverages etc. to achieve efficient allocation of resources.* For the same reason they are also warranted on demerit goods, which the community collectively considers bad for the society. Besides the above reasons, when incomes cannot be taxed adequately for administrative reasons, sales taxes may be resorted to (see Atkinson and Stiglitz (1980) on this issue). In developing countries like India quite a large part of the aggregate income originates in the unorganized sector. It is extremely costly to keep

252

track of such incomes and thereby bring them under the income tax net. Number of important suppliers of goods and services is much less than that of income earners. Hence the government has to resort to sales and excise taxes as a major source of revenue. Sales taxes may be general or selective. *General sales taxes refer to those sales taxes that apply to sales of all goods and services at the same rate. Selective sales taxes in contrast apply only to a specific good or a specific set of goods.* Unlike income taxes, sales taxes are taxes on expenditure. Sales taxes may be unit or ad valorem depending upon how the rates of these taxes are defined. We discuss these taxes below.

Table 8.1: Tax revenue as per cent of gross tax revenue

	2007–08	2008–09	2009–10	2010–11	2011–12	2012–13
Indirect	47.0	44.5	39.2	43.4	44.0	46.8
Customs	17.6	16.5	13.3	17.1	16.8	17.3
Excise	20.8	17.9	16.5	17.4	16.3	18.0
Service tax	8.6	10.1	9.4	9.0	11.0	11.5

Source: Economic Survey 2006–2007, Government of India.

8.2 RATES OF SALES TAXES: UNIT AND AD VALOREM

Sales taxes are imposed on a unit basis as well as on an ad valorem basis. *When the rate of the sales tax is specified as a given absolute amount of money to be paid as sales tax per unit of a commodity sold, the sales tax is a unit-based sales tax.* Thus, if the rate of sales tax on a commodity X is Rs. 5 per unit of the commodity X sold, it is a unit-based sales tax. On the other hand, *if the rate of a sales tax is specified as a given percentage of the value of sales of a commodity, the sales tax is an ad valorem one.* If the rate of a sales tax is defined as 10% of the value of sales of the commodity X, whose price is Rs. 10, the tax is an ad valorem one. Sellers of X under this tax will have to pay Re. 1 as sales tax per unit of X sold. Ad valorem sales tax has the following advantage over unit-based sales tax. If an ad valorem sales tax is imposed at the same rate on every good and service including leisure, buyers and sellers will face the same relative prices. Hence, there will not be any price distortions and inefficiency. Let us explain. Disregard leisure for the present. Suppose that only two goods are produced in an economy, X and Y whose supply prices in the pre-tax situation are P_X and P_Y respectively. Now an ad valorem sales tax at the rate t is imposed on both the goods. As a result the seller has to pay a tax of tP_X (tP_Y) per unit of $X(Y)$ sold. Therefore, supply prices of X and Y will rise to $(1 + t)P_X$ and $(1 + t)P_Y$ respectively. Thus buyers and sellers will face the same relative price of X, $[P_X(1 + t)/P_Y(1 + t)] = [P_X/P_Y]$. Hence, as we have seen in Chapter 4, this sales tax will not give rise to any inefficiency or excess burden, provided leisure can also be taxed at the same rate. In contrast, if the tax is a unit tax and the tax rate is t, supply prices of X and Y in the post-tax situation will be $P_X + t$ and $P_Y + t$ respectively. Hence relative prices of X faced by the buyers and sellers will be $(P_X + t)/(P_Y + t)$ and (P_X/P_Y) respectively and they are different. Hence this unit sales tax will give rise to excess burden.

8.3 GENERAL SALES TAX

Bases of a general sales tax may be different. It may be the value of all transactions or the GDP or the value of all consumer goods only. When the base of a general sales tax is all transactions, it is called a turnover tax. We focus on it first.

8.3.1 Turnover Tax: A General Sales Tax on All Transactions

Under the turnover tax every commodity is taxed at every stage of its production. Thus sales of wheat by the farmers to the millers, who turn this wheat into flour, are taxed. Again, the sales of flour, which includes the value of wheat, by the millers to the bakers who produce bread are taxed. Again sales of bread, which includes the value of flour, by the bakers to the consumers of bread are taxed. Thus the base of the turnover tax is many times larger than GDP and, therefore, a low rate of tax yields a large amount of revenue. Hence it is appealing to the politicians. However, it is inefficient as well as iniquitous. We shall illustrate these points with a simple example below.

Suppose that only two goods, X and Y, are produced in the economy at the final stage of production. X is produced with only one input, X_m, which in turn is produced with only one input, X_{m-1} and so on. Thus at the first stage of production of X the input X_1 is produced, which is used to produce X_2. At each stage of production only one unit of the input is used per unit of output. Every market is competitive. Price of X_i in the pre-tax situation is denoted by P_{Xi}, $i = 1, 2, 3, \ldots\ldots, m$. X_1 is produced with only labour and a fixed quantity of labour is required per unit of output of X_1. Therefore, P_{X1} equals fixed per unit labour cost of production of X_1. $P_{X2} = P_{X1}$ as P_{X1} is the marginal and average costs of production of X_2. Thus the pre-tax price of every X_i, $i = 1, 2, \ldots\ldots, m$ and X is P_{X1}. Now, suppose that a turnover tax is imposed at the rate, t. Then the producers of X_1, whose price is P_{X1}, will have to pay a tax of tP_{X1} per unit of X_1 sold. Hence supply price of X_1 to the producers of X_2 and hence marginal and average costs of producing X_2 and, therefore, its price will rise to $P_{X1}(1 + t)$. But producers of X_2 will have to pay a tax of $tP_{X1}(1 + t)$ on every unit of X_2 sold. Hence supply price of X_2 to the producers of X_3 will rise to $P_{X1}(1 + t)^2$. Proceeding in this manner one can easily deduce that the supply price of X to the final buyers will rise to $P_{X1}(1 + t)^m$. Consider another good, Y. Suppose its production structure is the same as that of X except for the fact that it involves n stages of production instead of m. Suppose that the commodity Y_n directly enters as input in the production of Y, it is the only input used and just one unit of this input is required per unit of output of Y. Again, only the commodity Y_{n-1} enters directly in the production of Y_n and just one unit of this input is required per unit of the output of Y_n and so on. In the first stage of production of Y, the good Y_1 is produced; it is produced only with labour and only one unit of labour is required per unit of the good produced. All the markets are also perfectly competitive. Let us denote the price of Y_i by P_{Yi}, $i = 1, 2, \ldots, n$. In the pre-tax situation therefore, just as in the case of X, the price of Y will be P_{Y1}. Following the imposition of the turnover tax, the supply price of Y to the buyers will rise to $P_{Y1}(1 + t)^n$. Thus, in the post-tax situation, as opposed to the pre-tax scenario, buyers and sellers of X and Y face different price ratios. The latter face $P_{X1}(1 + t)^{m-1}/P_{Y1}(1 + t)^{n-1}$, while the former face $P_{X1}(1 + t)^m/P_{Y1}(1 + t)^n$ giving rise to excess burden or inefficiency. The point is that *under a turnover tax the amount of tax that is paid on a commodity is an increasing function of the number of stages that its production involves.* In our example, producers of X pay a tax of $tP_{X1}(1 + t)^{m-1}$ per unit of X sold. Clearly, the tax burden on the producers of X is an increasing function of the number of stages involved in the production of X, m. If production of every commodity involves equal number of stages, then, as our example illustrates, relative prices faced by buyers and producers will be the same. But this condition is never met in reality. Hence *turnover tax causes price distortions and thereby generates inefficiency.*

The other problem the turnover tax gives rise to is that it induces the producers operating at different stages to merge and thereby reduce tax burden. Thus, for example, if the producers of X_1 and X_2 merge, their joint total tax liability will fall from $P_{X1}t + P_{X1}(1 + t)t$ to only $P_{X1}t$. (Explain this point yourself). *The tax, in other words, will generate strong inducements for vertical integration and thereby reduce competition.*

Finally, as is clear from our example, under a turnover tax the higher-up a producer in the production structure, the larger is her tax burden. This is because the whole value of the inputs used by a producer inclusive of the taxes paid by the input producers gets into the value of her sales. Thus the tax base of a producer is necessarily larger than that of her suppliers of inputs. In our example, the tax base of the producers of X_1 per unit of X_1 is P_{X1}, while that of the producers of X_2 per unit of X_2 is $P_{X1}(1 + t)$. This phenomenon is called pyramiding of taxes or cascading effect. *The turnover tax is, therefore, discriminatory to the producers who are higher-up in the production structure.* This discrimination is completely arbitrary. It is in no way true that the producers higher-up in the production structure are better or worse off than those in the lower rungs of the production structure. Clearly, therefore, the tax is inequitable.

8.3.2 Other Bases of a General Sales Tax

As we have mentioned above, *besides all transactions, there may be three other different bases of a general sales tax, namely, GDP, national income and aggregate consumption expenditure.* The most popular is the consumption-base-type general sales tax. GDP-based sales tax may be a single-stage or a multistage tax. In case of the former it applies usually at the retail level to sales of both consumer and capital goods. It may also apply at the wholesalers' or manufacturers' level for administrative convenience. In case of the multistage tax, it takes the form of a value added tax (VAT). It applies to the gross value added of every firm. This tax is not popular as it goes against the commonly accepted norm that tax should apply only to income, which is net of the cost incurred in earning the income. Depreciation is a component of the cost that the firm incurs to earn its income. Hence it should be deducted to arrive at the amount of the taxable income originating in the firm. This takes us to the case of the general sales tax with the national income as its base, since net domestic product in most countries is very close to national income. However, the problem with this kind of sales tax is that its base is almost the same as that of the income taxes, personal and corporation. This kind of sales tax is, therefore, not adopted to avoid double taxation of the same base. For these reasons consumption-based sales tax is quite popular. It may be implemented either through a single-stage tax on the sales of consumer goods at the retail level or through a multistage value added tax, which we shall discuss shortly.

8.3.3 Single-stage Sales Tax

A GDP-type or a consumption-type sales tax is implemented, as we have mentioned already, either as a single-stage tax or as a multistage value added tax. The choice is a matter of administrative convenience as the economic impact of such taxes is independent of whether they are implemented as a single-stage or as a multistage tax. Let us illustrate this proposition with a simple example. Take our familiar example of the farmer, flour miller and baker. The farmer produces 100 kg of wheat and sells it to the flour miller at Re. 1 per kg. The flour miller uses it to produce 100 kg of flour and sells it to the baker at Rs. 2 per kg. The baker uses the flour to produce 200 pounds of bread and sells it to the consumers at Rs. 2 per pound. The value addeds of the farmer, miller and the baker are Rs. 100, Rs. 100 and Rs. 200 respectively. Now suppose a single-stage sales tax at the rate of 10% is imposed on the sales of bread. The minimum price at which the baker is willing to sell 200 pounds of bread is Rs. 2. However, she now has to pay 10% of Rs. 2, which is Rs. 0.2, as tax. She will, therefore, raise her supply price to the buyers to Rs. 2.2 so that she receives Rs. 2 after paying the tax. This example illustrates the fact that, if a single-stage sales tax is imposed on a commodity at a given rate, its supply price under competitive market conditions will rise in the same percentage as the tax rate corresponding to every given level of supply or sales. We shall now show with the help of our example that this is the case even when the sales tax is implemented as a multistage value added tax. Suppose that the sales tax applies at the rate of 10% to the pre-tax value added at every stage of production of bread, i.e., it applies to the pre-tax value addeds of the farmer, miller and the baker at the rate of 10%. The farmer will then have to pay Rs. 10 as tax on its value added. Therefore, the tax she will pay per unit of the wheat sold is Re. 0.1. So, she will raise her supply price of wheat to the miller by the same amount so that she continues to receive the amount she was receiving earlier, as that is the minimum price at which she is willing to sell 100 kg of wheat. Thus to the miller the cost of intermediate inputs per unit of flour produced rises by 10%. She also has to pay Rs. 10 as tax on her pre-tax value added of Rs. 100. Thus her cost per unit of flour produced rises by Re. $(0.1 + 0.1 = 0.2)$, i.e., by 10%. So, she will raise her supply price by 10% also. For the same reason cost to the baker per pound of bread produced rises by Re. 0.1 + Re. 0.1, as she has to pay Re. 0.1 extra for the amount of flour required per pound of bread produced and Re. 0.1 as VAT on the value added of Re. 1 per pound of bread produced. So, she will also raise her supply price from Rs. 2 by 10% to Rs. 2.2. This example illustrates the point that, if a sales tax at a given rate is implemented in multistages as VAT, the supply price at every quantity of supply under competitive conditions at every stage including the final stage will rise in the same percentage as the tax rate. Hence the supply schedule of the final good on which the sales tax is imposed as VAT will shift upward in the same percentage as the tax rate. This is exactly the case if the sales tax is imposed on a final good as a single-stage tax. Moreover, both the single-stage sales tax and the multistage VAT yield the same amount of tax revenue to the government. In our example, both the taxes yield the same amount of tax revenue.

Let us first focus on the single-stage tax. The issue that is relevant in this context is, at what level should such a tax be imposed? Normally, it should be imposed at the retail level, otherwise a part of the GDP or the value of consumption expenditure will remain untaxed. For example, if the tax is imposed at the manufacturers' level, value addeds originating at the wholesalers' and retailers' levels will remain outside the tax net. However, since the number of manufacturers or wholesalers is much less than that of the retailers, it may be convenient to administer a single-stage tax at the manufacturers' or wholesalers' levels. This is particularly true in case of developing countries where there is an overwhelming preponderance of small retailers relative to wholesalers or manufacturers. In what follows, we shall discuss the value-added tax in much greater detail.

8.3.4 Value Added Tax (VAT)

In European countries value added tax has replaced a turnover tax for all the problems, as we have discussed above, that the latter gives rise to. A value added tax may be GDP-based or income-based or consumption-based. A value added tax applies to every firm and not just to firms catering only to final demand. In case of a GDP-based value added tax, it applies to the gross value added of every firm. Gross value added of a firm is defined as total sales of the firm net of the value of intermediate inputs purchased from other firms. When the value added tax is based on national income, the tax applies to net value added of every firm, which is defined as gross value added of the firm net of the amount of depreciation incurred by the firm. Consumption-based value added tax applies to the gross value added of every firm net of the amount of investment made by the firm. Investment of a firm consists of additions to the inventory and to the stock of fixed capital made by the firm. If we add up the tax base of every firm, we shall approximately get aggregate consumption inclusive of households' investment, provided trade balance is insignificant. Note that aggregate consumption here consists of not only personal consumption but also public or government consumption net of wages and salaries in government administration and defence.

VAT can be collected in two ways: Firms may be asked to furnish information regarding their tax base, assess their tax liability on the basis of the tax base and the tax rates specified in the tax statute and pay the tax. In the GDP-type VAT, for example, every firm may be asked to furnish information regarding its gross value added and assess its tax liability on the basis of this tax base and the tax rates specified in the tax statute. Suppose that the value of sales of a firm is Y, the value of intermediate inputs it used is M and the tax rate specified is t. Then the firm's tax liability, denoted by T, is $(Y - M)t$. Under the method of collection being discussed here the firm has to furnish information regarding Y and M, assess its T and pay it to the government. However, calculation of VAT is not as simple as it seems from above. The computation is complicated on account of the fact that here M stands for the value of the intermediate inputs the firm used net of the taxes paid on the intermediate inputs sold to the given firm by the producers of the intermediate inputs. In what follows we shall describe a method of calculating the value of M and thereby that of VAT.

However, before discussing it we shall clarify certain points. Note that M is a part of the gross value addeds of the firms that took part in its production. Hence Mt is a part of the tax liability of these firms. Let us illustrate this point with an example. Consider a farmer which in a given period produced and sold wheat of Rs. 200 to a flour miller who converted this wheat into flour and sold it at Rs. 300 to a baker who, in turn, produced bread using this flour and sold the product at Rs. 400 to the consumers. Suppose that a GDP-type VAT applies to these firms at the rate of 10%. The tax liability of the baker is Rs. $[400\ (Y) - 300\ (M)](1/10)$. Note that here the value of intermediate input used by the baker equals the sum of the gross value addeds of the flour miller and the farmer who produced the flour directly and indirectly and paid a tax of Rs. 300 (1/10) ($= Mt$). This suggests the other method of collection of VAT. Under this method each producer is asked to assess her VAT liability on the basis of her gross sales and claim the tax paid by her suppliers of intermediate inputs on their sales of intermediate inputs to her as credit. This method is called tax credit method in India. This means that the taxpayer can claim deduction of the tax paid by her suppliers of intermediate inputs on their sales of intermediate inputs to her from her tax liability. Thus the baker has to first show ($Yt =$) Rs. 400 (1/10) = Rs. 40 as her VAT liability and then claim deduction from her tax liability the amount of tax paid by the flour miller on the flour sold to her, which is ($Mt =$) Rs. 300 (1/10) = Rs. 30. To claim the tax credit every firm has to secure proofs of tax payments from its suppliers of intermediate inputs. Thus the baker in our example has to secure from the miller the proof that she has paid Rs. 30 as VAT on the flour sold to the baker. The miller in her turn will have to go through the same procedure as the baker. Even though this collection method has a higher compliance cost, it has the advantage that every producer makes sure that her suppliers have paid their due taxes. This method, therefore, has a built-in check against tax evasion. For this reason this method of collection has been adopted in the European countries. This method is also adopted in India.

8.4 INCIDENCE OF SALES TAX

We have pointed out in the chapter on tax incidence that the burden of selective indirect taxes on luxury goods is likely to be progressively distributed, while the burdens of selective sales taxes and excises on necessities are likely to be regressively distributed.

Regarding general sales taxes, we know that a consumption-type general sales tax aims at taxing consumption expenditures of individuals. We have already explained in the chapter on tax equity that if consumption expenditures of every individual is taxed at the same rate, as happens in the case of a general consumption-based sales tax, horizontal equity is ensured, i.e., every individual having the same present value of lifetime income end up paying the same present value of lifetime tax. However, there is no guarantee that such a tax ensures vertical equity too, even though it makes people with larger lifetime incomes pay larger amounts of tax over their lifetimes.

8.5 SALES TAX IN INDIA

8.5.1 Central and Local Sales Taxes

Sales taxes in India are levied by both the central and the state governments. Central Sales Taxes (CSTs) are governed by the Central Sales Tax Act 1956. CST applies to sales of all manufactured goods when the sales are made outside of the state where the seller is located. These sales, when confined to India, are called interstate sales. Every dealer in manufactured goods engaged in interstate sales has to pay CST on such sales. Let us illustrate with an example. Suppose that a dealer, A, located in West Bengal sells motor cars to a trader operating in Bihar. Such a sale is referred to as interstate sale and CST applies to it. CST, however, does not apply to sales made within the state where the seller is located. These sales are called intrastate sales. Thus, if A sells motor cars to a trader who operates in West Bengal, the sale is intrastate sale and it does not attract CST. The ceiling rate of CST was 4% in 2006–2007. It is, however, revised from time to time. CST also applies to imports of manufactured goods into and exports of manufactured goods outside India. CST is a single-stage or a single-point tax. CST is collected from the sellers, but recoverable from the buyers. CST is imposed on the dealers of the taxed commodity. The dealers charge the CST to the buyers and pay it to the central government.

State sales taxes or local sales taxes (LSTs) apply to intrastate sales, i.e., sales within a state, as we have already explained. LSTs are governed by State Sales Tax Acts of respective states. Rates of LSTs are subject to legislations of respective states and they vary from state-to-state and from time-to-time. However, the ceiling rate of LST in 2006–2007 was 15%. LSTs are also single-point taxes. Besides LSTs, states are empowered to impose surcharges, additional taxes etc. on sales. LST, just like CST, is also paid by the seller and recoverable from the buyers.

The problem with the structure of sales taxes in India is the following. Sales taxes apply to almost every good: not only to the final products catering to final demand, but also to intermediate inputs. Thus, for example, CSTs and LSTs are levied not only on sales of motor cars but also on sales of tires, steel, iron etc. and usually at different rates. This leads to pyramiding of taxes or cascading effect. Thus, if a producer of a commodity X uses intermediate inputs worth $M(1 + t)$, where M denotes the value of the intermediate inputs used by the given producer excluding the tax and t is the sales tax rate applicable to M, then the value of sales of the producer will include the whole of $M(1 + t) > M$. Thus the output of X will include not only the value of intermediate inputs, but also the amount of taxes paid by the suppliers of the intermediate inputs. This phenomenon, as we have already mentioned, is referred to as the pyramiding of taxes or the cascading effect. Hence, as we have pointed out already, sales tax base of producers higher-up in the production structure will necessarily be larger than those lower down in the production structure. This problem can be removed by introducing VAT. Both the central and the state governments are aware of this problem and efforts are on to replace the current structure of sales taxes through a nationwide system of VAT. Most of the states in India replaced their sales tax structures with VAT in April 2005. However, Tamil Nadu and the union territory of Pondicherry are yet to implement it. See Box 8.2 in this context.

8.5.2 Central and State Excises

Besides sales taxes, there are *central and state excise duties, which are imposed on the manufacturers by the central and the state governments respectively. State excise duties apply only to the manufacture of alcohol. Central excise duties apply to the manufacture of a large number of manufactured products, called excisable products, with rates varying from 0 to 12%.* There are only about seven items, motorcars, tiers, aerated soft drinks, chewing tobacco and air conditioners, which attract duty at the rate of 32%. Petrol also carries a high level of excise duty. The central excise is, however, implemented through a system of VAT called central VAT or CENVAT. CENVAT is based on the input credit system. Every manufacturer has to first assess her tax liability on the basis of the value of her total output and then claim the duty paid by the suppliers of her intermediate inputs on the intermediate inputs supplied to her as credit. Besides CST and central excise, the central government also collects service tax. Details of this tax are presented below.

8.5.3 Service Tax

Service sector at present is the largest and the fastest growing sector in India. It accounts for about 40% of GDP. However, services were outside the indirect tax net until 1993–1994. The bulk of the indirect tax revenue came from the manufacturing sector, which contributed only about a quarter of GDP. The omission clearly produced distortions and inequity. The major reasons for the non-inclusion of services in the tax net were the following. Quite a large number of services were in the informal sector and they did not have a regular system of accounting. Tax potential of many of the services did not warrant the administrative costs of tax assessment

---

Box 8.1: Responses to VAT in India

Governments' attempts at replacing the single-stage local and central sales taxes by VAT created widespread resentment. Even though most of the state governments have welcomed and implemented VAT by April 1, 2005, a few such as Uttar Pradesh, Tamil Nadu and the union territory of Pondicherry are yet to implement it. Apprehensions against VAT are due to the following reasons:

(i) It is viewed as regressive. Since it is a sales tax, its impact falls on purchases or expenditures of the people. Since the poor people typically spend a larger proportion of their income, it is argued that they pay a larger proportion of their income as VAT. The criticism applies actually to sales tax. VAT is just a means of implementing the sales tax. Its advantage is that it eliminates the cascading effect or pyramiding of taxes and thereby makes the regime of sales tax transparent, efficient and less inequitable. To mitigate the problem pointed out here, essential items of consumption such as food, crude clothing, medicine etc. should be taxed at low rates. This is, however, what is normally done everywhere.

(ii) There is also the apprehension that VAT will burden small businesses with a large amount of compliance cost. Since VAT is collected from every firm, small businesses are not spared. The cost of keeping records and accounts necessary for VAT is quite large for small businesses. Such costs come to quite a sizeable proportion of their income. These costs in contrast are quite a small percentage of the incomes of large businesses. Thus the former are discriminated against under VAT. The problem can be redressed by allowing for deductions from VAT liabilities of small businesses so that their compliance cost is covered to the required extent. It should, however, be noted here that Income Tax (Accounts and Records) Regulation of 1980 enjoins on every person to keep detailed records of all his/her transactions. Compliance with this is enough for VAT.

(iii) It is also pointed out that VAT is inflationary. This criticism, however, applies to sales tax. Imposition of sales tax raises supply prices and thereby market prices, as we showed in the Chapter on Tax Incidence. This is inevitable irrespective of whether the sales tax is implemented as a single-stage or as a multistage VAT. VAT in fact in Indian context where almost every good is taxed, will bring transparency to the price change following the imposition of the sales tax by eliminating the pyramiding of taxes or the cascading effect, as we have noted earlier.

and collection. Moreover, value added varied widely across firms within a sector and also across sectors. This wide variation could give rise to disputes. Despite these difficulties central government imposed a tax, called the service tax, on a few services such as services of telephones, non-life insurance and stockbrokers on July 1, 1994 at the rate of 5%. To circumvent the problem of variability of value added mentioned above, a procedure of self-assessment has been introduced for tax collection. Taxpayers have to assess their tax liabilities themselves on the basis of a set of simple rules. The Jurisdictional Superintendent of Central Excise is authorized to cross verify the correctness of self-assessed returns.

Successive budgets have widened the service tax net to include more and more services. In June 2003 the rate was raised to 8%. Efforts are also on to integrate the indirect taxes on goods and services. In fact, a committee was formed under the chairmanship of Vijay Kelkar to implement Fiscal Responsibility and Budget Management Act. The committee recommended Goods and Services Tax (GST), a unified scheme of taxation that will cover both goods and services. As a first step towards integrating indirect taxes on goods and services, budget for 2004–2005 extended the credit of service tax and excise duty across goods and services. This means that at the present CENVAT credit is available to the service taxpayers and the service tax credit is available to the payers of excise duty. Previously, the service taxpayers could claim credit only for the taxes paid by their suppliers on services that the service taxpayers used as inputs. They could not claim credit for the taxes paid by their suppliers on goods they used as intermediate inputs. Now they can claim credit on both. Thus at the present they pay service tax only on their value added. Similarly, CENVAT credit covers only goods, not services, used as intermediate inputs. Previously, manufacturers paying central excise duty could claim credit only on taxes paid on goods they used as intermediate inputs. Now they can claim credit also on taxes paid on services used as intermediate inputs. To make up for the loss in revenue resulting from these concessions the service tax rate was raised to 10% in the 2004–2005 budget.

8.6 CONCLUSION

Quite a large part of India's income originates in the informal sector and number of income earners is very large. Hence it is extremely costly to bring the whole of India's national income within India's income tax net. The government, therefore, seeks to bring the GDP under the tax net through the sales and excise taxes and the service tax. For this reason indirect taxes in general and sales and excise taxes in particular are the predominant source of revenue to the government (see Table 8.1). *The most important feature that strikes one, as one studies India's sales and excise tax structure, is that it is highly complex.* Both the state and the central governments levy sales taxes. Sales within a state, referred to as intrastate sales, are taxed by the state government while sales made outside the state, called interstate sales, are taxed by the central government. The rates charged by the two governments are different. It is quite difficult to define intrastate and interstate sales in practice. A seller, A, may, for example, sell a commodity to B, who may reside in some other state. But he may use the commodity bought in the state of the seller. Similarly, the opposite situation may also occur, i.e., B may reside in the same sate as A, but may use the commodity bought in some other state. You can in fact think of many situations where it is difficult to identify a sale as interstate or intrastate sale. Since tax rates on these two types of sales are different, sellers try to take advantage of any loophole or ambiguity in the definitions.

Moreover, sales taxes apply to the total sales of almost every good and the rates are different not only across goods but also across states. State governments have the power to fix the tax rates independently. These features have a number of worrisome implications. First, since both final products and intermediate inputs are taxed and the sales taxes fall on total sales and not on value added, these taxes lead to pyramiding of taxes or cascading effect. The tax base is also many times larger than GDP. Second, multiplicity of tax rates along with the coexistence of central and sales taxes lead to high-compliance costs and, therefore, act as an important barrier to business expansion. It also adversely affects international competitiveness of Indian business. This is, to say the least, a matter of great worry in the present context of globalization. Finally, state governments often use the sales tax rates as instruments of competition with other states to attract investment. Frequent changes in tax rates create confusion and uncertainty and thereby hamper investment. Fortunately, governments are aware of the problems noted above. They have agreed to desist from engaging in competition with one another through the lowering of the sales tax rates. Majority of the states have adopted VAT since April 2005 to avoid pyramiding or cascading of taxes. Only Tamil Nadu, Uttar Pradesh and the union territory of Pondicherry are yet to implement it. CENVAT has also been reformed. It now applies at the uniform rate of 16%. Despite these moves, India's tax structure is still complex. Even though the CENVAT rate is uniform, there are still many selective concessions and allowances, which perpetuates the regime of multiple rates. Moreover, the procedure of claiming service tax credit under the CENVAT is still highly complex. The problem with state VATs is that they do not cover services, as they are not empowered by the constitution to levy taxes thereon. Besides, there are still stamp duty, a tax levied by the states on transfer of properties, octroi or entry tax on the entry of goods, a tax imposed by local bodies on the entry of goods in the local area for use, and state taxes on some services such as entertainment. All these sundry taxes should have been merged with the VAT.

From the above it follows that there is a case for general sales taxes and excises in India. It can be shown that a general sales tax at a uniform rate on all goods and services including leisure do not lead to any excess burden as it does not make the prices faced by buyers and sellers different. However, for the sake of efficient allocation of resources goods that generate positive externalities and the merit goods should be taxed at lower rates, while the goods that create negative externalities and the demerit goods should be taxed at higher rates. However, taxing leisure is infeasible as its valuation is extremely difficult. In this situation a general sales tax will lead to excess burden. To minimize excess burden, Ramsey rule or inverse elasticity rule, explained in Chapter 4 in the Box 4.1, is to be followed so that tax rates on goods vary inversely with their own price elasticities. This means taxing the necessities at high rates and the luxuries at low rates. This obviously is grossly inequitable. In a country like India where quite a large section of the people are poor, taxing the necessities, such as food, with low-price elasticities, which are usually the mass consumption goods, at high rates and the luxuries, such as cars, air conditioners etc., with high-price elasticities, which are usually items of elitist consumption, at low rates, is unacceptable.

Box 8.2:   Goods and Services Tax (GST)

In the budget speech of 2006–2007 the Finance Minister, Mr. P. Chidambaram has hinted at replacing the present commodity taxation in India with a nationwide goods and services tax by 2010. Perhaps this announcement was made on the basis of the recommendation of a goods and services tax made by the Kelkar task force on the implementation of VAT. The task force recommended replacement of the current local and central sales taxes, central excises and the service tax with a nationwide goods and services tax. This tax is envisaged as a VAT covering every stage of production up to the final consumer. This tax will apply to almost every good and service. The input credit method will be followed, i.e., every seller will assess her tax liability on the basis of her total gross output and then claim the taxes paid on both goods and services used as intermediate inputs as credit. The tax is also conceived, as Bagchi (2006) calls it, as dual VAT, where both the centre and the states participate. Both impose tax on the same base consisting of the value added of almost every good and service at every stage of production. The tax rate for most goods is pegged at 20% of which 16% will be imposed by the centre and 4% by the states. Let us illustrate with an example. Suppose that a farmer in West Bengal produced wheat worth Rs. 100, sold it to a flour miller, who in turn produces flour worth Rs. 300 using this wheat and sold it to a baker who produces with this flour breads worth Rs. 400 and sold them to consumers. Thus the farmer produced a value added of Rs. 100, the flour miller produced a value added of Rs. 200 and the baker produced a value added of Rs. 100. Under the tax recommended, both the central government and the Government of West Bengal will tax each of these value addeds, at the rates of 16%, and 4% respectively. The flour miller will assess her tax liability as Rs. 60 (Rs. 48 as the central tax liability and Rs. 12 as the tax liability of the state) and claim the tax of Rs. 20 (Rs. 16 to the central government and Rs. 4 to the state government) as tax credit. Therefore, she will pay Rs. 40 as tax, Rs. 32 to the centre and Rs. 8 to the state. Besides the rate of 20%, two other rates have been proposed, a floor rate of 6% of which 4% will be imposed by the states and a middle rate of 12% of which 8% will be imposed by the states.

Even though the proposed GST will make India's chaotic commodity tax structure orderly, it is not free from problems either. It has been pointed out by Bagchi (2006) that it will rob the states of their financial autonomy. This is so because under the proposed scheme every state will have to tax the commodities at a uniform agreed upon rate. Another major problem is that its implementation will require major constitutional amendment.

Since it is not possible for the government to follow the Ramsey rule or the inverse elasticity rule, the best it can do is that it can go in for a general sales tax implemented through a countrywide VAT imposed on all goods and services at a uniform rate. However, exceptions need be made for the merit and the demerit goods. The former should be taxed at above average rates and the latter at below average rates to bring about efficient allocation of resources. The uniformity of tax rates for most goods will make the tax structure simple and transparent. Multiplicity of tax rates leads to controversies and thereby makes tax collection extremely costly. To give a simple example (see Mukherjee (2002)), a coconut seller claimed that coconut is a vegetable since vegetables are exempted from sales taxes and asked for tax exemption on his sales. The legal dispute that broke out went up to the Supreme Court. Even there all the judges could not come to an agreement. For this reason uniformity in tax rates is called for with the exception of a few significant merit and demerit goods.

SUMMARY

1. Sales taxes may be selective or general. The former applies to one or a few goods. The latter applies to all goods at the same rate. Efficient allocation of resources calls for selective sales taxes on goods that generate negative externalities and demerit goods. General sales taxes are warranted when it is difficult to bring the whole of the national income adequately under the income tax net. In case of developing countries like India quite a large part of the national income originates in the informal sector. It is extremely costly to tax such incomes through the income tax as number of income earners is very large and there is no regular system of accounting. Hence the government has to resort to general sales taxes as a source of revenue.

2. Sales taxes may be unit or ad valorem depending upon how the rates are specified. Unit sales taxes specify the tax rate as an absolute amount of money to be paid as sales tax per unit of sales. Ad valorem sales taxes on the other hand specify the tax rate as a given percentage of the total value of sales. Ad valorem sales taxes have the following advantage over unit sales taxes. If a general sales tax applies to all goods and services including leisure at a given ad valorem rate, it will not create any price distortions and, therefore, excess burden. But a general sales tax applicable to the same base as the above at a given unit rate will distort prices and thereby generate excess burden.

3. The base of a general sales tax may be all transactions. This kind of sales tax is referred to as the turnover tax. The base of such a sales tax is much larger than GDP. Hence a low-tax rate may yield quite a large amount of tax revenue. This makes such a tax attractive to the politicians. However, a turnover tax gives rise to many problems. Taxes paid on intermediate inputs get included in the value of output and thereby become a part of the tax base of the producer. This phenomenon is referred to as pyramiding of taxes or cascading effect. This makes the tax base of producers higher-up in the production structure larger than those of the producers lower down the production structure. Tax burden of this tax on the seller of a commodity also varies directly with the number of stages that the production of the commodity involves. It, therefore, induces sellers to integrate vertically to reduce tax burden. This tends to reduce competition. A turnover tax also distorts prices and thereby generates inefficiency when final goods do not involve equal number of stages of production.

4. Besides all transactions, general sales taxes may have three other bases, viz., GDP, national income and consumption. Consumption-type general sales tax is the most popular of the three. A sales tax may be implemented as a single-stage or as a multistage VAT. The choice between the two is a matter of administrative convenience as both have the same kind of economic impact. A single-stage sales tax may be applied to the retailers,

wholesalers or manufacturers. However, it is usually applied at the retail level. Otherwise, a part of the GDP consisting of the value added originating at the retail level and at the level of the wholesalers, if the tax is levied on the manufacturers, remains outside the tax net. However, in developing countries like India, number of retailers is very large relative to wholesalers and manufactures. Hence for administrative reasons sales taxes may be levied on the wholesalers or the manufacturers.

5. VAT may be GDP-type, income-type or consumption-type. GDP-type VAT applies to the gross value added of every firm. Income-type VAT applies to the net value added of every firm. Consumption-type VAT applies to gross value added of every firm net of its investment expenditure. Methods of collection of VAT revenue may also be different. Under one method each firm is asked to furnish information on its tax base, gross value added or net value added or gross value added net of its investment expenditure as the case may be and assess its tax liability on the basis of its tax base and the tax rate specified in the tax statute and pay the tax. Under another method, called the input credit method, each firm assesses its tax liability on the basis of its gross sales or net sales or gross sales net of its investment expenditure as the case may be and claim the tax paid by its suppliers of intermediate inputs as credit. The advantage of this method is that it has a built in check against tax evasion, as each firm has to furnish proof of the amount of tax paid by its intermediate input suppliers to claim the tax credit. For this reason this method has been adopted in Europe and India.

6. Burden of selective sales taxes on luxuries is progressively distributed, while burden of selective sales taxes on necessities is regressively distributed. Through a consumption-type general sales tax, consumption expenditure is taxed at a given rate. Such a tax ensures horizontal equity as every individual having the same lifetime income pays the same amount of tax over her lifetime. However, such a tax may not ensure vertical equity even though it makes people having larger amounts of lifetime income pay larger amounts of tax over their lifetimes.

7. In India both the central government and the state governments levy sales taxes. Sales taxes imposed by the state governments and the central government are called local sales taxes (LSTs) and central sales taxes (CSTs) respectively. The former apply to intrastate sales, while the latter applies to interstate sales. State governments fix the rates of LSTs independently and these rates vary across states and also across goods within every state. Both LSTs and CSTs are levied on almost every good, both final and intermediate. Hence they lead to pyramiding of taxes or cascading effect. Such a tax, just like the turnover tax, is inequitable and inefficient. Hence most of the states to the exception of Uttar Pradesh, Tamil Nadu and the union territory of Pondicherry replaced their taxes with VAT in April 2005.

8. Besides CST and LST, there are central and state excises. Excises are duties on manufactures and are levied on the manufacturers. Central excises apply to almost every manufactured good. State excises apply only to the manufactures of alcohol. Central excises are administered as VAT and are called CENVAT.

9. Sales taxes in India apply only to goods and not to services. Only the central government has the power to levy taxes on services. Until 1994 services were outside the indirect tax

net. Only a few services were brought under the tax net in July 1994. Since then successive budgets have continuously widened the service tax net to include more and more services. At the present service tax is implemented as VAT and the revenue is collected through the input credit method. Initially, a service provider could claim credit only for the services used as intermediate inputs. Now the credit has been extended also to goods. Similarly, under CENVAT tax credit was initially allowed for only goods used as intermediate inputs. Now the tax credit has been extended to services used as intermediate inputs as well.

10. There are a number of problems with India's sales tax structure. It is still highly complex. Rates differ across goods and states. Rates of LSTs on intrastate sales differ from those of CSTs on interstate sales and these divergences give rise to disputes. Separate taxation of goods and services is also not warranted. Though majority of the states have implemented VAT, a few are yet to adopt it. State VATs do not cover services either. The procedure of claiming CENVAT credit under service tax is still highly complex. Efforts are, however, on to remove these problems and bring all the different taxes under one common VAT to be called the Goods and Services Tax (GST). The Finance Minister has planned to implement GST by 2010.

KEY CONCEPTS

✓ General sales tax
✓ Unit sales tax
✓ Turnover tax
✓ Multiple stage sales tax
✓ Central sales tax (CST)
✓ Central excise duty
✓ CENVAT
✓ Goods and service tax (GST)
✓ Octroi
✓ Selective sales tax

✓ Ad valorem sales tax
✓ Single-stage sales tax
✓ Value added tax (VAT): GDP-type
✓ NI-type and consumption-type
✓ Input credit method
✓ Local sales tax (LST)
✓ State excise duty
✓ Service tax
✓ Stamp duty

REVIEW QUESTIONS

1. Distinguish between general sales tax and selective sales tax.
2. What are the justifications of imposing selective sales taxes?
3. Is it justified to impose general sales tax in addition to income taxes?
4. Distinguish between unit and ad valorem sales taxes. Is there any reason to prefer one to the other?
5. Define a turnover tax.
6. Explain why turnover taxes are inequitable and inefficient.
7. Why does the burden of a turnover tax vary directly with the number of stages of production the commodity involves?

8. Why is the tax burden of a turnover tax higher-up in the production structure greater?

9. Besides all transactions, what are the other bases of a general sales tax?

10. What are the reasons to prefer a consumption-type general sales tax?

11. Explain why the choice between a single-stage sales tax and a multistage sales tax is a matter of administrative convenience.

12. At what level should a single-stage tax be imposed?

13. What is VAT? What are the different types of VAT?

14. What are the different methods of collection of VAT revenue?

15. Is there any reason to prefer the input credit method of collection of the VAT revenue?

16. Define intrastate and interstate sales in the context of the Indian economy. To what kinds of sales do CSTs and LSTs apply?

17. What problems do the CSTs and LSTs give rise to? How can they be resolved?

18. Do central and state excises apply to manufactures?

19. What is CENVAT?

20. What problems multiplicity of tax rates give rise to?

21. What is service tax?

22. Why was service tax not introduced in India before 1994?

23. Why is India's commodity tax structure being replaced with VAT?

24. What is goods and services tax? Why is it being implemented in India?

═══════ PROBLEMS AND APPLICATIONS ═══════

1. Consider an economy where all the individuals are identical in every respect and taxation of leisure or lump sum tax is not available as an option. What kind of commodity tax structure will you recommend for this kind of economy? Will you recommend the same kind of commodity tax structure for an economy like India where income distribution is highly skewed?

   (*Hint:* Inverse elasticity rule or Ramsey rule may be applied to design the optimal commodity structure. However, such a rule recommends higher rates of taxes on necessities and lower rates of taxes on luxuries. This is surely highly iniquitous in the context of countries like India.)

2. Consider the example of the farmer, miller and baker given in the text. Suppose that a turnover tax is in place. What should its rate be to yield tax revenue of Rs. 50? How much tax is paid by each of these producers? Is there anything wrong with this pattern of tax distribution? Suppose this turnover tax is replaced with VAT. What should the rate of the VAT be to yield the same tax revenue as the turnover tax? Is the difference in the requisite tax rates to generate a given amount of tax revenue a likely deterrent for replacing a turnover tax with VAT? Explain your answer.

3. Even when it is not possible to tax leisure, it may be advisable to tax commodities at uniform rates. Do you agree with this position? Explain your answer.

4. Consider the example of the farmer, miller and baker given in the text. Suppose that a turnover tax at a given rate is in place. Now suppose that the baker buys out the flour mill and the wheat farm and continue to produce the three commodities in the same quantities. What will happen to his tax burden? Does you answer suggest anything regarding the desirability of a turnover tax?

5. Books can now be digitized and mailed to buyers. Cell phones can be recharged over phones without purchase and sell of recharge coupons. What are the implications of this kind of technological advancement in a country where goods are taxed, but services are not? Can you think of any reason why goods and services instead of being covered by the same sales tax or VAT need be taxed separately as is done in India?

6. Suppose that the supply of labour does not respond to changes in the wage rate. Will commodity taxation at a uniform rate generate excess burden in such a situation?

    (*Hint:* It will not, because it will not distort people's choice between income and leisure.)

7. A general sales tax is regarded as regressive since it is a tax on expenditure and consumption expenditure of the people rises less than proportionately with respect to income. However, this is true in the short run only. If you take a long run view a general sales tax will ensure horizontal equity and make the richer people pay more. Do you agree with this view? Explain.

    (*Hint:* If a general sales tax is imposed at the rate t, consumption expenditure of everyone is taxed at the rate t also. Show that under such a tax people with the same amount of lifetime income will pay the same amount of tax over their lifetime.)

8. Cigarettes, alcohol etc. are necessities to those who are addicted to them. Still they are taxed at high rates in India. Do you support this policy? Explain your position.

REFERENCES

General:

Atkinson, A.B. and Stiglitz, J.E. (1980): *Lectures on Public Economics*, McGraw-Hill, New York.

Bagchi, A. (2006): Towards GST: Choices and trade-offs, *Economic and Political Weekly*, April 8.

Minarik, J.J. (Ed.)(1979): *What to Tax: Income or Expenditure?* Brookings, Washington.

Mukhopadhyay, S. (2004): Taxation and constitution, *Economic and Political Weekly*, August 14.

For value added tax:

Shoup, C.S. (1969): *Public Finance*, Aldin, Chicago.

and their sustainability. Section 9.3 deals with different issues in public debt. Section 9.4 addresses the issue of long run sustainability of public debt. Section 9.5 extracts this issue of sustainability of public debt in Indian context. Section 9.6 analyses the roles of taxation and borrowing in financing public expenditure. Section 9.7 compares internal and external borrowing and the final section concludes.

9.2 DIFFERENT CONCEPTS OF DEFICIT IN GOVERNMENT'S BUDGET

9.1 INTRODUCTION

There are two methods of financing public expenditure besides money creation: taxation and borrowing. Here we focus on the latter. Borrowing may be internal or external. Internal borrowing refers to borrowing from private domestic economic agents. There are two important questions relating to it, namely, whether it imposes any burden on the community and, if it does, then on whom the burden falls. External borrowing on the other hand means borrowing from foreigners. The major question that emerges in this context is why the government chooses to borrow from external sources instead of domestic economic agents. Another question that intrigues people is why should the government borrow at all to finance its expenditure instead of resorting only to taxation. Finally, the question that has gained considerable importance in recent years is that of sustainability of public debt in the long run. All these issues are discussed at length in this chapter. It is arranged as follows. Since government resorts to borrowing to finance its deficit, Section 9.2 discusses different concepts of deficit in the government's budget and their significance. Section 9.3 deals with the burden of internal public debt. Section 9.4 addresses the issue of long run sustainability of public debt. Section 9.5 examines the issue of sustainability of public debt in Indian context. Section 9.6 assesses the roles of taxation and borrowing in financing public expenditure. Section 9.7 compares internal and external borrowing and the final section concludes.

9.2 DIFFERENT CONCEPTS OF DEFICIT IN GOVERNMENT'S BUDGET

Public debt is due to government borrowing and government borrows to meet its fiscal deficit. Hence before beginning the discussion on public debt, it is advisable to explain the concept of fiscal deficit in detail. Government's budget in India has two accounts, revenue account and capital account. Government's expenditures and receipts of any given year are recorded in the government's budget of the given year. Total expenditure of the government consists of both revenue expenditure and capital expenditure. *Revenue expenditures refer to those expenditures, which do not directly affect future incomes of the government.* These expenditures are recorded in the revenue account of the government's budget and consist of public consumption, subsidy, interest payment on public debt and transfer payments. *Capital expenditures on the other hand refer to those expenditures of the government, which affect directly the future income of the government.* They comprise of the investment expenditures (of PSUs) of the government. These items of expenditure are recorded in the capital account of the government's budget. Similarly, government's income consists of revenue receipts and capital receipts. *Revenue receipts refer to those receipts that do not directly affect future incomes or expenditures of the government.* These receipts are recorded in the revenue account of the government's budget. *Capital receipts on the other hand are those receipts that directly affect future incomes or expenditures of the government.* These receipts are recorded in the capital account of the government's budget. Revenue receipts consist of tax and non-tax income (comprising of fees charged on various public services provided by the government administration and defence) and PSU profit. Capital receipts are made up of receipts from the sale of shares of PSUs and physical assets, proceeds from recovery of past loans and also loans taken by the government.

The excess of government's revenue expenditure over its revenue receipts is called the revenue deficit of the government. In Box 9.1, we have shown how persistent revenue deficit can, a la Krugman (1979), lead to severe balance of payments crisis. The excess of government's total expenditure (comprising of both revenue and capital expenditure) over its total revenue receipts and non-debt creating capital receipts consisting of proceeds from sales of shares of PSUs and physical assets, and recovery of past loans is called the fiscal deficit of the government. Fiscal deficit is a measure of the increase in government's indebtedness. If we subtract from fiscal deficit interest charges on outstanding public debt, we get primary deficit of the government. Since interest paid by the government is due to deficits created in the past, i.e., due to activities carried out in the past by the government, primary deficit measures the deficit that arises out of current activities of the government. (For a discussion of the concept of fiscal deficit in Indian context, see Chelliah (2005).)

Box 9.1: Revenue Deficit and Balance of Payments Crisis

Krugman (1979) shows how revenue deficit of the government makes a country in a fixed exchange rate regime crisis-prone. We present his argument briefly below. He considers an open economy where the central bank pursues a fixed exchange rate policy. Wages and prices are perfectly flexible so that there is full employment in every period. Private saving, denoted S, is an increasing function of income, Y, and a decreasing function of wealth, W. Of the two the former is given at the full employment level. S is a decreasing function of wealth and this implies that consumption is an increasing function of W, since Y is given. Thus

$$\dot{W} = S = S(Y, W), \text{ where } \dot{W} \equiv dW/d\tau, \ \tau \equiv \text{time .and } (dS/dW) < 0 \qquad \text{(B.9.1)}$$

Since Y is given at its full employment level, we can derive from (B.9.1) the value of W that makes S or $\dot{W}$ zero. We denote this value of W by W_0.

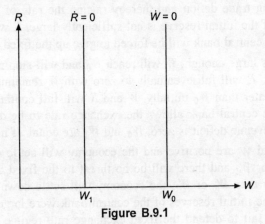

Figure B.9.1

Ignoring investment for simplicity, we can write the goods market equilibrium condition as

$$\Big/ \ Y = C + G + X - M$$
$$\Rightarrow \qquad (Y - T - C) - (G - T) = X - M$$
$$\Rightarrow \qquad S(Y, W) - (G - T) = X - M \qquad \text{(B.9.2)}$$

Here S is taken as a function of Y because T (and also G) are assumed to be given. From the above equation it follows that, if government's revenue deficit, $(G - T)$, exceeds private saving, there is trade deficit, i.e., demand for foreign exchange is larger than its supply and the central bank has to sell foreign exchange from its reserves to keep the exchange rate stable. Denoting reserves of foreign exchange held by the central bank by R, we have

$$\dot{R} = S(Y, W) - (G - T) \qquad \text{(B.9.3)}$$

(Contd.)...

(Contd.)...

The value of revenue deficit is given by assumption in this model. Given the value of revenue deficit, there is a unique value of W that makes $\dot{R}$ zero. Let us denote this value of W by W_1. Now W_1 is less than W_0, if revenue deficit is positive. If revenue deficit is zero, the two are equal. The sets of combinations of R and W that make $\dot{W}$ and $\dot{R}$ zero are shown in the (W, R) plane by the two vertical lines in Figure B.9.1. We shall now explain why persistent revenue deficit makes the economy crisis-prone with the help of Figure B.9.1. For W less than W_1 both $\dot{R}$ and $\dot{W}$ are positive. For $W_1 < W < W_0$, $\dot{R} < 0$, but $\dot{W} > 0$. However, for $W > W_0$, both $\dot{R} < 0$ and $\dot{W} < 0$. Now the initial value of W of the economy can be anywhere. Suppose it is less than W_1. In this case R and W will both be rising. Once W is equal to W_1, S equals the given amount of revenue deficit. Hence trade deficit becomes zero and so does $\dot{R}$. At W_1, however, $\dot{W}$ is positive. Hence W will rise from W_1 widening trade deficit and thereby raising the rate of depletion of reserves of the central bank. If the initial reserve is not sufficiently large, R will fall to zero before W rises to W_0 and the central bank will be forced to give up the fixed exchange rate policy.

If the initial reserve is large enough, W will reach W_0 and will stop rising. $\dot{R}$ is, however, negative at W_0 and so R will fall eventually to zero with W remaining unchanged at W_0. Similarly, if W is greater than W_0 initially, W and R will fall continuously until reserves get exhausted and the central bank allows the exchange rate to be determined by market forces. However, if revenue deficit is zero, W_0 and W_1 are equal. If initially W is less than this value, both $\dot{R}$ and $\dot{W}$ are positive and the economy will settle down to steady state with W equal to W_0 or W_1 and there will be no threat to the fixed exchange rate policy. If initially W is larger than W_0 or W_1, the economy will settle down to steady state with W_0 or W_1, provided the initial reserves of the central bank were large enough. Otherwise, the central bank will fail to defend the fixed exchange rate regime. Thus in the face of persistent revenue deficit, the central bank will fail to maintain a fixed exchange rate.

9.3 BURDEN OF INTERNAL PUBLIC DEBT

In purely accounting sense internally held public debt, i.e., loans raised by the government from domestic economic agents, constitutes a government liability, which is matched by an asset of equal value of the private sector. Loans given to the government are income-yielding or interest-bearing financial assets of the lenders to the government. Thus, when the private sector extends a loan to the government, the latter acquires a financial liability, while the former acquires a financial asset of equal value, which represents a claim on the future incomes of the government. Therefore, if we consider the economy as a whole, which consists of both the private sector and the government or the public sector, internal public debt does not represent a burden at all. The asset of the private sector just cancels out the liability of the public sector. For the economy as a whole internal public debt is neither an asset nor a liability. It is a debt, which we owe to ourselves. This should be clear from the simplified asset–liability accounts of the government and the private sector represented below, which have been drawn up under the assumption that there is no external borrowing or lending. The government sector consists of the government administration and defence, the central bank and the public sector enterprises.

In the asset–liability account of the government (Table 9.1), its liabilities consist of the stock of high-powered money, denoted by H, and the total net outstanding internal loans (i.e., internal loans taken from net of loans given to domestic economic agents), denoted by L_G. The assets on the other hand consist of its total stock of physical assets, K_G. Obviously, values of the assets and liabilities are unlikely to match as part of the assets may be acquired with tax or other receipts of the government and/or the loans and the high-powered money may at least partly be used to finance subsidy or transfer payments or payments of wages and salaries and interest in government administration and defence. Hence B_G is a balancing item. Table 9.2 repreents the asset-liability account of the private sector. In the absence of external borrowing and lending, which we ignore for simplicity, assets of the private sector include the stock of physical assets it owns, K_P, the stock of high-powered money, H, issued by the central bank and the government and, therefore, held by the private sector and the net amount of loans it has extended to the government, L_G. The private sector here is a net lender to the government and hence does not have any liabilities. B_P is just a balancing item. It is clear from the balance sheets of the government and the private sector that the liabilities of the government are exactly matched by the financial assets of the private sector and hence in the consolidated account for the economy as a whole, represented in Table 9.3, these liabilities and assets cancel out each other. The economy as a whole has only assets consisting of the stocks of physical assets of the government and the private sector. B is just a balancing item.

Table 9.1: Asset–liability account of the public or the government sector

Liability	Assets
H	K_G
L_G	B_G

Table 9.2: Asset–liability account of the private sector

Liability	Assets
B_P	K_P
	H
	L_G

Table 9.3: Asset–liability account of the economy as a whole

Liability	Assets
B	$K = K_P + K_G$

Servicing of public debt, i.e., repayment of and interest payment on public debt, is made with tax proceeds. These payments also do not affect the income of the private sector as a whole. *What is collected as taxes to service public debt is paid back as interest on and repayment of public debt. Hence aggregate income of the private sector remains unaffected. Thus, it seems that even servicing of public debt does not impose any burden on the private sector.* The view presented above was propagated by Lerner (1948) and was widely held in the 40s. However, there is a consensus today that internal public debt, despite the above observations, burdens the private sector in many different ways. These are presented below.

The first and the major point that follows from the above is that at the time government borrowing takes place, private sector gives away a part of its wealth as loan to the government. However, the government services this debt only by taxing the private sector so that private sector's income remains unchanged. Thus, in return for the loan the private sector, when we consider it as a whole, does not get anything. Obviously, therefore, public borrowing imposes a burden on the private sector. Let us now identify exactly what the private sector loses, as it gives a loan to the government. Suppose that the government uses the loan to finance its expenditure. If that is the case, then we shall show below that the private sector will have to make do with lower levels of investment and consumption. In other words, *government borrowing from domestic economic agents to finance an increase in government consumption (G) burdens the private sector by crowding out private investment and consumption.*

This proposition can be established using the IS–LM model, given by the following equations:

$$Y = C(Y - T) + I(i) + G \tag{9.1}$$

$$\frac{\bar{M}}{P} = L(i, Y) \tag{9.2}$$

Notations in the above equations have their usual meanings. Let us establish the first proposition with the help of Figure 9.1 where real GDP, denoted by Y, is measured along the horizontal axis, while the nominal interest rate, denoted by i, is measured along the vertical axis. The *IS* and *LM* schedules are plotted in the first quadrant of Figure 9.1. IS_0 and LM_0 represent the initial *IS* and *LM* schedules. The initial equilibrium, therefore, corresponds to the point of intersection of IS_0 and LM_0, with the equilibrium value of Y equal to Y_0. In the second quadrant positive values of investment are measured along the horizontal axis in the leftward direction and the *II* schedule represents the investment function. In the fourth quadrant on the other hand positive values of consumption are measured in the downward direction along the vertical axis and the *CC* schedule represents the consumption function. Following an increase in *G* financed with internal borrowing, the *IS* shifts to the right, while *LM* remains unaffected. Hence the equilibrium values of both Y and i go up. Accordingly, equilibrium level of investment falls from I_0 to I_1. Less investment means smaller capital stock and, therefore, lower level of potential output in the future period. Thus, public borrowing to finance public consumption burdens the private sector by lowering future capital stock and thereby future level of potential output. If consumption were a function of interest rate, it could have gone down too, despite being an increasing function of income, if it were sufficiently highly sensitive to interest rate.

However, following qualifications to the above proposition must be noted. First, investment may be an increasing function of Y as well. An increase in Y brings about a higher rate of utilization of capacity and, therefore, a higher profit rate. This might induce producers to undertake larger investment. In this scenario the *II* schedule will shift to the left with the rise in Y. The new equilibrium II schedule, which corresponds to the new equilibrium value of Y, Y_1, is labelled II'. Since the II schedule shifts to the left with the increase in Y, investment in the new equilibrium may be larger, as shown in the figure, despite the rise in the interest rate. Thus a loan-financed increase in G may exert a crowding-in effect on private investment along with the crowding-out effect and the former may be stronger than the latter. Given the possibility that investment may be an increasing function of Y, loan-financed increase in government consumption will necessarily crowd out private investment if and only if the economy operates with the full employment level of output.

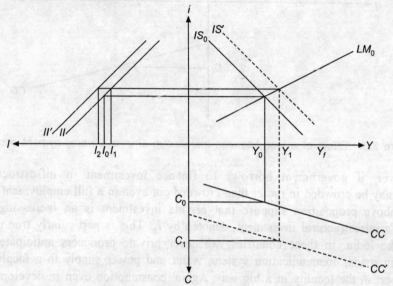

Figure 9.1: Effect of a loan-financed increase in G in a demand deficient economy.

In this situation the economy is in equilibrium with the full employment level of output, Y_f. The IS and LM in this case are represented by IS_f and LM_0 respectively in Figure 9.2. Following the increase in G financed with internal borrowing, the IS shifts rightward and the new IS is labelled IS_{f1}. The LM remains unaffected. Thus an excess demand for goods and services is created at the initial equilibrium (Y, i). Here it is not possible for the producers to expand Y any further. Hence dissatisfied buyers will start bidding up the prices. With the rise in P the LM schedule will start shifting leftward and eventually the equilibrium will occur when the LM intersects the new IS, IS_{f1}, at Y_f. In this case investment falls by the whole amount of the increase in G. Thus, when the economy operates with the full employment level of output, a loan-financed increase in government consumption crowds out private investment and thereby burdens the private sector unambiguously. If consumption were a function of interest rate, consumption would have fallen too and the increase in G would have been accommodated through a decline in both private investment and consumption. Note in this connection that to the extent an increase in public expenditure is accommodated through a reduction in consumption, future capital stock stays unchanged and, therefore, the burden of the loan-financed increase in government expenditure remains confined to the present generation.

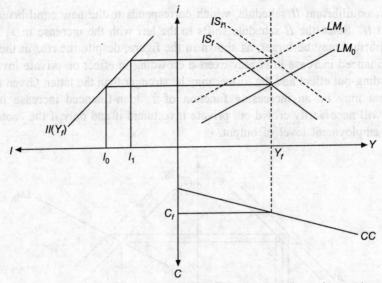

Figure 9.2: Effect of a loan-financed increase in G in a full employment economy.

However, if government borrows to finance investment in infrastructure, private investment may be crowded in rather than crowded out even in a full employment economy. To prove the above proposition suppose that private investment is an increasing function of government's infrastructural investment, denoted by I_g. This is particularly true in developing countries like India. In these countries, whenever private producers anticipate government investment in roads, communication system, water and power supply in a locality, they also begin to invest in the locality in a big way. Again, consumption even in developing countries like India is a decreasing function of interest rates, as loans for financing consumption particularly of durable consumption goods are readily available to a large section of consumers. Incorporating these assumptions, we rewrite (9.1) and (9.2) as

$$Y = C(Y - T, i) + I(i, I_g) + G + I_g \qquad (9.3)$$

$$\frac{\bar{M}}{P} = L(i, Y) \qquad (9.4)$$

Note that here, as before, $I(.)$ represents private investment function. The equilibrium yielded by (9.3) and (9.4) is shown in Figure 9.3 where the initial IS and LM labelled IS_f and LM_o intersect at Y_f. Following the loan-financed increase in I_g from, say, I_g^0 to I_g^1, the private investment function labelled $II(Y_f, I_g^0)$ shifts to the left to $II(Y_f, I_g^1)$ and the IS, accordingly, shifts to the right to IS_{f1}. Excess demand for goods and services emerges at the initial equilibrium (Y, i). Since producers cannot raise output, the price level rises shifting the LM to the left. New equilibrium is restored when price rises to such an extent that the LM cuts the new IS, IS_{f1}, at Y_f. If responsiveness of private investment to public investment is sufficiently high relative to the interest elasticity of private investment, in the new equilibrium private investment, as shown in Figure 9.3, will be larger. The rise in i lowers consumption by the same amount as the rise in aggregate investment.

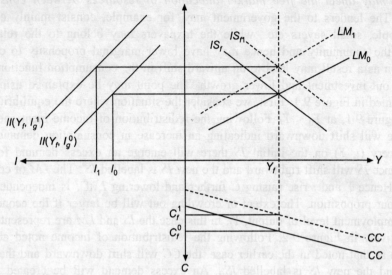

Figure 9.3: Effect of a loan-financed increase in public investment in a full employment economy.

We may summarize the results derived above as follows. *A loan-financed increase in government consumption necessarily crowds out private investment in a full employment economy lowering future levels of capital stock and output and thereby burdening the private sector. It may crowd out consumption also, if consumption is a function of interest rate. However, this crowding out of private investment may not occur in a full employment economy if the government borrows to finance infrastructural investment. In this case only consumption may be crowded out. The crowding out of private investment and also private consumption may not occur in a demand deficient economy operating with less than full employment level of output even when government borrows to finance its consumption.*

Besides the point noted above, government borrowing may impose many other kinds of burdens on the economy. Taxes that are raised to service public debt redistribute income from the taxpayers to the lenders to the government. This may be socially undesirable and, therefore, may reduce social welfare. We shall dwell on this issue further later.

We have also seen in Chapter 4 on tax efficiency that both direct and indirect taxes, which are not a lump sum, are distortionary and hence involve excess burden. These taxes make the prices faced by buyers and sellers different in some or all markets and thereby saddle the economy with deadweight losses. Hence, *if the government raises direct and indirect tax rates to service public debt, the gap between the prices faced by buyers and sellers will widen raising the amount of deadweight loss or excess burden.* (Using the formula that measures excess burden in a market, compute the increase in excess burden following an increase in the tax rate applied to the purchase or sale of the given good.)

In addition to the points noted above, *servicing of public debt may produce some macroeconomic effects. The redistribution of income from the taxpayers to the lenders to the government may affect the free market allocation of resources between consumption and investment.* The lenders to the government may, for example, consist mainly of pensioners, salaried people, small savers etc., while the taxpayers may belong to the relatively richer sections of the community and hence may have lower marginal propensity to consume. The redistribution as a result may lead to an upward shift in the consumption function and thereby may crowd out investment and lower growth. The point may be explained using the *IS–LM* model presented in Figure 9.1. First, we consider the situation where the equilibrium occurs, as shown in Figure 9.1, at $Y_0 < Y_f$. Following the redistribution of income mentioned above, the *CC* schedule will shift downward indicating an increase in consumption demand at every Y. Hence at every (i, Y) on the initial *IS* there will emerge an excess demand for goods and services. Hence *IS* will shift rightward and the new *IS* is labelled *IS'*. The *LM* of course remains unaffected. Hence Y and i rise raising C further and lowering I, if I is independent of Y. This establishes our proposition. The extent of crowding out will be larger if the economy operates at the full employment level of output, Y_f. In this case the *IS* and *LM* are represented by IS_f and LM_0 respectively in Figure 9.2. Following the redistribution of income noted above, for the same reason as that noted in the earlier case, the *CC* will shift downward and the *IS* will shift rightward and the new *IS* is labelled IS_{f1}. An excess demand will be created at the initial equilibrium (Y, i). Here it is not possible for the producers to expand Y any further. Hence dissatisfied buyers will start bidding up the prices. With the rise in P the *LM* schedule will start shifting leftward and eventually the equilibrium is achieved when the *LM* intersects the new *IS*, IS_{f1}, at Y_f. In this case investment will definitely fall. The extent of crowding out of investment is larger than that in the earlier case because in the earlier case a part of the initial increase in consumption demand is accommodated through a rise in Y. Hence the amount of investment crowded out through the increase in the interest rate is less. (Prove this point in greater detail yourself.) In the earlier case crowding out may not occur at all if investment is an increasing function of Y.

Again, the *larger the amount of public debt, given the tax rate, as a proportion of GDP, the greater is the proportion of tax proceeds spent in servicing public debt and the higher is the disposable income relative to GDP since interest payment on public debt is transfer income.* Let us explain the above proposition. The disposable income is given by $[PY + iL - tPY]$, where L, i, t and P denote the nominal value of the outstanding public debt, nominal interest rate, tax rate net of the ratio of transfers to GDP and price level respectively. Hence nominal disposable income as a proportion of nominal GDP becomes $[1 - t + ib]$, where $b \equiv (L/PY)$. Note that $[1 - t + ib]$ also gives the ratio of real disposable income, $([PY + iL - tPY]/P)$, to real GDP, $[(PY)/P]$. Therefore, the consumption function may be written as $C((1 - t + ib)Y)$ where $(1 - t + ib)Y$ is the real disposable income. Therefore, if b rises, given t, ratio of disposable income to GDP goes up raising consumption demand at every Y. This will also, as in the earlier case, crowd out investment and thereby lower growth rate. (Consumption is an increasing function not only of disposable income, but also of wealth. Since lenders to the government normally regard public debt as a part of their net wealth, the rise in b, which means an increase in wealth corresponding to every given Y, will raise consumption demand corresponding to every Y and thereby lower growth rate through the wealth effect also.) (Prove all these points rigorously using the *IS–LM* model yourself.) (For the impact of a loan-financed increase in government expenditure see Yellen (1989), Anand and Winbergen (1989), Rakshit (2000) and Buiter (1988).)

9.3.1 Burden of Internal Public Debt and Future Generations

Future generations refer to the generations who were not born or were too young to earn and lend to the government at the time government borrowing took place. Government borrowing burdens future generations in the following ways. First, as we have pointed out above, government borrowing may reduce private investment and thereby lower future capital stock and potential output. Hence future generations may have smaller levels of goods and services for use. Second, public debt is serviced by taxing people. A part of the tax imposed by the government for servicing its debt may fall on future generations transferring income from the future generations to the generation who lent to the government.

9.3.2 Ricardian Equivalence

Results derived above constitute the mainstream view regarding the burden of public debt. However, there is an important different view in this regard. It is known as *Ricardian equivalence. It states that loan-financed government expenditure and tax-financed government expenditure are equivalent in the sense that they have the same impact on macro-variables.* This proposition was made by Barro (1974, 1989). Barro assumes that individuals are altruistic towards their descendants (which include not only their own children but also their grand children, children of their grand children and so on) so much so that to them their descendants' consumption is as important as their own. Extending the life cycle and permanent income hypothesis of consumption, Barro assumes that an individual's consumption depends not only on the present value of her own lifetime disposable income but also on the present value of the lifetime disposable income of her family, which is infinitely lived. Extending the case of an individual to that of the government, Barro further assumes that just like an individual a government cannot go on borrowing indefinitely. It has to just like an individual pay off all its debts from its income within its lifetime, which is of course infinitely long. This means that, if the government borrows in the current period, then, given its expenditures, it has to raise taxes at some point of time in the future to service this debt. This implies that the present value in the current period of these additional future taxes imposed by the government to service the debt should equal the amount of borrowing. Let us illustrate this point with an example. Suppose that the government borrows an amount A in period zero at the rate of interest, i. In period 1 it pays off the debt along with interest by taking fresh loans. The amount of loan it has to take in period 1 for this purpose is $[A(1 + i)]$. In period 2 also the government does the same thing and, therefore, borrows $[A(1 + i)^2]$, assuming interest rate to remain the same for simplicity. Borrowing to service past debt is called Ponzi game. Barro assumes that a government cannot go on playing this Ponzi game forever. Hence, given its expenditures, at some point of time it has to raise its taxes to pay off its debts. Suppose that the government does this in period τ. Additional taxes the government collects in period τ is, therefore, $A(1 + i)^\tau$. Its present value in period zero is the amount of borrowing, A. Finally, Barro assumes that all families are identical in every respect. From the above assumptions it follows that, if the government lowers taxes in the current period keeping its expenditure unchanged and finances the deficit by borrowing, it will impose additional taxes in future to service this debt and the present value of these additional taxes in the current period will equal the amount of borrowing. Since all families are identical, both public debt and the additional taxes imposed to service it will be equally distributed among all the families. Hence the present value of lifetime disposable income of every family will remain unchanged despite this switching from tax to borrowing. Therefore, consumption expenditure of every family will remain unaffected. This implies that the IS and, therefore, equilibrium values of all the macro-variables will remain the same. Thus, if the government replaces taxes with borrowing or the reverse to finance its expenditure, all macro-variables will remain unchanged and no crowding out of private investment will take place. Under conditions of Ricardian equivalence the equation of the IS in period zero is given by

$$Y = C\left(\sum_{\tau=0}^{\infty} \frac{Y_\tau}{(1+r)^\tau} - \sum_{\tau=0}^{\infty} \frac{T_\tau}{(1+r)^\tau} \right) + I(i) + G$$

where $Y_\tau \equiv$ aggregate income in period τ and $T_\tau \equiv$ aggregate tax collection in period τ.
If tax in period zero is reduced and the resulting deficit is financed with borrowing, future taxes will go up so that the present value of the tax remains unchanged. Hence consumption demand and, therefore, the IS remain unaffected.

Empirical evidences carried out to test Ricardian equivalence do not support it—see in this context Gramlich (1989), Bernheim (1990), Haque and Montiel (1987). This is not surprising in view of the kind of unrealistic assumptions on the basis of which the equivalence proposition is derived. First, consider the assumption that all individuals and all families are identical. This is obviously a gross distortion of truth. More precisely, different individuals lend different amounts to the government and the tax burden is also unequally distributed among the people. Distribution of public debt and that of tax burden among individuals may vary widely, i.e., those who lend to the government may be largely different from those who pay taxes. For example, loans to the government may come mainly from the pensioners and small savers, while taxes may come mainly from the rich. Thus burden of future taxes imposed to service current borrowing may not fall on those who extend the loan in the current period. Moreover, individuals may not be as altruistic as assumed by Barro. They may not bother about what will happen thirty or forty years later. It is also extremely difficult to predict government's fiscal policies even in near future. Government can sustain deficits over long periods without any difficulty. Thus, despite borrowing, taxes may not rise for long periods of time. Debts can also be serviced by reducing public expenditure and money creation. For example, the government can retire its debts in times of recession by printing money without any cost to the society. Such a policy may in fact give a boost to both income and investment and also raise consumption. For all these reasons in the event of government borrowing, rational lenders to the government and also other members of the present generation can reasonably consider themselves better off relative to the situation where they pay the same amount as tax. For more on this line see Bernheim and Bagwell (1988). Hence, when taxes are replaced with borrowing, consumption expenditure is likely to rise and therefore the IS curve is likely to shift to the right exerting an expansionary impact on macro-variables.

9.4 PUBLIC DEBT: LONG RUN ISSUES

There are three approaches to the long run analysis of public debt: Domar approach, which examines the long run sustainability of public debt, solvency approach, which analyses the long run implications of public borrowing from the point of view of the solvency of the treasury and Ricardian equivalence. We shall discuss each of these approaches and compare them below.

9.4.1 Domar Approach

Before the Keynesian ideas gained currency, deficit in government's budget was considered bad and balanced budget was the norm. Following the publication of *The General Theory of Employment, Interest and Money* in 1936, Keynesian ideas came into dominance. Keynesians recommended budget deficit in times of recession and budget surplus in times of boom and inflation to stabilize the economy at the full employment level of output. Thus, Keynesians recommended more or less a cyclically-balanced budget, i.e., balanced budget over a cycle. However, in the post-war period there was a widespread belief that demand deficiency was the norm rather than a cyclical phenomenon in a mature capitalist economy. This belief was based on high propensities to save and low propensities to invest evinced in this type of economies. Hence it was felt that persistent budget deficit was needed to keep these economies at full employment levels of output. Persistent budget deficit was viewed as the sole instrument for stabilization because monetary policy was found to be largely ineffective owing to high-interest elasticity of money demand and low interest sensitivity of aggregate demand for goods and services. In this backdrop, Domar (1944) examined whether persistent budget deficit was sustainable. Keynesian consensus, encapsulated above, collapsed since the seventies. The belief today is that forces operating through the price system keep market economies close to the natural rate of output and deviations of output from its natural rate due to shifts in demand are transient phenomena. However, Domar enquiry remains relevant even today for two reasons. First, despite changes in beliefs, many governments the world over are plagued with persistent large fiscal deficits. Second, long recessions in Japan in the early nineties and in India since 1997 signal, a la Krugman (1999), return of depression economics. In both the countries attempts at reviving the economies led to large fiscal deficits.

Persistent fiscal deficit and the consequent growth in public debt may become unsustainable in the long run. It becomes unsustainable when interest charges on public debt as a proportion of GDP go on rising over time. If interest charges on public debt as a proportion of GDP keep on increasing over time, then eventually they will exhaust the entire taxable capacity of the economy and beyond that point the government will be unable to raise additional taxes to meet its interest obligations. As a result public borrowing will become unsustainable. The government will be forced to suspend its borrowing programme. In fact, government borrowing will become unsustainable much before the above-mentioned point is reached since the increase in interest charges as a proportion of GDP will start crowding out many kinds of public expenditures, which are absolutely essential for the smooth running of the economy. Of course the government can finance its debt obligations by creating money or by additional borrowing, but that, as we have already pointed out, will generate income in the hands of the people in addition to GDP and thereby, as we have explained above, may lead to crowding out of private investment even when the economy operates with less than full employment level of output. If the economy operates at the full employment level of output, creation of interest income in addition to GDP will exert upward pressure on prices generating inflation and, as we have already explained, may crowd out private investment fully. Formally, an increase in (ib) financed by money creation or borrowing will raise disposable income, $(1 - t + ib)Y$, corresponding to any given Y, and thereby produce the kind of impact on the consumption function and IS as explained earlier. The increase in money supply that occurs when the increase in (ib) is financed by money creation on the other hand will shift the LM to the right. If the debt–GDP ratio, b, is sufficiently large, the equilibrium Y will be at or quite close to the full employment level of output. (Explain this point.) In this situation, if the government resorts to creation of money or borrowing from the public to finance interest charges, it will make the IS intersect the LM beyond the potential or full employment level of Y generating, as we have pointed out earlier, strong inflationary pressure. Therefore, if ib rises to a sufficiently high level, money or debt financing of interest charges will lead to severe macroeconomic instability and, therefore, will be infeasible. Borrowing to pay interest charges on public debt, as we have mentioned already, is called Ponzi game. From the above it is clear that the government cannot go on playing the Ponzi game forever, when interest charges on public debt as a proportion of GDP is rising continuously. Sooner or later it will generate macroeconomic instability of serious proportions. Therefore, if debt–GDP ratio rises to a sufficiently high level, the government will be forced to stop borrowing. It will not be able to take any more loans.

Domar (1944) was the first who formally addressed the problem of sustainability of public debt in the long run. Domar derived the conditions under which public debt becomes unsustainable in the long run, when government runs a fiscal deficit every period. Domar considered the situation where the ratio of government's consumption to GDP and that of taxes net of subsidies and transfers to GDP are fixed. These ratios are denoted by E and R respectively. There is no government investment. Real GDP of the economy grows at a constant exponential rate, g. Government borrows at a fixed real rate of interest, r_0. Note that at any point of time outstanding public debt increases by the amount of government borrowing taking place at that point of time. In this situation fiscal deficit and, therefore, public borrowing in period τ is given by

$$\frac{d\tilde{D}}{d\tau} = (E - R)Y_0 e^{g\tau} + r_0 \tilde{D}_\tau \tag{9.5}$$

where $\tilde{D} \equiv$ real value of outstanding public debt, $Y \equiv$ real GDP, $\tau \equiv$ time and $Y_0 \equiv$ initial value of real GDP. Solving (9.5) and dividing by Y, we get

$$d\left(\equiv \frac{\tilde{D}}{Y}\right) = \left(d_0 - \frac{E - R}{g - r_0}\right)e^{-(g - r_0)\tau} + \frac{E - R}{g - r_0}, \quad d_0 \equiv \frac{\tilde{D}_0}{Y_0} \tag{9.6}$$

where $\tilde{D}_0 \equiv$ initial value of $\tilde{D}$. From (9.6) it follows that d will approach a stable value over time if and only if $g \geq r_0$. However, public borrowing is unsustainable if $r_0 > g$.

Following Fischer and Easterly (1990), we can derive the Domar condition for sustainability of public debt in a slightly modified form in the following way: Denoting the nominal value of outstanding public debt, as we have done before, by L and the ratio of L to nominal GDP, PY, by b, we get

$$b = \frac{L}{PY} \quad \Rightarrow \quad \log b = \log L - \log P - \log Y$$

Differentiating the above equation with respect to τ, we have

$$\hat{b} = \hat{L} - \hat{P} - \hat{Y}; \hat{b} \equiv \frac{db/d\tau}{b} \equiv \frac{\dot{b}}{b}, \hat{L} \equiv \frac{dL/d\tau}{L} \equiv \frac{\dot{L}}{L}; \hat{P} \equiv \Pi \equiv \frac{dP/d\tau}{P} \equiv \frac{\dot{P}}{P}$$

and

$$\hat{Y} \equiv g \equiv \frac{dY/d\tau}{Y} \equiv \frac{\dot{Y}}{Y} \tag{9.7}$$

Denoting primary deficit by Z and fiscal deficit by F, we have (ignoring seigniorage or financing by money creation for simplicity)

$$\frac{dL}{d\tau} = F = Z + iL \tag{9.8}$$

Substituting (9.8) into (9.7), we can rewrite it as

$$\hat{b} = \frac{(Z + iL)}{L} - \Pi - g = \frac{(Z/PY)}{(L/PY)} + i - \Pi - g = \frac{z}{b} + r - g$$

$$\Rightarrow \qquad \dot{b} = z - b[g - r]; \quad z \equiv (Z/PY), r = i - \Pi \tag{9.9}$$

where $r \equiv$ real rate of interest.
Equation (9.9) implies the following

$$\dot{b} > 0 \quad \Leftrightarrow \quad z > b[g - r] \tag{9.10}$$

The above inequality implies that, to prevent b from rising over time, i.e., to avoid the problem of sustainability of public debt, the government should not allow z to exceed $b[g - r]$. If we calculate the value of $b[g - r]$ on the basis of the data of the year 2003 for the Indian economy, it comes to 1% (since $b \cong (1/2)$, $\Pi \cong 6\%$, $g \cong 6\%$ and $i \cong 10\% \Rightarrow$ RHS = (1/2) $[6 - 4] = 1\%$). Restriction on z amounts to restricting the size of the fiscal deficit as a proportion of nominal GDP as well. Denoting the amount of fiscal deficit as a proportion of nominal GDP by f, we have (see (9.8))

$$f = z + ib \tag{9.11}$$

From (9.11) it follows that, if the ceiling on z is 1%, then that on f on the basis of the data of the given year is 6% (since $ib = (1/2)$ 10% = 5%). *Domar approach, therefore, recommends a ceiling on the size of the fiscal deficit as a proportion of nominal GDP to avoid the problem of sustainability of public debt.* (One can see Anand, R. and S.V. Winbergen (1989) in this context.)

9.4.2 Solvency of the Treasury

A government is solvent if it is in a position to service its debts. Let us first derive the condition, which, if satisfied, makes the government solvent. Consider first a two period horizon—period 0 and period 1. Suppose that in period zero, government's debt was L_0. If in period 1 government has a primary surplus (which is the negative of primary deficit) of S_1 so that $L_0 = S_1/(1 + i)$, where $i \equiv$ interest rate on government loans, then obviously the government will be able to service its debts. If, however, $L_0 > S_1/(1 + i)$, the government will not be able to service its debt and thereby will become insolvent. Let us now extend the time horizon to three periods, period 0, period 1 and period 2. Also suppose that the outstanding public debt in period zero is L_0 as before. Then, if primary surpluses of the government in periods 1 and 2 denoted by S_1 and S_2 respectively are such that

$$L_0 = \frac{S_1}{1+i} + \frac{S_2}{(1+i)^2} \tag{9.12}$$

the government is just able to service its debt. Let us explain. Suppose that the government uses S_1 to service its debt in period 1. Then, its total debt liability in period 1 reduces to $[L_0(1 + i) - S_1]$. Note that S_1 may be negative as well. Government's debt service charges in period 2 therefore become $[L_0(1 + i) - S_1](1 + i)$. When (9.12) is satisfied, $S_2 = [L_0(1 + i) - S_1](1 + i)$. Hence the government is able to service its debt. Note that S_2 is negative if $S_1 > L_0(1 + i)$. It also follows that, if $L_0 > [S_1/(1 + i)] + [S_2/(1 + i)^2]$, the government is unable to service its debt and, therefore, is insolvent. Thus, if S_1 and S_2 are such that (9.12) is satisfied, the government is just able to service its debt. Also note that either of S_1 and S_2 can be negative. Extending (9.12) to the infinite time horizon, we can state that the government is just solvent if

$$L_0 = \sum_{\tau=1}^{\infty} \frac{S_\tau}{(1+i)^\tau} \tag{9.13}$$

Equation (9.13) is referred to as the intertemporal budget constraint of the government. The government is, therefore, solvent if and only if

$$L_0 \le \sum_{\tau=1}^{\infty} \frac{S_\tau}{(1+i)^\tau} \tag{9.14}$$

The solvency approach, see, for example, Buiter (1990), assumes individuals to be infinitely lived. If these individuals apprehend that (9.14) will be violated, they will stop lending to the government and thereby force the government to stop its borrowing programme. This is the importance of the solvency condition or the intertemporal budget constraint.

At this point it may be advisable to compare the solvency condition (9.14) to the Domar sustainability condition. Domar sustainability condition states that, when real rate of interest is less than the growth rate of real GDP, public borrowing is sustainable even if every S_τ is negative. Therefore, (9.14) makes government's borrowing programme Domar sustainable, but a Domar sustainable borrowing programme need not satisfy the solvency condition. For the solvency approach in Indian context, one can go through Lahiri and Kannan (2004) and Buiter and Patel (1997).

9.4.3 Ricardian Equivalence and Sustainability of Public Debt

Ricardian equivalence, as we have already discussed, states that tax financing and debt financing are equivalent. It posits, as you should be able to recall, that the government services its debt by imposing additional taxes in future periods so that the present value of these additional future taxes in the current period equals the value of the outstanding public debt in the current period. In other words, Ricardian equivalence assumes that the government abides by the inter-temporal budget constraint, (9.13). Hence, government is always solvent and public borrowing always sustainable.

9.4.4 Evaluation of the Three Approaches: Superiority of the Domar Approach

We shall now evaluate the three approaches following the line suggested by Rakshit (2005). We have already noted some of the reservations against the Ricardian equivalence approach. Besides the points made earlier, it can be criticized on the following grounds also. It is derived from the intertemporal budget constraint of the government. However, a government may be profligate and violate it. Moreover, as follows from Domar approach, when real rate of interest is less than the growth rate, public borrowing is sustainable even if the government runs primary deficit every period indefinitely—see (9.6) and (9.10). Hence in such a situation there is nothing to prevent the government from violating the intertemporal budget constraint. When individuals realize this, they will not expect a rise in future taxes as they lend to the government and consider themselves better off at least relative to the situation where they pay the same amount as tax.

There are many problems with the solvency approach as well. Like the Ricardian approach this approach also presumes that the individuals have infinite time horizon. We have already noted the objections to this assumption. Most important problem with the solvency approach is that, when real rate of interest is less than the growth rate of real GDP, government faces no difficulty in servicing its debt even when it runs primary deficit every year and thereby violates the solvency condition. When people realize this, there is no reason why they will stop lending to the government even when they find that the solvency condition is violated, as long as primary deficits remain within limits. From the above discussion it follows that Domar approach to the sustainability of public debt is superior to the other two approaches.

9.4.5 Shortcomings of Domar Approach

There is a major shortcoming of the Domar approach as well. It treats g and r as exogenously given. In reality, however, z, g and r may all be related to one another. Recent research in growth theory, for example, no longer regards the long run rate of growth as exogenous, as in the neoclassical growth model, and seeks to endogenise or explain it. The modern theory of growth, which is referred to as the endogenous theory of growth, makes the long run rate of growth of GDP an increasing function of the investment ratio (ratio of investment to GDP) (Barro and Sala-i-Martin (1995)), and the proportion of productive resources invested in education and health (Lucas (1988)), infrastructure (Barro (1990)) and R&D (Romer (1990)). Thus, if an increase in z is due to a rise in public investment in the areas specified above and if this larger public investment leads to an increase in the investment ratio and a rise in the proportion of productive resources devoted to the sectors mentioned above, g will rise. In fact, the increase in g may be much greater than that in z. Thus the ceiling on z irrespective of the composition of government expenditure does not have much theoretical support even from the long run point of view. There is, therefore, urgent need for research in this area. The problem of sustainability of public debt may be regarded as a short run problem as well. In fact, one important objective of economic policies of most of the governments including Government of India is to prevent the debt–GDP ratio from rising in the short run, i.e., from one year to the next. This is done by imposing ceilings on actual annual values of z and f in accordance with (9.10) and (9.11) respectively instead of their trend values or average values over cycles. If (ib) can be kept stable in every short run, it will remain stable in the long run as well. In the short run prices and wages are usually sticky. As a result i and r are equal, Y may be much less than its potential or full employment level and g, r and b are likely to be quite closely related to one another. Let us explain. If primary deficit rises because of an increase in public investment, say, and if there is slack in the economy so that Y is below its potential or full employment level, GDP will rise relative to its previous level raising the growth rate, g. If the increase in public investment holds the promise of improving the future supplies of essential infrastructural inputs, private investment may also rise making the rise in Y and g larger. We can derive this result using the IS–LM model. The increase in public investment and the consequent rise in private investment will lead to a rightward shift in IS raising Y and thereby $g \equiv [(Y - Y_{-1})/Y_{-1}]$, where $Y_{-1} \equiv$ the previous year's output. What will happen to the interest rate, i, depends upon the state of the money and the loan market. If the interest rate is low, economic agents may have little incentive to part with liquidity and, therefore, may hold real balance far in excess of what they need to carry out transactions, i.e., the economy may be in a situation of a liquidity trap. Hence the excess or idle real balance in the hands of the economic agents may be sufficient to meet the additional demand for real balance that is created with the rise in Y so that there is no need to withdraw funds from the loan market. The loan market equilibrium and the equilibrium interest rate may, therefore, remain unaffected despite the rise in Y.

The situation is presented in Figure 9.4 where the IS intersects the LM and, therefore, the equilibrium occurs, at the latter's horizontal stretch or in the liquidity trap region. Thus, if the IS intersects the LM at a low-interest rate at which the LM is horizontal as shown in Figure 9.4, the increase in public and private investment will have little impact on i. The rise in GDP due to the increase in public investment may even lower z instead of raising it. Thus a rise in public investment may lower z, raise g and leave i unaffected. As a result interest charges as a proportion of GDP may go down instead of rising with the rise in primary deficit. In this case the increase in public debt does not affect i and may lead to a more than proportionate increase in Y lowering (ib). Even if the economy is not in the liquidity trap, the rise in i may not be much following the rise in public and private investment for the following reasons. First, an increase in Y raises firm's profit and, therefore, a larger proportion of them may be in a position to repay their loans and pay interest on them. Hence default rate may go down. This reduces risk of extending loans and the banks as a result may reduce excess reserves and extend more loans. See Blinder (1987) in this context. This lowers the reserve deposit ratio of the banks raising the value of the money multiplier. Thus the stock of inside money and, therefore, that of aggregate money supply may rise along with the increase in Y making the LM quite flat. In other words, economy's money supply may be an increasing function of Y making the LM flatter than usually assumed. This will lead to a small increase in i, if it rises at all. Second, an increase in public investment in infrastructure may give such a strong boost to business sentiments that private investment may rise substantially. Banks' outlook regarding the future business prospect of firms may also brighten and induce them to lower excess reserves and thereby raise the stock of money supply. Thus the LM may also shift rightward along with the IS making the expansion in Y larger and the rise in interest rate less. In fact, the interest rate may also fall in this case. Thus the LM may not only be quite flat, it may also shift to the right following an increase in public investment in infrastructure.

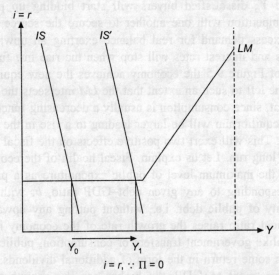

Figure 9.4: Effect of a loan-financed increase in public investment in liquidity trap.

Moreover, the central bank may have an interest rate target and adjust money supply to keep the interest rate at the target level. In this case the LM will again be horizontal at the target interest rate.

Finally, the government may finance the rise in primary deficit by borrowing from the central bank. In this situation the LM shifts to the right along with the IS making the expansion in Y larger and the rise in interest rate less. i may fall as well.

In all these cases i may remain unchanged or its rise may be insignificant. It may even fall in two of the above cases. Thus, if there is slack in the economy and the rise in primary deficit is due to additional investment in growth-enhancing areas, the increase in $b(g - r)$ may be more than that in z and as a result (ib) may fall instead of rising, see (9.10). The implication of the above is that, *the size of the primary or the fiscal deficit is a poor indicator of the fiscal health of the economy or of the sustainability of public debt. The composition of government expenditure and the mode of financing it, the state of the economy, the nature of the monetary policy of the central bank are all important in determining economy's fiscal health and the sustainability of public debt.* We shall dwell on this point further below.

So far we mainly focused on the situation where there exist substantial excess capacity and unemployment. Let us now turn to the case where the economy operates with the full employment level of output. We shall argue below that even in this situation a loan-financed increase in public investment will produce some favourable impact on the fiscal health of the economy in the medium and the long run, while an increase in government consumption or transfers financed with borrowing is likely to exert just the opposite impact. We shall explain the point using Figure 9.5 where the initial equilibrium of the economy corresponds to the point of intersection of the *IS* and *LM* at the full employment level of output, Y_f. Now suppose that public investment in crucial areas rises. It may, as we have already pointed out, stimulate private investment as well and shift the *IS* to the right. The new *IS* in Figure 9.5 is labelled IS_1. There will thus emerge excess demand at the initial equilibrium (Y, i). Since here producers cannot expand output beyond Y_f, dissatisfied buyers will start bidding up prices. Buyers will be engaged in a price competition with one another to secure the scarce good. The increase in prices will generate excess demand for real balance exerting an upward pressure on i. The upward spiral in prices and interest rates will stop when the rise in i fully crowds out private expenditure. In terms of Figure 9.5 the economy achieves the new equilibrium, when the rise in P shifts the *LM* to the left to such an extent that the *LM* intersects the new *IS*, IS_1, at Y_f. The point to note here is that, since consumption is usually a decreasing function of i too, aggregate investment in the new equilibrium will be larger leading to a rise in the investment ratio (ratio of investment to GDP). This will exert two positive effects on the fiscal health of the economy in the medium and the long run. Let us explain. Fiscal health of the economy, as follows from (9.10), is indicated by the maximum level of public expenditure as a proportion of GDP that can be sustained corresponding to any given debt–GDP ratio, b, without giving rise to the problem of sustainability of public debt, i.e., without putting any upward pressure on b. An increase in the investment ratio raises the growth rate of the economy in the medium and the long run. Moreover, unlike government transfers or consumption, public investment in private and mixed goods yields some return in the form of additional dividends. Therefore, the higher the ratio of public investment to GDP, the higher are the growth rate and the level of government's income as a proportion of GDP in the medium and the long run. Now, z is given

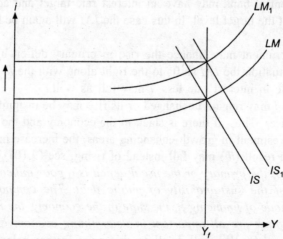

Figure 9.5: Effect of a loan-financed increase in government expenditure in the situation of full employment.

by the excess of public expenditure excluding interest payments over government's income as a proportion of GDP. Hence, the higher the level of public investment as a proportion of GDP, (then, everything else including total government expenditure as a proportion of GDP remaining the same), the less is z and the higher is g and, therefore, as follows from (9.10), the larger is the amount of public expenditure as a proportion of GDP that can be sustained without giving rise to the problem of sustainability of public debt in the medium and the long run. In contrast, an increase in government transfer payments or consumption will lower g in the medium and long run by crowding out private investment, when the economy operates with the full employment level of output. Nor will it augment future income of the government. It is thus quite clear that, even when the economy operates with the full employment level of output, the larger the proportion of public investment in any given level of total public expenditure, the better is the fiscal health of the economy in the medium and the long run.

As follows from the above, one major shortcoming of imposing a ceiling on fiscal deficit is that, the policy regards all kinds of government expenditure on an equal footing with regard to sustainability of public debt. The inappropriateness of this approach may be best illustrated with an example. Suppose that NTPC sets up a power plant and finances it with borrowing. This, therefore, raises the size of the fiscal deficit by the amount of this investment. The power plant will obviously yield a return. If this rate of return exceeds or equals the rate of interest on the loan, NTPC will have no problem in servicing its debt. Hence this increase in fiscal deficit does not contribute to the problem of sustainability of public debt. On the other hand, if the government buys armaments and finances it with borrowing, it will tend to make public debt unsustainable as the increase in the stock of armaments does not yield any future income to service the debt.

From the above it follows that the fiscal health of the government depends crucially on the composition of public expenditure. We shall also show below that it also depends on the modes of financing used. Size of the fiscal deficit is a poor indicator of the government's fiscal health since it treats every kind of expenditure and every source of receipt on an equal footing. Let us elaborate on this point further by analyzing the implications of different methods of financing public expenditure on government's debt burden.

9.4.6 Ceiling on Fiscal Deficit and Sustainability of Public Debt: Some Problems

Fiscal deficit is defined as total government expenditure net of total revenue receipts plus total non-debt creating capital receipts consisting of recovery of loans plus disinvestment of PSU shares. Note first that, if fiscal deficit is financed with borrowing from the central bank, it does not add to government's debt since central bank is a part of the government. Hence, *to what extent fiscal deficit will add to government's debt burden depends upon how much of fiscal deficit is financed by borrowing from the central bank.*

Again, suppose that in a given period the government lowers fiscal deficit by reducing total amount of outstanding loans extended by the government through an increase in the recovery of loans. This will, however, in the later years reduce government's interest income. Hence, everything else remaining the same, primary and fiscal deficit as a proportion of GDP will rise in later years worsening the fiscal health and aggravating the problem of sustainability of public debt. In fact, impact of financing public expenditure with an increase in the recovery of loans will be exactly the same as that of taking fresh loans. In the former case the interest income falls, while in the latter case interest payments rise exactly by the same amount in future periods. In both cases, therefore, everything else remaining the same, size of the fiscal deficit as a proportion of GDP goes up by the same amount in future periods. Hence in both cases fiscal health and the problem of sustainability of public debt worsen to the same extent.

Reducing fiscal deficit through disinvestment of PSU shares is costlier than taking fresh loans or raising the amount of recovery of past loans. This is because holding PSU shares is risky, while extending loans to the government is riskless. Economic agents are normally risk averse and hence they will buy PSU shares if and only if these are expected to yield a higher rate of return than loans to government. Therefore, if fiscal deficit is reduced by a given amount through disinvestment, dividend incomes in future periods will fall by quantities larger than the amount of decline in interest income that occurs in the case where fiscal deficit is reduced by the same amount through an increase in the recovery of loans. Hence in the present case, everything else remaining the same, sizes of fiscal deficits corresponding to any given amount of public expenditure will increase by larger amounts than those in the earlier two cases in future periods.

From the above discussion it follows that *public liability (PL), which is defined as public debt net of central bank's holding of government securities, i.e., central bank's loans to the government, is the true indicator of government's indebtedness to the rest of the economic agents.* Again, another indicator, *fiscal gap (FG), which is defined as fiscal deficit (FD) minus monetized deficit (i.e., that part of FD that is financed with borrowing from the central bank) plus non-debt creating capital receipts is a much better indicator than fiscal deficit of the impact of current budgetary operations of the government on the fiscal health of the government or sustainability of public debt.* Fiscal deficit minus monetized deficit gives yearly increase in government's debt to the rest of the economic agents. The second term, non-debt creating capital receipts, gives the reduction in government's financial assets (consisting mainly of outstanding government loans to the rest of the economic agents and shares of PSUs). Thus, as follows from our above discussion, FG is a much better measure than FD of the increase in government's debt burden due to current budgetary operations. We are now in a position to examine the issue of sustainability of public debt or the fiscal health of the government in the nineties in India, as done in Box 9.1.

9.5 INDIA'S PUBLIC DEBT: SUSTAINABILITY IN THE LONG RUN

Following Rakshit (2000), we discuss here India's current debt scenario. The figures in Table 9.4 reveal a disquieting trend regarding the fiscal health of the government in the nineties. In the first phase of reforms, i.e., from 1990–1991 to 1996–1997, both public debt and FD as proportions of GDP declined steadily, but in the last three years both evince a sharply rising trend. Growth–interest differential also remained more or less stable till 1995–1996, but declined sharply thereafter. We have pointed out above that PL is a much better indicator than public debt as defined officially of government's debt burden and FG is a truer measure than FD of the increase in government's debt burden. Data presented in Table 9.4 show that PL–GDP ratio increased steadily throughout the nineties. FG–GDP ratio also rose steadily till 1994–1995, dropped in 1995–1996 and increased sharply thereafter. These figures show that the fiscal health of the government not only deteriorated in the later part of the 90s but also in the earlier part.

Table 9.4:   Indicators of fiscal sustainability: 1990–2000
(Figures are as percentage of GDP)

	1990–1991	1991–1992	1992–1993	1993–1994	1994–1995	1995–1996	1996–1997	1997–1998	1998–1999	1999–2000
Public debt	65.5	64.5	64.1	65.4	63.3	61.5	60.0	62.1	62.0	65.1
FD	10.0	7.4	7.4	8.3	7.1	6.6	6.4	7.3	8.9	9.9
$g + \Pi$	15.7	14.5	15.4	14.4	17.9	15.0	13.9	9.8	13.7	
i		8.8	9.2	9.5	9.3	9.2	9.7	9.5	9.9	
$g + \Pi - i$ $= g - r$		5.7	6.2	4.9	8.6	5.8	4.3	0.3	3.8	
PL	48.9	49.2	50.2	53.8	53.3	51.2	50.9	53.2	53.4	57.4
FG	8.0	8.7	7.9	9.0	8.3	5.6	6.9	7.3	8.6	
RD[1]	4.5	3.6	3.4	4.2	3.7	3.2	3.6	4.1	6.3	6.7
I_g^2	6.4	5.9	5.1	4.8	4.9	4.1	3.6	3.9	3.9	
$(I_g/IFL)^3$	58.8	62.6	60.5	53.5	56.9	55.9	49.8	48.4	40.4	
$(g - \rho)^4$		9.3	10.0	7.9	10.9	8.0	6.8	2.6	5.7	
NIRR[5]	18.5	18.9	18.7	6.5	17.2	16.7	16.5	14.8		

RD[1] $\equiv$ revenue deficit, $I_g^2 \equiv$ public investment, $IFL^3 \equiv$ incremental financial liability $\equiv$ fiscal deficit plus non-debt creating capital receipts, $(g - \rho)^4 \equiv$ growth–net interest rate differential and NIRR[5] $\equiv$ net cost of government borrowing defined as interest cost net of return on government's assets.
Source: Rakshit (2000).

We pointed out above that the larger the proportion of public investment in total government expenditure, the better is the fiscal health of the economy. From the data it is also clear that RD–GDP ratio increased, while the ratio of capital expenditure to GDP declined steadily all through the nineties. This implies that during the nineties larger and larger proportion of pubic borrowing plus non-debt creating capital receipts of the government financed revenue expenditure at the cost of capital expenditure. This is also evident from the steady decline in capital expenditure as percentage of IFL (incremental financial liability), which is defined as fiscal deficit plus non-debt creating capital receipts of the government. This decline in the importance of capital expenditure in the total expenditure of the government is also reflected in the steady rise in the net cost of government borrowing defined as interest cost net of return on government's assets and the steady fall in the growth–net interest rate differential. Thus, throughout the nineties fiscal health of the government declined steadily and unless the trend is reversed, it will lead sooner or later to serious fiscal and economic crisis.

Besides fiscal deficit, revenue deficit and primary deficit, two other concepts of deficit that are used in Indian context are budgetary deficit and deficit financing. The former is defined as total expenditure minus total receipt excluding net sale of treasury bills, while the latter means increase in net RBI credit to the government. The latter gives the increase in the stock of high-powered money.

9.6 TAXATION OR BORROWING

According to the benefit principle taxes raised to finance the cost of providing social goods should be distributed among the beneficiaries in line with the benefits they receive. Capital expenditure of the government yields benefits in future periods. Hence it should not be financed by taxation. To put the burden of the cost of government investment on its beneficiaries, it has to be financed with borrowing and this loan is to be serviced by taxing the beneficiaries of the investment. According to the benefit principle, therefore, revenue expenditures of the government comprising wages and salaries, debt servicing charges etc., which constitute the current cost of providing social goods should be met with taxation, while capital expenditures should be met with borrowing.

One problem with the above scheme of financing public expenditure is that in LDCs like India tax base is quite narrow, tax evasion is rampant, political costs of raising tax rates is very high and prices of most of the goods the government provides are either zero or much less than their equilibrium values. Hence return on public investment, by way of profit and taxes, is very low. Hence financing public investment with borrowing at market rate of interest is unsustainable. The problem in the pre-nineties era in India was resolved through a system of statutory liquidity ratio (SLR) under which banks were under the compulsion to hold a fixed percentage of their deposits in the form of certain types of unencumbered government bonds, which paid very low-interest rates. These low-interest rate bank loans made it possible for the government to finance adequate levels of investment in infrastructure without getting into the problem of sustainability of public debt. The SLR has been diluted to a large extent in the post-liberalization period on the ground that it threatens the financial health of the banks. This apprehension, however, may be baseless. Increase in public investment crowds in private investment giving a boost to bank business and, therefore, bank profit. Hence lower interest rate on loans given to the government may increase bank profit rather than reduce it. This area requires serious research. In many countries governments imposed interest rate controls to make their borrowing programme Domar sustainable. But these measures led to capital flights—see in this context Coddington (1986). However, SLR is unlikely to give rise to these problems by lowering banks' deposit rates, as in India there are restrictions on domestic financial investment in foreign assets. Moreover, the crowding in effect of additional public investment may more than compensate for banks' losses due to low-interest rate SLR loans. See Problem 5 in this context. There is of course the problem of unproductive public investment—see Gelb (1988).

9.7 EXTERNAL PUBLIC DEBT

External public debt is raised from foreigners, i.e., from the international credit market. *The most important feature that distinguishes external public debt from the internal public debt is that it has to be serviced with foreign exchange, which a country receives, excepting external loans, only in return for exports or by way of aid or transfers from foreigners. It is often difficult to transform domestic output into foreign exchange as a country's exports are usually constrained by demand. This problem of converting internal resources into external resources is referred to as transfer problem.* We shall first ignore this problem in comparing internal and external debt.

9.7.1 Comparison of Internal and External Public Debt

For simplicity consider a two-period economy. Suppose that wages and prices are perfectly flexible so that there is full employment of productive resources in every period. Suppose that the government wants to borrow an amount A to finance G. If the government borrows this amount from internal sources, it will reduce, as we have pointed out earlier, either consumption or investment expenditure or both by A in the period in which the borrowing takes place. If it reduces investment expenditure, output in the next period will go down by $A(1 + \rho)$, where $\rho \equiv$ marginal productivity of capital. Moreover, in equilibrium $\rho = r$, where r denotes the domestic real rate of interest. Thus the total cost of internal borrowing is the reduction in period 2's output consumption by $A(1 + r)$. This is equivalent to the loss in period 1's consumption or output by A. Following the internal borrowing, therefore, the private sector loses either A amount of consumption in period 1 or $A(1 + r)$ amount of goods and services in period 2 or both in paris. Hence the cost of the internal borrowing to the private sector is either A amount of goods and services in period 1 or $A(1 + r)$ amount of goods and services in period 2. In period 2 the government pays back the debt along with interest. This the government does by taxing the individuals. So, servicing of internal public debt leaves incomes of all the individuals taken together unaffected in period 2. If, however, the government raises the loan from external sources at a real rate of interest, say, r^*, the community loses nothing in the first period as the government buys the goods and services from abroad with this external loan. However, in the next period it has to pay $A(1 + r^*)$ to service this debt. This the government does by taxing the community so that the individuals lose $A(1 + r^*)$ amount of income to the foreign lenders. Thus, in case of internal loans the cost to the community in terms of period 2's output is $A(1 + r)$, while in case of the external loans the cost is $A(1 + r^*)$. Hence, *if the transfer problem is ignored, the only basis of comparison of these two types of loans is the interest rates at which these loans are available to the government.* If interest rates on both these types of loans are the same, then they are equivalent. Otherwise, the loan that is available at a lower interest rate is preferable. It should be noted in this context that if the economy operates with unutilized productive resources, an increase in government expenditure financed with internal borrowing, as we have already explained, may be costless as the additional government expenditure will be met through an expansion in output. In fact, the sum of consumption and investment in the first period will rise. Consumption and investment are each likely to increase too.

The *most important problem related to external public debt particularly in the context of developing countries consists in the problem of converting domestic output into foreign exchange*, as the amount of export is demand-constrained. If external public debt grows, but export does not increase commensurately, external debt service charges will increase steadily as a proportion of export earning and render such borrowing unsustainable. Steady increase in the proportion of debt servicing charges in export earning will erode the borrowing country's credit-worthiness in the international credit market. They will apprehend that the borrowing country will soon default on external debt service obligations. Thus, if the amount of debt servicing charges as a proportion of export earning goes beyond a point, it will cause panic among international lenders and they might seek to withdraw their funds en masse leading to a severe balance of payments crisis. Thus, *in case of developing countries external borrowing is sustainable if and only if such borrowing contributes to the country's export capacity to such an extent that the country is able to earn additional foreign exchange that is sufficient to service the external debt.*

One important shortcoming of the approaches to the long run sustainability of public debt discussed above is that they do not distinguish between internal and external borrowing, i.e., they treat these two sources of borrowing as equivalent. Even though Domar originally considered internal public debt alone, the restriction that Domar approach imposes on fiscal deficit is interpreted nowadays to apply to total borrowing of the government, external and internal—see Fischer and Easterly (2005) in this connection. However, in the context of developing countries, the government should be very careful about external public borrowing even if they are available at the same interest rate as or lower interest rates than internal loans because of the transfer problem. Box 9.2 exemplifies the dangers of external borrowing in case of developing countries.

Box 9.2:   Current Account Deficit and Currency Crisis

There is a general consensus that large and persistent current account deficits along with pegged exchange rate often leads to currency crisis. This view is propagated by L. Summers and the IMF. Large and persistent current account deficit brings about rapid increase in external debt. If this is not accompanied by commensurate increase in export earnings so that ratio of external debt service charges to export earnings also rises steeply, domestic and foreign investors become sceptical of the domestic economy's ability to service foreign debt in near future and therefore they apprehend large scale capital flight, suspension of exchange rate peg and, therefore, a drastic depreciation in domestic currency. Since returns on domestic assets are denominated in domestic currency, apprehension of large depreciation in domestic currency implies a steep fall in expected returns on domestic assets in foreign currency. This induces foreigners to withdraw their capital from domestic financial assets en masse precipitating the crisis. Sudden substantial depreciation of domestic currency plunges domestic companies including domestic banks and financial institutions with large external debts denominated in foreign currency into deep financial crisis. They go bankrupt, default on their debt service obligations leading to a collapse of the financial system of the domestic economy as a whole. The economy as a result experiences deep recession. As Table B.9.1 shows, in both Mexico and Thailand currency crisis followed a period of large and persistent current account deficit. However, in Thailand unlike in Mexico the persistent current account deficit did not weaken the fundamentals of the economy, i.e., it did not lead to a rise in debt service charges as a proportion of export earning. In fact the ratio showed a mildly declining

---

(Contd.)...

(Contd.)...

trend. Despite that the crisis occurred. This points to the irrationality of the foreign investors and underscores further the dangers of external borrowing.

Table B.9.2: Key macroeconomic indicators: Thailand

	1975	1980	1990	1992	1993	1994	1995	1996
Current account balance (as percentage of GDP)	− 4.2	− 4.3	− 8.7	− 5.7	− 5.6	− 5.5	− 7.9	− 7.9

	1985	1994	1995	1996
Total debt service/exports	31.9	11.3	11.0	11.1

	1988	1989	1990	1991	1992	1993	1994
Current account balance (as percentage of GDP: Mexico)	− 1.4	− 0.1	− 1.3	− 3.2	− 5.6	− 4.4	− 5.6

SUMMARY

1. Government's budget, which records its receipts and expenditures has two accounts, revenue account and capital account. Receipts and expenditures that have no direct bearing on the future income and expenditure of the government are recorded in the revenue account and those, which have are recorded in the capital account. Revenue deficit is defined as the excess of total revenue expenditure over total revenue receipt. Fiscal deficit on the other hand is defined as the excess of total revenue and capital expenditures of the government over its total revenue and non-debt creating capital receipts. Primary deficit is fiscal deficit net of interest payments.

2. In a purely accounting sense public debt does not impose any burden. It is a liability of the government. At the same time it is an asset of the private sector. Hence, for the economy as a whole, which consists of both the private and the public sector, public debt is neither an asset nor a liability.

3. Servicing of public debt is done by collecting taxes from individuals. Taxes collected from individuals are again paid back to them as interest on and repayment of loans. So servicing of public debt does not make the individuals, when we consider all of them together, worse off. Hence it does not impose any burden either. However, it burdens the economy in the following ways:

   (i) A loan-financed increase in government consumption crowds out private investment and also private consumption. To the extent it lowers private investment, it reduces future capital stock and potential output. However, in a demand deficient economy if investment is a function of GDP or/and the loan is used to finance public investment in infrastructure, private investment may be crowded in. In a full employment economy also if the loan finances public investment in infrastructure, private investment may be crowded in. In the latter case, therefore, only private consumption is crowded out.

(ii) If direct and indirect tax rates are raised to service internal public debt, the excess burden or deadweight loss will increase.

(iii) Redistribution of income from the taxpayers (who are relatively rich with low-consumption propensity) to the lenders (who are relatively poor with high-consumption propensity) brought about by the servicing of public debt will raise consumption and thereby may crowd out investment lowering growth. The redistribution itself may be undesirable and will, therefore, reduce social welfare.

4. Ricardian equivalence proposition states that if government reduces taxes and finances the resulting deficit by borrowing, it will leave every macro-variable unaffected. Hence taxation and borrowing as modes of financing government expenditure are equivalent. Empirical evidences do not support this proposition.

5. One important question regarding the long run aspect of public borrowing is whether it is sustainable in the long run. There are three approaches to this question: Domar approach, Solvency approach and Ricardian equivalence. When interest charges on public debt as a proportion of GDP keep on rising over time, it will eventually exhaust the taxable capacity of the economy. Government borrowing at that point will become unsustainable. Domar shows that, if the government in every period borrows a fixed proportion of GDP, public debt will become unsustainable if real rate of interest exceeds the growth rate of GDP. More generally, when growth rate of GDP exceeds the real rate of interest, government will be able to sustain primary deficit every year within a given ceiling.

6. Solvency approach states that government or treasury is solvent if the present value of the future primary surpluses of the government over an infinite time period is less than or equal to the current liability or debt of the government. If infinitely lived individuals apprehend that the solvency condition is going to be violated, they will stop lending to the government forcing the government to abandon its borrowing programme. Ricardian equivalence presumes that the solvency condition is always satisfied. If government's borrowing programme satisfies solvency condition, it fulfils Domar's sustainability condition too. But the converse is not true. Problems with the solvency approach and Ricardian equivalence are the following. Individuals do not have infinite time horizons. They are not as altruistic as is assumed in these approaches. It is extremely difficult to predict government's fiscal policies even five years later. As long as Domar condition is fulfilled, the government can violate solvency condition without any harm. Domar approach thus seems superior to the other two.

7. Domar approach puts a ceiling on the sizes of primary and fiscal deficits as proportions of GDP to avoid the problem of sustainability of public borrowing in the long run. However, careful scrutiny of this position has shown that the size of the primary or the

fiscal deficit is a poor indicator of the fiscal health of the economy or of the sustainability of public debt. The composition and the mode of financing government expenditure, the state of the economy, the nature of the monetary policy of the central bank are all important in determining economy's fiscal health and the sustainability of public debt.

8. Public liability (PL), which is defined as public debt net of central bank's holding of government securities, is the true indicator of the government's indebtedness to the rest of the economic agents, domestic and foreign. Again, another indicator, fiscal gap (FG), which is defined as fiscal deficit (FD) minus monetized deficit (i.e., that part of FD that is financed with borrowing from the central bank) plus non-debt creating capital receipts is a much better indicator than fiscal deficit of the impact of current budgetary operations of the government on the fiscal health of the government or sustainability of public debt. A brief survey of the relevant data of the Indian economy in the nineties reveals a steady decline in the fiscal health of government all through this period.

9. Benefit principle recommends financing of revenue expenditure by taxation and that of capital expenditure by borrowing.

10. LDCs like India have to be very careful about external loans even if they are available at the same rate of interest as or lower rates of interest than internal loans. External borrowing is sustainable if and only if it leads to as much increase in foreign exchange earnings as is sufficient to service the external loan.

KEY CONCEPTS

- ✓ Internal public debt
- ✓ Sustainability of public debt
- ✓ Revenue deficit
- ✓ Primary deficit
- ✓ Fiscal gap
- ✓ Future generation
- ✓ External loan
- ✓ Budgetary deficit

- ✓ Burden of internal public debt
- ✓ Solvency of treasury
- ✓ Fiscal deficit
- ✓ Public liability
- ✓ Incremental financial liability
- ✓ Ricardian equivalence
- ✓ Transfer problem
- ✓ Deficit financing

REVIEW QUESTIONS

1. Internal public debt is a debt which we owe to ourselves. Explain this statement.

2. How does internal public debt impose a burden on a community? Explain.

3. Compare the effects of tax-financed and loan-financed increase in government expenditure in the *IS–LM* model. Explain Ricardian equivalence in this context. What are the objections to Ricardian equivalence?

4. What do you mean by sustainability of public debt?

5. If the government borrows a fixed proportion of GDP every period, then under what conditions will public debt be sustainable?

6. Why is a ceiling on fiscal and primary deficit required for the sake of sustainability of public debt? Explain.

7. Under what conditions is the solvency of treasury ensured? Explain.

8. What does Ricardian equivalence imply about sustainability of public debt? Explain.

9. Compare the three approaches, namely, Domar approach, solvency approach and Ricardian equivalence, to the problem of sustainability of public debt. Which of three will you prefer and why?

10. What are the shortcomings of the Domar approach? Explain.

11. Why is public liability a better measure than fiscal deficit of the government's indebtedness to the rest of the economic agents? Explain.

12. Why is fiscal gap a better indicator than fiscal deficit of the impact of the current budgetary operations of the government on the fiscal health of the economy or on the sustainability of public debt? Explain.

13. Why are the tendencies evinced by the movements in the different indicators of the fiscal health of the Indian economy in the nineties are a matter of concern? Explain.

14. Under what conditions will the government prefer internal to external borrowing, when there is no transfer problem? Explain.

15. Under what conditions is external debt sustainable? Explain.

16. If fiscal deficit is reduced through disinvestments of PSU shares, or through recovery of past loans, fiscal health of the government or sustainability of public debt will not improve. Explain.

17. How will the government choose between taxation and borrowing in financing its expenditures? Explain.

PROBLEMS AND APPLICATIONS

1. Suppose that an economy is in recession with substantial quantities of unemployed labour and capital and the government wants to stabilize the economy and at the same time improve its fiscal health. Which component of public expenditure should the government choose to raise and what mode of financing should it choose? Explain your answer.

   (*Hint:* Recession is an opportunity for the government to invest on a large scale in infrastructure, retire its debts and finance its expenditures by money creation.)

2. The Government of India announced recently that it had set itself a target of eliminating revenue deficit within a stipulated period. Is there any justification for such a programme? Explain.

   (*Hint:* Benefit principle states that revenue expenditures should be financed with taxation and capital expenditure by borrowing. In recession financing revenue deficit by money creation may be costless. However, if in such a situation the opportunity of raising public expenditure is utilized fully to raise capital expenditure, benefit to the society is likely to be more. For these reasons eliminating revenue deficit may be justified.)

3. Suppose that consumption is a function of only disposable income, while investment is a function only of interest rate and the economy is operating with less than full employment level of output. An increase in loan-financed government expenditure in this scenario will burden the future generation in more ways than one. Can you think of any other method/methods of financing the increased public expenditure that will spare the future generation and contribute to stabilizing the economy?

   (*Hint:* Money creation is the only option. Even taxation crowds out investment.)

4. Suppose that Ricardian equivalence holds. Show in the framework of the *IS–LM* model that a loan-financed increase in government expenditure has the same effect as that of a tax-financed increase in government expenditure on consumption and investment.

   (*Hint:* In both the cases the present value of future income of the infinitely lived household is the same. Hence consumption demand corresponding to any (Y, r) is the same and, therefore, the *IS* schedule is also the same in both the cases.)

5. Consider a bank. Suppose that the interest it charges on loans is fixed. It is not fully loaned up, i.e., its lending is constrained by demand. Private investment is a decreasing function of interest rate and an increasing function of public investment. Public investment on the other hand is a decreasing function of interest rate. Is there any condition under which it may be profitable for the bank to lend to the government at a lower interest rate? If this condition is met, is there any optimum interest rate on government loans?

   (*Hint:* Suppose that interest rates charged to private borrowers and the government are $\bar{r}$ and r_g respectively. Total profit of the bank: $R = \bar{r}I_p[\bar{r}, I_g(r_g)] + r_g I_g(\cdot) - \bar{C} - c[I_p(\cdot) + I_g(\cdot)]$, where I_p, I_g and r_g denote private investment, public investment and interest rate on government loans respectively and $\bar{r}$ denotes the fixed interest rate charged to private borrowers by banks. $\bar{C} + c(I_p + I_g)$ gives the cost of extending loans. Derive the condition under which a fall in r_g raises profit. Find out the profit maximizing value of I_g.

6. Suppose exports in an economy are constrained by paucity of crucial infrastructure services. Should the government in this economy borrow from abroad to finance imports of armaments and foreign tours of bureaucrats and ministers? Explain your answer.

   (*Hint:* This will render external borrowing unsustainable.)

7. In India if an income taxpayer saves in the form of some specific types of government securities such as National Savings Certificates (NSCs) or in some government savings scheme such as Public Provident Fund (PPF), her total amount of tax payable falls by 20% of the savings invested NSCs or PPF. Will such a tax deduction scheme promote savings, i.e., will such a scheme really reduce the tax liability of the saver? Explain. (If Ricardian equivalence holds, lifetime tax liability of the infinitely lived households will not change. But, if it does not, tax liability is likely to fall. Explain these points.)

8. Suppose that a country is growing at a given exponential rate, α. What proportion of GDP can the government borrow so that the debt–GDP ratio of the country does not go beyond some pre-specified level, β? Explain. Suppose that the exponential growth rate of the economy depends on the investment ratio, which in turn depends upon the ratio of public investment to GDP. Suppose that in every period the full employment level of output is produced and the government borrows a fixed α proportion of GDP and also taxes a fixed

t proportion of GDP. Is there any way in which the government can reduce the long run debt–GDP ratio to a target level, if the real interest rate in the economy is fixed at $\bar{r}$? Try to derive your result formally making appropriate assumptions.

(*Hint:* Answer this question using the original Domar model.)

9. Consider the situation where the economy operates with the full employment level of output. Suppose that private investment is an increasing function of public investment besides being a decreasing function of the interest rate. Derive the conditions under which loan-financed increase in public investment will crowd in private investment. Under what conditions will there exist an optimum value of public investment that maximizes private investment. Answer this question using the *IS–LM* model.

10. Actual distribution of tax burden of both direct and indirect taxes among individuals is highly complex. In this scenario is it possible for the Ricardian equivalence to hold?

11. How is the ceiling on primary deficit modified if government finances by borrowing only investment expenditure, which yields as much return as the rate of interest?

12. If the government services its debt by reducing its expenditure, will the Ricardian equivalence hold? Explain.

REFERENCES

For different concepts of deficit in government's budget:

Chelliah, R.J. (2005): The meaning and the significance of fiscal deficit, *in*: Bagchi, A. (Ed.), *Readings in Public Finance*, Oxford University Press, New Delhi.

Rakshit, M. (2000): On correcting fiscal imbalances in the Indian economy, *Money and Finance*, 2(2), July–September.

——(2005): Budget deficit: Sustainability, solvency and optimality, *in*: Bagchi, A. (Ed.), *Readings in Public Finance*, Oxford University Press, New Delhi.

For burden of internal loan-financed increase in government expenditure:

Anand, R. and S.V. Winbergen (1989): Inflation and the financing of government expenditure: An introductory analysis with an application to Turkey, *World Bank Economic Review*, 3, (1), January.

Buiter, W.H. (1988): Some thoughts on the role of fiscal policy in stabilization and structural adjustment in developing countries, *NBER Working Paper*, No. 2603, May, Mass., Cambridge.

——(1985): A guide to public sector debt and deficits, *Economic Policy* 1, November.

Lerner, A.P. (1948): The burden of the national debt, *in*: Metzler, L.A., et al. (Eds.), *Income, Employment, Public Policy: Essays in Honour of Alvin Hansen*, W.W. Norton, New York.

Rakshit, M. (2000): On correcting fiscal imbalances in the Indian economy, *Money and Finance*, 2(2), July–September.

Yellen, J.L. (1989): Symposium on the budget deficit, *Journal of Economic Perspectives*, Spring.

For Ricardian equivalence:

Barro, R.J. (1974): Are government bonds net wealth?, *Journal of Political Economy*, 81(6), December.

——(1989): The Ricardian approach to budget deficits, *Journal of Economic Perspectives*, Spring.

Bernheim, D. (1987): Ricardian equivalence: An evaluation of theory and evidence, *NBER Macroeconomic Annuals*.

Bernheim and Bagwell (1989): Is everything neutral? *Journal of Political Economy*, April.

Gramlich, E.M. (1989): Budget deficits and national savings: Are politicians exogenous?, *Journal of Economic Perspectives*.

Haque, N. and Montiel, P. (1987): *Ricardian Equivalence, Liquidity Constraints, and the Yaari–Blanchard Effect: Tests for Developing Countries*, International Monetary Fund, Research Department, Washington DC.

For Domar approach:

Domar, E. (1944): Burden of the debt and the national income, *The American Economic Review*, 34, 798–827.

Fischer, S. and Easterly, W. (1990): Economics of the government budget constraint, *World Bank Research Observer*, 5(2), July.

Rakshit, M. (2000): On correcting fiscal imbalances in the Indian economy, *Money and Finance*, 2(2), July–September.

——(2005): Budget deficit: Sustainability, solvency and optimality, *in*: Bagchi, A. (Ed.), *Readings in Public Finance*, Oxford University Press, New Delhi.

——(1991): The macroeconomic adjustment programme: A critique, *Economic and Political Weekly*, 24 August.

For solvency approach:

Buiter, W.H. (1990): The arithmetic of solvency, *in*: Buiter W.H., (Ed.), *Principles of Budgetary and Financial Policy*, Mass., Cambridge, MIT Press.

Lahiri, A. and Kannan, R. (2004): India's fiscal deficit and their sustainability in perspective, *in*: Fararo E., and Lahiri, A., (Eds.), *Fiscal Policies and Sustainable Growth in India*, Oxford University Press, New Delhi.

Patel, U.R. (1997): Solvency and fiscal correction in India: An analytical discussion, *in*: Mundle, S. (Ed.), *Public Finance: Policy Issues for India*, Oxford University Press, New Delhi.

For comparison of internal and external debt:

Buchanon, J.M. (1958): *Public Principles of Public Debt*, Richard, D. Irwin (Ed.), 75–84.

For redistributive impact of a loan-financed increase in government expenditure in a full employment economy:

Kaldor, N. (1956): Alternative theories of distribution, *Review of Economic Studies*, 23.

For importance of demand deficiency in recent years:

Krugman, P. (1999): *The Return of Depression Economics*, W.W. Norton & Company, New York.

For the problems of public investment:

Gelb, A. (1988): *Oil Windfalls: Blessing or Curse?* Oxford University Press, New York.

For the problems of interest rate controls:

Cuddington, J.T. (1986): Capital flight: Estimates, issues and explanations, *Princeton Studies in International Finance*, 58, Princeton University Press.

For comparison of borrowing and taxation on efficiency grounds:

Feldstein, M.S. (1985): Debt and taxes in the theory of public finance, *Journal of Public Economics*, 28(2), November.

For seminal contributions in the endogenous growth theory:

Barro, R.J. and Sala-I-Martin, X. (1995): *Economic Growth*, McGraw-Hill.

Lucas, R.E., Jr. (1988): On the mechanics of development planning, *Journal of Monetary Economics*, 22(1), July.

Romer, P.A. (1990): Endogenous technical change, *Journal of Political Economy*, 98(5), October, Part II.

For the relationship between revenue deficit and BOP crisis:

Krugman, P. (1979): A model of balance of payments crisis, *Journal of Money, Credit and Banking*, August.

To know about how money supply and supply of bank credit are related to levels of aggregate output in the economy:

Blinder, A.S. (1987): Credit rationing and effective supply failures, *Economic Journal*, 97, 327–352.

10 | FISCAL FEDERALISM

Chapter Objectives

The objectives of this chapter are to explain

(i) the theoretical basis of fiscal federalism, i.e., the rationale of decentralization of government's economic activities. More precisely, it seeks to explain the theoretical basis for decentralization of the government's function of provision of social goods.

(ii) the reasons for centralizations of tax powers and the functions of stabilization and income distribution.

(iii) the concepts of vertical and horizontal imbalances and discuss the corrective measures.

(iv) the economic impacts of different types of grants.

(v) the structure of fiscal relations among different tiers of governments in India and assess them on the basis of the economic principles that should govern such relations.

10.1 INTRODUCTION

Many countries including India are federations, i.e., a union of a number of geographically separate political units. India, for example, consists of twenty-eight geographically-separate states, six union territories and one national capital territory (Delhi). There are many types of federations. On one extreme, *there are nation states where primary allegiance of every citizen is to the federation, i.e., to the nation state, and not to the constituent political unit of which she is a member. Here the nation state has sovereign power, but its constituent political units are not sovereign.* India is an example of this kind of a federation. It has a three-tier government: central government, state governments and local municipal bodies in urban areas and panchayats in rural areas. On the other extreme, a federation may consist of a number of sovereign geographically separate political units and in such a federation primary allegiance of a member is to the political unit to which she belongs and not to the federation.

Here we focus on a federation like India where the nation state is sovereign, but its constituent political units are not. In a federation powers and functions of the government do not remain concentrated in the hands of just the highest government, the centre. They are delegated at least partly to the lower level governments. Our primary objective in this chapter is to examine whether there is any theoretical ground of fiscal federalism. Fiscal federalism consists in decentralization of government's economic activities. Thus the main purpose of this chapter is to examine whether there is any economic reason for delegating at least partly government's economic activities to the lower level governments—the state governments and local bodies—instead of concentrating them all in the hands of the centre. Government has three major functions: provision of social goods, achieving a desired distribution of income and stabilization. The questions that emerge in the context of fiscal federalism are the following: How should these functions be performed? Should they be fully centralized so that all the functions are performed by the central government only or should they be decentralized and if the latter, then how should these activities be allocated among different tiers of governments? This chapter examines these issues in detail. This chapter also discusses the structure of fiscal relations among different tiers of governments in India and assesses them on the basis of the economic principles that should govern them.

10.2 PROVISION OF SOCIAL GOODS

It is possible to build a case for decentralized provision of social goods on the basis of the benefit principle. This principle states that the cost of providing public goods has to be met only by taxing their beneficiaries and the cost has to be distributed among them in line with the amounts of benefits received. The size of the geographical area over which the benefits of a social good spread varies from one social good to another. National defence, medical or agricultural research benefit the whole nation, while a park benefits a small locality. City streets principally benefit the people living in the city. Clearly, therefore, the cost of national defence, medical and agricultural research etc. should be met by taxing everyone living in the country, while the cost of providing park, city streets etc. should be met by taxing only the people living in the locality where the park is located and the city respectively. This may be efficiently done, if provisions of social goods with nationwide, statewide and local level benefits are left to the centre, states and local municipal bodies or panchayats respectively. Let us elaborate.

Better Information Regarding Local Needs

First note that local level governments cannot provide nationwide social goods as they benefit every citizen of the country and local governments can levy taxes only on the people living in their respective jurisdictions. Hence benefit principle cannot be followed if nationwide social goods are provided by the local governments. For similar reasons statewide social goods cannot be provided by the local municipal bodies. However, the centre can provide all kinds of social goods as it has the power to tax every citizen of the country. However, decentralized provision of social goods may be superior for the following reasons. First, a local government is closer to the people living within its jurisdiction. It has, therefore, better information regarding the needs of the local people for social goods. Let us illustrate with an example. Consider a gram panchayat of a village in India. It is a body of the elected representatives of the people living in the village. It, therefore, knows thoroughly the kinds of social goods the villagers need. It also has a fairly good knowledge regarding how the benefits of the social goods are likely to be distributed among people. Therefore, local governments are in a better position to provide efficiently local social goods whose benefits remain confined principally to their jurisdictions. For the reasons stated above decentralized provision of social goods is likely to be more efficient. Accordingly, nationwide, statewide and local social goods should be provided by the central, state and local governments respectively.

Scope for Experimentation

Another important advantage of decentralized provision of social goods is that the local bodies can experiment with social goods without putting all the people of the country to jeopardy. Such experiments, when fail, harm only a small section of the people living in the country. Experimentation in the provision of social goods is necessary as no one can be sure a priori as regards the best way of meeting a particular need. Kolkata's experiment with underground metro railway, for example, definitely helped other metropolitan cities to decide whether such modes of transport are of help to them or not. More precisely, other states can now decide better whether it is worthwhile to make the required level of expenditure and take the trouble of putting the facility in place for their cities. Similarly, West Bengal introduced teaching in only mother tongue and removed grading in primary schools to improve the performance of children at a later stage. The results of this experiment were certainly of great use to the other states.

Scope for Intergovernment Competition

Decentralized provision of social goods also creates scope for intergovernment competition. In a decentralized system, performance of a lower government will always be compared to that of others. If a lower government is inefficient in providing social goods relative to others, it will be noticed and written about in newspapers, government reports etc. Thus an inefficient lower government will be humiliated. As intercommunity movement is free, people and business may move out of the jurisdictions of inefficient lower governments to those of efficient ones. All this acts as a check against inefficiency.

Caveats: Externalities and Economies of Scale

There are, however, certain caveats in the above-mentioned scheme of decentralized provision of social goods. First of these is the externality generated by social goods. The benefits/costs of a local social good provided by a lower government may not remain confined entirely to its own jurisdiction. It may spill over to neighbouring areas to a certain extent. For example, an improvement in city streets made by Kolkata Corporation (the municipal body in charge of providing civic amenities to the residents of Kolkata) will benefit not only the residents of Kolkata but also those of the suburbs who commute daily to Kolkata to attend schools, colleges, offices etc. Hence these people must also be taxed to meet the cost of providing services of Kolkata streets. But Kolkata Corporation does not have that power. These externalities are, therefore, a leakage, which is a weakness of the decentralized provision of social goods. Local level social goods that generate substantial externalities have to be provided by the higher-level government. In India provision of state level social goods that generate substantial externalities is a joint responsibility of the centre and the states. A notable example of this type of goods is education. A state investing in education creates a skilled labour force. It is a source of skilled labour not only to the state making the investments but also to other states, as labour is freely mobile across states in a federation. Availability of skilled labour opens up investment opportunities and thereby gives a boost to investments in various areas not only in the state undertaking investment in education but also in other states. Thus the benefits of educational services provided by the state spill over to the other states as well. This type of services, therefore, has strong interstate spillover effects.

The other problem with decentralization consists in the economies of scale in the provision of certain social goods. Provision of certain social goods such as police service, which is provided in India by the state governments, may be subject to economies of scale. Centralized provision of these services will reduce unit cost of providing these services and thereby benefit the people. Economies of scale are often due to indivisibilities of certain inputs. To produce certain services, however small their quantities may be, some facilities of some minimum size have to be set up and these facilities may produce a much larger amount of the services than what the lower government produces. Therefore, to raise the outputs of these services from levels below the maximum that the above-mentioned facilities can support, quantities of all the inputs required for their production need not be raised until the outputs go beyond the maximum levels. Hence an increase in output of these services up to certain limits leads to a less than proportionate increase in the cost of production precipitating a fall in the unit cost of production. In case of police service, for example, communication and intelligence networks of some minimum sizes have to be set up to produce any positive amount of police service and often these networks are able to support much larger amounts of services than what is provided by the state governments. These economies of scale can, however, be reaped even in the decentralized scheme if the lower governments closely cooperate with one another and share the indivisible inputs.

10.2.1 Decentralized Provision of Social Goods: Theoretical Foundation

Theory of Clubs

We have built above a case for decentralized provision of social goods on the basis of spatial characteristics of social goods, i.e., on the basis of the fact that the size of the geographical area or the number of individuals a social good caters to varies from one social good to another. Buchanan (1965) in fact develops a model to classify social goods on the basis of the number of individuals they can optimally serve. He actually determines for every social good the optimum number of individuals it should serve and the optimum quantity in which it should be supplied. Buchanan's work was a reaction to the classification of goods into pure private goods and pure social goods by Samuelson and Musgrave. According to Samuelson and Musgrave a pure private good, as we have seen in Chapter 2, is rival and excludable. This means that a pure private good at any given point of time cannot be shared. It can cater to only a single individual at any given point of time. In contrast, a pure social good is one, which is non-rival and non-excludable. Since it is non-rival, an infinitely large number of individuals can consume it at the same time. These are, however, two extreme examples. Most of the goods, according to Buchanan, share the characteristics of both pure private and pure social goods. Even a given system of defence can cover only a finite area and, therefore, a finite number of individuals. Similarly, even a pair of shoes, though cannot be used by more than one individual at the same time, can be shared during a given period of time. Every social good is non-rival and, therefore, more than one individual can use it at the same time. However, there is a limit to the non-rivalness of every social good. Beyond a certain level an increase in the number of users of a social good will lead to a marked deterioration in the quality of its service to its consumers. Consider the example of national defence cited above. Similarly, the efficiency of a police force of a given size falls with the increase, beyond certain limits, in the area of the territory it serves. In fact, as shown by Buchanon, it is possible to think of an optimum number of consumers for every social good. Buchanon's theory, which is referred to as the theory of the clubs, determines the optimum number of individuals or the optimum size of the community or club for every social good. It does not stop just at that. It also determines the optimum scale of provision of every social good for its optimum club or community size. We present his model below.

Consider a social good. It is consumed by individuals who are all, for simplicity, assumed to be identical. The cost of providing the social good is distributed in line with the benefits received by the individuals. Since all individuals are identical, every individual derives the same amount of benefit from the social good provided. Hence everyone is charged the per capita cost of providing the social good. Suppose that Z denotes the total cost of providing the social good and $Z = Z(S)$; $Z' > 0$, where S stands for the amount of the social good supplied. The per capita cost of providing the social good is, therefore, given by $[Z(S)/N]$, where $N \equiv$ number of consumers of the social good. $[Z(S)/N]$ is the price that the government will charge every individual for the social good. Thus the larger the value of N, given S, the less is the price charged to a consumer.

However, with the increase in N, at least beyond a certain level, the quality of the service rendered by the good to each of its users deteriorates. Let us illustrate with an example. Suppose that the social good is a park. If the number of users of the park increases, then beyond a certain level the park gets congested and the service rendered by the park to each of its users deteriorates. This is true of most of the social goods. Think of a road or a bridge or of drainage and sanitation facilities or even of public administration and defence. Let us, for example, consider the case of defence. The larger the size of the population of a country, the greater is the difficulty of defending the people of the country, what with the problem of monitoring the activities of the suspected people, the extent of loss of life in case of ground or air attack etc. Hence the greater the density of population in a country, the less is the usefulness of a given system of national defence. Thus an increase in N inflicts a cost on the users of the social good. More precisely, corresponding to every N, every consumer of the social good suffers a given amount of disutility due to congestion or crowding. (This disutility may be negative, when N is small). The larger the value of N, the greater is this disutility. Buchanan assumes that this disutility can be measured in terms of money. Let us denote the money value of the disutility suffered by a representative consumer of the social good due to congestion by R. Obviously, R is an increasing function of N. Thus $R = R(N)$; $R' > 0$. Thus, total cost to a representative consumer of the social good consists of two components, namely, the per capita cost of providing the social good, $[Z(S)/N]$, and the money value of the disutility suffered by every consumer due to congestion, $R(N)$. Denoting this total cost by C, we have $C = [Z(S)/N] + R(N)$.

The optimum number of consumers or the optimum community or club size for a given social good is defined as the one corresponding to which C is minimum.

Let us now turn to the issue of the optimum level of output of the social good. The optimum scale of provision of the social good is defined as the one that best satisfies consumers' preferences. More precisely, provision of the social good is optimum, when supply price of the social good to the representative consumer equals her demand price for the social good. We denote the representative consumer's demand price by P^D. Obviously, $P^D = P^D(S)$; $P^{D\prime} < 0$, where $P^D(S)$ is the inverse demand function for the social good of the representative consumer. The supply price of the social good to the representative consumer, as we have already explained, is $[Z(S)/N]$, the per capita cost of providing the social good. At the optimum level of provision of the social good, as we have already pointed out, $P^D(S) = [Z(S)/N]$. Let us explain this condition a little more. Consider a level of S corresponding to which $P^D(S) > (<)[Z(S)/N]$. $[Z(S)/N]$ is the per capita cost of providing the social good. It is also the price charged to every consumer for the social good. Hence at the given level of S there is excess demand for (excess supply of) the social good at the price charged, i.e., at the price charged the representative consumer wants more (less) of the social good than the given S. Hence every consumer's demand is exactly met, i.e., every consumer's preference is best satisfied, when for the representative consumer $P^D(S) = [Z(S)/N]$. Thus in the optimal community or club for the social good where (i) the number of members or the number of consumers of the social good is optimum and (ii) the supply of the social good is also optimum, the following conditions are satisfied:

$$C = [Z(S)/N] + R(N) \text{ is minimum and}$$

$$\frac{Z(S)}{N} = P^D(S) \tag{10.1}$$

Thus, the optimal values of S and N are such that C is minimized and (10.1) is satisfied. We can derive the optimum values of S and N in the following manner. Corresponding to any given S we can find out the value of N that minimizes C. We shall get this value of N as a function of S, as given by $N(S)$. This function gives us corresponding to every value of S the value of N that minimizes C. Substituting this value of N in (10.1), we can solve it for the value of S that satisfies it. Putting this value of S in $N(S)$, we shall get the value of N that minimizes C corresponding to the given S. Thus we get the optimum values of S and N. In what follows, we derive these values.

The FOC of minimizing C with respect to N is given by

$$\frac{Z(S)}{N^2} = R'(N) \tag{10.2}$$

The LHS of (10.2) gives, given S, the fall in the per capita cost of providing the social good if the number of consumers rises by 1 unit. It, therefore, gives the marginal benefit of a rise in N. The RHS gives the increase in the cost to the representative consumer due to congestion following an increase in N. It, therefore, gives the marginal cost of a rise in N. At the optimum N the two are equal. By solving (10.2) we get the value of N that minimizes C, given S. In other words, solving (10.2), we get $N(S)$. Graphical derivation of this value of N is shown in Figure 10.1, where marginal benefit and marginal cost of N as given by the LHS and RHS of (10.2) and denoted by MBN and MCN respectively are measured on the vertical axis and N on the horizontal axis. The MB and MC schedules represent the LHS and RHS of (10.2) respectively. The MB schedule is drawn for a given value of S, S_0. The optimum value of N clearly corresponds to the point of intersection of the two schedules. This value of N is labelled N_0. For any N less (greater) than N_0, MBN is larger (less) than MCN. Hence, following a rise (fall) in N by 1 unit per capita cost of providing the social good will fall (rise) by a larger (smaller) amount than the increase (decrease) in R. Hence C will fall. This explains why the cost minimizing N corresponds to the point of intersection of the MBN and MCN schedules.

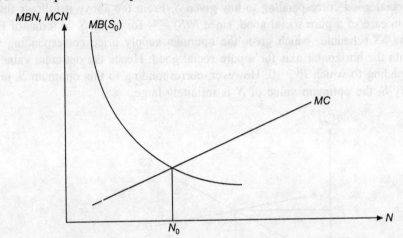

Figure 10.1: Determination of the cost minimizing N.

Following an increase in S—see (10.2)—the MC schedule will remain unaffected and the MB schedule will shift upward raising the optimum value of N. Thus N' of $N(S)$ is positive. Substituting $N(S)$ in (10.1), we can solve it for the optimum value of S and putting this optimum value of S in $N(S)$, we get the optimum value of N. Derivation of these values is shown graphically in Figure 10.2, where in the first quadrant we plot the demand price and supply price of S against S. The DD schedule represents $P^D(S)$, the inverse demand function for the social good. It gives the demand price, P^D, corresponding to every different S. It is downward sloping. The SS schedule on the other hand gives the supply price, $[Z(S)/N(S)]$, corresponding to every S. Since both Z and N increase with a rise in S, the slope of SS is ambiguous. We show it as an upward sloping line in Figure 10.2. The optimum value of S corresponds to the point of intersection of DD and SS. It is labelled S^*. In the fourth quadrant NS represents the function $N(S)$. The optimum value of N clearly corresponds to the optimum value of S on NS. It is labelled N^*.

The major implication of the model presented above is that it classifies social goods in accordance with the optimum number of consumers or the optimum community size they cater to. First, consider the case of the pure public good as defined by Musgrave and Samuelson. It is non-rival without any limit. It means that, if the number of consumers of a pure social good increases, it will not lead to any congestion. The quality of its service to the consumers will remain unaffected. However, with an increase in the number of consumers of the pure social good, the per capita cost of providing the social good will fall. Thus, in case of a pure social good, corresponding to any given S marginal benefit of a rise in N is positive, but marginal cost of a rise in N is nil for every N. The optimum value of N corresponding to any given S is, therefore, infinitely large. One can derive this result also using Figure 10.1, where the MC schedule in the case of a pure public good coincides with the horizontal axis. MB schedule, however, remains as usual above the horizontal axis for every N, when $S > 0$—see the LHS of (10.2). Hence the optimum value of N corresponding to every non-zero S is infinitely large.

Let us now focus on Figure 10.2. $[Z(S)/N(S)]$—see (10.1)—gives the optimum supply price of a social good corresponding to any given S. From the above it follows that it is zero for every S in case of a pure social good, since $N(S) = \infty$ for every S. In terms of Figure 10.2, therefore, the SS schedule, which gives the optimum supply price corresponding to every S, coincides with the horizontal axis for a pure social good. Hence the optimum value of S is the one corresponding to which $P^D = 0$. However, corresponding to this optimum S, just as in the case of every S, the optimum value of N is infinitely large.

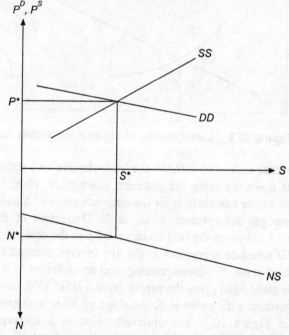

Figure 10.2: Determination of the optimum values of N and S.

From the above it follows that, given the cost of provision of a social good, the closer the good to a pure social good, i.e., the greater the extent of its non-rivalness, the lower is $R'(N)$, the marginal cost of a rise in N, i.e., the lower is the MC schedule in Figure 10.1. Hence, the larger is N or the community size corresponding to any given S. Again, given Z, the larger the community size corresponding to any given S, the lower is the optimum supply price corresponding to every S, i.e., the lower is the SS schedule in Figure 10.2. Hence, given the demand function, the optimum values of both N and S will be larger. Similarly, one can also easily deduce that, given other factors, the greater the demand for a social good, the larger are its optimum values of N and S. *Since degrees of non-rivalness and demands of different social goods are different, optimum community sizes of different social goods are also different. Buchanon's model, therefore, gives a theoretical foundation for classifying social goods on the basis of the number of consumers they should optimally cater to. Thus, social goods, whose optimum community sizes equal the whole population of the country, are nationwide social goods. Social goods whose optimal community sizes more or less equal the average population of a state are statewide social goods and so on. For reasons discussed in the earlier section there is a case for keeping the responsibility of providing only nationwide social goods with the centre and delegating the provision of statewide and local social goods to the states and the local bodies respectively.*

Mechanism of Preference Revelation under Decentralized Provision of Social Goods: Voting by Feet

In addition to the reasons for decentralized provision of social goods discussed earlier, an important and interesting argument in its favour has been provided by Tiebout (1956). His argument is presented below. Samuelson showed that in case of social goods there is no mechanism for preference revelation. Accordingly, social goods cannot be produced in optimum quantities. (We have explained these points in Chapter 2.) Tiebout argues that though this is true in case of centrally-provided nationwide social goods, there does exist a mechanism of preference revelation in case of statewide and local social goods, when their provision is decentralized and delegated to the states and the local bodies. Tiebout argued that even though people cannot move freely across nations, they can do so across jurisdictions of states and local bodies. Therefore, *if in a state tax burden is high relative to the quality and quantity of the social goods provided, people will leave such states and migrate to states where the situation is better. This phenomenon is referred to as 'voting by feet'. Tiebout argued that through this voting by feet a country will achieve an efficient outcome in respect of provision of statewide and local social goods.*

Let us illustrate his argument using Buchanan's model presented above. The model shows that every social good has an optimum community size. If the community size of a local social good is larger (smaller) than the optimum, it means that the per capita cost of providing the social good, though low (high), is too high (low) relative to the quality and quantity of the social good provided. In other words, in larger (smaller) than optimum communities, people are paying more (less) for social goods through taxes than what they are willing to. This we see clearly in Figure 10.2, where we find that in larger (smaller) than optimum communities, with $N > (<)N^*$, supply price of social goods is higher (lower) than the demand price. Hence people will leave larger than optimum communities to smaller than optimum communities and thereby tend to make the size of every community optimum.

Thus, more generally, if statewide and local social goods are provided by the states and the local bodies respectively, per capita availability of these social goods and their quality (the factors that determine the demand price of these social goods) and per capita tax burden (the supply price of these social goods) are likely to vary widely across communities. Hence the mechanism of voting by feet is likely to operate tending to make all community sizes optimum. People will move away from communities where the supply price exceeds the demand price to join the communities where just the opposite holds. This mechanism will not operate if these goods are provided by the centre. Under centralized provision, per capita availability of these goods and their quality and per capita tax burden will be uniform in every community ruling out any scope for the mechanism of voting by feet to operate. Thus, *Buchanan's theory of clubs together with Tiebout's voting by feet argument constitute a strong theoretical basis for decentralized provision of social goods. More precisely, these two studies together show that if statewide and local social goods are provided by the states and local bodies respectively, their provision will be socially efficient.*

The problem with Tiebout's argument is that an individual's decision regarding where to live is governed not only by the quality and quantity of social goods available and tax burden but also by job opportunities. Thus people may not leave a larger than optimum community if job opportunities are plentiful there. To what extent the mechanism of voting by feet will operate depends upon the relative importance of other factors such as job opportunities in the choice of location of the individuals. This is an empirical matter and has to be settled empirically.

10.3   TAXATION

It follows from our above discussion that the nationwide, statewide and local social goods should be provided by the centre, states and local bodies respectively. The question that now emerges is whether tax powers should also be decentralized so that every level of government gets the power to tax people within its jurisdiction to meet the cost of provision of the social goods it provides. It is implicit in our discussion above that every government should tax the beneficiaries of the social goods it provides to defray the cost of provision of social goods. However, there are certain problems with such a scheme in a federation. People and factors are freely mobile across jurisdictions of lower governments and this creates considerable problems for decentralization of tax powers. We just pointed out above that such mobility may lead to voting by feet, which has a beneficial impact on society. However, if issues of income distribution are taken into account, voting by feet may aggravate income disparities among communities. Let us illustrate this point with an example. Consider a state with a high concentration of the poor. Its per capita income is, therefore, low. Need for social goods in this state may be high. The poor have to depend on publicly provided education, health care, sanitation, drinking water etc. as they cannot afford to spend on such services. On the other hand, high concentration of the poor may lead to greater incidence of crime, drunkenness etc. and hence the rich might also require higher levels of police and other administrative services for protection. The poor may have little taxable capacity. Their income may be too low to generate any surplus after meeting the basic necessities of food, shelter and clothing. Hence it may not be possible to tax the poor even though they derive considerable benefits from the government-provided social goods. The government, therefore, cannot help taxing only the rich to meet the cost of social goods. As a result taxes on the rich in this state may be considerably higher relative to the benefits of social goods reaped by them compared to the states where there is smaller concentration of the poor. This may induce the rich to vote by feet and move away from the poor state to rich states with lower concentration of the poor. This will reduce the per capita income and, therefore, the tax base of the poor state. Along with the rich, capital may also move away leading to considerable economic stress for the poor state. Thus, when there exists considerable economic inequality among communities, decentralization of tax powers may induce the rich to move from poorer communities to richer ones aggravating income disparities, worsening the tax base of the poor communities and thereby seriously undermining their capacities to meet the needs for social goods of their poor members. For these reasons decentralization of tax powers is usually not recommended. When tax powers rest with the centre, tax rates will be uniform across all states. Hence moving away from one state to another will not give any tax relief. Even though it is not all that difficult to move from one state to another within a federation, it is quite difficult to move from one country to another. Hence, even if the centre imposes taxes at high rates, it will usually not be possible for people to move away to low tax countries to escape the tax burden.

More generally, there is usually considerable income disparity across states in a federation. As a result ability to provide social goods varies substantially across states. Rich states have high per capita income and low incidence of poverty. Hence they have large tax bases. People in these states, being rich, need not depend much on publicly-provided goods. Such states, therefore, have in their command a large resource base relative to their needs. Poor states with low per capita income and high incidence of poverty on the other hand have command over a woefully inadequate resource base relative to their needs. This *disparity in the states' abilities to provide the social goods they have to provide is considered undesirable in every federation. If tax powers rest with the centre, it can distribute the tax revenue that it collects in excess of its own needs equitably among states so that their abilities to provide social goods become equal.*

Moreover, there are substantial economies of scale in tax collection. For these reasons *tax powers in almost all federations are concentrated in the centre. Most of the taxes everywhere are levied and collected by the centre and only a few are left to the states and local bodies.*

10.4 VERTICAL AND HORIZONTAL FISCAL IMBALANCES

From the above it follows that *in a federation provision of social goods has to be decentralized, but most of the tax powers have to be vested in the centre. This will obviously lead to considerable fiscal imbalance between the centre and the states. The former will have much larger amount of tax collection than what it needs to provide the social goods that it has to provide, while the states or the lower bodies will have in their command much less resources than what they need for providing the social goods that they should provide. This imbalance is referred to as vertical fiscal imbalance.* This problem is removed through transfers of incomes from the centre to the lower level governments. These transfers are called *grants*. Grants may be of various types. We shall discuss them below.

Besides the imbalance between the centre and the lower level governments, there may be, as we have pointed out above, substantial fiscal imbalance among fiscal positions of states as well. This imbalance is referred to as horizontal imbalance. Fiscal position of a state refers to its ability to provide the social goods that it is required to provide. Obviously, fiscal position of a state depends upon the amount of revenue that it can collect relative to the amount of revenue that it needs to provide the social goods at the required level. The amount of revenue that a state can raise depends upon its tax base and its tax effort. The latter is the tax rate that the state applies to its tax base. *Tax base of a state is called its fiscal capacity.* The revenue that a state needs to provide social goods depends upon the unit cost of providing social goods and the need for social goods. The latter in turn depends, among others, upon the size of the population, the area of the state, the proportion of poor people in the population etc. Let us illustrate with an example. States in India provide police service. The larger the area of the state and/or the greater the size of the population, the greater is the scale on which police service is to be provided. Consider two states. Suppose that one state's population size is twice that of the other. Clearly, monitoring the activities of a larger population is more difficult and costly. Similar argument holds for the area as well. Again, the poor have to depend on public provision for most of the goods, as their income is barely sufficient for the basic necessities such as food and clothing. Thus the revenue need is determined by a host of factors. Some of these are the unit cost of providing social goods, the area of the state, the size of the population and incidence of poverty. (Try to think of other possible determinants of the need for social goods. Also try to identify the determinants of the unit cost of providing social goods.) *Fiscal position of a state is determined by its fiscal capacity relative to its revenue or fiscal need. The greater a state's fiscal capacity relative to its need, the better is its fiscal position.* Every federation wants every state to have equal fiscal position, i.e., every federation wants to remove horizontal fiscal imbalance. Every federation, therefore, designs its transfers or grants in such a manner that both vertical and horizontal imbalances are removed. We shall discuss the issues of horizontal and vertical imbalances in detail in the Indian context later.

It should be noted here that there might also exist vertical imbalance between a state and its rural/urban local bodies. There may exist horizontal fiscal imbalance among the local bodies within a state too. These are, just as in the earlier case, corrected through transfer of incomes from the state to its local bodies. Let us now focus on these income transfers.

10.5 ECONOMICS OF GRANTS

Incomes, as we have mentioned above, *have to be transferred from the centre to the states and from the states to the local bodies to remove vertical and horizontal imbalances. These transfers are called grants.* Grants may be divided into two broad categories, conditional and unconditional. Conditional grants in turn may be either matching grant or earmarked grant. The latter is also called specific grant. We shall examine the economic effects of these grants below.

10.5.1 Unconditional Grant

To examine the economic impact of grants we consider a very simple example of a community, which consumes just one private good, X, and a public good, Y. Its income in terms of the private good is M. Individual members of the community spend the whole of their disposable income on X. The price at which the lower government, which is in charge of providing social goods to the community, can purchase Y to supply it to the members of the community is P_Y.

This price is given in terms of the private good. The combinations of X and Y that the community can consume is, therefore, given by the budget equation

$$M = X + P_Y Y \qquad (10.3)$$

The social welfare function of the community is given by $U(X, Y)$. The lower government, by assumption, knows this function and the budget constraint and chooses the tax rate and Y in such a manner that the community's welfare is maximized subject to the budget constraint. The government decides on G and the tax rate by carrying out the following exercise:

$$\max_{Y, X} U(Y, X)$$

$$\text{subject to } \quad M = X + P_Y Y \qquad (10.4)$$

Suppose that the solution of this exercise is given by (X_0, Y_0). The tax that the government collects is, therefore, given by $P_Y Y_0$ and the tax rate that it applies to community's income, M, equals $(P_Y Y_0 / M)$. The lower government buys with this tax revenue the optimal quantity of the social good. The community uses the rest of its income, its disposable income, to purchase X. It therefore, purchases, the optimum quantity of X, X_0. The situation is depicted in Figure 10.3, where AB represents the community's budget line, as given by (10.3). Its vertical intercept AO equals M and the absolute value of its slope equals P_Y. The optimum point on AB is labelled Q. The tax rate is given by (AX_0/AO), where AX_0 gives the amount of income that will remain with the community after it has consumed X_0 amount of X.

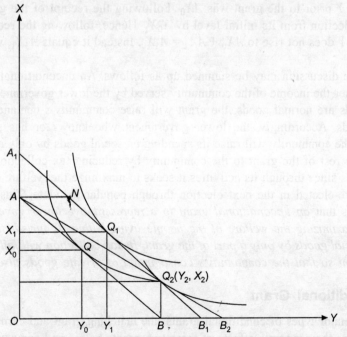

Figure 10.3: Unconditional and matching grants.

Now, suppose that an unconditional grant of G is given to the lower government. *An unconditional grant is one, which a higher government gives to a lower government without imposing any conditions regarding how it should be used.* It is just like a transfer income received by the community from the higher-level government. The lower government, being representative of the members of the community, spends it in such a manner that the community's social welfare is maximized. Thus the budget line of the community becomes

$$M + G = X + P_Y Y \qquad (10.5)$$

The lower government now chooses Y and the tax rate in such a manner that U is maximized subject to the new budget constraint. If X and Y are both normal goods, G will be allocated between both and the whole of G will not be spent only on Y. Suppose that maximization of U subject to the budget constraint requires spending of only $G_0 < G$ on Y over and above the initial expenditure of $P_Y Y_0$. Then the government, which wants to maximize the welfare of the community will pass on the remaining part of the grant, $(G - G_0)$, to the community so that this amount gets spent on X. This the government can do by reducing total tax collection, which was $P_Y Y_0$ prior to the receipt of the grant, by $(G - G_0)$. The situation is shown in Figure 10.3, where $A_1 B_1$ is the new post-grant budget line, as given by (10.5). AA_1 measures the amount of the grant, G. The optimum point on this budget line is Q_1, which contains more of both X and Y than Q. This means that maximization of social welfare requires the lower government to raise its spending on Y by only a part of the grant received. $X_0 X_1$ represents the part of the total grant that the lower government transfers to the community by reducing tax collection so that its consumption of X rises by $X_0 X_1$. The initial tax collection and expenditure on Y prior to the grant was AX_0. Following the receipt of the grant, government reduces tax collection from its initial level by $X_0 X_1$. Hence, following the receipt of the grant, expenditure on Y does not rise to $AX_0 + AA_1 = A_1 X_0$. Instead it equals $A_1 X_1$, which is less than $A_1 X_0$ by $X_0 X_1$.

The above discussion may be summed up as follows. An unconditional grant to a lower government raises the income of the community served by the lower government. If both private and social goods are normal goods, the grant will raise community's demand for both private and social goods. Accordingly, the lower government who knows or has some idea of the preferences of the community will raise its spending on social goods by only a part of the grant and pass on the rest of the grant to the community by reducing tax collection. This the lower government does since through its activities it seeks to maximize the welfare of the community so that it gets re-elected in the next election through popular mandate. This simple example, therefore, shows that *an unconditional grant to a representative lower government, which is interested in maximizing the welfare of the people living within its jurisdiction, will raise its spending on social goods by only a part of the grant. Its tax collection will fall by the remaining part of the grant so that the community's consumption of private goods also rises.*

10.5.2 Conditional Grant

There are two major types of conditional grants, the matching grant and earmarked or specific grant. We discuss the economic effects of these two grants below and compare them with each other and also with the unconditional grant.

Matching Grant

A matching grant is one, which matches the lower government's expenditure on some specific good or goods. Suppose that the higher government wants the lower government to provide more of social goods or more of some specific social good. It can seek to achieve that through a matching grant. It can specify that for every rupee spent by the lower government on social goods or on some specific social goods, as the case may be, it will give a matching grant of a given amount, which may be Re. 1 or some other given amount. Let us illustrate with an example. The central government may announce that for every rupee spent on education by any state government, it will give to the state government a grant of Re. 1. This grant is a matching grant. We shall first examine the economic impact of a matching grant and then compare the economic impact of this grant to that of an unconditional grant. We shall compare an unconditional grant and a matching grant of the same amount. We shall carry out these exercises using the same simple framework used above to examine the impact of an unconditional grant.

Suppose that the higher government gives a matching grant of v (measured in terms of the private good, X) per unit of expenditure (also measured in terms of the private good, X) of the local government on the social good, Y. Thus, if the local government spends P_Y, which denotes the price of Y in terms of X, on Y, it will get a matching grant of $P_Y v$. Therefore, to buy one unit of Y the local government will now have to spend only $[P_Y/(1 + v)]$ and not P_Y. (Explain this point yourself.) The local government gets the difference between P_Y and $[P_Y/(1 + v)]$ as matching grant per unit of the social good purchased. A matching grant, therefore, reduces the price of the commodity on which it is given. The matching grant being discussed here reduces the price of Y from P_Y to $[P_Y/(1 + v)]$. However, it does not affect the income of the community or prices of other goods. Hence in our simple example the budget line of the community under the matching grant considered here becomes

$$M = X + [P_Y/(1 + v)]Y \tag{10.6}$$

The local government as before will choose Y and the tax rate in such a manner that the community's welfare is maximized subject to the above budget constraint. Let (X_2, Y_2) be the optimum combination of X and Y that maximizes welfare of the community subject to the above budget constraint. The local government will, therefore, spend $[P_Y/(1 + v)]Y_2$ on Y exclusive of the matching grant. It will, therefore, collect $[P_Y/(1 + v)]Y_2$ amount of tax revenue so that the private sector consumes X_1 amount of X. The local government in equilibrium receives a total matching grant of $v [P_Y/(1 + v)]Y_2$, where Y_2 is also a function of, among other factors, v. Thus the total amount of matching grant, given P_Y, M and the utility function, is a function of v. AB_2 in Figure 10.3 represents the post-grant budget line (10.6). Its vertical intercept is clearly M, which is the same as that of the pre-grant grant budget line AB representing (10.3). Its slope (absolute value) is, however, $[P_Y/(1 + v)]$, which is less than P_Y. P_Y is the absolute value of the slope of the pre-grant budget line. The matching grant budget line will, therefore, lie above the pre-grant budget line. Along the matching grant budget line real income of the community is larger than that along the pre-grant budget line as the community is able to attain higher social indifference curves. The matching grant will, therefore, raise the consumption of the social good through the income effect, if it is a normal good. In addition, the matching grant reduces the price of the social good. This will produce a substitution effect as well. The fall in the price of the social good will induce the community to substitute the social good for the private good. Thus *the matching grant will raise community's expenditure on social goods through both the substitution and the income effect.* In Figure 10.3 the community chooses from AB_2 the point Q_2, which contains more Y than Q, which is the optimum point on the pre-grant budget line AB. (*Exercise:* Decompose the increase in Y from the pre-grant to the post-grant situation into substitution and income effect.)

We shall now compare the economic impact of a matching grant to that of an unconditional grant of equal value. We have already pointed out above that the total amount given in equilibrium as matching grant depends on the matching grant's rate, v. We assume here that the higher government chooses v in such a manner that the total matching grant equals G, the amount of the unconditional grant considered above. This assumption is made just for the sake of comparing the economic effects of the matching grant to that of an unconditional grant. Unless the grants are of equal value, no meaningful comparison can be made. Thus, by assumption v is chosen in such a manner that the total amount of matching grant in equilibrium equals G. Let us denote this v by v^*. We assume that the budget line (10.6) with $v = v^*$ is represented by AB_2 in Figure 10.3. Thus the pair (X_2, Y_2), as shown in the figure, is the optimum point for the community in the post-matching grant situation, when $v = v^*$. The total equilibrium amount of matching grant received by the lower government is, therefore, $v^*[P_Y/(1 + v^*)]Y_2 = G$ (by assumption). Obviously, (X_2, Y_2) satisfy the budget constraint, (10.6). Hence

$$M = X_2 + [P_Y/(1 + v^*)]Y_2$$

$$\Rightarrow \qquad M = X_2 + [P_Y/(1 + v^*)]Y_2 + v^*[P_Y/(1 + v^*)]Y_2 - v^*[P_Y/(1 + v^*)]Y_2$$

$$= X_2 + P_Y Y_2 - G$$

$$\Rightarrow \qquad M + G = X_2 + P_Y Y_2 \qquad\qquad (10.7)$$

Thus (X_2, Y_2) satisfy the unconditional grant budget equation, (10.5), also. (X_2, Y_2) will, therefore, lie on both the matching grant budget line, AB_2 and the unconditional budget line, A_1B_1. In other words, it is given by the point of intersection, Q_2, of the two budget lines as shown in Figure 10.3.

The reason why (X_2, Y_2) should lie on the unconditional grant budget line is not far to seek. The matching grant reduces the price of the social good effectively faced by the lower government. This is because per unit of the social good purchased the lower government receives a given amount of matching grant. Hence the fall in the price of the social good to the lower government in the post-grant situation is nothing but the amount of matching grant received by the lower government per unit of the social good purchased. It has no impact on either the income of the community or the prices of other goods. Check this point yourself. Let us illustrate with an example. Suppose that the price of the social good was Re. 1 in the pre-grant situation. Now the higher government sanctions a matching grant of Re. 1 for every rupee spent by the local government on the social good. Thus, to purchase one unit of the social good the lower government now has to spend only Re. 0.5, since it will get a matching grant of Re. 0.5 for its expenditure of Re. 0.5 on the social good. Thus the price of the social good to the lower government in the post-grant situation falls to Re. 0.5 and this *fall in the price of the social good to the lower government in the post-grant situation is nothing but the amount of matching grant received by the lower government per unit of the social good purchased.* This means that the *total amount of matching grant received by the lower government in equilibrium is nothing but the absolute amount of fall in the price of the social good multiplied by the equilibrium quantity of the social good purchased.* Again, if we compare the pre-grant and the post-grant situations, *the only difference in prices is that the price of the social good (the good on which the matching grant is given) effectively faced by the lower government is less.* Income of the community is unaffected. Hence, *the value of the post-grant equilibrium (X, Y) evaluated at the post-grant prices is equal to the community's income.* From the above statements given in italics it follows that the value of the post-grant equilibrium (x, y) evaluated at the pre-grant prices should exceed the community's income by the total amount of the matching grant received by the lower government in equilibrium. In our example, therefore, the value of post-grant equilibrium (X, Y) evaluated at pre-grant prices should exceed the community's income, M, by G, the equilibrium amount of the matching grant. Thus the post-grant equilibrium (X, Y) satisfy the unconditional grant budget equation also. However, at the (X, Y) chosen under the matching grant from the unconditional grant budget line $mrs_{Y,X} = [P_Y/(1 + v)] < P_Y$, the slope of the unconditional grant budget line. At the equilibrium (X, Y) chosen under the unconditional grant $mrs_{Y,X} = P_Y$. At every point to the left (right) of this equilibrium point on the unconditional grant budget line $mrs_{Y,X} > P_Y$ $(mrs_{Y,X} < P_Y)$. Hence the matching grant equilibrium (X, Y) will lie to the right of the unconditional grant equilibrium (X, Y) on the unconditional grant budget line. Hence under the matching grant consumption of the social good will be larger.

The reason for the result is not far to seek. The amount of grant is the same in the two cases, i.e., in both cases the same amount of income is transferred from the higher to the lower government. Hence the income effect is the same in the two cases. But in the matching grant case, price of the social good also becomes less. Hence the matching grant produces a substitution effect along with the income effect. This substitution effect induces the community to substitute the cheaper social good for the private good. The consumption of the social good under the matching grant is larger because of this substitution effect. The result of our exercise may, therefore, be summed up as follows. *If a matching grant of a given amount is given to a lower government, a larger part of this grant will be spent in the desired direction compared to the situation where the same amount is given in the form of an unconditional grant.* Clearly, a matching grant on a particular commodity or a particular set of commodities, unlike an unconditional grant, constitutes interference with the community's choice. It interferes with the community's choice by lowering the price of the good on which the grant is given from its true price. Thus, a higher government gives a matching grant on a commodity, when it regards the commodity as a merit good.

Close-ended Matching Grant

When there is a ceiling on the total amount of matching grant, it is a close-ended matching grant. Let us illustrate with an example. Consider the case presented above where the higher government gives a matching grant of v for every unit of expenditure by the lower government on the social good. To buy a unit of the social good, Y, therefore the lower government has to spend only $[P_Y/(1 + v)]$, as it gets the remaining part, $[vP_Y/(1 + v)]$, as matching grant. Thus the lower government gets a matching grant of $[vP_Y/(1 + v)]$ per unit of Y purchased. Suppose that the ceiling on the total amount of matching grant is Q. Then the lower government will get matching grant as long as its purchase of Y is less than or equal to Y_0, where Y_0 is such that

$[vP_Y/(1 + v)]Y_0$ equals Q. Therefore, for purchases of Y in excess of Y_0 the effective price of Y to the lower government will no longer be $[P_Y/(1 + v)]$. It will again be P_Y. Thus the budget line under the close-ended matching grant will be given by (10.6) for $Y \le Y_0$ and by

$$M + Q = X + P_Y Y \text{ for } Y > Y_0 \tag{10.8}$$

Let us explain. Suppose that the value of X that satisfies (10.6), when $Y = Y_0$ is X_0. Putting these values of X and Y in (10.6), we have

$$M = X_0 + [P_Y/(1 + v)]Y_0$$
$$= X_0 + [P_Y/(1 + v)]Y_0 + v[P_Y/(1 + v)]Y_0 - v[P_Y/(1 + v)]Y_0$$
$$= X_0 + P_Y Y_0 - Q$$
$$\Rightarrow \qquad M + Q = X_0 + P_Y Y_0$$

Thus (X_0, Y_0) satisfies (10.8). (Explain this point yourself.) If now the community seeks to purchase more Y, it will have to pay P_Y for every additional unit of Y purchased. The community exhausts all its income in purchasing (X_0, Y_0), whose value at pre-grant prices is $M + Q$. Therefore, for every additional unit of Y purchased beyond Y_0, the community will have to lower purchase of X from X_0 by P_Y. Thus, the value of every (X, Y) that contains larger than Y_0 amount of Y evaluated at pre-grant prices is the same as that of (X_0, Y_0) evaluated at pre-grant prices. Every such (X, Y) will, therefore, satisfy (10.8).

The close-ended matching grant budget line is shown graphically in Figure 10.4. It is represented by ABB_1. The vertical intercept of the budget line, OA, is given by M. Its slope (absolute value) for $Y \le Y_0$ is $[P_Y/(1 + v)]$. B represents the combination (X_0, Y_0). However, for $Y > Y_0$ the budget line is given by (10.8) represented by A_1BB_1. Hence for $Y > Y_0$ the budget line is given by BB_1, which is steeper than AB. A_1BB_1 is the unconditional grant budget line,

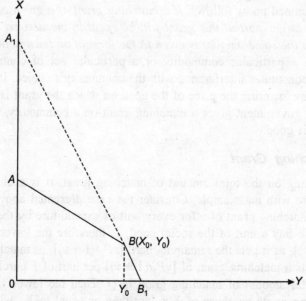

Figure 10.4: Close-ended matching grants.

when community's income in terms of X including the unconditional grant equals $M + Q$ and the prices of X and Y are P_X and P_Y respectively. Its vertical intercept is $(M + Q)$ and absolute value of its slope is P_Y. Clearly, AA_1 equals Q, the ceiling amount of the matching grant in terms of the private good.

We shall now compare the economic effect of a close-ended matching grant to that of an unconditional grant of the same amount. Let the amount of these grants be G. If the ceiling on the close-ended matching grant is Q, then only two situations are possible: in one $Q > G$ and in the other $Q = G$. Obviously, if $Q < G$, equilibrium amount of matching grant can never be equal to G. Here also equilibrium values of X and Y under the close-ended matching grant will depend upon the rate of the matching grant, v, given the social welfare function, community's income and the prices of X and Y. We assume for the sake of comparison that the higher government chooses v in such a manner that the equilibrium amount of total matching grant received equals G. Consider first the case where $G < Q$. If in this situation there exists a v that makes the equilibrium amount of total matching grant equal to G, the equilibrium will obviously occur in the interior of the flatter portion of the close-ended matching grant budget line. It will occur for reasons discussed in the case of the matching grant at the point of intersection of the close-ended budget line and the unconditional grant budget line, with the amount of grant equal to G, as shown in Figure 10.5(A). At the equilibrium point, as before, $mrs_{YX} = P_Y/(1 + v) < P_Y$, the slope of the unconditional grant budget line. Hence, for reasons discussed earlier, the close-ended matching grant equilibrium (X, Y) will lie to the right of the unconditional grant equilibrium (X, Y) on the unconditional grant budget line. Hence under the close-ended matching grant consumption of the social good will be larger.

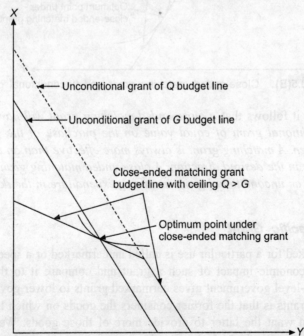

Figure 10.5(A): Close-ended matching grant and unconditional grant I.

Now consider the case where $G = Q$. In this case, if there exists a v that makes the equilibrium amount of the total matching grant equal to G, then the equilibrium will obviously occur on the steeper portion of the close-ended matching grant budget line and this portion coincides with the unconditional grant budget line corresponding to Q amount of grant, as shown in Figure 10.5(B). Hence, in this case it will have the same effect as the unconditional grant.

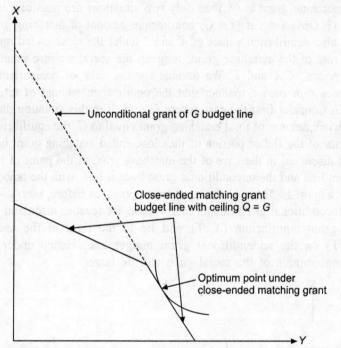

Figure 10.5(B): Close-ended matching grant and unconditional grant II.

From the above it follows that *a close-ended matching grant will have at least the same impact as an unconditional grant of equal value on the purchase of the good on which the matching grant is given. A matching grant is always more effective than an unconditional grant in raising expenditure in the desired direction. A close-ended matching grant on the other hand is more effective than an unconditional grant in raising expenditure in the desired direction, but not always.*

Earmarked or Specific Grant

A grant that is earmarked for a particular use is called an earmarked or a specific grant. We shall examine below the economic impact of such a grant and compare it to the grants discussed above. Often a higher-level government gives earmarked grants to lower governments. The only justification of such grants is that the former considers the goods on which the grants are given to be merit goods and want the latter to provide more of those goods. We shall examine the economic impact of the earmarked grant using the same framework used earlier. Suppose that a local government gets G amount of earmarked grant (measured in terms of the private good, X) and it is earmarked for the social good, Y. We can examine its impact in terms of Figure 10.3. Let us focus on the budget line. Suppose that the pre-grant budget equation is given by (10.3), which is represented by AB in the figure. Following the receipt of the earmarked grant of G, the community can raise its purchase of Y by (G/P_Y) corresponding to every level of X it could purchase earlier. The budget line will, therefore, shift to the right by the amount (G/P_Y), with the maximum possible consumption of X remaining equal to $OA(=M)$. The new budget line, therefore, coincides with the unconditional grant budget line A_1B_1, given by (10.5). (Explain yourself.) However, it will not include the portion A_1N (why?). Thus the new budget line is NB_1. Clearly, the earmarked grant will have the same impact as the unconditional grant if the optimum point at which $mrs_{YX} = P_Y$ on A_1B_1 is located on NB_1. In this case, therefore, the community consumes more of both X and Y. Hence the grant, G, despite being earmarked, is spent on both Y and X. Let us explain how this becomes possible. Since the grant is earmarked, it is spent fully on Y. However, the government reduces its tax collection and thereby its spending exclusive of the grant to such an extent that the total expenditure on Y including the grant falls in the post-grant situation. The reduction in tax collectin enables the community to consume more X. However, if it is located in the interior of A_1N, the community's welfare will be maximized at N (why?) In this case, clearly, the earmarked grant raises the community's expenditure on Y more than an unconditional grant of equal amount. Thus an earmarked grant is at least as effective as an unconditional grant of equal amount in raising a lower government's expenditure in the desired direction.

The result that we get from our above analysis is that an earmarked grant does not necessarily lead to an additional expenditure equal to the grant amount in the desired direction. There may be leakage and a part of the grant may be used to reduce taxes. Thus, *if the higher government identifies certain social goods as merit goods and want the lower government to provide more of these, it will do better if it provides a matching or an earmarked grant. The former is necessarily better than, while the latter is at least as good as the unconditional grant.*

10.6 FLYPAPER EFFECT

From our discussion of the unconditional grant it follows that its impact is equivalent to that of a transfer income of equal amount given to the community. In both cases the community's budget line will be the same and hence the community will choose the same combination of X and Y. Hence in both cases expenditures on private and social goods, i.e., private expenditure and public expenditure, will increase by the same amounts. Empirical investigations carried out in the US, however, do not support this. They show that, if the grant is given to the local government, public expenditure increases more and private expenditure rises less compared to the situation where the same amount is given as transfer income to the community. This phenomenon is known as the flypaper effect, as the money tends to remain in the sector where it is initially given. It is not hard to explain this phenomenon. Even though the local government has some idea about the tastes and preferences of the community, it does not know the social welfare function exactly. When it receives a grant, it knows that the community will want to allocate it between both types of goods. Hence it should spend only a part of it on social goods and use the rest for reducing taxes. However, it by no means knows the exact allocation of the grant desired by the community. It, therefore, has to depend upon the reaction of the people following the receipt of the grant in determining its allocation. If following the receipt of the grant there is a strong demand for tax reduction, it goes in for a substantial tax cut. Otherwise, it uses the major part of the grant for raising its own expenditure. In reality, when a lower government receives a grant, demand for a tax reduction is not usually strong. This may happen on account of the fact that most of the people may remain unaware of the receipt of the grant. Hence major part of the grant is used to finance additional public expenditure. Similarly, when the community receives transfer income, it usually does not demand strongly for a tax increase, may be because of the free rider problem explained in Chapter 2. Hence major part of the transfer is used to purchase private goods. This may explain the asymmetry.

10.7   INCOME DISTRIBUTION

Reduction in inequality and achieving an optimum income distribution are a major task of the government. Decentralization of this function may not be feasible for the following reasons. There are usually no restrictions on people moving across states or jurisdictions of local bodies in a federation. Under these conditions if the states or local bodies attempt at redistributing income, their efforts are likely to be frustrated. Let us illustrate with an example. Consider two states, one with a higher degree of inequality than the other. The former accordingly taxes the rich at higher rates and gives transfers to the poor at higher rates also. This will obviously induce its rich to move out to and the poor to move in to it from the latter. This will lead to a drastic shrinkage in the tax base of the former making the redistribution programme infeasible. Thus, if the function of income redistribution is decentralized, the rich may flock to the states with the lowest tax rates and the poor may move to the states with the highest rate of transfer. Hence the country will fail to achieve the desired income distribution. If, however, the task of redistribution is given to the centre, rates of taxes on the rich and those of transfers to the poor will be uniform across all states. Hence there will be no incentive to move from one state to another. For this reason *the task of redistribution of income usually rests with the centre.* The scheme works because it is quite difficult for people to move from one country to another.

10.8   STABILIZATION

The function of stabilization should also rest with the centre for the following reasons. Economies of the constituent political units in a federation—economies of the states in India, for example—are closely interrelated. Every political unit exports quite a substantial part of its aggregate production to the rest of the federation and imports a sizable portion of the rest of the country's GDP. Hence the constituent political units cannot adopt stabilization policies independently. Expansionary programme in one unit will lead to expansion in other units and vice versa. Thus, if one unit adopts an expansionary policy and the other a contractionary one, they will tend to neutralize one another. Even when all the states adopt expansionary (contractionary) programmes, if there is no coordination among them, the expansionary (contractionary) stimulus will be far too strong relative to the desired leading to strong inflationary (recessionary) pressure. More generally, given the strong interdependence among the states, stabilization programmes adopted independently by the states may either oppose one another and thereby become ineffective or reinforce one another in an unforeseen manner and thereby generate strong inflationary or recessionary pressure. Hence *the stabilization function should be left to the centre.*

10.9 FISCAL FEDERALISM IN INDIA

We have discussed above how the functions of the government, namely, provision of social goods, distribution of income and stabilization, and the power to tax should be allocated among centre, states and local bodies. We shall now focus on India, which is a federation. We shall examine below how the functions and powers mentioned above are distributed among the centre, states and local bodies in India and whether they conform to the economic principles laid down above.

Until the nineties India had a two-tier federal structure consisting of the centre and the states. There was also a marked bias in the distribution of powers in favour of the centre. Though rural and urban local bodies—the panchayats in rural areas and municipalities in urban localities—existed, they did not have much power. Following liberalization since the beginning of the nineties, efforts started being made to move to a three-tier structure of government. The seventy-fourth amendment to the constitution made in the nineties conferred constitutional status on the local bodies.

10.9.1 Delegation of Functions

Indian Constitution specifies powers and functions of the centre and the states. It does not directly specify any powers or functions of the local bodies. The states may delegate some powers and functions assigned to it by the Constitution to the local bodies. There are three lists of powers and functions in the Constitution, namely, the union list, the state list and the concurrent list. These three lists distribute government's powers and functions between the centre and the states. The union list specifies the powers and functions of the centre. The state list lays down the powers and functions of the states. The concurrent list specifies the powers and functions that are the joint responsibility of the centre and the states. The delegation of powers and functions to the centre and the states is based on the economic principles discussed above. Thus provision of social goods that have nation-wide benefits such as defence, international relations, atomic energy and space, national highways, airways, international waterways and railways and stabilization functions including all functions relating to money supply, external borrowing etc. are delegated to the centre. States have been given the responsibility of providing social goods whose benefits and costs remain confined to their respective jurisdictions. Thus public order and police, local government, health, agriculture, irrigation, land rights, fisheries and industries, intrastate communications and transport, trade and commerce and minor minerals have been assigned to the states. The states in their turn may devolve some of these functions to the rural and urban local bodies. Provision of social goods that generate strong externalities or spillover effects have been put in the concurrent list so that they become the joint responsibility of the centre and the states. Some of the important items in the concurrent list are education, social security and social insurance.

10.9.2 Delegation of Powers

Distribution of tax powers in India also broadly conforms to the principles of economic theory discussed above. Accordingly, most of the tax powers are delegated to the centre. Tax powers of different governments are clearly specified in the Constitution. The Constitution applies the principle of separation in assigning the tax powers. This principle means that the tax powers assigned by the Constitution to the centre and the states do not overlap, i.e., they do not cover the same tax base. The centre is empowered to levy income taxes (except on agricultural income), customs duties, central excise and sales tax and service tax (i.e., tax on services). The states can impose taxes on agricultural income, sales tax (only on intrastate sales), state excises (only on the manufacture of alcohol), land revenue (tax on land used for agricultural or non-agricultural purposes), taxes on entertainment and professions and callings. Local bodies have the power to impose taxes on properties (buildings etc.), octroi (taxes on entry of goods for use within the jurisdiction of the local body), tax on markets and tax/user charges on public utilities such as drainage, water supply etc. All residual powers have been given to the centre, i.e., the centre is empowered to impose any tax not mentioned in the constitution. It should be noted here that the principle of separation is violated in case of state sales taxes and central excises. Legally, these two taxes are separate since the former falls on the sales of goods, while the latter applies to the production of manufactured items. But the bases of these two taxes clearly overlap. To illustrate, suppose that states impose sales tax on the sales of motor cars by dealers, while the centre imposes excise duties on the manufacture of motor cars by the manufacturers. The manufacturers sell what they produce to the dealers who in their turn sell the motor cars to the consumers. Thus the base of the sales tax and that of the central excise on motor cars are the same, namely, the value of the motor cars. The only difference is that the base of the central excise on motor cars does not include the dealers of motor cars' value added, which is a small percentage of the total value of motor cars.

10.9.3 Vertical Fiscal Imbalance

Tax powers, as we have already mentioned, are concentrated in the centre. But functions are more or less evenly distributed between the centre and the states. This has created substantial vertical imbalance, i.e., as we have explained above, imbalance between the centre and the states in respect of their incomes relative to needs. The centre has too much income relative to the functions assigned to it. Just the opposite is true in case of the states. The situation is worsened by the fact that states' earning from agricultural income and land revenue is insignificant. The only important source of revenue for the states is the sales tax. As a result the states are able to cover only a small part of their total expenditure from their revenue receipts. In 2000–2001, for example, the states could finance only 42% of their total expenditure including capital expenditure (investment) from their revenue receipts. According to the Eleventh Finance Commission (EFC) two-thirds of the total tax collection of India is made by the centre, while the state governments and the local bodies collect the remaining part, but each of the three tiers of the government makes one-third of the total government expenditure. The gaps between revenues and expenditures of the states and the local bodies are filled up largely from income transfers received from the centre. (See Table 10.1.)

10.9.4 Horizontal Fiscal Imbalance

Horizontal fiscal imbalance, as we have explained above, means fiscal imbalance among states and also among local bodies within a state. Here we focus mainly on horizontal fiscal imbalance among states. While functions assigned by the Constitution to different states are the same, they differ widely in respect of their abilities to raise tax revenue, the unit costs they have to incur for providing social goods and their needs for social goods. In other words, fiscal positions of different states differ considerably. These differences are mainly due to wide disparities in economic conditions, geographical characteristics, areas and population sizes among the states. The needs for social goods depend not only on population size and the area, but also, among others, on the state of infrastructural development, incidence of poverty and natural factors. Thus a well-endowed state with good infrastructure, low incidence of poverty and favourable natural factors has much less need for social goods than a dry land area or a state prone to flooding with high incidence of poverty and low level of infrastructure development. As a result of all these there is substantial variation in fiscal positions across states leading to considerable horizontal fiscal imbalance. (To have an idea of the wide disparities in fiscal capacities indicated by per capita SDPs of the states, see Table 10.1.)

Table 10.1: Revenue pattern of states (2011–12) (All figures are in rupees)

States	Per capita SDP	RR/GSDP	OTR/GSDP	ONTR/GSDP	CT/GSDP	Poverty ratio
HIS						
Gujarat	57,508	10.2	6.6	1.02	2.5	16.63
Goa	1,12,602	16.8	7.3	6.5	3.0	5.09
Haryana	62,078	10.9	6.8	1.5	2.6	11.16
Kerala	53,877	12.9	8.7	0.83	3.3	7.05
Maharashtra	62,457	10.3	7.1	0.8	2.4	17.35
Punjab	46,364	12.8	8.3	1.3	3.2	8.26
Tamilnadu	57,131	14.0	9.7	0.817	3.4	11.28
MIS						
Andhra Pradesh	42,119	16.8	9.4	2.1	5.4	9.2
Karnataka	41,959	14.6	9.6	0.8	4.1	20.91
West Bengal	14,874	12.4	5.2	0.6	6.6	19.98
LIS						
Bihar	13,210	23.0	5.2	1.2	16.7	33.74
Chhattisgarh	26,979	18.8	7.2	3.14	8.5	39.93
Jharkhand	25,634	23.2	6.6	2.7	14.0	39.96

(Contd.)...

Table 10.1: Revenue pattern of states (2011–12) (All figures are in rupees) *(Contd.)*...

States	Per capita SDP	RR/GSDP	OTR/GDSP	ONTR/GSDP	CT/GSDP	Poverty ratio
Madhya Pradesh	24,395	21.7	8.7	2.3	10.8	31.65
Orissa	24,134	17.0	5.7	1.77	9.5	32.59
Rajasthan	28,851	15.7	6.4	1.93	7.3	14.71
Uttar Pradesh	18,217	20.1	7.7	1.9	10.6	29.43
Special category states						
Arunachal Pradesh	36,877	61.3	2.3	3.0	55.9	34.67
Assam	22,910	5.6	2.8	19.4	24.1	31.98
Himachal Pradesh	48,923	23.4	6.7	3.3	13.4	8.06
Jammu & Kashmir	28,999	50.7	7.9	3.1	39.7	10.35
Manipur	23,953	57.7	3.1	4.5	50.1	36.89
Meghalaya	36,397	33.7	3.5	2.4	27.8	11.87
Mizoram	39,546	51.9	2.4	3.3	46.3	20.4
Nagaland	43,267	46.2	2.1	1.6	42.5	18.88
Sikkim	70,477	66.7	4.3	20.4	42.0	8.19
Tripura	39,542	30.4	4.0	0.7	25.7	14.05
Uttarakhand	50,303	16.8	5.5	1.9	9.4	11.26

SDP–State Domestic Product, RR–Revenue Receipt, OTR–Own Tax Receipt, ONTR–Own non-tax receipt, CT–Current transfers from the central government.

Source: RBI

10.9.5 Vertical and Horizontal Fiscal Imbalances: Corrective Measures

The vertical and horizontal imbalances are corrected through transfers of income from the centre to the states. The states receive income transfers from the centre from two sources, namely, the Finance Commission and the Planning Commission. They also receive transfers for implementing central government schemes and shared-cost projects. We shall discuss each of these three transfers below.

Finance Commission Transfers

In accordance with the Constitution's recommendations Finance Commissions (FCs) are set up every five years to resolve the problems of vertical and horizontal fiscal imbalances. FCs determine in the main states' share in the tax revenue of the centre and the distribution of this share among different states. The FC does its job in the following manner. It estimates for each state the expenditure the state has to incur, given a standard level of efficiency, to discharge the functions assigned to it by the Constitution during the term of the FC. It also estimates for the same period the revenue that each state should be able to raise, given its tax powers and a standard level of tax effort and efficiency. In sum the FC estimates for each state its revenue need and fiscal capacity and thereby the gap between the two during its term. It corrects the vertical and horizontal imbalances by filling up this gap through income transfers from the centre (Table 10.2). These income transfers take two forms, namely, tax devolution and grants-in-aid. *Both these types of transfers are unconditional grants.* We shall explain them below.

Table 10.2: Shares of different categories of
states in the total transfers of Finance Commission in percentage terms

	1987–1988	1991–1992	1993–1994	1994–1995	1995–1996	1996–1997	1997–1998	1998–1999	1999–2000
LIS*	50.44	52.37	50.41	51.2	50.96	49.77	50.83	48.43	48.24
MIS**	31.73	32.03	32.45	32.87	33.66	33.7	34.89	34.65	35.74
HIS***	17.83	15.59	17.14	15.93	15.38	16.53	14.28	16.93	16.02

*Low-income states

**Middle-income states

***High-income states

Source: Finance Accounts of State Governments.

The FC also estimates the amount of revenue that the centre should be able to raise, given its tax powers and a standard level of efficiency and tax effort. On the basis of this estimate and all the other estimates mentioned above the FC decides on the percentage of the central tax revenue that should devolve to the states. It then determines the share of each state in the total amount of central tax revenue that devolves to the states. The amount of central tax revenue that each state gets as a result of this exercise is referred to as tax devolution. If the tax devolution fails to fill up the estimated gap between the revenue need and fiscal capacity of a state, the FC fills it up with grants-in-aid. Thus grants-in-aid refer to income transfers that states receive from the FC over and above tax devolution so that fiscal positions of all states are equalized. The last Finance Commission, The Twelfth Finance Commission (TFC), which was set up on November 1, 2002, in its report submitted on November 30, 2004 covering the period between 2005–2010 raised states' share in the tax revenue of the centre from 29.5% to 30.5%. See Box 10.1 for the major recommendations of the TFC.

The FCs' practice of filling up the gap between projected revenue need and fiscal capacity of a state with tax devolution and grants-in-aid is referred as 'gap filling'. One major criticism of the practice of gap filling by the FCs is that it has produced a perverse incentive effect in India. It has induced the states to spend as much as they can and collect as little as possible from its own sources. The reasons may be stated as follows. The FC is supposed to estimate revenue need and fiscal capacity of the states objectively and independently on the basis of the functions and tax powers assigned to the states and some standard level of efficiency and tax effort. These estimates are not supposed to have any link with the actual revenues and expenditures of the states. The actual revenues and expenditures of a state can substantially deviate from these estimates. A state may be inefficient and profligate and, therefore, its actual expenditure may far exceed the amount of expenditure ideally required for the functions it has to discharge. Again, due to inefficiency and lack of political will tax collection of a state may be far less than what it reasonably should be, given its tax powers and tax base. The FCs are supposed to take their decisions on tax devolution and grants-in-aid on the basis of their own objective assessment of the required expenditure levels and reasonable levels of tax collections of the states. In practice, however, every FC made its estimates on the basis of the actual expenditures and revenues of the states. Thus the amount of flow of central fund to a state virtually depended on how large its expenditure actually was relative to its tax collection from its own sources. This might have induced the states to maximize its expenditure and minimize its tax collection efforts. This perverse incentive impact of 'gap filling' has perhaps led to the increasing dependence of the states on central funds. The proportion of states' current expenditure financed with own revenue receipt has steadily declined over time from 69% in 1955–1956 to 52% in 2002–2003.

Box 10.1: Thirteenth Finance Commission

Until now thirteen FCs made their recommendations. The latest one, the Thirteenth Finance Commission (TFC) was appointed on November 13, 2007 and it made its recommendations on December 29, 2009. Its recommendations cover the period 2010–2015. The tasks assigned to the TFC were the following: It was to determine the share of the states in the tax revenue of the centre and also the share of each state in it. It had to specify the principles determining the amounts of grants-in-aid for each state. Along with these it was asked to suggest ways by means of which the center and states could raise tax collection as a proportion of GDP, reduce fiscal deficits and make public borrowing more sustainable. In addition the TFC was assigned the task of suggesting measures to augment the resources of local bodies of the states. Some of the major recommendations of the TFC for tax devolution and grants-in-aid are the following: States' share in the central taxes is to be raised to 32 per cent from 30.5 per cent. It recommended grants-in-aid for improvements in elementary education, health, infrastructure etc. It also recommended non-plan revenue grant for eight states. To improve finances of the centre and the states, it suggested a 'Grand Bargain' between the centre and the states to implement Goods and Services Tax. It also urged the states to take steps for closing down all non-working state PSUs and privatising existing state PSUs. It suggested measures to minimize losses in the power sector and asked the states to expedite the process of migration to the new pension scheme.

Tax Devolution

Here we shall discuss some key features of the procedure followed by the FC for distributing the total amount of tax devolution among the states. The objective of this distribution consists in equalization of fiscal positions of different states. However, the FC does not use its own estimates of fiscal positions of different states for the purpose of determining the amount of tax devolution for each state. This is perhaps because the FC is aware of its estimates' shortcomings, which we have pointed out above. Instead the FC uses a formula, which takes into account a large number of diverse factors that the FCs think determine a state's fiscal position relative to others. These factors again have varied from one FC to another. However, the factors that the Eleventh Finance Commission (EFC) have considered are the following: The distance of the per capita SDP (State Domestic Product) of a state from the highest per capita SDP. This is taken to be a major indicator of the fiscal capacity of a state relative to that of the state having the highest per capita SDP. The greater this distance, the less is the fiscal capacity of the state relative to the one having the highest fiscal capacity and hence the greater is the state's need for income transfers from the states' share of the central pool. The formula used by the EFC for tax sharing gives it a weight of 62.5%. EFC also picked up area, population size and an index of infrastructure development as the major indicators of the needs for social goods and, therefore, needs for revenue. They had the weights of 10%, 7.5% and 7.5% respectively in the formula. Since the practice of 'gap filling' produces adverse incentive effects, the EFC also accommodated some indicators of tax efforts and fiscal discipline in the formula with weights of 5% and 7.5% respectively. Thus, states that made greater tax efforts and showed greater fiscal responsibility were rewarded. However, this attempt at distributing states' share in central taxes equitably among states makes little impact, as the FC meets any excess of the gap between projected revenue need and fiscal capacity of a state over tax devolution through grants-in-aid. Hence the FC transferred more resources to those states, which actually or historically had larger gaps between expenditure and revenue. Hence, despite efforts at removing horizontal imbalance through tax devolution, disparities among states are steadily growing over time. Table 10.2 shows that in recent years flow of FC transfers to the middle-income states has increased at the expense of the low-income states. (See Box 10.2 for a comparison of the schemes of distribution of the states' share in central resources among the states of Canada and India.)

Box 10.2:   Income Transfers to States: Canada and India

Canada is a federation like India. It is made up of different provinces. It may be instructive to know how the provinces' share in the central pool of tax revenue is distributed among different provinces. It may also be useful to compare this scheme of distribution to the corresponding system of distribution of India. In Canada, provinces' share in the central resources is distributed among the provinces on the basis of the following formula:

$$E_i = \sum_j t_j \left(\frac{B_{Rj}}{P_R} - \frac{B_{ij}}{P_i} \right) P_i \qquad \text{(B.10.1)}$$

(Contd.)...

(Contd.)...

$E_i \equiv$ entitlement of the province i

$B_{Rj} \equiv$ total tax base of the country of the jth tax or duty

$P_R \equiv$ total population of the country

$B_{ij} \equiv$ tax base of the jth tax in the ith province

$P_i \equiv$ population of the ith province

$t_j \equiv$ national average tax rate for the jth tax $\equiv \dfrac{\sum\limits_i TR_{ij}}{\sum\limits_i B_{ij}}$

$\sum\limits_i TR_{ij} \equiv$ total tax revenue earned by the country from the jth tax

$\sum\limits_i B_{ij} \equiv$ total tax base of the jth tax for the whole country

Equation (B.10.1) gives the total amount of income transfer or grant to the ith province from the central pool. Let us explain it. (B_{Rj}/P_R) gives the per capita tax base of the jth tax for the whole country. (B_{ij}/P_i) on the other hand gives the per capita tax base of the jth tax in the ith province. $(B_{Rj}/P_R) - (B_{ij}/P_i)$, therefore, gives the excess of the country's per capita tax base of the jth tax over that of the ith province. $t_j[(B_{Rj}/P_R) - (B_{ij}/P_i)]$ accordingly gives the excess of the country's per capita revenue from the jth tax over the ith province's per capita revenue from the jth tax, when it applies the national average tax rate of the jth tax to the tax base of the jth tax. $t_j[(B_{Rj}/P_R) - (B_{ij}/P_i)]P_i$, therefore, gives the amount of grant or income transfer that will make up ith province's shortfall of per capita earning from the jth tax from the national average, provided it applies the national average tax rate of the jth tax. Hence $\sum\limits_j t_j[(B_{Rj}/P_R) - (B_{ij}/P_i)]P_i$ gives the total amount of grant that will make up the jth province's shortfall of per capita earning from all taxes from the national average per capita earning from all taxes, provided the jth province applies the national average tax rate for every tax. It should be noted that equation (B.10.1) holds only for positive values of E_i. Thus provinces whose per capita earning from all taxes under the average tax rate exceeds national average per capita earning from all taxes under the national average tax rate need not part with any part of their tax revenue. They simply do not get any grant from the centre. Canada, therefore, gives grants to provinces in such a manner that every province's per capita command over resources at least equals the national average provided that every province makes national average amount of tax effort, i.e., every province applies the national average tax rate for every tax. Thus, grants based on (B.10.1) makes every province's fiscal capacity at least equal to the national average, if every province's tax effort equals the national average. The problem with this formula is that it focuses only on fiscal capacity and not on fiscal position and thereby ignores revenue need of the provinces. A reasonable tax distribution formula that seeks to remove horizontal imbalance, as we have pointed out, should aim at equalizing fiscal positions of provinces or states.

(Contd.)...

(Contd.)...

Unlike Canada the tax devolution formula used by India to remove horizontal imbalance focuses not only on fiscal capacities but also on revenue needs of the states. The objective in India is, therefore, equalization of or at least reduction in disparities in fiscal positions of the states. Canada uses a direct measure of the shortfall of the fiscal capacity of every province relative to the national average. India, however, does not use direct measures of fiscal positions of different states in its tax devolution formula. Instead, it uses certain indicators of relative fiscal positions of states such as the shortfall of per capita income of a state from the highest per capita income of the country, area of the state, size of the population, degree of infrastructure development etc. The first of these factors is the indicator of the relative fiscal capacity, all the other factors are, as we have explained in the text, indicators of revenue need. Besides, India's tax devolution formula also accommodates such factors as tax efforts and fiscal discipline and rewards those states that make greater tax efforts and display greater fiscal discipline.

Planning Commission Transfers

Another source of central funds to the states is the Planning Commission (PC), which was set up by the central government to implement five-year plans. The PC gives grants and loans to the states to implement programmes specified in the five-year plans. The PC lays down investment targets for five years for each sector in each state. On the basis of these targets and 'the states' own estimates of their own resources (including transfers from the Finance Commission) that can be used to finance plan expenditure and expected grants and loans from the PC, the states formulate their own state plans. They have to submit their plans to the PC for its approval. The PC approves the plans after a process of bargaining over the grants and loans asked for from the PC. The bargaining takes place through the National Development Council (NDC) comprising of the PC and the Chief Ministers of the states. Following the approval, the PC gives the states the grants and loans decided on in the process of bargaining. Since 1969 distribution of the transfers of the PC among the states is determined by the Gadgil formula. According to this formula 30% of these transfers are reserved for the special category states, states that are of strategic importance for national security, and the remaining 70% is reserved for the general category states. Ninety per cent of the transfers to the special category states are given in the form of grants and 10% in the form of loans. The 30% of the Planning Commission transfers reserved for the special category states are distributed among them on the basis of the sizes of their plans and the history of their past expenditures. The remaining 70% of the transfers are distributed among the general category states on the basis of a formula, which encompasses a number of factors such as population (with 60% weight), per capita income (25% weight), fiscal performance (7.5% weight) and special problems (7.5% weight). Thus, the formula seeks to attach importance to both equity and efficiency. The larger the population the greater is the need for state-provided goods. The lower the per capita income the less is the fiscal capacity. Hence equity calls for larger allocation of PC transfers to states with larger population and lower per capita income. However, to ensure efficient and timely utilization of resources and to induce the states to raise as much tax as possible from its own sources, importance has also been given to the fiscal performance of the states. Planning Commission grants are all conditional-specific purpose grants (earmarked grants).

Central Ministry Transfers

The central ministry transfers constitute the third source of central funds to the states. The central ministries make transfers to their counterparts in the states for specific projects, which may be wholly funded by the centre or funded by both the centre and the states. The former are called central sector projects (CSP), while the latter are referred to as centrally-sponsored schemes (CSS). The justification of these transfers is that the projects they finance either have strong interstate spillover effects so that the whole cost of these projects should not be borne alone by the state undertaking the project or these projects are merit goods, which the centre wants the states to provide. The importance of these transfers is growing in recent years.

Intergovernmental Loans

Another implicit source of central funds to the states is the intergovernmental loans. States get loans from the centre at subsidized rates. The subsidy constitutes an implicit transfer of funds from the centre to the states. It has been alleged that the states often borrow substantially and thereby contribute to fiscal deficit of the government. States can borrow from different sources, namely, centre, market, small savings schemes and provident fund. They can also borrow from the RBI in the form of ways and means of advances and overdraft. Borrowings from the small savings schemes and provident fund are highly attractive to the states. This is because these schemes carry central government guarantee, which makes them 100% safe. Hence they can attract funds at lower than market rates of interest. To the states, therefore, they constitute a cheap source of loans. States can also take ways and means advances from the RBI. These loans are given by the RBI to enable the states to meet temporary shortfalls in cash due to mismatch between receipts and payments. These are short-period loans and have to be repaid within three months. There is a ceiling on ways and means of advances. If the states' loans from the RBI exceed this ceiling, the excess is called overdraft. There is a ceiling on overdrafts also. The only restriction on these loans from the RBI is that they have to be kept within the ceiling always. Thus, the states can maintain these loans at the ceiling level always despite the short-term nature of the loans. Immediately after paying back these loans, the states can take these loans again.

Since the function of stabilization rests with the centre and unrestrained borrowing by the states may have serious destabilizing impact, the Ministry of Finance in coordination with the RBI and the Planning Commission imposes a ceiling on the total borrowing by the states from all sources, even though the states have fiscal autonomy. However, the states have found ways of evading this ceiling through off the budget ways of raising loans such as contingent liabilities. Let us explain. To implement a project, construction of a bridge, say, the states can set up a state enterprise and this enterprise can raise loans from the market. These loans do not figure in the state budget. It is extremely difficult to keep track of these borrowings. The importance of this kind of borrowings is increasing in recent years.

The centre also indulges in the practice of writing-off states' debts, if they reach unsustainable heights. It also guarantees loans given by external agencies to the state enterprises. This means that in case the state enterprises fail to meet their debt obligations, the centre will meet them. These practices create moral hazard problems for the states. They are induced to spend their loans irresponsibly on wasteful low-return projects, as they know that in case they fail to repay the loans or if interest charges rise to unsustainable heights, the centre will bail them out through debt write-offs etc. The centre is aware of the problems and has made efforts to discipline the states by forcing the states asking for debt write-offs to abide by certain fiscal prudential norms. However, political factors often stand in the way of being strict with the states.

Rural/Urban Local Bodies

Given the functions and tax powers assigned to the local bodies, there also exists considerable vertical imbalance between the state and its local bodies. Prior to the nineties this was addressed through transfers from the state governments. These transfers were discretionary and ad hoc. This means that these transfers were not based on any rules or principles or any objective assessment of the extent of vertical imbalance. The scenario, however, started changing since the nineties when these local bodies gained constitutional status. Now the states set up their own State Finance Commissions to determine the sharing of state taxes between the state government and the local bodies. Despite these developments, firm objective criteria for tax sharing to remove vertical imbalance at this level are yet to emerge. Devolution of state taxes to local bodies is still far too inadequate relative to needs. This area still requires a lot of reform and constructive thinking.

Evaluation of the Structure of Intergovernmental Transfers in India

It has been pointed out by many experts that the system of intergovernmental transfers in India has made only a limited impact on disparities in fiscal positions of the states. In fact data on state-wise distribution of federal resources reveal an increase in the share of the middle-income states at the expense of the low-income states (see Table 10.2). This failure to make substantial impact on interstate inequality in fiscal positions has been attributed principally to two factors, namely, the failure of the FCs to assess independently the expenditure requirement and the revenue potential of the states and the increasing importance in recent years of central ministry transfers, which do not have equalization of fiscal positions as an objective. Let us explain the former.

Low-income states historically have low per capita revenue, as their tax base is small. They also have low per capita expenditure, as they cannot afford high levels of expenditure. As a result the gap between per capita expenditure and per capita revenue in low-income states is also small relative to that in the higher-income states. Gap between 500 and 400, for example, is much smaller than that between 5000 and 4000. Since the FCs, while calculating these gaps for the states, rely on the actuals, their estimated deficits are also small for the low-income states. FCs' objective is to bridge these gaps through tax devolution and grants-in-aid. Accordingly, they transferred smaller amount of funds to the low-income states. In other words, FCs' reliance on actual or historical revenues and expenditures of the states in distributing central funds among the states led to the perpetuation of the historical inequality among the fiscal positions of the states. In fact, despite the system of intergovernmental transfers in place, disparity in per capita income among states is steadily increasing over time and the system is perhaps contributing to it to a certain extent.

From the above it follows that *consolidation of the sources of central funds to the states and objective assessment of the fiscal positions of the states are the key to the resolution of the problems of vertical and horizontal imbalances.*

SUMMARY

1. A federation is a union of a number of geographically-separate political units. There are many types of federation. In the most common type of federations, of which India is an example, only the federation has sovereign power and the citizens owe their primary allegiance to the federation and not to the constituent political units of which they are members.

2. In a federation, powers and functions of the government are decentralized. Fiscal federalism, which consists in decentralization of economic functions of the government, is a key feature of every federation. The main objective of this chapter is to discuss the rationale of fiscal federalism. There are three major functions of the government, namely, provision of social goods, redistribution of income and stabilization. There is a case for decentralizing the function of provision of social goods. Areas covered by social goods vary from one social good to another. Social goods, which benefit all the people in a country, are called nationwide social goods. Social goods whose benefits remain confined to the jurisdiction of a state are statewide social goods, while social goods whose benefits cover only a small locality are local social goods. There are reasons to believe that considerable efficiency gain can be made if provision of social goods is decentralized and responsibilities of providing statewide and local social goods are delegated to the states and local bodies respectively. Decentralization leads to efficiency gain because it creates ample scope for intergovernment competition and experimentation. Efficiency gains also result from the fact that lower governments have better information regarding local needs.

3. Buchanon (1965) and Tiebout (1956) provide a theoretical basis for fiscal federalism. Buchanon shows that every social good has an optimum community size and an optimum scale of provision. Tiebout shows that if provision of social goods whose optimum community sizes are equal to the population of a state or smaller, is decentralized, provision of these social goods will be optimum through a mechanism called voting by feet.

4. Tax powers in all federations are usually concentrated in the centre. The reason is the following. Fiscal positions vary substantially across states. Fiscal position is defined as a state's ability to provide social good. It depends on a state's fiscal capacity (tax base) and its revenue need. The latter in turn is determined by unit cost of providing social goods and need for social goods. However, every federation wants every state to have equal fiscal position. If tax powers are concentrated in the centre, it will be possible for the centre to distribute its excess tax revenue equitably among states so that fiscal positions of states become equal. Moreover, there are substantial economies of scale in tax collection.

5. Provision of social goods in a federation is decentralized to a considerable extent. However, tax powers are concentrated in the hands of the centre. As a result the centre

gains command over a large tax base, which is much in excess of its needs, whereas states' tax base falls woefully short of their needs. This imbalance in the fiscal positions of the centre and the states is referred to as vertical imbalance. There is also horizontal imbalance in a federation. This refers to the wide disparity in the fiscal positions of states. These imbalances are corrected through transfers of income from the centre to the states. These income transfers are called grants.

6. Grants are of various types. Some of these are unconditional grants, matching grants, close-ended matching grants and earmarked or specific grants. An unconditional grant is one, which the recipient lower government can use in whatever manner it wants. An unconditional grant is used only partly to provide more social goods. The remaining part is used to reduce tax burden of the community.

7. Sometimes a higher government gives a given amount in grant for every rupee spent by the lower government on a particular good or a particular set of goods. This kind of a grant is called a matching grant. It is more effective than an unconditional grant in raising the recipient lower government's expenditure in the desired direction. If there is a ceiling on the total amount of a matching grant, it is called a close-ended matching grant. A close-ended matching grant is not as effective as a matching grant, but it is at least as effective as an unconditional grant in raising the recipient government's expenditure in the desired direction.

8. When a higher government gives a grant and specifies on what good or goods it has to be spent, it is called an earmarked grant or specific grant. The recipient government does not necessarily spend even an earmarked grant wholly in the desired direction. It may use a part of it to lower the tax burden of the community.

9. Function of income distribution in a federation usually rests with the centre. Since people are mobile across states, if a state with a high incidence of poverty attempts at redistributing income, the rich may leave the state frustrating its redistributive efforts.

10. Since economies of individual states within a federation are highly interdependent, stabilization efforts of individual states may be in conflict with one another. Hence the function of stabilization rests with the centre.

11. India is a federation. Accordingly government's functions in India are decentralized. Distribution of functions between the centre and the states conforms broadly to the economic principles that should govern such distribution. Thus the responsibility of providing nationwide social goods is given to the centre, while the task of providing statewide and local social goods is delegated to the states. Provision of social goods with strong spillover effects has been made the joint responsibility of the centre and the states. The centre has also been given the responsibility of stabilization. Tax powers are also concentrated in the centre.

12. Vertical and horizontal imbalances are corrected through income transfers from the centre. There are three main sources of central funds to the states, namely, the Finance Commission (FC), Planning Commission (PC) and central ministry transfers.

13. FC is a constitutional body. It is set up every five years to remove the vertical and horizontal imbalances. FC estimates for each state the gap between its revenue need and

fiscal capacity. FC removes vertical and horizontal imbalances by filling up these gaps. Income transfers made by the FCs to fill up these gaps take two forms, namely, tax devolution and grants-in-aid. This practice of filling up the gap between revenue need and fiscal capacity is referred to as 'gap filling'. As FCs' estimates of the gaps were based on actual gaps of the states, the practice of 'gap filling' might have produced a perverse incentive effect.

14. Since the FCs are aware of the shortcomings of their own estimates of the gap between the fiscal capacity and revenue need of the states, it uses, in lieu of its own estimates of the gaps, a formula to determine the amount of tax devolution to each state. The formula varies from one FC to another. The formula used by the EFC takes into account the shortfall of a state's per capita SDP from the highest per capita SDP, area, population size, index of infrastructure development and some indicators of fiscal discipline.

15. Planning Commission gives income transfers to states to implement Five Year Plans. On the basis of the investment targets for the states specified in the Five Year Plans, the states formulate their own state plans. The PC gives the states income transfers in the form of both grants and loans to help them implement their plans. The distribution of PC transfers among states is based on Gadgil formula.

16. Different ministries of the central government make income transfers to their counterparts in the states to finance various projects partly or fully. These projects are either merit goods or goods with strong spillover effects. These transfers are referred to as central ministry transfers.

17. States get loans from the centre at subsidized rates. The subsidy constitutes an implicit transfer of fund from the centre to the states. Even though the centre imposes a ceiling on states' total amount of loans for purposes of stabilization, its practice of writing off states' debts when they reach unsustainable heights has created moral hazard problem for the states.

18. Despite the existence of the system of intergovernmental transfers, inequality in the fiscal positions of the states is growing over time. FCs' practice of basing their projections of the states' gaps between their revenue needs and revenue potential on historical or actual deficits in states' budgets has perhaps contributed to the widening disparity in the fiscal positions of the states.

KEY CONCEPTS

✓ Federation
✓ Spatial characteristics of social goods
✓ Intergovernment competition in the provision of social goods
✓ Economies of scale in the provision of social goods
✓ Optimum community/club size
✓ Vertical imbalance

✓ Fiscal federalism
✓ Decentralization of the provision of social goods
✓ Experimentation in the provision of social goods
✓ Spillover effects and decentralized provision of social goods
✓ Voting by feet

✓ Tax base
✓ Fiscal capacity
✓ Fiscal position
✓ Unconditional grant
✓ Close-ended matching grant
✓ Flypaper effect
✓ Tax devolution
✓ Gap filling
✓ Gadgil formula
✓ Central sector projects (CSP)
✓ Ways and means of advances
✓ Contingent liability

✓ Horizontal imbalance
✓ Tax effort
✓ Revenue capacity
✓ Grant
✓ Matching grant
✓ Earmarked/specific grant
✓ Finance Commission
✓ Grants-in-aid
✓ Planning Commission transfers
✓ Central ministry transfers
✓ Centrally-sponsored scheme (CSS)
✓ Overdraft

REVIEW QUESTIONS

1. Explain the spatial characteristics of social goods.

2. On what grounds will you recommend decentralized provision of social goods?

3. What are the problems with decentralized provision of social goods?

4. Identify the factors that determine the optimum club or community size of a social good. Answer this question using Buchanon's framework.

5. Works of Buchanon and Tiebout together provided a theoretical basis for the decentralized provision of social goods. Explain this statement.

6. What are the reasons for centralization of tax powers?

7. Explain the reasons for vertical and horizontal fiscal imbalances in a federation. How are they removed? Explain in this context the concepts of fiscal or revenue capacity and fiscal position.

8. Explain why an unconditional grant by a higher to a representative lower government will raise the latter's expenditure on social goods only by a part of the grant, when both private goods and social goods are normal goods?

9. Explain why a matching grant will raise the consumption of the commodity on which the grant is given by a larger amount than an unconditional grant? Explain why the commodity on which a matching grant is given is considered to be a merit good by the higher government?

10. Explain why a close-ended matching grant is at least as effective as an unconditional grant of the same amount in raising the consumption of the good on which the matching grant is given.

11. Under what conditions will an earmarked grant succeed in raising lower government's expenditure in the desired direction more than an unconditional grant of the same amount as the earmarked grant and when will it fail?

12. Why should the distribution function of the government be centralized?

13. Why should stabilization function of the government be centralized?
14. How are powers and functions distributed between the centre and states in India?
15. Why are there vertical and horizontal imbalances in India?
16. How do the FCs determine the amount of tax devolution to the states?
17. Why does the PC give income transfers to the states? How are PC transfers distributed among the states?
18. What are central ministry transfers? What is the rationale of these transfers?
19. What are the different sources of loans to the states? What are the difficulties in controlling states' borrowings? Why does the centre's practice of debt write-offs create moral hazard problems for the states?
20. Is there any reason to believe that the system of intergovernment transfers in India is contributing to the perpetuation of the inequality in the fiscal positions of the states? Explain.

========= **PROBLEMS AND APPLICATIONS** =========

1. Suppose that the cost of provision of a social good is given by $Z = 5S$ and the cost due to crowding to the representative consumer of this social good is given by $R = N$. The inverse demand function of the representative consumer is given by $P = 100 - (1/2)S$. Determine the optimum number of consumers and the optimum scale of provision of this social good. Illustrate the solution graphically. How will your results change if (i) the cost of provision of social goods falls and (ii) marginal benefit derived by the representative consumer from the social good rises? Illustrate your answers graphically.

    (*Hint*: $S^* = 146$ (approx.) $P^* = 27$ and $N^* = 27$ (approx.) Work out the rest.)

2. Suppose that the municipality of an urban area plans to set up tube wells to improve drinking water supply to a slum. Suggest a practical way of applying the Buchanon's framework to determine the number of tube wells to be set up.

    (*Hint*: Z consists of the annual interest charges on the loan needed to set up the tube well plus the cost of maintenance. Denoting this by $\overline{C}$, we have $Z(S) = \overline{C}S$, $S \equiv$ number of tube wells. R here is mainly the income lost by the average slum dweller annually due to waiting. R clearly depends not only on N but also on S. If S doubles, the waiting period, given N, is more or less halved. The cost due to waiting can be derived by multiplying the average period of waiting of an average slum dweller by the average wage rate earned by the slum dwellers. Thus $R(N, S)$ is likely to have this kind of a form: $(1/S)\overline{W}\alpha N$ (for $N > S$), where $\overline{W} \equiv$ the average wage rate of the slum dwellers and $(\alpha N/S)$ gives the average period of waiting of a slum dweller. Note that for $N \leq S$, there is no crowding and, therefore, no waiting. As a result $R = 0$. Obviously, in the optimal situation, N has to be greater than S. Hence we consider only such situations here. Now compute the benefit of an average slum dweller from tube wells. Suppose first that there is no crowding and, therefore, no waiting for taking water from the tube well. In this situation the benefit to an average slum dweller from the tube well consists in the income gained due to saving of the time that had to be spent annually to fetch water from some distant source. This gain is $\overline{WL}$, where $\overline{L}$ is the time saved. However, if $N > S$, there is waiting. The cost of waiting due to N exceeding S is given by $(1/S)\overline{W}\alpha N$. Hence total benefit of an average slum dweller from tube wells is $\overline{WL} - (1/S)\overline{W}\alpha N$. Marginal benefit of S is, therefore, $(1/S^2)\overline{W}\alpha N$. The inverse demand function of an average slum dweller is, therefore, $P = (1/S^2)\overline{W}\alpha N$. Work out the rest.)

3. Suppose that a community consumes just two goods, a private good and a public good denoted by X and Y respectively. The social welfare function and the budget constraint of the community are given by $U = X^{0.8}Y^{0.2}$ and $100 = X + Y$ respectively. Here the private good is the numeraire. Suppose that the government in charge of providing the social good to the community knows these functions and wants to discharge its responsibility in such a manner that the community's welfare is maximized subject to its budget constraint. Now suppose that this government gets an unconditional grant of G from the higher government. Derive the lower government's expenditure on the social good, amount of tax collection and the tax rate as functions of G. How do they behave with an increase in G? Is there any reason to believe that this behaviour will be replicated in reality? If the higher government wants the lower government to raise its expenditure on the social good by 10, then by how much should it raise G? Explain.

   (*Hint:* $Y = 20 + G/5$. Work out the rest.)

4. Suppose that the social welfare function of a community is given by $U = X^{0.8}Y^{0.2}$, where X is a private good and Y is a public good. Community's income is Rs. 100. Prices of X and Y are Re. 1 and Rs. 2 respectively. Suppose that the higher government gives the lower government in charge of providing the community with social goods a matching grant of Rs. v for every rupee spent on the social good, Y. Derive the equilibrium amount of the matching grant as a function of v. For the total amount of matching grant to be Rs. 50 what value of v should the government choose? How much Y will the individual choose when the total amount of matching grant given is Rs. 50. If Rs. 50 is given as unconditional grant, how much Y will be chosen? Explain the difference.

   (*Hint:* Equilibrium amount of matching grant $= (100/9)v$).

5. Consider the framework of Problem 4. Compare the effect of a close-ended matching grant of Rs. 50 to that of an unconditional grant of (i) Rs. 30 and (ii) Rs. 50. Explain the results.

6. Can you think of any circumstances under which the higher government will opt for the close-ended matching grant in lieu of the matching grant? Explain your answer.

   (*Hint:* When the higher government knows the budget constrain and utility function of the community, it can derive the community's expenditure on the public good as a function of the rate of the grant. In this case, therefore, to make sure that the lower government provides a desired amount of public good, it need not choose the close-ended matching grant. However, when it does not know these functions, in that case if it wants the lower government to provide more social good and at the same time if it does not want its expenditure to exceed a given level, it has to choose the close-ended matching grant.)

7. Consider a community, which consumes one private good, X and one public good, Y. Prices of X and Y are Re. 1 and Rs. 2 respectively. Social welfare function of the community is given by $X^{0.7} Y^{0.3}$. Community's money income is M. The lower government in charge of this community gets an earmarked grant of Rs. 100. Can you derive the condition under which it will raise the community's expenditure on Y more than an unconditional grant of Rs. 100?

   (*Hint:* Suppose that the community gets an unconditional grant of Rs. 100. Derive the post-grant optimum value of X as a function of M. This is given by $(14/20)M + 70$. Set it equal to M and then solve for M. The solution is given by $M = (1400/6)$. For all $M < (1400/6)$, the desired result will obtain. Explain it.)

8. Make an evaluation of the system of intergovernment transfers in India. What measures should be adopted to improve its performance?

REFERENCES

Major references for the theory of fiscal federalism:

Bhajan, G., Brennan, G. and Matthew, R.L. (1980): *The Economics of Fiscal Federalism*, Australian National University, Canberra.

Buchanan, J.M. (1965): An economic theory of clubs, *Economica*, February.

Musgrave, R.A. (1981): Approaches to a fiscal theory of political federalism, *in: Public Finances, Needs, Sources and Utilization*, National Bureau of Economic Research, Princeton, N.J., Princeton.

Oates, W.E. (1971): *Fiscal Federalism*, Harcourt-Brace, New York.

Tiebout, C.M. (1956): A pure theory of local government expenditure, *Journal of Political Economy*, October.

Major references for fiscal federalism in Indian context:

Bagchi, A. (2000): On the need to strengthen equalizing role of fiscal transfers in India, *Report of the Eleventh Finance Commission*, Government of India.

Rao, M.G. and Singh, N. (2005): *The Political Economy of Indian Federalism*, Oxford University Press, New Delhi.

Srivastava, D.K. (2000): *Fiscal Federalism in India: Contemporary Challenges*, National Institute of Public Finance and Policy, New Delhi.

Symposium on the Report of the Twelfth Finance Commission, *Economic and Political Weekly*, 40(31), July 30–August 5, 2005.

Twelfth Finance Commission (2003): *Fifty Years of Fiscal Federalism in India*, Twelfth Finance Commission, New Delhi.

INDEX